Cataloging
and Classification
An Introduction

Second Edition

Cataloging and Classification
An Introduction

Lois Mai Chan
University of Kentucky

McGraw-Hill, Inc.

New York   St. Louis   San Francisco   Auckland   Bogotá
Caracas   Lisbon   London   Madrid   Mexico City   Milan
Montreal   New Delhi   San Juan   Singapore
Sydney   Tokyo   Toronto

Cataloging and Classification: An Introduction

Acknowledgments appear on page 503, and on this page by reference.

12 13 14 15 DOC/DOC   0 3 2 1 0

ISBN 0-07-010506-5

This book was set in Palatino by ComCom, Inc.
The editors were Judith R. Cornwell and John M. Morriss;
the production supervisor was Richard A. Ausburn.
The cover was designed by Carla Bauer.
Project supervision was done by Editorial Services of New England, Inc.
R. R. Donnelley & Sons Company was printer and binder.

Library of Congress Cataloging-in-Publication Data

Chan, Lois Mai.
    Cataloging and classification: an introduction / Lois Mai Chan.—
2nd ed.
        p.   cm.
    Includes bibliographical references and index.
    ISBN 0-07-010506-5 (alk. paper)
    1. Cataloging—United States.   2. Classification—Books.
I. Title.
Z693.5.U6C48   1994   93-22606
025.3—dc20

About the Author

Lois Mai Chan is a professor at the College of Library and Information Science, the University of Kentucky. She is the author of several books in the field of cataloging and classification, including *Library of Congress Subject Headings: Principles and Application*, *Immroth's Guide to the Library of Congress Classification*, and *Thesauri Used in Online Databases: An Analytical Guide*, as well as numerous articles appearing in *Library Resources & Technical Services*, *Cataloging & Classification Quarterly*, *Information Technology and Libraries*, and other journals. She coedited *Theory of Subject Analysis: A Sourcebook*. She is a member of the Decimal Classification Editorial Policy Committee and served as its chair from 1986 to 1991. In 1989 she received the American Library Association's Margaret Mann Citation for Outstanding Professional Achievement in Cataloging and Classification.

To
S.K., Jennifer, and Stephen

Contents

Preface   xix

PART ONE   Introduction   1

Background Reading   1
Further Reading   1

Chapter 1   Bibliographic Control and Library Catalogs   3
Bibliographic Control   3
Library Catalogs   4
    General Characteristics   4
    Forms of Catalogs   5
    Access Points in a Catalog   9
    Arrangement of Records in a Catalog   9
Cataloging Operations   10
    Cataloging Files   11
    Cataloging Procedures   12
Record Examples   15
    The Bibliographic Record   15
    The Authority Record   23
Conclusion   26

PART TWO   Descriptive Cataloging   29

Basic Tools   29
Background Reading   29
Further Reading   30

Chapter 2   Development of Cataloging Codes   33
British Museum Cataloguing Rules   33
Jewett's Rules   34
Cutter's Rules   34
AA 1908   35

Prussian Instructions   36
Vatican Code   36
ALA Draft (1941)   37
LC 1949   37
ALA 1949   38
AACR (1967)   38
   International Standard Bibliographic Description   41
   AACR, Chapters 6, 12, and 14, Revised   43
AACR2 (1978)   43
   Universal Bibliographic Control   44
AACR2R (1988)   45
   Options   46
Library of Congress Rule Interpretations   47

Chapter 3   Description   49
Types of Library Materials   49
ISBD(G)   50
Organization of the Description   53
Sources of Information   53
Punctuation   63
   Brackets   63
   Colon   63
   Comma   63
   Dash   64
   Diagonal Slash   64
   Ellipses   64
   Equals Sign   64
   Full Stop   64
   Hyphen   64
   Mark of Omission   65
   Minus Sign   65
   Parenthesis   65
   Period   65
   Plus Sign   66
   Question Mark   66
   Semicolon   66
   Slash   66
   Space   66
   Square Brackets   66
Levels of Description   67
   Cutter's Levels   67
   Levels of Description in AACR2R   67
   Examples   68
Exercise A   69

Areas of Description   69
    Title and Statement of Responsibility Area   70
    Edition Area   75
    Material (or Type of Publication) Specific Details Area   76
    Publication, Distribution, etc., Area   78
    Physical Description Area   82
    Series Area   90
    Note Area   92
    Standard Number and Terms of Availability Area   96
Supplementary Items   97
    As a Separate Item   97
    As a Dependent Item   97
Analytics   97
    Analytics of Monographic Series and Multipart
        Monographs   98
Exercise B   99

Chapter 4   Choice of Access Points   107
Concepts   108
    Main Entry   108
    Authorship   108
Choice of Main Entry   112
    Types of Main Entry   112
    Conditions of Authorship   112
    Rules for Choice of Entry   113
    Changes in Title Proper   120
    Changes of Persons or Bodies Responsible for a Work   120
Added Entries   121
    Added Entries under Personal Names   121
    Added Entries under Corporate Names   121
    Added Entries under Titles   122
    Added Entries under Series   122
    Analytical Added Entries   122
    Tracing   122
Exercise A   122

**Chapter 5   Name Authority Control and Forms
of Headings and Uniform Titles**   123
Name Authority Control   123
Forms of Headings   125
    Principles of Uniform and Unique Headings   126
Headings for Persons   126
    Choice of Name   127
    Choice of Form of Name   129

Choice of Entry Element   130
Additions to Names   131
Distinguishing Persons with the Same Name   133
Geographic Names in Headings   134
Language   134
Changes of Name   134
Additions to Place Names   134
Headings for Corporate Bodies   135
Definition   135
Choice of Name   136
Choice of Form   136
Modifications   137
Choice of Entry Element   138
Conferences, Congresses, Meetings, etc.   140
Governments and Government Bodies   140
Government Officials   141
Uniform Titles   141
Anonymous Classics Written before 1501   142
Special Rules for the Bible   143
Other Sacred Scriptures   144

Chapter 6   References   145
Personal Name Headings   147
See References   147
See also References   148
Names of Corporate Bodies and Geographic Names   148
Uniform Titles   148
Exercise A   149
Topics for Discussion-Descriptive Cataloging   149

PART THREE   Subject Access
in Library Catalogs   153

Basic Tools   153
Background Reading   153
Further Reading   154

Chapter 7   Subject Cataloging   155
History of Subject Access in Library Catalogs   156
The Classed or Classified Catalog   157
The Alphabetical Specific Catalog   157
The Online Catalog   158
Subject Cataloging Systems   158

General Principles of Subject Cataloging	159
The User and Usage	160
Uniform and Unique Headings	161
Specific and Direct Entry	161
Consistent and Current Terminology	162
Cross-references	163
Subject Authority Control	164
Levels of Subject Authority Control	164
Functions of a Subject Authority File	165
General Methods of Subject Analysis	166
Assigning Subject Headings: General Guidelines	167
Depth of Subject Cataloging	167
Specific (Coextensive) Entry	167
Number of Headings	168
Multitopical and Multielement Works	168

Chapter 8 Library of Congress Subject Headings	171
Format of Headings and MARC Coding	172
Subject Authority Records	172
Subject Headings in Bibliographic Records	174
Main Headings: Functions, Types, Syntax, and Semantics	176
Topical and Form Headings	176
Headings for Named Entities	179
Subdivisions	182
Form Subdivisions	183
Topical Subdivisions	183
Free-Floating Form and Topical Subdivisions	184
Chronological Subdivisions	188
Exercise A	189
Geographic Subdivisions	190
Order of Subdivisions	193
Exercise B	194
Cross-References	195
Equivalence Relationships	195
Hierarchical Relationships	196
Associative Relationships	197
General References	198
Assigning Subject Headings—Special Materials	199
Subject Headings for Literary Works	199
Works about Individual Works	204
Subject Headings for Biography	205
Exercise C	208
Subject Headings for Children's Literature	208
Library of Congress List of Juvenile Headings	208
Subject Cataloging of Children's Materials	209

Chapter 9   Sears List of Subject Headings   211
Main Headings   213
    Single-Noun Headings   213
    Phrase Headings   213
Cross-References   214
    Specific *See* References   214
    Specific *See also* References   215
    General References   216
    Examples of Cross-References   216
Subdivisions   217
    Subject or Topical Subdivisions   217
    Form Subdivisions   218
    Exercise A   219
    Period or Chronological Subdivisions   220
    Place, Local, or Geographic Subdivisions   220
    Exercise B   221
Classes of Headings Omitted   221
    Proper Names   222
    Common Names   224
    Exercise C   224
Subject Headings for Special Types of Materials   225
    Subject Headings for Biography   225
    Subject Headings for Literature   227
    Exercise D   229

Chapter 10   Medical Subject Headings and Other Subject Cataloging Systems   231
Medical Subject Headings   231
    Brief History   231
    Format   232
    Structure of Headings   236
    Cataloging Instructions   239
PRECIS   244
COMPASS   251
Topics for Discussion-Subject Analysis   253

PART FOUR   Classification   255

Basic Tools   255
Background Reading   256
Further Reading   256

Chapter 11   General Principles of Classification   259
Definition   259
Basic Concepts   260

Notation   262
How to Classify   262
    Choosing a Number: General Guidelines   263
    Choosing a Number: Multitopical Works   264
Call Numbers   266
MARC Coding for Classification and Item Numbers   266
Modern Library Classification Systems   267

Chapter 12   Dewey Decimal Classification   269
History   269
    The Beginning   269
    Early Editions   270
    Fifteenth Edition   271
    Sixteenth Edition and Later Editions   271
    Abridged Dewey Decimal Classification   272
Revision   272
    Current Procedures for Revision   272
    Forms of Revision   273
Basic Principles   275
    Classification by Discipline   275
    Structural Hierarchy   277
Notation   278
    Symbols   278
    Notational Hierarchy   278
    Mnemonics   279
Evaluation   280
    Merits   280
    Weaknesses   281
Assigning Call Numbers   282
Class Numbers   282
Number Building: Full Edition   282
    Combining Schedule Numbers   283
    Exercise A   284
    Adding Notation(s) from the Auxiliary Tables
        to a Base Number   285
    Exercise B   291
    Exercise C   295
    Classification of Literature   296
    Exercise D   301
    Segmentation   302
Number Building: Abridged Edition   303
    Combining Schedule Numbers   304
    Exercise E   304
    Adding Notation(s) from the Auxiliary Tables
        to a Base Number   305

Exercise F   309
Classification of Biography   312
Exercise G   313
Book or Item Numbers   314
    Cutter Numbers   315
    Unique Call Numbers   317
    Exercise H   318
    Prefixes to Call Numbers   324
    Exercise I   325

Chapter 13   Library of Congress Classification   327
History   328
Basic Principles and Structure   329
    Overall Characteristics   329
    Main Classes   330
    Subclasses   332
    Divisions   333
Notation   333
    Symbols   333
    Hospitality   336
    Mnemonics   336
Evaluation of the Library of Congress Classification   337
    Merits   337
    Weaknesses   338
The Schedules: Revision and Publication Patterns   338
    Revision   338
    Publication Patterns for Revised Schedules   339
    Indexes   340
Applying the Library of Congress Classification: Instructions
  and Examples   340
    Format of Schedules   341
    Class Numbers   341
    Cutter Numbers   343
    Dates in Call Numbers   348
    Works Entered under Corporate Headings 349
    Exercise A   350
Tables   351
    Tables of General Aplication   352
    Tables of Limited Application   356
    Exercise B   366

**Chapter 14   National Library of Medicine Classification
and Other Modern Classification Systems**   369
National Library of Medicine Classification   369
    Brief History and Current Status   370
    Basic Principles and Structure   370

Notation   372
Index   374
Classification of Special Types of Materials   375
Cataloging Examples   377
Other Modern Library Classification Systems   379
   Expansive Classification (Charles Ammi Cutter,
     1837–1903)   379
   Universal Decimal Classification   382
   Subject Classification (James Duff Brown, 1862–1914)   387
   Colon Classification (Shiyali Ramamrita Ranganathan,
     1892–1972)   389
   Bibliographic Classification (Henry Evelyn Bliss,
     1870–1955)   392
Topics for Discussion-Classification   397

PART FIVE   USMARC Formats and Production of Cataloging Records

PART FIVE   USMARC Formats and Production
of Cataloging Records   401

Basic Tools   401
Background Reading   401

Chapter 15   USMARC Formats   403
USMARC: History   403
Types of MARC Formats   404
Architecture of USMARC Formats   406
   Elements of a MARC format   407
   Units in a MARC Record   407
   Component Parts of a MARC Record   409

Chapter 16   Producing Cataloging Records   413
Major Sources of Cataloging Copy   415
   Library of Congress   415
   Bibliographic Utilities   417
Computer-Assisted Cataloging   418
   Online Cataloging Activities   419
   Conversion and Maintenance of Cataloging Records 421
Conclusion   422

Appendix A   Bibliographic Records in Card and MARC
Formats   423

Appendix B   Authority Records in MARC Format   433

Appendix C   First Level of Description   439

Appendix D   General Tables from the Library of Congress
Classification   441

Appendix E   Key to Exercises   449

Glossary   479

Bibliography   493

Acknowledgments   503

Index   505

Preface

Cataloging And Classification: An Introduction, Second Edition, is intended as a text for beginning students and a tool for practicing cataloging personnel.

The book's overall scope remains largely the same. As in the first edition, this second edition contains a discussion of the analysis and representation of library materials in catalogs, and it presents the essence of library cataloging and classification in terms of the three basic functions: descriptive cataloging, subject access, and classification, along with authority control as well as the processing of cataloging records both in the manual and machine-readable cataloging modes. Throughout the book, I have attempted to reflect current practice in the field.

NEW TO THIS EDITION

Many of the chapters have been reorganized internally to provide a more logical progression of ideas and factual details. All chapters have been rewritten to incorporate recent developments, particularly the tremendous impact technology has had on cataloging and classification. Because of the great variety of online systems and the idiosyncracies of each, online catalogs are discussed in this edition in general and broad terms, with cataloging examples taken from a number of online systems. Emphasis is placed on the computer processing of cataloging information in the MARC (MAchine-Readable Cataloging) formats.

The discussion of USMARC formats has been expanded considerably. The MARC system and formats are introduced in Chap. 1. The development and architecture of USMARC formats are discussed in greater detail in Chap. 15, wherein the reader will find an emphasis on the formats' underlying structure and principles.

Chapter 15 on the structure of the USMARC formats is placed near the end of the book because it refers to concepts introduced throughout the earlier chapters. I believe readers will more easily grasp its details after they understand the complexities of what must be coded. However, those who wish to study or teach the MARC formats along with catalog-

ing operations may use this chapter and the earlier chapters simultaneously.

Each part of the book (there are five) begins with a list of background
readings that include many works considered to be classics in the field.
For those who wish to pursue the subject in greater depth, a list of further
readings is given. The readings are designed to help the reader gain an
overview of the subject to be presented. Additional works are listed in
the bibliography. Each of Parts two through five also includes a list of
tools used in the preparation and processing of that part of the cataloging
record.

In each part, I have placed an emphasis first on the historical development and principles that are essential to the understanding of cataloging and classification. Discussion and examples of the provisions in
the basic tools are then presented in order to illustrate the operations of
cataloging and classification. Throughout this edition, principles and
practice in name and subject authority control are interspersed where
appropriate.

THE PLAN OF THE BOOK

Part One, "Introduction," provides a general overview of bibliographic
control and cataloging and classification.

In Part Two, "Descriptive Cataloging," the revised second edition of
Anglo-American Cataloguing Rules is used as the basis for the part's five
chapters. Chapter 2, on the development of cataloging codes, places the
current code in a historical context that sets up the organic nature of the
current code and points out the inevitability of future changes; an
exposition of the rules follows.

Part Three, "Subject Access in Library Catalogs," is based on the
latest editions of the *Library of Congress Subject Headings* (Chap. 8) and
Sears List of Subject Headings (Chap. 9.) In Chap. 10, a brief introduction
to a specialized system, *Medical Subject Headings,* is added in this edition
along with other subject cataloging systems.

Part Four, "Classification," contains a discussion of classification
and examples based on the 20th edition of the full version and the 12th
edition of the abridged version of the *Dewey Decimal Classification* (Chap.
12) and the most recent editions of *Library of Congress Classification* (Chap.
13.) In Chap. 14, a discussion of *National Library of Medicine Classification*
is also included as is a brief treatment of other classification systems.
Systems that are seldom or no longer used—but that are not necessarily
inferior to those in use—are included both to expose students to ideas
that challenge current practice and also help illustrate principles and
theory in different manifestations.

The chapters on the individual subject headings systems and classification schemes are designed so that they may be used as a whole or selectively. For example, Chap. 9 on *Sears List of Subject Headings*, may be used without first studying Chap. 8, on *Library of Congress Subject Headings*. And in Chap. 12, the sections of the abridged edition of *Dewey Decimal Classification* can be used without first studying the section of the full edition. As a result, some overlap of discussions of similar points occurs in these chapters. I have used this method of presentation so that the text will be equally as useful to those library–information science programs that are designed for specific types of libraries and that do not cover all systems of subject cataloging or classification (e.g., school libraries).

This text is designed as an aid in the study of the operations and the basic tools and not as a substitute for the tools themselves. In other words, one cannot prepare a bibliographic description of a document without resorting to *Anglo-American Cataloguing Rules*, nor can one classify an item without a classification scheme. Therefore, the text's discussions concentrate on the essence of the rules; no attempt is made to replicate or reproduce the cataloging rules.

In each chapter dealing with major cataloging and classification operations, exercises are included to reinforce the concepts covered, and answers are given in Appendix E.

The text again contains a glossary, updated to reflect recent developments and current literature, and it includes common terms in cataloging and classification. A bibliography of cataloging tools and selected writings in the field is also given.

Over 95 percent of the examples used in this edition are parts of, or complete, records based on recent Library of Congress cataloging. Examples illustrating various cataloging operations consist of extracts from LC cataloging records. *Complete* MARC bibliographic and authority records are included in the appendixes to show how the parts fit together in the final cataloging product. Throughout this edition, one particular set of examples, the authority record for William A. Katz and the bibliographic record for the fifth edition of his book on reference, are used to illustrate the structure of and relationship between authority and bibliographic records and the various manifestations of the same records in different cataloging systems.

I am indebted to several individuals for their assistance in the preparation of this edition: Donna Sykes for inputting the original edition, Nancy Lewis for bibliographic assistance and proofreading, Valerie Boggs for proofreading some of the chapters, and Kate Seago and Barbara Pfeifle for their help in providing some of the illustrations. A special note of thanks is due to Dr. Theodora Hodges for reading the entire manuscript and making numerous invaluable suggestions. Dr.

Hodges also prepared the index. I would also like to thank the publisher's reviewers for their extremely valuable comments: Virgil L.P. Blake, Queens College, CUNY; Shirley L. Hopkinson, San Jose State University; Hemalata Iyer, SUNY-Albany; Patricia Oyler, Simmons College; Kathleen Reed, Drexel University; Jerry D. Saye, University of North Carolina, Chapel Hill; Elaine Svenonious, University of California, Los Angeles; and Amy Warner, University of Michigan.

Lois Mai Chan

Cataloging and Classification
An Introduction

PART I
INTRODUCTION

BACKGROUND READING

Bengtson, Betty G. "Bibliographic Control." In Irene P. Godden, ed., *Library Technical Services.* 2nd ed. San Diego: Academic Press, 1991. Pp. 147–203.

Cochrane, Pauline A. "Universal Bibliographic Control: Its Role in the Availability of Information and Knowledge." *Library Resources & Technical Services,* **34** (4):423–431, October 1990.

FURTHER READING

Hagler, Ronald. *The Bibliographic Record and Information Technology.* 2nd ed. Chicago: American Library Association, 1991.

Markuson, Barbara Evans. "Bibliographic Systems, 1945–1976." *Library Trends,* **25**:311–327, July 1976.

The Online Catalogue: Developments and Directions. Charles Hildreth, ed. London: Library Association, 1989.

Scott, Edith. "The Evolution of Bibliographic Systems in the United States, 1876–1945." *Library Trends,* **25**:293–310, July 1976.

Wilson, Patrick. "The Catalog as Access Mechanism: Background and Concepts." *Library Resources & Technical Services,* **27**(1):4–17, January/March 1983; also in *Foundations of Cataloging: A Sourcebook.* Michael Carpenter and Elaine Svenonius, eds. Littleton, Colo.: Libraries Unlimited, 1985. Pp. 253–268.

CHAPTER ONE
BIBLIOGRAPHIC CONTROL
AND LIBRARY CATALOGS

BIBLIOGRAPHIC CONTROL

The term *bibliographic control* refers to the operations by which recorded information is organized or arranged according to established standards and thereby made readily identifiable and retrievable. Indexing, classification, and descriptive and subject cataloging are some of the activities involved in bibliographic control. The most common tools used in bibliographic control are files or lists called *bibliographic files* or, if automated, *bibliographic databases,* and the individual units of such files or databases are called *bibliographic records.* A companion concept to bibliographic control is *authority control.* This is achieved in a given bibliographic file when uniform terms are used for names and topics as access points so that records pertaining to the same entity or concept are not dispersed among synonyms or variant name forms. In addition, authority control also resolves homonyms by distinguishing terms that are spelled the same but have different meanings.

Bibliographies, indexes, and catalogs are the most common types of bibliographic files. These exist in many forms, and within each form one file may differ considerably from another in type of bibliographic material covered, amount of information provided per record, how records are organized, and how records may be retrieved. Bibliographic databases, which are bibliographic files that have been converted to a form recognizable and manipulatable by the computer (in other words, made *machine-readable*), show even more variation than manually prepared files because of the versatility and power of computers in handling bibliographic data and allowing different designs of online systems.

Bibliographic records are the building blocks of a bibliographic file. Each bibliographic record pertains to an item in the collection represented in the file and contains two primary kinds of information: first, enough data for the item to be identifiable in the context of the file; and second, at least one "access point," i.e., a label by which the record can be retrieved or under which it is filed. In this sense, names of authors are access points, so are titles, and so are subject terms; so may be other entities, such as performers.

The amount and nature of information included in a record depend on the purposes for which the file is prepared. In some bibliographic files, such as scientific periodical indexes or catalogs of highly specialized libraries, it is appropriate that records provide extensive subject and/or descriptive information; in others, such as a short-title catalog of items published at a given place and time, very little information per item is sufficient.

LIBRARY CATALOGS
General Characteristics

A *library catalog* is a kind of bibliographic file. It differs from a bibliography or a periodical index in that all its records pertain to items in one or more libraries and carry information on where the items can be found. Most library catalogs represent a single institution's holdings (which may be distributed in many branches). Other catalogs show the holdings of several libraries or collections; these are called *union catalogs*.

Like other bibliographic files, a library catalog consists of a set of records that, like the records in other bibliographic files, provide data about the items in the collection or collections the catalog represents. The data on each record include, at least, (1) a bibliographic description giving the identification, publication, and physical characteristics of the document, and (2) a call number (consisting of the classification number based on the subject content and a book number based on the author, the title, or both) that indicates the location of the item in the collection. Most records—those for fiction are the usual exceptions—also include subject terms which state succinctly the subject content of the document.

Almost all library catalogs are *multiple-access* files. This means that they offer many ways to retrieve a particular record: by author, title, subject, and other characteristics. In a card catalog, there are usually several cards for the same item, each filed under a heading that represents a different access point. This way of providing information about items in a collection—multiple access to records that provide sufficient details for identification plus characterization of content—allows a user to locate particular items or to select relevant items for specific purposes.

In library cataloging, it has long been the practice to designate one of the access points as the chief access point, or *main entry*. In most cases, the main entry is based on the author if such can be determined. Otherwise, the main entry is based on the corporate body responsible for the content or on the title.

There are two reasons for main entry practice. First, it is the most efficient way to manage lists that are maintained manually. In the days of manually prepared cards, it was the convention to record all needed information on one card and to include only brief descriptions on other cards (called *added entries*) for the same item. For printed card sets, it is the record with the main entry heading that is duplicated; one card is filed as is, and added entry headings are typed on other cards as appropriate. Second, even for computer-stored lists, where the main entry–added entry distinction would seem unnecessary, it remains helpful to have a standard convention for the way a bibliographic item should be cited. The main entry pattern (in other words, author/title) is the usual way of referring to a text, a fact that adds to its effectiveness as a citation standard.

The catalogs of most general libraries in this country show a great deal of similarity—and also quite a few differences. With respect to the records in the catalogs, there is not much variation in the bibliographic information they show or in the style in which they are drafted. This is so because, over the last several decades, cataloging practice has become highly standardized. There are some differences in how much bibliographic detail is included per record, but even in this, accepted standards are followed.

The more specialized a library is, in the material it collects or the clientele it serves, the more its catalog is likely to vary from that of other libraries. This is particularly true for subject-access provisions. However, even for general libraries, there are many ways in which catalogs differ from each other even when their records reflect standard practice. Among these are (1) the physical form the catalog takes, (2) the access points provided, and (3) the principle governing how the records are sequenced. They also may differ considerably in how individual records are formatted, that is, what they look like on cards, pages, or microform or computer screens. These differences are discussed below.

Forms of Catalogs

The primary forms for library catalogs are the *card catalog*, the *book catalog*, the *microform catalog*, and the *computer-accessed catalog;* the last is usually referred to as an *online catalog*. When catalog records were manually produced—handwritten, typed, or typeset—there were only a few options for physical form: book, card, and, to a limited extent, microform. Within these forms, considerations of cost and bulk placed a severe limit on the amount of information that could be included in a given record and on the number of access points that could be provided for it. As it did with access points, the advent of catalog automation made a major difference in the potential forms catalogs could take and in the variety of features an individual catalog could exhibit. The following brief account treats the major catalog forms both historically and as they exist today.

Card catalog

In this type of catalog, cataloging entries are recorded on 3 by 5 cards, one entry per card or set of cards. Each entry can then be revised, inserted, or deleted without affecting other entries. Before the card catalog, most library catalogs were in book form, either printed or looseleaf. When the card catalog was first introduced in the latter part of the nineteenth century, its advantage in ease of updating was immediately perceived, and libraries throughout the United States began adopting this form. The Library of Congress printed-card service, begun in 1901, which distributes ready-made catalog cards to other libraries, contributed to its widespread use. For nearly a century, the card catalog was the predominant form of catalog in American libraries. Catalog automation eventually changed the picture, but not for well over a decade after its introduction: early catalog databases were used primarily to print sets of catalog cards.

The mode of display of information on a catalog card conforms to the size and shape of the card. Most commonly, the call number resides in the upper left corner. The main entry heading is on one or more lines (most take only one line), with the rest of the bibliographic information following in several short paragraphs. Near the bottom of the card are what are called *tracings*, which are records of the secondary headings (or added entries) under which the record is filed. At the very bottom there may be various control numbers. This description fits what is called a *unit card*. When a record will not fit on one card, its information is continued on subsequent cards under a brief representation of the main entry heading. For an example of a catalog card, see page 16.

Book catalog

The book catalog is a list in book form of the holdings of a particular library collection or group of collections, with the cataloging records displayed in page format. This is the oldest form of library catalog. Its items may be recorded by handwriting as in a manuscript catalog, by typing, or by a printing process. The oldest manuscript catalog goes back as far as the *Pinakes* compiled by Callimachus for the Alexandrian library. The book-form catalog was the predominant form of library catalog until the late nineteenth century, when the use of the card catalog began to spread. Even so, manually prepared book catalogs continued to be issued in small numbers for many years.

In comparison with card catalogs, the major advantages of book catalogs are portability and the ease of producing multiple copies. Copies of a book catalog can be placed in all the branches of a library so that each branch can have a record of the holdings of the entire system; copies of the card catalog cannot be so readily or economically reproduced. The major disadvantage of the book catalog in the early days was the difficulty and cost of revision. It also was highly susceptible to wear and tear.

As libraries turned to automation during the 1960s, technological advances in the equipment related to book-catalog production spawned a renewed interest in the book catalog. The major advances were the availability of a high-speed sequential card camera coupled with improvement in offset printing and the development of a 120-character print chain for computers along with advances in computer typesetting methods. Earlier book catalogs were often produced by arranging catalog-card images in a page layout and photographing them. Book catalogs can now be produced from a machine-readable database, a change that greatly facilitates updating and increases the variety of ways catalog information can be presented. Nonetheless, once there is a printout from the database, the resulting catalog has all the disadvantages of the book form, the worst of which is inhospitality to corrections, changes, and additions.

With respect to display of information, the records in book catalogs that were produced from photocopies of catalog cards showed the same record format, although usually at a reduced size. One advantage is that a given number of records on a page can be scanned in a shorter time than the same records can be browsed in a card drawer. With the advent of computer-produced book catalogs, there were new display options. A particular book catalog may be a single-entry list or a multiple-access list, and the amount of information given in each record also may vary according to the purpose of the catalog.

Microform catalog

A microform catalog is a variant of the book catalog. It contains cataloging records in microimage and requires the use of a microform reader for viewing. There are various media for the microform catalog, such as microfilm (continuous negative), microcard (positive), and microfiche (negative). The prevalent form of microform catalog is on microfiche.

Earlier microform catalogs were made by photographing catalog cards or pages of book catalogs. A more recent method enables production of a microform catalog directly from machine-readable records. This method is called *computer-output microform* (COM). The COM device converts the digital information contained on computer-generated magnetic tape into print display on microform. Thus, in catalog production, computer technology combines with micrographics to ensure lower costs and more efficient updating.

As with the book catalog, the microform catalog has the advantage of economy in duplication. Once a microform catalog is produced, it is much cheaper to duplicate than a book catalog. Furthermore, the microform catalog carries the primary advantage of book catalogs—portability—to an extreme. This device enables every branch or department of a library to possess a copy of the entire library catalog, a luxury unthinkable before the development of micrographics. The major disadvantage of microform occurs at the use stage. The need for a microform reader, the handling of the fiche or film, and the display image become psychological barriers for many users. Nonetheless, the microform catalog is considered to be a viable backup device to supplement and complement a machine-readable database or an online catalog. Furthermore, many libraries with catalog databases are not yet able to mount an online catalog and are caught between two sets of rising costs: card catalog maintenance and book catalog production. For them, a COM catalog may serve as an interim to an online catalog or even be considered a satisfactory long-term alternative.

Online catalog

When a library's users can retrieve catalog records directly from a computer database, the library is said to have an *online catalog*. The usual mode of display in an online catalog is through a computer terminal. In this mode, individual cataloging records or parts thereof are retrieved by means of access points or search keys and are displayed instantly on a monitor. Many of the terminals are accompanied by printers, which may be used to print out desired items.

The records that are the base for an online catalog may be stored in a mainframe or a minicomputer to which public-access terminals are connected. In either case, users are literally "on line" to the database.

There is another catalog form that is also generally referred to as an online catalog. This is the CD-ROM (compact disk—read-only memory) catalog. For CD-ROM catalogs, a catalog database is periodically copied onto compact disks, which can be accessed through stand-alone microcomputers.

Users gain numerous advantages from online catalogs, including instant feedback during the retrieval process and the availability of more access points than any manual catalog can offer. Furthermore, they allow remote access so that the user does not have to be physically present in the library in order to search in the catalog.

An online catalog can be integrated with other library operations such as cataloging, acquisitions, and circulation, resulting in an integrated online system. With an integrated system, the user is able not only to identify an item but also to ascertain whether the item is currently available for browsing or circulation. In some integrated systems, it is also possible to find out whether a particular item is on order. An added advantage is that an online catalog is not subject to physical wear and tear, as is a card or book catalog. (Early online systems were plagued by "down time," making the system temporarily unavailable to patrons.

However, this, or any other mechanical malfunction, is rarely a problem with modern online installations.)

Machine-readable cataloging (MARC) records form the basic units of an online catalog. For a cataloging record to be machine-readable, not only must it be input to a computer, but also its various elements must be tagged or labeled in such a way that they can be stored, manipulated, and eventually retrieved in all the ways that are appropriate for technical and reference services in libraries. In the early 1960s, in consultation with other major libraries, the Library of Congress began work on developing a protocol for coding bibliographic records. The emerging protocol was called the *MARC format*. There are other protocols for coding various kinds of records for computer storage and retrieval. For library records, MARC is the system that has prevailed in this country and in many others. The MARC format is briefly explained at the end of this chapter, and it is discussed in greater detail in Chapter 15.

Access Points in a Catalog

Probably one of the most significant ways in which catalogs differ is in the number and nature of their *access provisions*—the ways a given item may be retrieved. Most traditional card catalogs have entries filed under headings for author(s) or other responsible agent(s), first word in the title not an article, the first word of an alternative title, series name if applicable, and (except for most fictional works) one or more subject headings. Each access point is represented on a separate card or entry. There has been considerable change over the years in just what aspects of records should be made access points and what the style of headings should be, but in the manual cataloging environment at least, the overall level of access has remained about the same.

Catalog automation brought a fundamental change because it allowed retrieval over a wide range of access points. Some early computer-printed lists, hardcopy or microform, listed a given item under each of its major title words. Most online and CD-ROM catalogs allow keyword searching, i.e., searching on any word in titles, subject heading strings, and other parts of the record. Many also allow combined searches, through Boolean operations that enable patterns like "both X and Y in one record," "either X or Y," "X but not Y," and so on in even more complicated groupings.

Arrangement of Records in a Catalog

In manually prepared catalogs, how the records or entries are arranged determines how they can be retrieved. There are two primary ways in which individual bibliographic entries are organized or arranged into a coherent file: alphabetical and systematic (or classified).

In a *classified* catalog, the entries are arranged according to a chosen system of classification, resulting in subject collocation. This is a form of catalog arrangement that was popular in the nineteenth century but which, as a public tool, has become all but extinct in American libraries. However, as a working tool for catalogers, a variant of the classified catalog exists in the form of the *shelflist* (a full set of main entry catalog records filed in call-number order). A classed catalog that is intended for library users needs an author-title index if it is to be an effective access tool.

In an *alphabetical,* or *dictionary,* catalog, entries are organized in alphabetical sequence, with author, title, and subject headings interfiled. This form was introduced in the latter part of the nineteenth century and soon became predominant in this country. In some libraries, the dictionary catalog may be divided into two alphabetical sequences: one for author and title entries and the other for subject entries. In others, all name entries may be in one sequence and all subject and title entries interfiled in another. Over the years, standards for filing in library catalogs have been developed by the American Library Association and the Library of Congress.[1] Nonetheless, many libraries developed their own filing policies or modified the existing standards.

Some catalogs are in what is called *accession order:* records are filed chronologically by when they were added to the catalog, and indexes are provided to give systematic access. Such catalogs are rarely intended for use by the public.

In an online catalog, the internal arrangement of stored records depends on how a given system is designed. The arrangement is not relevant to a user's search because he or she sees only a small segment of the catalog at any given time. How retrieved items appear on the screen also depends on the design of the system, and here several options may be open to the searcher. Some systems display retrieved items in alphabetical order, while others display them in chronological or reversed chronological order; some systems also allow display of retrieved items in classified order.

CATALOGING OPERATIONS

One cannot discuss cataloging in today's library environment without acknowledging that catalogers in local libraries make heavy use of bibliographic records prepared elsewhere, a practice called *copy catalog-*

[1]*ALA Filing Rules.* Chicago: American Library Association, 1980; and *Library of Congress Filing Rules.* Washington, Library of Congress, 1980.

ing. Sources of such records are the Library of Congress (LC) and, for those who are members of networks or consortia, records prepared by other members. A *network* or *consortium* is an association of libraries with the main purpose of sharing resources, including cataloging information. It maintains a cataloging database of contributed records that also includes records from the LC MARC database. Member libraries have direct online access to the database and may use its records for verification of items to be purchased by the local library, for identification of items for interlibrary loan purposes, or for producing records for the local catalog. The largest networks in this country are the Online Computer Library Center (OCLC), the Research Libraries Information Network (RLIN), and the Western Library Network (WLN).

Despite the large role that copy cataloging plays in local libraries today, all professional catalogers have to be able to do full cataloging for an item—a process called *original cataloging.* For items for which no cataloging copy exists, one must rely on original cataloging.

Cataloging Files

Before considering the procedures entailed in the cataloging operation, it should be noted that a library's bibliographic apparatus may contain several files, each made up of individual records. Files relating to the cataloging operation are (1) the bibliographic file, (2) the shelflist, and (3) the authority file or files.

1. The bibliographic file represents the library's holdings; in other words, it is what is ordinarily known as "the catalog." It contains a bibliographic record for every cataloged item in the collection, with multiple access under main and added entries represented by headings formulated in standard terms. It also contains two kinds of cross-references, those which lead a searcher from an unused term to the equivalent authorized term (*see* references) and those which link related headings (*see also* references).

2. A shelflist is a copy of a subset of the bibliographic file. It consists of an array of duplicates of main entry records arranged in shelf order (i.e., by call numbers). The purpose of a shelflist is twofold: for inventory control and for facilitating the part in the cataloging process that requires fitting book numbers into a preexisting array. In addition to basic bibliographic information, a shelflist record often contains information regarding acquisition of the item, the library's holdings, locations of individual copies, and such notes as "Missing." Traditionally, libraries maintained a shelflist in card form and kept it in the cataloging department as a working tool, and this is usually still the case for libraries with

card catalogs. In some such libraries, however, the shelflist is made available to the public as a means of providing, in part, the classified approach. Libraries with online catalogs do not need to keep a separate shelflist for either record keeping or shelf-order access, but nevertheless some of them still maintain manual shelflists, in part because of how they facilitate the shelf-reading aspect of taking inventory.

3. The authority file records the standardized forms of names and topical terms that have been authorized as headings, i.e., access points, along with their associated cross-references. The need for an authority file and the work that goes into building one are described below under "Authority Work." In manual systems, authority files are often maintained separately, one authority file for names and another for subject headings. In online systems, they may either be one or two separate files, and either way, they may or may not be integrally linked to the bibliographic file.

Cataloging Procedures

Several distinct cataloging procedures are part of preparing an individual bibliographic record for a library: (1) *descriptive cataloging* (the preparation of bibliographic descriptions and the determination of bibliographic access points), (2) *subject analysis,* which includes subject heading assignment (often referred to as *subject cataloging,* which involves the selection of subject access points for individual bibliographic records) and classification (the assignment of class numbers and book numbers), and (3) *authority work* (the determination of the standardized forms of subject terms and names). For those doing online cataloging, an additional procedure is MARC tagging. Each of these activities is the focus of one or more later chapters in this book. Only a brief account of these activities is given in this introductory chapter.

Descriptive cataloging

Descriptive cataloging consists of

1. Drafting a set of information that includes the item's title, the agent responsible (most often the author), the edition, the place and date of publication, the publisher, a physical description, series membership if any, and any appropriate notes (such as "Includes index" or "Sequel to ...").
2. Deciding what elements in the description should be the basis for access points, in other words, what the main and added entries should be.

3. Determining the proper form for the names and titles selected as main and added entries. (This last is called *name authority work,* which is described below.)

Descriptive cataloging in this country, and indeed in much of the world, is carried out according to accepted standards. The standards that have prevailed over the years are described in Part Two of this book. The one that is used in most English-speaking countries is *Anglo-American Cataloguing Rules,* second edition, revised (referred to as *AACR2R*), which was published in 1988.

Subject cataloging

For each bibliographic record, appropriate subject headings are chosen from an authorized list. Most general libraries in this country use one of two authorized lists, *Library of Congress Subject Headings* (LCSH) for large libraries and *Sears List of Subject Headings* for smaller ones. For specialized libraries, special subject headings lists, such as *Medical Subject Headings,* may be used. In some libraries, subject headings under which there are local listings are registered in a local subject authority file.

Traditionally, subject headings have been assigned from authorized lists only. In online catalogs, subject terms not derived from an authorized list are sometimes assigned to augment, or to take the place of, the authorized terms.

Classification

Classification requires fitting the primary topic of a work to the provisions in the classification scheme being used. Most American libraries use either the *Library of Congress Classification* (LCC) or the *Dewey Decimal Classification* (DDC). Specialized libraries often use subject-oriented systems such as *National Library of Medicine Classification.* After the appropriate class number has been chosen, a book number is added to form a call number. This too is done according to standard patterns, somewhat different for each system. It also calls for adjusting the numbers indicated in the standards to fit the new item into the shelf array of existing items.

Authority work

Authority work entails a procedure that spans both descriptive and subject cataloging. In order to fulfill the objective of the catalog as a tool for retrieving all works by a given author or all works on a given subject, the access points to bibliographic records are normalized and standardized. In other words, all works by a given author or on a given subject are listed under a uniform heading for that author or subject. To this end, each author's name and the name of each subject is "established" when used for the first time, and the decision is recorded in a record called the *authority record*. Furthermore, to allow access through variant names and different forms of a name or a subject, cross-references to a given heading are provided in the catalog and also are recorded in the authority record for that heading. The same is true for references between related headings. A fact worth noting is that while each bibliographic record represents a physical item or group of items in a collection, each authority record refers to a person, corporate body, common title, or subject that may appear in any number of bibliographic records. The activities of authority control include both integrating standardized authority records into the local system and preparing authority records for those names and subjects not available from standard authority files.

When a new authority record must be made, it often requires considerable checking in reference and other sources and considerable consultation as well to arrive at the decisions that are ultimately registered in it. Authority work, therefore, has long been regarded as the most time-consuming, costly aspect of cataloging.

MARC tagging

In an automated cataloging environment, the cataloger also must supply the codes and other information needed for computer processing. In MARC records, for instance, there is considerably more information relating to the item than is called for in a standard bibliographic description. This added information includes various computer tags as well as codes for language, type of publication, and other attributes of the item being cataloged. In American libraries, records are set up according to the various USMARC formats,[2] a set of related standards for handling different kinds of records, including those for bibliographic and authority data.

A MARC record is made up of three parts, the first two of which contain information that aids in processing the record and are not the direct responsibility of catalogers; in modern installations, this information is "system supplied." It is the provisions that cover the data in the main part of a MARC record that catalogers must learn how to use. This part of a MARC record is organized into fields and, for most fields, into component subfields. Each field is identified by a three-digit numerical code called a *field tag*, and each subfield is identified by an alphabetic or

[2]For a more detailed discussion of the USMARC formats, see Chapter 15 of this book.

numeric *subfield code.* Certain fields contain two *indicators* containing values (in the form of a numeric character or a blank) that interpret or supplement the data in the field, e.g., whether a personal name includes a surname or what kind of title is presented.

Table 1-1 shows the major MARC field tags for a bibliographic record, and Table 1-2 shows those for an authority record. Each is explained and illustrated by a coded record example, which also is explained in turn.

RECORD EXAMPLES

The following pages, which conclude this chapter, take two records pertaining to a two-volume monographic work by William A. Katz—its bibliographic record and the authority record for Katz—and use them to explain and illustrate what has just been said about cataloging operations.

The Bibliographic Record

The basic cataloging data, prepared by the cataloger, include the following:

1. Classification data
   Class number and book number: Z711 .K32 1987 (based on Library of Congress Classification)
   or *Class number:* 025.52 (based on Dewey Decimal Classification)
2. Descriptive data
   a. Bibliographic description

Title:	Introduction to reference work
Statement of responsibility:	William A. Katz
Edition statement:	5th ed.
Publication:	New York : McGraw-Hill, c1987.
Physical description:	2 v. ; 24 cm.
Series:	McGraw-Hill series in library education
Note:	Contents: v. 1. Basic information sources — v. 2. Reference services and reference processes.
Note:	Includes bibliographical references and indexes.
Standard numbers:	ISBN 0-070-33537-0 (v. 1) : $28.95 ISBN 0-070-33538-9 (v. 2) : $27.95

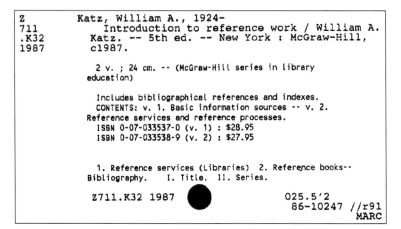

```
Z          Katz, William A., 1924-
711            Introduction to reference work / William A.
.K32       Katz. -- 5th ed. -- New York : McGraw-Hill,
1987       c1987.

           2 v. ; 24 cm. -- (McGraw-Hill series in library
           education)

           Includes bibliographical references and indexes.
           CONTENTS: v. 1. Basic information sources -- v. 2.
           Reference services and reference processes.
           ISBN 0-07-033537-0 (v. 1) : $28.95
           ISBN 0-07-033538-9 (v. 2) : $27.95


           1. Reference services (Libraries)  2. Reference books--
           Bibliography.    I. Title.  II. Series.

           Z711.K32 1987          ⬤           025.5'2
                                              86-10247 //r91
                                                         MARC
```

FIGURE 1-1   A catalog card.

  b. Bibliographic access points
    Author (main entry):   Katz, William A., 1924-
    Title: Introduction to reference work
    Series: McGraw-Hill series in library education
  3. Subject cataloging data
    Subject heading: Reference services (Libraries)
    Subject heading: Reference books—Bibliography.

In a card catalog, the data are arranged in the format shown in Figure 1-1. A complete set of catalog cards for this book appears in Appendix A.

In Figure 1-1, which represents the *main entry* card, the call number appears in the upper left-hand corner. The main entry under the author's name appears on the first line, followed by descriptive details in separate paragraphs. The paragraph that appears at the bottom of the second card is called *tracings.* It traces the subject and bibliographic access points. The two subject entries are preceded by arabic numerals, and the two added entries for title and series follow roman numerals. Instead of repeating the words in the titles and the series, the tracings for the added entries carry the words *Title* and *Series,* indicating that these added entries are the same as in the body of the record.

A coded bibliographic record

To make the cataloging data machine-readable, each of the elements shown above must be coded. Figure 1-2 shows the coded bibliographic record for the Katz book from the OCLC union catalog, the largest MARC database in existence.

To understand this MARC record, it is necessary to look at it in conjunction with Table 1-1 and the accompanying explanation.

TABLE 1-1   Tags for Frequently Occurring Variable Data Fields in a Bibliographic Record

Tag	Name
008	Coded control information
010	Library of Congress Control Number
020	International Standard Book Number
040	Cataloging Source
043	Geographic Area Code
050	Library of Congress Call Number
082	Dewey Decimal Call Number
090	Local call numbers
100	Main Entry—Personal Name
110	Main Entry—Corporate Name
111	Main Entry—Meeting Name
130	Main Entry—Uniform Title
245	Title Statement
250	Edition Statement
260	Publication, Distribution, etc. (Imprint)
300	Physical Description
400	Series Statement/Added Entry—Personal Name
410	Series Statement/Added Entry—Corporate Name
440	Series Statement/Added Entry—Title
500	General Note
504	Bibliography Note
505	Formatted Contents Note
600	Subject Added Entry—Personal Name
610	Subject Added Entry—Corporate Name
611	Subject Added Entry—Meeting Name
650	Subject Added Entry—Topical Term
651	Subject Added Entry—Geographic Name
653	Index Term—Uncontrolled
700	Added Entry—Personal Name
710	Added Entry—Corporate Name
730	Added Entry—Uniform Title
740	Added Entry—Variant Title
800	Series Added Entry—Personal Name
810	Series Added Entry—Corporate Name
811	Series Added Entry—Meeting Name

Explanation of Table 1-1

In the earlier discussion of MARC it was pointed out that the MARC record is divided into various fields. All the field tags are three digits long. The various kinds of fields are often referred to as the 00X fields, the 0XX fields, and the 1XX, 2XX, ... fields.

The information ordinarily thought of as catalog data is recorded in that part of the MARC structure called the *variable fields*. The variable

```
▶ OCLC:      13559686        Rec stat:    c
  Entered:    19860421        Replaced:    19910308    Used:     19920506
  Type: a              Bib lvl: m          Source:        Lang:  eng
  Repr:                Enc lvl:            Conf pub: 0    Ctry:  nyu
  Indx: 1              Mod rec:            Govt pub:      Cont:  b
  Desc: a              Int lvl:            Festschr: 0    Illus:
                       F/B:      0         Dat tp:   s    Dates: 1987,      ¶
▶   1  010      86-10247//r91 ¶
▶   2  040      DLC ‡c DLC ¶
▶   3  020      0070335370 (v. 1) : ‡c $28.95 ¶
▶   4  020      0070335389 (v. 2) : ‡c $27.95 ¶
▶   5  050 00   Z711 ‡b .K32 1987 ¶
▶   6  082 00   025.5/2 ‡2 19 ¶
▶   7  090      ‡b  ¶
▶   8  049      KUKK ¶
▶   9  100 1    Katz, William A., ‡d 1924- ¶
▶  10  245 10   Introduction to reference work / ‡c William A. Katz. ¶
▶  11  250      5th ed. ¶
▶  12  260      New York : ‡b McGraw-Hill, ‡c c1987. ¶
▶  13  300      2 v. ; ‡c 24 cm. ¶
▶  14  440 0    McGraw-Hill series in library education ¶
▶  15  504      Includes bibliographical references and indexes. ¶
▶  16  505 0    v. 1. Basic information sources -- v. 2. Reference services and
  reference processes. ¶
▶  17  650 0    Reference services (Libraries) ¶
▶  18  650 0    Reference books ‡x Bibliography. ¶
```

FIGURE 1-2   A MARC bibliographic record from the OCLC database.

fields, in turn, comprise two types: (1) variable control fields and (2) variable data fields.

The variable control fields (00X) contain control numbers and other control and coded information used in processing MARC records. (In Figure 1-2, these are shown without codes in the first seven lines.)

The variable data fields (01X–8XX) contain cataloging data. (These are shown line by line in Figure 1-2.) Fields 010–082 contain numbers and codes, such as standard book number, Library of Congress control number, and call numbers. Fields 100–8XX contain bibliographic and subject cataloging data: elements of a bibliographic description, main and added entries, and subject headings. In OCLC records used as examples throughout this book, field 049 is used for local holdings information.

Some of the field tags can be seen to fall into groups. The 1XX fields are for different categories of main entry. The 4XX and 8XX fields pertain to series. The 5XX fields are for notes. The 6XX and 7XX fields are for subject added entries and name and title added entries, respectively.

Most fields are divided into subfields, identified by alphabetical or numeric codes preceded by the symbol ‡ (a dagger), called a *delimiter*, e.g., ‡b, ‡2, etc. Generally, the first element in a field is subfield ‡a, followed by other subfields. For instance, in the publication details field (260), ‡a is for place of publication, ‡b is for publisher, and ‡c is for date; and in the Dewey Decimal call number field (082), ‡a is for classification number, ‡b is for item number, and ‡2 is for edition number (i.e., the number of the edition of DDC from which the classification number is taken). Some subfield codes have mnemonic value; for instance, ‡d in fields 100, 700, and 800 for personal name entries is for date of birth or birth/death dates, and ‡l in fields 1XX, 4XX, and 7XX is for language of work. Table 1-1 does not show subfield codes, but some are shown in Figure 1-2, the coded Katz record. (In record display, the ‡a subfield code is often implicit and does not show.)

Explanation of Figure 1-2
Figure 1-2 shows the "full" MARC record for the Katz book. *Full* means here that virtually all elements and codes contained in the record are displayed. It is primarily library personnel who need to see coded records; in most cases, users of online catalogs are offered abbreviated or full but noncoded displays. Although some of what appears in the Katz MARC record has no obvious relation to what normally appears on a traditional library catalog card, most of what can be seen is simply a different manner of displaying standard catalog information, with each element showing the codes that enable the data to be processed by machine. The following explanation goes through the Katz MARC record element by element.

The first line gives the OCLC control number and shows that the record has been corrected (Rec stat: c); the second line gives the dates for when the record was first entered, replaced, and last used.

Most of the data in the next five lines come from field 008, which gives various coded information about the record. Although of no direct interest to users and often not displayed in the public catalog, this coded information is essential to efficient record processing, especially in systems that allow searchers to specify such things as "only English language material" or "only if there are illustrations" or "only if published since 1980."

The next eighteen lines of the record, *variable data fields* 010–650, present what many would call the heart of the MARC record. The number after each line number is its MARC field tag. The data in the first subfield begins a few spaces over. Line by line, the Katz MARC record shows

010 LC control number
040 Cataloging source was LC
020 ISBN for first volume
020 ISBN for second volume
050 LC call number (Class number is first subfield; subfield b is for the book number.)
082 Dewey call number
090 Reserved for local call numbers
049 Local holdings symbol
100 Personal name main entry heading for Katz (Subfield d is for date of birth.)
245 Title and statement of responsibility (The latter is subfield c; if there were a subtitle, it would be subfield b.)

```
PUBLIC CATALOG                                   Searching: KY/KENTUCKY

  Katz, William A., 1924-
    Introduction to reference work /  William A. Katz.
    5th ed.
  New York : McGraw-Hill, c1987.
    2 v. ; 24 cm.

    McGraw-Hill series in library education
  Includes bibliographical references and indexes.
  v. 1. Basic information sources -- v. 2. Reference services and reference
  processes.

    Reference services (Libraries)
    Reference books.

  Press RETURN to continue:
  PUBLIC CATALOG                                 Searching: KY/KENTUCKY

  Katz, William A., 1924-
    Introduction to reference work /  William A. Katz.
    5th ed.
  New York : McGraw-Hill, c1987.
    2 v. ; 24 cm.

  LOCATION          CALL#/VOL/NO/COPY            STATUS

  KG/KING REF       Z711 .K32 1987 v.1 c.1       Available
  KG/KING REF       Z711 .K32 1987 v.2 c.1       Available
```

```
(END) Press RETURN to continue or /ES to start a new search:
```

(a)

```
PUBLIC CATALOG                                   Searching: KY/KENTUCKY

  MAIN ENTRY AUTHOR: Katz, William A., 1924-
  TITLE:            Introduction to reference work /  William A. Katz.
  EDITION:          5th ed.
  PUBLISHER:        New York : McGraw-Hill, c1987.
  PHYSICAL DESC:    2 v. ; 24 cm.
  SERIES:           McGraw-Hill series in library education
  NOTES:            Includes bibliographical references and indexes.
                    v. 1. Basic information sources -- v. 2. Reference
                    services and reference processes.

    SUBJECTS:       Reference services (Libraries)
                    Reference books.

  LOCATION          CALL#/VOL/NO/COPY            STATUS

  KG/KING REF       Z711 .K32 1987 v.1 c.1       Available
  KG/KING REF       Z711 .K32 1987 v.2 c.1       Available
```

```
(END) Press RETURN to continue or /ES to start a new search:
```

(b)

FIGURE 1-3   Public display of MARC records in an LS2000 online catalog. (a) A full bibliographic record. (b) A bibliographic record with field labels. (c) A brief bibliographic record.

```
PUBLIC CATALOG                              Searching: KY/KENTUCKY

  Katz, William A., 1924-
    Introduction to reference work /  William A. Katz.
    5th ed.
  New York : McGraw-Hill, c1987.
    2 v. ; 24 cm.

  LOCATION        CALL#/VOL/NO/COPY                  STATUS

  KG/KINGZ711 .K32 1987 c.1Available
```

```
(END) Press RETURN to continue or /ES to start a new search:
```
(c)

FIGURE 1-3   (Continued)

250   Edition statement
260   Place of publication, publisher (subfield b), and date of publication (subfield c)
300   Number of volumes (number of pages for a one-volume work) and size (subfield c)
440   Title of the series the book appears in
504   Bibliography note
505   Contents note for the titles of each of the volumes
650   First topical subject heading
650   Second topical subject heading

The numerals 0 and 1 that appear between some field tags and the first subfield are *indicators,* the meanings of which are defined uniquely for each field. For details, consult *USMARC Concise Formats.*[3]

Once coded, the information contained in the MARC record can be manipulated by the computer to produce various cataloging products: catalog card (as shown in Fig. 1-1), microform catalog entry, online catalog entry, acquisitions list, etc. While the layout of a catalog card has been standardized, online display of records varies from system to system. Within a particular system, records also may be displayed in long or short formats. Figures 1-3 and 1-4 show different displays of the same cataloging information in two different systems (LS2000 and NOTIS) of online catalogs, some of which show different configurations of the same data.

[3]*USMARC Concise Formats.* Prepared by Network Development and MARC Standards Office. Washington: Cataloging Distribution Service, Library of Congress, 1991.

```
Search Request: T=INTRODUCTION TO REFERENCE WORK      University of Kentucky
BOOK - Record 8 of 8 Entries Found                            Long View
--------------------------------------------------------------------------
Author:         Katz, William A., 1924-
Title:          Introduction to reference work / William A. Katz.
Edition:        5th ed.
Published:      New York : McGraw-Hill, c1987.
Description:    2 v. ; 24 cm.

ISBN            0070335370 (v. 1) : $28.95
                0070335389 (v. 2) : $27.95

Contents:       v. 1. Basic information sources -- v. 2. Reference services
                and reference processes.
Notes:          Includes bibliographical references and indexes.
Subjects:       Reference services (Libraries)
                Reference books--Bibliography.
--------------------------------------------- + Page 1 of 2 -------------
STArt over       HOLdings                    <F8>  FORward page
HELp             BRIef view                  <F5>  PREvious record
OTHer options    INDex

NEXT COMMAND:

Search Request: T=INTRODUCTION TO REFERENCE WORK      University of Kentucky
BOOK - Record 8 of 8 Entries Found                            Long View
--------------------------------------------------------------------------
Title:          Introduction to reference work

Series:         McGraw-Hill series in library education.
--------------------------------------------------------------------------
LOCATION:        CALL NUMBER:               STATUS:
King Reference   Z711 .K32 1987             Enter HOL 1 for holdings
(Non-Circulating)




--------------------------------------------- + Page 2 of 2 -------------
STArt over       HOLdings                    <F7>  BACk page
HELp             BRIef view                  <F5>  PREvious record
OTHer options    INDex

NEXT COMMAND:
```

(a)

```
Search Request: T=INTRODUCTION TO REFERENCE WORK      University of Kentucky
BOOK - Record 8 of 8 Entries Found                            Brief View
--------------------------------------------------------------------------
Author:         Katz, William A., 1924-

Title:          Introduction to reference work / William A. Katz.

Edition:        5th ed.
Published:      New York : McGraw-Hill, c1987.
Series:         McGraw-Hill series in library education.

Description:    2 v. ; 24 cm.
--------------------------------------------------------------------------
LOCATION:        CALL NUMBER:               STATUS:
King Reference   Z711 .K32 1987             Enter HOL 1 for holdings
(Non-Circulating)


--------------------------------------------- Page 1 of 1 ---------------
STArt over       HOLdings                    <F5>  PREvious record
HELp             LONg view
OTHer options    INDex

NEXT COMMAND:
```

(b)

FIGURE 1-4 Public display of MARC records in a NOTIS online catalog. (a) A full bibliographic record. (b) A brief bibliographic record.

The Authority Record

An authority record contains essentially the following elements:

1. The established heading for a person or a corporate body, the uniform title[4] of a work, or a subject
2. Cross-references from other names, titles, or terms not used for the heading and to and from related headings
3. The sources used in establishing the heading

The name authority record for William A. Katz includes the following data:

> *Established heading*
> **Katz, William A., 1924-**
>
> *Cross-references*
> Katz, Bill, 1924-
> Katz, Willis Armstrong, 1924-
> Katz, William, 1924-
>
> *Sources used*
> Library Buildings Institute, Chicago, 1963. Problems in planning library facilities, 1964-
> His Your library, c1984: CIP t.p. (William Katz, SUNY at Albany)

A coded authority record

Figure 1-5 shows a coded authority record from the OCLC union database representing the authority data for the catalog heading for William A. Katz.

As was the case with the coded Katz bibliographic record and the table of MARC bibliographic tags, it can be best understood in conjunction with Table 1-2, which shows the major fields in the MARC authorities format, along with their field tags. Some of the fields parallel those in the format for bibliographic data: the control fields and 1XX fields (with the authorized headings reflecting different types of names: 100 personal, 110 corporate, 111 meeting, and so on). Others are quite different; the 4XX fields show "*see* references"; the 5XX fields are for "*see also* references"; and the 6XX fields are variously defined: complex references, history notes, source for name choice, and notes identifying the sources used in establishing the heading.

---

[4]A standardized title for a work that has appeared under different titles; for a fuller discussion, see Chapter 5 of this book.

```
▶ ARN:      324772           Rec stat:    n
  Entered:  19840819         Replaced:    19840819
  Type:      z       Enc lvl:    n     Source:          Lang:
  Roman:     ∎       Upd status: a     Mod rec:         Name use: a
  Govt agn:  ∎       Ref status: a     Subj:       a    Subj use: a
  Series:    n       Auth status: a    Geo subd: n      Ser use:  b
  Ser num:   n       Auth/ref:   a     Name:       a    Rules:    c ¶
▶  1  010      n  79092477  ¶
▶  2  040      DLC ǂc DLC ¶
▶  3  100 10   Katz, William A., ǂd 1924- ¶
▶  4  400 10   Katz, Bill, ǂd 1924- ¶
▶  5  400 10   Katz, Willis Armstrong, ǂd 1924- ¶
▶  6  400 10   Katz, William, ǂd 1924- ¶
▶  7  670      Library Buildings Institute, Chicago, 1963. ǂb Problems in
planning library facilities, 1964. ¶
▶  8  670      His Your library, c1984: ǂb CIP t.p. (William Katz, SUNY at
Albany) ¶
```

FIGURE 1-5   A MARC authority record from the OCLC data base.

In Figure 1-5, showing the MARC name authority record for the heading for William A. Katz, the first two lines give the authority file control number, indicate that it is a new record, and give the date when it was entered and the date when it was replaced (in this case, the

TABLE 1-2   Tags for Frequently Occurring Variable Data Fields in an Authority Record

Tag	Name
008	Coded control information
010	Library of Congress Control Number
040	Cataloging Source
050	Library of Congress Call Number
100	Heading—Personal Name
110	Heading—Corporate Name
111	Heading—Meeting Name
130	Heading—Uniform Title
151	Heading—Geographic Name
400	See From Tracing—Personal Name
410	See From Tracing—Corporate Name
411	See From Tracing—Meeting Name
430	See From Tracing—Uniform Title
450	See From Tracing—Topical Term
451	See From Tracing—Geographic Name
500	See Also From Tracing—Personal Name
510	See Also From Tracing—Corporate Name
511	See Also From Tracing—Meeting Name
530	See Also From Tracing—Uniform Title
550	See Also From Tracing—Topical Term
551	See Also From Tracing—Geographic Name
663	Complex See Also Reference—Name
664	Complex See Reference—Name
670	Source Data Found
675	Source Data Not Found
680	Public General Note

same). The third through seventh lines (unnumbered) show other control data. The remaining lines, containing variable data fields, are analyzed below:

010   LC control number
040   Record originated with LC
100   Authorized personal name heading for William A. Katz, with his birth date
400   Form of name not used as the heading for Katz, from which a *see* reference would be made to the preferred heading
400   Another nonpreferred form of name for Katz, from which a *see* reference also would be made
400   A third nonpreferred form of name for Katz, from which a *see* reference also would be made
670   One of the sources in which the chosen form of Katz's name was found
670   Another source used in establishing Katz's name

As in the case of a bibliographic record, the coded authority record can be used to generate authority records for different kinds of catalog. Figure 1-6 shows the authority record for Katz in the card format.

The authority record, in whatever physical form, shows the standardized heading for use as an access point in the catalog and also provides data for generating cross-references that link variant names and forms to the authorized heading. Again, the cross-references may be displayed in different ways in the public catalog. Figures 1-7 through 1-9 show examples of such references in the card catalog and in two online catalogs.

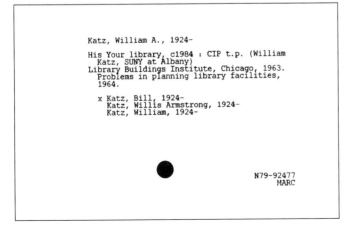

FIGURE 1-6   An authority record in card format.

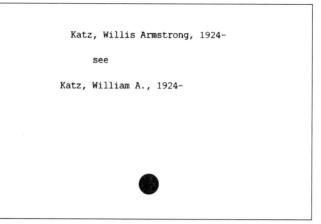

FIGURE 1-7   Cross-reference in card format.

CONCLUSION

This introductory chapter has attempted to set the framework for a study of bibliographic control in the library environment, particularly in the environment of the general library. It began with the general picture, defining bibliographic control and noting the various ways of achieving it in all environments but showing how its demands vary according to the nature of the material to be brought under control. Abstracting and indexing services differ from libraries in terms of both ultimate product and the details of how listed items are analyzed and tagged for retrieval. They are both engaged in bibliographic control, however, and both use similar identification and retrieval mechanisms.

The discussion then turned to library catalogs, spelling out their similarities and differences and discussing the impact of library automation. It proceeded to the operations entailed in producing and maintaining a library catalog and its subsidiary files. Finally, it illustrated those operations through extended analysis of a bibliographic record and an authority record in terms of their essential features: how they are coded for machine storage, manipulation, and retrieval; and how they are displayed in various forms of catalogs.

All these topics are treated in extensive detail in subsequent chapters. Their order reflects the order of activities in producing a bibliographic record: drafting a description, deciding on name access points and forms of names, assigning subject headings, and classification. Emphasis is on standard North American cataloging practice, reflecting Library of Congress practice, but along the way alternative means and

```
PUBLIC CATALOG                              Searching: KY/KENTUCKY


AUTHOR:   KATZ, WILLIS

REF   TITLES   AUTHOR
---   ------   ------
R1       39    KATZ, WILLIS ARMSTRONG, 1924-
(END)




CHOICE: R1
```
(a)

```
PUBLIC CATALOG                              Searching: KY/KENTUCKY


PERSONAL NAME:   KATZ, WILLIAM A., 1924-

REF   TITLES   PERSONAL NAME
---   ------   -------------
R1       39    Katz, William A., 1924-
               *REPLACES: KATZ, WILLIS ARMSTRONG, 1924-

R2        2    - ed
(END)




CHOICE: R1
```
(b)

```
PUBLIC CATALOG                              Searching: KY/KENTUCKY


PERSONAL NAME:   KATZ, WILLIAM A., 1924-
        FOUND:   39

REF   DATE   TITLES                          AUTHOR
---   ----   ------                          ------
R1    1989   The Acquisitions budget /
R2    1988   Finance, budget, and management
R3    1987   Introduction to reference work / Katz, William A.,
R4    1987   Current trends in information :
R5    1987   Reference services today :
R6    1987   The Publishing and review of ref
R7    1986   Magazines for libraries :        Katz, William A.,
R8    1986   Personnel issues in reference se
R9    1986   Reference and information servic
R10   1986   Reference and online services ha
(MORE)

CHOICE: R
```
(c)

FIGURE 1-8   Public display of cross-references in an LS2000 online catalog. (a) Screen 1: Catalog user enters name: Katz, Willis. Online catalog responds with number of postings. User chooses R1. (b) Screen 2: Display of authorized heading. User chooses R1 to see bibliographic records. (c) Screen 3: Display of index to bibliographic records.

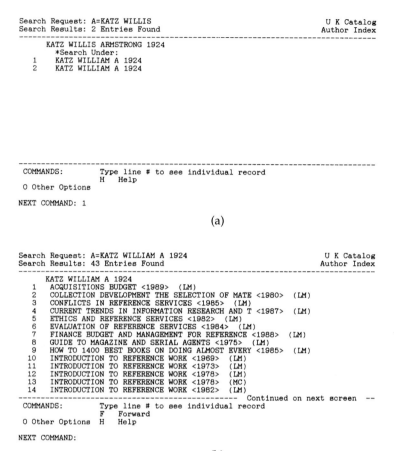

```
Search Request: A=KATZ WILLIS                                    U K Catalog
Search Results: 2 Entries Found                                  Author Index
------------------------------------------------------------------------------
        KATZ WILLIS ARMSTRONG 1924
          *Search Under:
    1     KATZ WILLIAM A 1924
    2     KATZ WILLIAM A 1924




------------------------------------------------------------------------------
    COMMANDS:        Type line # to see individual record
                     H   Help
    O Other Options

    NEXT COMMAND: 1
```

(a)

```
Search Request: A=KATZ WILLIAM A 1924                            U K Catalog
Search Results: 43 Entries Found                                 Author Index
------------------------------------------------------------------------------
        KATZ WILLIAM A 1924
    1   ACQUISITIONS BUDGET <1989>  (LM)
    2   COLLECTION DEVELOPMENT THE SELECTION OF MATE <1980>  (LM)
    3   CONFLICTS IN REFERENCE SERVICES <1985>  (LM)
    4   CURRENT TRENDS IN INFORMATION RESEARCH AND T <1987>  (LM)
    5   ETHICS AND REFERENCE SERVICES <1982>  (LM)
    6   EVALUATION OF REFERENCE SERVICES <1984>  (LM)
    7   FINANCE BUDGET AND MANAGEMENT FOR REFERENCE <1988>  (LM)
    8   GUIDE TO MAGAZINE AND SERIAL AGENTS <1975>  (LM)
    9   HOW TO 1400 BEST BOOKS ON DOING ALMOST EVERY <1985>  (LM)
    10  INTRODUCTION TO REFERENCE WORK <1969>  (LM)
    11  INTRODUCTION TO REFERENCE WORK <1973>  (LM)
    12  INTRODUCTION TO REFERENCE WORK <1978>  (LM)
    13  INTRODUCTION TO REFERENCE WORK <1978>  (MC)
    14  INTRODUCTION TO REFERENCE WORK <1982>  (LM)
------------------------------------------------ Continued on next screen  --
    COMMANDS:        Type line # to see individual record
                     F   Forward
    O Other Options  H   Help

    NEXT COMMAND:
```

(b)

FIGURE 1-9   Public display of cross-references in a NOTIS online catalog. (a) Screen 1: Catalog user enters name: Katz Willis. Online catalog responds with cross-reference to authorized heading in main library collection and medical library collection. User chooses 1 (main library collection). (b) Screen 2: Display of index to bibliographic records.

tools are discussed. Details of MARC coding are left to the end (Chap. 15), even though it is now a part of all the rest, because its details cannot be understood until the complexities in what must be coded are mastered.

PART II
DESCRIPTIVE
CATALOGING

BASIC TOOLS

Anglo-American Cataloguing Rules. 2nd ed., 1988 revision. Prepared under
the direction of the Joint Steering Committee for Revision of AACR,
a committee of: the American Library Association, the Australian
Committee on Cataloguing, the British Library, the Canadian Committee on Cataloguing, the Library Association, the Library of Congress. Michael Gorman and Paul W. Winkler, eds. Chicago: American Library Association, 1988.
Gorman, Michael. *The Concise AACR2, 1988 Revision.* Chicago: American
Library Association, 1989.
Library of Congress Rule Interpretations. 2nd ed. Washington: Cataloging
Distribution Service, Library of Congress, 1989.

BACKGROUND READING

Cutter, Charles A. *Rules for a Dictionary Catalog.* 4th ed. Rewritten.
Washington: Government Printing Office, 1904. Republished, Lon-
don: The Library Association, 1953. (First published under the title
Rules for a Printed Dictionary Catalogue in 1876.)
Dunkin, Paul S. *Cataloging U.S.A.* Chicago: American Library Associa-
tion, 1969. Chaps. 3–4.
Gorman, Michael. "Descriptive Cataloguing: Its Past, Present, and Fu-
ture." In Michael Gorman et al., eds., *Technical Services Today and
Tomorrow.* Englewood, Colo.: Libraries Unlimited, 1990. Pp. 63–73.
International Conference on Cataloguing Principles, Paris, 1961. "State-
ment of Principles." In A. H. Chaplin and Dorothy Anderson, eds.,
Report of International Conference on Cataloguing Principles. London:
Organizing Committee of the International Conference on Cata-
loguing Principles, 1963. Pp. 91–96.

Jewett, Charles C. "Smithsonian Catalogue System." In *Smithsonian Report on the Construction of Catalogues of Libraries and of a General Catalogue and Their Publication by Means of Separate, Stereotyped Titles with Rules and Examples.* 2nd ed. Washington: Smithsonian Institution, 1853. Pp. 3–19. Also in Michael Carpenter and Elaine Svenonius, eds., *Foundations of Cataloging: A Sourcebook.* Littleton, Colo.: Libraries Unlimited, 1985. Pp. 51–61.

Lubetzky, Seymour. *Cataloging Rules and Principles: A Critique of the ALA Rules for Entry and a Proposed Design for Their Revision.* Washington: Library of Congress, 1953.

Lubetzky, Seymour. "Principles of Descriptive Cataloging." In *Studies of Descriptive Cataloging.* Washington: Library of Congress, 1946. Pp. 25–33. Also in Michael Carpenter and Elaine Svenonius, eds., *Foundations of Cataloging: A Sourcebook.* Littleton, Colo.: Libraries Unlimited, 1985. Pp. 104–112.

Osborn, Andrew D. "The Crisis in Cataloging." *Library Quarterly,* **11:**393–411, October 1941.

Pettee, Julia. "The Development of Authorship Entry and the Formulation of Authorship Rules as Found in the Anglo-American Code." *Library Quarterly,* **6:**270–290, July 1936. Also in Michael Carpenter and Elaine Svenonius, eds., *Foundations of Cataloging: A Sourcebook.* Littleton, Colo.: Libraries Unlimited, 1985. Pp. 75–89.

FURTHER READING

Auld, Larry. "Authority Control: An Eighty-Year Review." *Library Resources & Technical Services,* **26:**319–330, October/December 1982.

Boll, John. "The Future of AACR2 (in the OPAC Environment)." *Cataloging & Classification Quarterly* **12**(1):3–34, 1990.

Clack, Doris Hargrett. *Authority Control: Principles, Applications, and Instructions.* Chicago: American Library Association, 1990.

Henderson, Kathryn Luther. "'Treated with a Degree of Uniformity and Common Sense': Descriptive Cataloging in the United States—1876–1975." *Library Trends,* **25:**227–271, July 1976.

Kelm, Carol R. "The Historical Development of the Second Edition of Anglo-American Cataloging Rules." *Library Resources & Technical Services,* **22:**22–33, Winter 1978.

Maxwell, Margaret F. *Handbook for AACR2, 1988 Revision: Explaining and Illustrating the Anglo-American Cataloguing Rules.* Chicago: American Library Association, 1989.

Perreault, Jean. "Authority Control, Old and New." *Libri,* **32:**124–148, 1982.

Swanson, Edward. "Choice and Form of Access Points According to AACR2." *Cataloging & Classification Quarterly,* **11**(3/4):35–61, 1990.

Taylor, Arlene G. "Research and Theoretical Considerations in Authority Control." *Cataloging & Classification Quarterly,* **9**(3):29–57, 1989.

Tillett, Barbara B. "Considerations for Authority Control in the Online Environment." *Cataloging & Classification Quarterly,* **9**(3):1–13, 1989.

Wajenberg, Arnold S. "Authority Work, Authority Records, and Authority Files." In Michael Gorman et al., eds., *Technical Services Today and Tomorrow.* Englewood, Colo.: Libraries Unlimited, 1990. Pp. 86–94.

CHAPTER TWO
DEVELOPMENT OF
CATALOGING CODES

This chapter provides background for the study of descriptive cataloging. Today, descriptive cataloging in this country and in Great Britain, as well as in many English-speaking countries, is largely governed by a jointly developed cataloging code, the current version of which is the 1988 revision of the second edition of *Anglo-American Cataloguing Rules.* (The first edition appeared in 1967; the second, in 1978.) This chapter shows the current version in its historical context.

The emergence and development of cataloging codes illustrate the growth of an idea: that standardization in some practices has advantages for libraries. In the early days of library service, cataloging was largely an individual activity for each library. Each library constructed its own catalog in a way deemed most suitable for its purposes. Bibliographic records were presented in forms and styles that varied from library to library.

Gradually, librarians realized the advantages of standardization of practice and of cooperation among libraries. The need for codification of cataloging practice became increasingly apparent, especially for cooperative or shared cataloging. Compatibility of cataloging records in the catalogs of different libraries facilitates services to users who move from library to library. It enables library cooperation and economizes library operations through centralized or cooperative cataloging. It is also important in a union catalog or a union database.

Since the middle of the nineteenth century, a series of cataloging codes has been developed. Each new code sought to improve on the preceding ones. Most of the earlier codes represent the efforts of individuals, and the later ones result from corporate undertakings. Following is a brief discussion of the development of the codes.

BRITISH MUSEUM CATALOGUING RULES

Panizzi, Sir Anthony, et al. "Rules for the Compilation of the Catalog." *Catalogue of Printed Books in British Museum.* London: British Museum. Printed by order of the trustees, 1841. Vol. 1, pp. v–ix.

British Museum. Department of Printed Books. *Rules for Compiling the Catalogues of Printed Books, Maps and Music in the British Museum.* Rev. ed. London: British Museum. Printed by order of the trustees, 1936.

The British Museum Cataloguing Rules (BM), also known as Panizzi's ninety-one rules, were developed in 1839 as a guide for the compilation of the British Museum catalogs. They reflect the functions of these particular catalogs as inventory lists and finding lists.

This set of rules is considered to be the first major cataloging code and has influenced later codes.

JEWETT'S RULES

Jewett, Charles C. *Smithsonian Report on the Construction of Catalogs of Libraries, and Their Publication by Means of Separate, Stereotyped Titles, with Rules and Examples.* 2nd ed. Washington: Smithsonian Institution, 1853. Reprinted, Ann Arbor, Mich.: University Microfilms, 1961.

Jewett's code contains thirty-three rules largely based on Panizzi's rules. Jewett's discussion of subject headings represents the earliest call for codifying subject heading practice.

Jewett was noted for his proposal of centralized and cooperative cataloging by means of a union catalog which would provide "stereotyped" cataloging entries for all libraries.

CUTTER'S RULES

Cutter, Charles Ammi. *Rules for a Dictionary Catalog.* 4th ed. Rewritten. Washington: Government Printing Office, 1904. Republished, London: The Library Association, 1953.

The first edition appeared in 1876 with the title *Rules for a Printed Dictionary Catalogue,* which formed Part II of the U.S. Bureau of Education Publication, *Public Libraries in the United States.* It contains 369 rules covering descriptive cataloging, subject headings, and filing.

Cutter's purpose was to "investigate what might be called the first principles of cataloging"; because of this, his code has had greater influence on subsequent codes than any other work in the area of cataloging. It became the basis for the dictionary catalog, which was to become the predominant form of catalogs in general libraries in the United States.

Cutter's code contains the well-known statement of the objects of the catalog and the means for attaining them.[1]

Objects

1. To enable a person to find a book of which either
   a. the author ⎤
   b. the title   ⎬ is known
   c. the subject ⎦
2. To show what the library has
   d. by a given author
   e. on a given subject
   f. in a given kind of literature
3. To assist in the choice of a book
   g. as to its edition (bibliographically)
   h. as to its character (literary or topical)

Means

1. Author entry with the necessary references (for a and d)
2. Title entry or title reference (for b)
3. Subject entry, cross-references, and classed subject table (for c and e)
4. Form entry and language entry (for f)
5. Giving edition and imprint, with notes when necessary (for g)
6. Notes (for h)

The essence of this statement is still discernible in the present Anglo-American cataloging code.

AA 1908

Catalog Rules: Author and Title Entries. American ed. Chicago: American Library Association, 1908.

AA 1908 represented the first joint effort between American and British librarians in developing a cataloging code. However, the two groups did not reach full agreement on all details, and the code was published in two editions (English and American).

AA 1908 reflected the influence of previous codes—BM, Cutter—and, to a large extent, current practice of the Library of Congress, which

---

[1]Charles Ammi Cutter, *Rules for a Dictionary Catalog,* 4th ed. Rewritten. Washington: Government Printing Office, 1904; republished, London: The Library Association, 1953. P. 12.

had begun distributing printed cards in 1901. It owed a great deal to Cutter's rules; however, it excluded Cutter's statements of objects and means, and the rules for subject headings also were omitted. The major aim of the code was to meet the requirements of larger academic and research libraries. To a considerable extent, this statement set the tone of the subsequent codes, which have been drawn up primarily to respond to the needs of large research libraries. The needs of smaller libraries are only occasionally recognized in the provision of alternative rules.

PRUSSIAN INSTRUCTIONS

The Prussian Instructions: Rules for the Alphabetical Catalogs of the Prussian Libraries. Translated from the 2nd ed., authorized August 10, 1908, with an introduction and notes by Andrew D. Osborn. Ann Arbor, Mich.: University of Michigan Press, 1938.

Originally developed as a standardized system of cataloging for Prussian libraries, the Prussian Instructions (PI) were adopted by many libraries in Germanic and Scandinavian countries.

The rules reflected two major differences in cataloging between the Germanic and the Anglo-American traditions. PI prescribed grammatical rather than mechanical (or literal) title. For title entries, the entry word was the first grammatically independent word of the title instead of the first word of the title disregarding an article. The second difference was in the fact that PI did not recognize corporate authorship (i.e., a corporate body being treated as the author of a publication).

VATICAN CODE

Vatican Library. *Rules for the Catalog of Printed Books.* Translated from the 2nd Italian ed. by the Very Rev. Thomas J. Shanahan, Victor A. Schaefer, and Constantin T. Vesselowsky. Wyllis E. Wright, ed. Chicago: American Library Association, 1948. (3rd ed. in Italian appeared in 1949.)

These rules were developed for the purpose of compiling a general catalog of printed books in the Vatican Library after its reorganization in the 1920s. The persons responsible were either Americans or American-trained librarians. Therefore, American influence and bias are evident. It has been called an "international code with a definite American bias."[2] Its significance for American librarians lies in the fact that for

---

[2]K. G. B. Bakewell. *A Manual of Cataloguing Practice.* Oxford: Pergamon Press, 1972. P. 32.

many years the Vatican code was, as Wright states in the Foreword to the English translation, "the most complete statement of American cataloging practice."[3]

Probably the most comprehensive and best-structured code at the time, the Vatican code contains rules for entry, description, subject headings, and filing, with ample examples throughout.

ALA DRAFT (1941)

ALA Catalog Rules: Author and Title Entries. Preliminary American 2nd ed. Chicago: American Library Association, 1941.

During the early 1930s, there was a general feeling of the need for a revised ALA cataloging code. A Catalog Code Revision Committee under the American Library Association was established for this purpose. Its intention to cooperate with the Library Association of Great Britain and other national library associations was not fully realized because of the eruption of World War II.

The draft code was completed in 1941. The 88-page pamphlet AA 1908 had blossomed into a 408-page document. The reason for the elaboration, as stated in the Preface, was the need for standardization required by centralized and cooperative cataloging. The committee felt that elaborate and precise detail was the means to accomplish this end. The code consists of two parts, one dealing with entry and headings and the other with description. Again, the rules for subject headings were omitted.

The 1941 draft code was dealt a heavy blow in June 1941 by Andrew D. Osborn's article entitled "The Crisis in Cataloging."[4] Osborn criticized the code for attempting to provide a rule for every situation or question that may come up, an approach he referred to as "legalistic." The consequence, Osborn maintained, was unnecessary multiplication of rules.

LC 1949

Library of Congress. *Rules for Descriptive Cataloging in the Library of Congress Adopted by the American Library Association.* Washington: Library of Congress, 1949.

[3]Vatican Library. *Rules for the Catalog of Printed Books.* Translated from the 2nd Italian ed. by the Very Rev. Thomas J. Shanahan, Victor A. Schaefer, and Constantin T. Vesselowsky. Wyllis E. Wright, ed. Chicago: American Library Association, 1948. P. [v].
[4]Andrew D. Osborn. "The Crisis in Cataloging." *Library Quarterly,* **11**:393–411, October 1941.

Because of the extensive use of Library of Congress printed catalog cards by libraries in the United States, the need was felt for the publication of the Library of Congress (LC) rules, which were not totally compatible with the ALA rules.

In 1946, the Library of Congress published its *Studies of Descriptive Cataloging: A Report to the Librarian of Congress by the Director of the Processing Department,* which advocated simplification of cataloging details. On the basis of the principles (which are reminiscent of Cutter's "objects") and the recommendations in the report, the Library of Congress proceeded to complete the work on the rules for description. A preliminary edition appeared in 1947, and a final edition appeared in 1949 (LC 1949).

The rules cover bibliographic description only, excluding choice of entries (i.e., of access points), and forms of headings. Many types of materials are considered: monographs, serials, maps, relief models, globes and atlases, music, facsimiles, photocopies and microfilms, and incunabula.

ALA 1949

ALA Cataloging Rules for Author and Title Entries. 2nd ed. Clara Beetle, ed. Chicago: American Library Association, 1949.

Since the Library of Congress was revising its rules for description, the American Library Association decided to omit that portion of the rules from the 1941 draft and include only the rules for entry and heading in the ALA rules. This decision was made partly because individual libraries had been following LC practice (owing to the availability of LC printed cards) and partly because that portion of ALA 1941 had not been very well received. As a result, the rules in ALA 1949 cover entry and headings only and must be used in conjunction with LC 1949.

ALA 1949 and LC 1949 served as the standards for descriptive cataloging for American libraries until the appearance of the *Anglo-American Cataloging Rules* in 1967.

The criticism of Osborn did not seem to have a great deal of effect on ALA 1949, for the rules in this code, in the opinion of many, are as pedantic, elaborate, and often arbitrary as those in the preliminary edition of 1941.

AACR (1967)

Anglo-American Cataloging Rules. Prepared by the American Library Association, the Library of Congress, the Library Association, and the Canadian Library Association. North

American text. Chicago: American Library Association, 1967. Reprinted in 1970 with supplement of additions and changes.

The strongest criticism of ALA 1949 was voiced by Seymour Lubetzky, whose *Cataloging Rules and Principles*[5] provided a thorough and penetrating analysis of ALA 1949 and proved to be the most important document for subsequent development in the field of descriptive cataloging. Lubetzky criticized ALA 1949 for being unnecessarily long and confusing because it provided duplicate and overlapping rules to meet identical conditions. Related rules were scattered, he maintained, and there was a lack of logical arrangement and organization of the rules.

Lubetzky's work is divided into three parts. Part I presents a detailed analysis of specific rules in ALA 1949. Part II takes up the question of the "corporate complex" (again providing a perceptive analysis of the confusion regarding corporate authorship in existing codes), condemning ALA 1949 for many unnecessary rules, such as those distinguishing between kinds of corporate bodies. In Part 3, "Design for a Code," Lubetzky sets forth two objectives: "(1) to enable the user of the catalog to determine readily whether or not the library has the book he wants; (2) to reveal to the user of the catalog, under one form of the author's name, what works the library has by a given author and what editions or translations of a given work."

Lubetzky's report was received favorably, and another ALA Catalog Code Revision Committee, with Wyllis Wright as chairman, was established for the purpose of drafting a new code. In 1956, Lubetzky was appointed the editor of the new code.

In 1960, Lubetzky's *Code of Cataloging Rules, Author and Title Entry: An Unfinished Draft*[6] appeared. It begins with a statement of objectives, followed by specific rules developed on the basis of these objectives. Although not completed, the draft code gives indication of what can be accomplished by basing specific rules on basic principles. One major departure from previous codes is the determination of entry based on the conditions of authorship rather than on types of work.

Lubetzky's work was both exciting and frightening to those involved in cataloging. It presaged a new era for cataloging, yet many were concerned about the cost such drastic changes would incur. This concern was to become a major force in ensuing code revision work.

In 1961, one of the most important events in the evolution of cataloging codes took place. The International Conference on Cataloguing Principles was held in Paris, October 9–18, 1961, with delegations from fifty-three countries and twelve international organizations. The discus-

---

[5]Seymour Lubetzky. *Cataloging Rules and Principles*. Washington: Library of Congress, 1953.
[6]Seymour Lubetzky. *Code of Cataloging Rules, Author and Title Entry: An Unfinished Draft*. Chicago: American Library Association, 1960.

sion of principles of cataloging was based on a draft statement of principles circulated before the meeting.

As a result of the conference, a statement of principles, which has become known as the "Paris Statement" or the "Paris Principles," was issued. It drew heavily on Lubetzky's draft code of 1960. The scope is limited to the choice of entry and the forms of headings only. It opens with a statement of the functions of the catalog, which represents a restatement of Lubetzky's and Cutter's objectives. The principles that follow rest logically on these objectives and are stated in specific terms in considerable detail.

The Paris Statement represented a great step forward toward international agreement. One frequently cited feature of this document is its endorsement of corporate entry and natural, rather than grammatical, arrangement of title, which removes the major differences between the Anglo-American and the Germanic traditions of cataloging.

Lubetzky resigned as editor of the new code in 1962 and was succeeded by C. Sumner Spalding. Code revision proceeded on the basis of the work already done under Lubetzky and the Paris Principles. Cooperation between the American and British library associations also was initiated.

Time and again, the concern for the cost of change caused compromises. The most notorious example was the retention of the practice (appearing as rules 98 and 99) of entering certain corporate bodies under the names of places—a drastic departure from the Paris Principles, which entered corporate bodies directly under their names. On this point and certain other points the American and the British committees could not reach complete agreement. This disagreement entailed the publication of two separate texts of the *Anglo-American Cataloging Rules*, the North American text and the British text, a fact considered by many to be regrettable.

It was decided that the new code should include rules for both entry and description. Since the Paris Principles deal with the problems of entry and headings only and there were no international guidelines for the development of the rules for description, LC 1949 was used as the basis for Chapters 6 and 7 for description of monographs and serials, as well as for the rules for cataloging nonbook materials in the North American text.

The new code appeared in 1967 and was received with mixed feelings. The logical arrangement and its emphasis on the conditions of authorship rather than on types of work were considered to be a great improvement over the previous codes. Some critics lamented the compromises made because of practical considerations and the inadequate handling of nonbook materials.

Implementation of the new rules was quite a different matter from

theoretical considerations. The major problem was how to reconcile the conflicts between existing entries in the catalog and new entries prepared according to the new rules without incurring prohibitive costs. It would be extremely expensive to revise existing headings in the catalog in accordance with the new code. The Library of Congress adopted the policy of superimposition. Although the rules for entry and description were to be followed in cataloging all works new to its collection, the rules for headings for persons and corporate bodies were to be applied only to headings being established for the first time. Headings previously established according to former codes continued to be used in cataloging new works. For example, the heading **Porter, William Sydney, 1862–1910** continued to be used in cataloging works by O. Henry, even though the new code required the use of the latter name as the heading. Libraries around the country, on the whole, adopted a similar policy.

In the next two or three years, the application of the new code proved that some of the rules were ambiguous and a few others not satisfactory. A supplement of additions and changes was issued in 1970 and appeared in later printings of the code. Changes occurring after 1970 were announced in *Cataloging Service*.[7] Further changes appeared in separately published supplements.

Since the appearance of the Paris Principles, many other cataloging codes have been revised or developed according to their provisions, notably the German code (*Regeln für die alphabetische Katalogisierung*, (RAK)), the Swedish code, and the Danish code. The RAK represents a major revolution in Germanic cataloging in that the concept of corporate entry was introduced and the mechanical, rather than grammatical, title was accepted.

International Standard Bibliographic Description

> *ISBD(M): International Standard Bibliographic Description for Monographic Publications*. Prepared by the Working Group on the International Standard Bibliographic Description. 1st standard ed. London: IFLA Committee on Cataloguing, 1974.

> *ISBD(S): International Standard Bibliographic Description for Serials*. Recommended by the Joint Working Group on the International Standard Bibliographic Description for Serials set up by the IFLA Committee on Cataloguing and the IFLA Committee on Serial Publications. London: IFLA Committee on Cataloguing, 1974. 1st standard ed., London: International Office for UBC, 1977.

---

[7]A serial publication issued by the Library of Congress. The title was changed to *Cataloging Service Bulletin* in 1978.

ISBD(G): *International Standard Bibliographic Description
(General): Annotated Text.* Prepared by the Working Group on
the General International Bibliographic Description. London:
IFLA International Office for UBC, 1977.

After the Paris conference, the next step toward greater international
agreement was taken at the International Meeting of Cataloguing Experts
held in Copenhagen in 1969. At this meeting, an international
working group was established with the purpose of developing a standard
order and content for the description of monographic material. The
objectives of the new format for bibliographic description were defined
as follows:

> ... first, that records produced in one country or by the users of one language
> can be easily understood in other countries and by the users of other
> languages; second, that the records produced in each country can be inte-
> grated into files or lists of various kinds containing also records from other
> countries; and third, that records in written or printed form can be converted
> into machine-readable form with the minimum of editing.[8]

To fulfill these requirements, the order of bibliographic elements to be
presented on a record was standardized, and a special punctuation
pattern distinguishing these elements was prescribed.

A document entitled ISBD(M): *International Standard Bibliographic
Description (for Single Volume and Multi-Volume Monographic Publications)*
was issued in 1971. In the following years, this format was accepted and
adopted by many national bibliographies. Again, in the course of its
applications, many ambiguities and a lack of detail in some areas were
brought out. These were discussed at the International Federation of
Library Associations (IFLA) Conference held in Grenoble in 1973. After
this conference, two documents were published in 1974: the first standard edition of ISBD(M) and a set of recommendations for ISBD(S) (for
serial publications). The first standard edition of ISBD(S) was published
in 1977.

After the development of ISBD(M) and ISBD(S), in retrospect, it was
considered desirable to develop a *general* ISBD that could serve as the
framework for specific ISBDs. ISBD(G): *International Standard Bibliographic Description (General)* was published in 1977. Since then, other
ISBDs also have been developed, including those for cartographic materials, nonbook materials, printed music, antiquarian materials, component parts, and computer files.

[8]*ISBD(M): International Standard Bibliographic Description for Monographic Publications.*
Prepared by the Working Group on the International Standard Bibliographic Description.
1st standard ed. London: IFLA Committee on Cataloguing, 1974. P. vii.

AACR, Chapters 6, 12, and 14, Revised

Anglo-American Cataloging Rules: North American Text. Chapter 6: Separately Published Monographs. Chicago: American Library Association, 1974.

Anglo-American Cataloging Rules: North American Text. Chapter 12 Revised: Audiovisual Media and Special Instructional Materials. Chicago: American Library Association, 1975.

Anglo-American Cataloging Rules: North American Text. Chapter 14 Revised: Sound Recordings. Chicago: American Library Association, 1976.

In order to adopt the ISBD in this country, its provisions must be incorporated into the cataloging rules. After the publication of the 1971 edition of ISBD(M), the Library of Congress, upon the request of the American Library Association, undertook the preparation of a revised version of Chapter 6 of AACR. The revision, completed in the summer of 1974 after the publication of the first standard edition of ISBD(M), was published as a separate pamphlet by the American Library Association. The Library of Congress began implementation in September 1974, followed by the libraries around the country. The prescribed punctuation gave the cataloging entry a completely new look. The revised format represented yet another giant step toward international standardization.

The revised Chapter 6 was followed by *Chapter 12 Revised* (1975) for audiovisual media and special instructional materials and *Chapter 14 Revised* (1976) for sound recordings.

AACR2 (1978)

Anglo-American Cataloguing Rules. 2nd ed. Prepared by the American Library Association, the British Library, the Canadian Committee on Cataloguing, the Library Association, the Library of Congress. Michael Gorman and Paul W. Winkler, eds. Chicago: American Library Association, 1978.

By 1973, it was felt that the appropriate time had come for an overhaul of the Anglo-American cataloging code. Certain significant developments since the publication of AACR in 1967 pointed to the desirability of a revision.[9] First, rapid progress toward the formulation of interna-

---

[9]"AACR 2: Background and Summary." *Library of Congress Information Bulletin*, **37**:640, October 20, 1978.

tional standards for the description of monographs, serials, and other media indicated the need to redraft the AACR provisions for bibliographic description so that the code would facilitate the effort to promote international exchange of bibliographic data. Second, the rules for nonbook materials in AACR (1967) had been considered inadequate from the beginning, a situation which resulted in the proliferation of various cataloging codes for nonbook materials. Only a complete revision of the rules for nonprint media could provide the standardization needed in this area. Third, the points of divergence between the separate North American and British texts of AACR had been gradually reconciled, leading to the prospect of a unified code. Furthermore, there had been numerous piecemeal revisions and changes in the rules since 1967, which rendered the code rather inconvenient to use. Yet another goal was to make the code more in tune with computer possibilities. Finally, the announced intention of the Library of Congress to abandon the policy of superimposition and to close its card catalogs contributed to the momentum toward the decision to produce the second edition, which came to be known as AACR2.

Universal Bibliographic Control

A major consideration in the revision of AACR (1967) was the ideal of universal bibliographic control (UBC). This ideal, which was the theme of the Thirty-Ninth International Federation of Library Associations (IFLA) Meeting in 1973, was adopted as a goal for ultimate international cooperation. The basic idea is to have each document cataloged only once, as near to the source of publication as possible, and to make basic bibliographic data on all publications issued in all countries universally and promptly available in a form that is internationally acceptable.[10] In 1974, IFLA established an International Office for UBC with Dorothy Anderson as director.

The fact that such a dream was even conceivable was due to the many encouraging developments toward international cooperation and standardization in the field of cataloging. The Paris Conference and the International Meeting of Cataloguing Experts in Copenhagen were two milestones on the road toward achieving the goal of UBC. The standards and agreements produced by these conferences played an important role in the revision of the *Anglo-American Cataloguing Rules.*

Work began in 1974 toward the preparation of the second edition of AACR. A Joint Steering Committee for Revision of AACR was formed, with representatives from the United States, Britain, and Canada. The

[10]Dorothy Anderson. *Universal Bibliographic Control: A Long Term Policy—A Plan for Action.* Munich: Verlag Dokumentation, Pullach, 1974. P. 11.

objectives of the revision were defined on the outset: (1) to reconcile in a single text the North American and the British texts, including official changes since 1967, and (2) to consider for inclusion amendments and changes and work currently in progress, with attention paid to international interests. Work on the revision began in early 1975. Paul W. Winkler was appointed editor, with Michael Gorman from Britain serving as associate editor. The five authors were designated: the American Library Association, the British Library, the Canadian Committee on Cataloguing, the (British) Library Association, and the Library of Congress.

In the revision, the joint steering committee decided to conform to international agreements and standards, particularly the Paris Principles and the ISBD.

The Anglo-American Cataloguing Rules, second edition (AACR2, 1978), was divided into two parts: (1) description and (2) headings, uniform titles, and references. Part One was based on the *International Standard Bibliographic Description* (ISBD) for general materials and those for special types of material. Part Two was based on the Paris Principles.

The experience gained in implementing AACR (1967) resulted in a delay in implementing AACR2 until January 2, 1981, to allow time for preparation of transition. The Library of Congress decided to effect three operations simultaneously: (1) abandoning superimposition, (2) freezing its card catalog, and (3) implementing AACR2. As a result, all cataloging records created after January 2, 1981 would conform to AACR2 in headings as well as bibliographic description. Efforts were made to revise headings already in the LC MARC database that were not compatible with AACR2 provisions. The freezing of the card catalog eliminated the need to revise pre-AACR2 records in that catalog. As a result, while headings in the card catalog and corresponding headings in the LC MARC database may not agree, the headings are consistent at least within each catalog, thereby maintaining what is known as the *integrity of the catalog*.

For libraries that were not ready to freeze their card catalogs because their computer-produced catalogs were not yet in place, both pre-AACR2 headings and AACR2 headings appeared, sometimes for the same author (linked by cross-references) but without an attempt to maintain the integrity of the catalog.

AACR2R (1988)

Anglo-American Cataloguing Rules. 2nd ed., 1988 revision. Prepared under the direction of the Joint Steering Committee for Revision of AACR, a committee of: the American Library

Association, the Australian Committee on Cataloguing, the British Library, the Canadian Committee on Cataloguing, the Library Association, the Library of Congress. Michael Gorman and Paul W. Winkler, eds. Chicago: American Library Association, 1988.

In the early 1980s, three supplements containing revisions to AACR2 (1978) were issued. In addition, revisions also were approved by the Joint Steering Committee for the Revision of AACR (JSC) that had never been published. Furthermore, a draft revision of Chapter 9 for computer files was prepared and published in 1986 in response to the ever-changing nature of computer files. With these changes, it was considered appropriate to issue a revised edition of AACR2. The JSC decided to call the new edition *Second Edition 1988 Revision* instead of the "third edition," perhaps because of the "anguished howls and monumental upheaval that greeted the advent of the original AACR2 in 1978"[11] or the fact that "the rules have not been radically recast [nor was there] basic rethinking."[12]

Michael Gorman and Paul W. Winkler again served as the editors of the revised edition, which was published in 1988. The Library of Congress began implementation of the revised edition in the latter part of 1989, after preparatory work was done to ease the transition.

The changes in AACR2R (1988) include revisions of rules approved since the publication of AACR2 (1978); incorporation of the revised chapter on computer files; revision of a number of rules regarding music; rethinking of the concept of separate bibliographic identities; the treatment of titles, author headings, geographic names, and corporate bodies; and provisions for describing material for the blind and otherwise visually impaired. At the same time, many existing rules and examples were corrected or clarified.

Options

AACR2R (1988) contains a number of options, indicated by *Optional addition, Alternative rule,* or *Optionally.* These allow individual libraries or cataloging agencies to make decisions based on individual considerations in cases where two or more provisions are equally valid. Each library or cataloging agency must decide on the application of each optional provision. Libraries using LC cataloging data will most likely conform to Library of Congress practice.

[11]Margaret F. Maxwell. "AACR2R: *Anglo-American Cataloguing Rules.*" *Library Resources & Technical Services,* **33**(2):179, April 1989.

[12]Michael Gorman. "AACR2R: Editor's Perspective." *Library Resources & Technical Services,* **33**(2):181, April 1989.

LIBRARY OF CONGRESS RULE INTERPRETATIONS

In the implementation of AACR2R, the Library of Congress has made a number of modifications. Furthermore, some of the rules are open to different interpretations. To ensure consistency in application, the Library of Congress has been publishing its decisions regarding options, modifications, and interpretations in *Cataloging Service Bulletin*.[13] These decisions are cumulated in a publication entitled *Library of Congress Rule Interpretations* (LCRI)[14] Libraries that make use of Library of Congress cataloging data consult LCRI regularly in order to achieve consistency between their own cataloging and that of the Library of Congress.

[13]*Cataloging Service Bulletin.* No. 1– , Summer 1978– .
[14]*Library of Congress Rule Interpretations.* 2nd ed. Washington: Cataloging Distribution Service, Library of Congress, 1989.

CHAPTER THREE
DESCRIPTION

The first part of *Anglo-American Cataloguing Rules,* second edition, 1988 revision (AACR2R),[1] contains rules on the bibliographic description of library materials. These rules give instructions on how to represent the bibliographic and physical characteristics of the material being cataloged. The following discussion concerns Part One of AACR2R only. Choice of access points, forms of headings, and cross-references are treated in Part Two of AACR2R and are discussed in Chapters 4, 5, and 6 of this book.

TYPES OF LIBRARY MATERIALS

For the purpose of bibliographic description, the following types of library materials have been identified in AACR2R:

> Books, pamphlets, and printed sheets
> Cartographic materials
> Manuscripts
> Music
> Sound recordings
> Motion pictures and videorecordings
> Graphic materials
> Computer files
> Three-dimensional artefacts and realia
> Microforms
> Serials

For definitions of these terms, see AACR2R (pp. 615–624) and the Glossary of this book.

The first chapter of AACR2R is devoted to bibliographic description of all types of materials and can be considered a general-guidance

---

[1]*Anglo-American Cataloguing Rules.* 2nd ed., 1988 revision. Prepared under the direction of the Joint Steering Committee for Revision of AACR, a committee of: the American Library Association, the Australian Committee on Cataloguing, the British Library, the Canadian Committee on Cataloguing, the Library Association, the Library of Congress. Michael Gorman and Paul W. Winkler, eds. Chicago: American Library Association, 1988.

chapter. Each of the chapters numbered 2 through 12 in AACR2R provides rules for the description of a specific type of material. The rules in these later chapters often refer to Chapter 1 for details applicable to all types of materials. Thus neither Chapter 1 nor any of the subsequent chapters for rules of description can be used alone. In cataloging, the cataloger begins with the chapter dealing with the specific type of material being cataloged, e.g., Chapter 2 for printed monographs, and then uses that chapter along with Chapter 1. In some cases, two or more chapters dealing with specific types of materials may be required if the item being cataloged manifests more than one medium, e.g., a serial map or a book in microform. To facilitate use, the rules in these chapters have been numbered with a mnemonic device; for example, rule 1.5 deals with the physical description area, and so do rules 2.5 (for books), 3.5 (for cartographic materials), 4.5 (for manuscripts), and so on.

The introduction to AACR2R (p. 8) states that in choosing the appropriate chapter or chapters to be used in cataloging a particular item, the cataloger should start with the physical form of the item being cataloged, not the original or any previous form in which the work has been published. For example, a monographic publication in microform should be described according to the rules in Chapter 11 (for microforms), augmented by those in Chapter 2 (for books) and Chapter 1 (general rules) when required.[2]

ISBD(G)

The *ISBD(G): International Standard Bibliographic Description, (General)* developed by agreement between the International Federation of Library Associations (IFLA) and the Joint Steering Committee for the Revision of AACR and published in 1977, serves as a single framework for the description of all types of publications in all types of media, thereby ensuring a uniform approach in bibliographic description. Its major provisions are shown in Table 3-1.

The ISBD(G) was incorporated into Chapter 1 of AACR2R as the general format for bibliographic description. Several specialized ISBDs for specific types of material also have been developed, and more are currently under development. Each of the chapters numbered 2 through 12 is based on a specialized ISBD if it exists. For example, the basis of the rules for the description of monographic materials in AACR2R is *The*

[2]The policy of the Library of Congress, however, is to emphasize the original item, with details relating to the reproduction given in the notes. See *Library of Congress Rule Interpretations*. 2nd ed. Washington: Cataloging Distribution Service, Library of Congress, 1989. Chap. 11, p. 1.

TABLE 3-1   The ISBD(G)

Area	Prescribed Preceding (or Enclosing) Punctuation for Elements	Element	
Note: Each area, other than the first, is preceded by a point, space, dash, space (. —).			
1. Title and statement of responsibility area		1.1	Title proper
	[]	1.2	General material designation
	=	1.3	Parallel title
	:	1.4	Other title information
		1.5	Statements of responsibility
	/		First statement
	;		Subsequent statement
2. Edition area		2.1	Edition statement
	=	2.2	Parallel edition statement
		2.3	Statements of responsibility relating to the edition
	/		First Statement
	;		Subsequent statement
	,	2.4	Additional edition statement
		2.5	Statements of responsibility following an additional edition statement
	/		First statement
	;		Subsequent statement
3. Material (or type of publication) specific area			
4. Publication, distribution, etc., area		4.1	Place of publication, distribution, etc.
			First place
	;		Subsequent place
	:	4.2	Name of publisher, distributor, etc.
	[]	4.3	Statement of function of publisher, distributor, etc.
	,	4.4	Date of publication, distribution, etc.
	(	4.5	Place of manufacture
	:	4.6	Name of manufacturer
	,)	4.7	Date of manufacture
5. Physical description area		5.1	Specific material designation and extent of item
	:	5.2	Other physical details

(Continued)

TABLE 3-1 (Continued)

Area	Prescribed Preceding (or Enclosing) Punctuation for Elements		Element
5. Physical description area	;	5.3	Dimensions of item
	+	5.4	Accompanying material statement
6. Series area		6.1	Title proper of series
	=	6.2	Parallel title of series
Note: A series statement is	:	6.3	Other title information of series
enclosed by parentheses.		6.4	Statements of responsibility relating to the series
When there are two or			
more series statements,			
each is enclosed by	/		First statement
parentheses.	;		Subsequent statement
	,	6.5	International Standard Serial Number of series
	;	6.6	Numbering within series
	.	6.7	Enumeration and/or title of subseries
	=	6.8	Parallel title of subseries
	:	6.9	Other title information of subseries
		6.10	Statements of responsibility relating to the subseries
	/		First statement
	;		Subsequent statement
		6.11	International Standard Serial Number of subseries
	;	6.12	Numbering within subseries
7. Note area			
8. Standard number (or alternative) and terms of availability area		8.1	Standard number (or alternative)
	=	8.2	Key title
	:	8.3	Terms of availability and/or price
	()	8.4	Qualification (in varying positions)

SOURCE: International Federation of Library Associations. Working Group on the General International Bibliographic Description, *ISBD(G): International Standard Bibliographic Description (General): Annotated Text.* London: IFLA International Office for UBC, 1977, pp 2–3.

International Standard Bibliographic Description for Monographic Publications, ISBD(M), which was developed under the auspices of the IFLA and published in 1974.

ORGANIZATION OF THE DESCRIPTION

The bibliographic description is divided into the following units, called *areas,* and presented in the order given:

Title and statement of responsibility
Edition
Material (or type of publication) specific details
Publication, distribution, etc.
Physical description
Series
Note(s)
Standard number and terms of availability

Each of these areas is further divided into a number of elements which vary according to the type of material. The following sections contain discussions of descriptive areas and elements across all types of materials.

SOURCES OF INFORMATION

AACR2R specifies sources of information to be used in describing a publication; in the case of a printed monograph, for example, such sources include the title page and the verso of the title page. Of these, the source of bibliographic data to be given first preference is called the *chief source of information.* The rules identify one or more chief sources of information for each type of material. In a particular item, bibliographic data such as the title and publication details are often repeated in slightly different forms in various locations, including the cover and spine of a book, the verso of the title page, and the container or accompanying material. Specifying the *chief source of information* helps to achieve consistency and uniformity in bibliographic description.

Table 3-2 lists chief sources of information for different types of materials.

In Chapters 2 to 12 (specific types of material), prescribed sources of information for individual bibliographic areas are given. Information taken from sources other than the prescribed ones is enclosed in brackets.

Examples of chief sources of information with corresponding bibliographic descriptions are shown in Figures 3-1 to 3-7 (pages 56-62).

TABLE 3-2   Chief Sources of Information

Type of Material	Source
Books, pamphlets, and printed sheets	Title page or its substitute
Cartographic materials (other than a printed atlas)	a. Cartographic item itself b. Container or case, the cradle and stand of a globe, etc.
Manuscripts	Manuscript itself Title page Colophon Caption, heading, etc. Content of the manuscript
Music	Title page or its substitute
Sound recordings	
Disc	Disc and label
Tape (open reel-to-reel)	Reel and label
Tape cassette	Cassette and label
Tape cartridge	Cartridge and label
Roll	Label
Sound recording on film	Container and label
Motion pictures and videorecordings	a. Item itself b. Its container (if integral part of item)
Graphic materials	Item itself, including any labels or the container
Computer files	Title screens or other formally presented internal evidence
Three-dimensional artefacts and realia	Object itself with any accompanying textual material and container
Microforms	Title frame
Serials (printed)	Title page

FIGURE 3-1   Half title page, title page, and verso of a book.

Description:
Mass media/mass culture : an introduction / Stan Le Roy Wilson. — 2nd ed. — New York : McGraw-Hill, c1992.
xvii, 460 p. : ill. (some col.) ; 24 cm. — (McGraw-Hill series in mass communication)
Includes bibliographical references and index.
ISBN 0-07-070816-9

Main entry:
Wilson, Stan Le Roy.

Added entries:
Title.
Series.

MASS MEDIA/ MASS CULTURE

AN INTRODUCTION

Second Edition

STAN LE ROY WILSON

College of the Desert

McGraw-Hill, Inc.

New York St. Louis San Francisco Auckland
Bogotá Caracas Lisbon London Madrid Mexico
Milan Montreal New Delhi Paris San Juan
Singapore Sydney Tokyo Toronto

MASS MEDIA/ MASS CULTURE

AN INTRODUCTION

Mass Media/Mass Culture
An Introduction

This book was set in Times Roman by Better Graphics, Inc.
The editors were Hilary Jackson, Carol Einhorn, and Tom Holton; the designer was Karen K. Quigley; the production supervisor was Denise L. Puryear.
The photo editor was Elsa Peterson.
Arcata Graphics/Halliday was printer and binder.

Cover Photo Credits
Top L: UPI/Bettmann; Lower L: Copyright © 1991 by The New York Times Company, reproduced with permission; Top R: CBS/Everett Collection; Center R: MGM 1939/Bob Cosenza/Superstock; Lower R: Copyright © 1989 by Random House, Inc.

Library of Congress Cataloging-in-Publication Data
Wilson, Stan Le Roy.
Mass media/mass culture: an introduction/Stan Le Roy Wilson.—2nd ed.
p. cm.—(McGraw-Hill series in mass communication)
Includes bibliographical references and index.
ISBN 0-07-070816-9
1. Mass media. 2. Communication and culture. 1. Title. II. Series.
P90.W494 1992
302.23—dc20 91-16406

This book was set in Palatino by Ruttle, Shaw & Wetherill, Inc.
The editors were David Follmer and Scott Amerman;
the text designer was Joan E. O'Connor;
the production supervisor was Leroy A. Young.
The cover was designed by Joan E. O'Connor and Karen K. Quigley.
The photo editor was Deborah Bull/Photosearch.
R.R. Donnelley & Sons Company was printer and binder.

COVER PAINTING:
The Metropolitan Museum of Art, Purchase,
Joseph Pulitzer Bequest, 1947. (47.11.5)
Greek. Vases, Black-Figured, Attic.
6th Century B.C., ca. 550–530 B.C.
Amphora, black-figured.
SIDE B: Men weighing merchandise.
Attributed to the Taleides Painter.
Said to be from Agrigento, Sicily.
Terracotta.
H. 11-5/8 in.

THE WESTERN EXPERIENCE
Volume I
Antiquity to the Middle Ages

2 3 4 5 6 7 8 9 0 DOC DOC 9 5 4 3 2 1

ISBN 0-07-010619-3

The Western Experience

FIFTH EDITION

VOLUME I

ANTIQUITY TO
THE MIDDLE AGES

MORTIMER CHAMBERS
University of California,
Los Angeles

RAYMOND GREW
University of Michigan

DAVID HERLIHY
Brown University

THEODORE K. RABB
Princeton University

ISSER WOLOCH
Columbia University

McGRAW-HILL, INC.

New York   St. Louis   San Francisco   Auckland   Bogotá
Caracas   Hamburg   Lisbon   London   Madrid   Mexico   Milan   Montreal
New Delhi   Paris   San Juan   São Paulo   Singapore   Sydney   Tokyo   Toronto

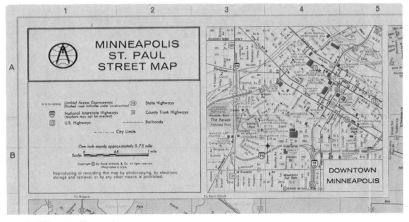

FIGURE 3-3   Part of a map.

Description:
Minneapolis–St. Paul street map / Rand McNally. — Scale
[ca. 1:47,520]. 1 in. equals approx. 0.75 mile. — [Chicago] : Rand
McNally, [1970]
1 map : both sides, col. ; 89 × 98 cm. on sheet 91 × 65 cm., folded
to 23 × 10 cm.
Insets: Downtown Minneapolis; Downtown St. Paul;
Minneapolis–St. Paul and vicinity.

Main entry:
Rand McNally and Company

Added entry:
Title.

FIGURE 3-2   Title page and verso of the first volume of a three-volume book.

Description:
The Western experience / Mortimer Chambers ... [et al.]. —
5th ed. — New York : McGraw-Hill, c1991.
3 v. : ill. (some col.), maps ; 24 cm.
Includes bibliographical references and indexes.
Contents: v. 1. Antiquity to the Middle Ages — v. 2. The early
modern period — v. 3. The modern era.
ISBN 0-07-010619-3 (v.1) — ISBN 0-07-010620-7 (v. 2) — ISBN
0-07-010621-5 (v. 3)

Main entry:
Title

Added entry:
Chambers, Mortimer.

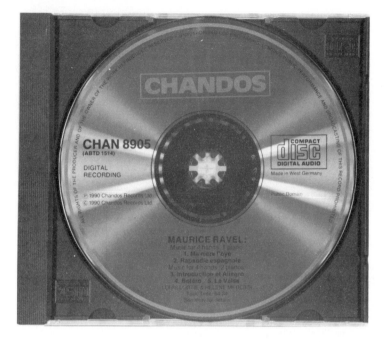

FIGURE 3-4 A compact disc and case.

Description:
Music for four hands, 1 piano [sound recording] / Maurice Ravel. — Colchester, England : Chandos Records, c1990.
1 sound disc (64 min., 44 sec.) : digital, stereo. ; 4¾ in.
Compact disc
Louis Lortie & Hélène Mercier, pianos.
Contents: Ma mère l'oye — Rapsodie espagnole — Introduction et Allegro — Bolero — La Valse.

Main entry:
Ravel, Maurice, 1875-1937.

Added entries:
Lortie, Louis, 1959-
Mercier, Hélène.
Title.

FIGURE 3-5 Title frames of a microfilm.

Description:

J.C.M. Hanson and his contribution to twentieth-century cataloging / by Edith Scott. — Chicago : Dept. of Photoduplication, University of Chicago Library, 1970.

1 microfilm reel : negative ; 35 mm. At head of title: The University of Chicago.

Thesis (Ph.D.) — University of Chicago, 1970.

Includes bibliographical references (p. 669–695)

Main entry:
Scott, Edith, 1918-

Added entry:
Title.

SCIENCE IN THE
COLLEGE CURRICULUM

*A Report of a Conference
Sponsored by Oakland University
and Supported by a Grant from the
National Science Foundation,
May 24–26, 1962*

ROBERT HOOPES

ROCHESTER, MICHIGAN
1963
(a)

*Copyright © 1963, Oakland University
Rochester, Michigan*
(b)

FIGURE 3-6   Title page and verso of a book.

Description:
Science in the college curriculum : a report of a conference
sponsored by Oakland University and supported by a grant from the
National Science Foundation, May 24-26, 1962 / [edited by] Robert
Hoopes. — Rochester, Mich. : [Oakland University], 1963.
x, 211 p. ; 22 cm.
"Conference on Education in Science for the Undergraduate
Non-Science Concentrator"—Pref.

Main entry:
Title

Added entries:
Hoopes, Robert.
Conference on Education in Science for the Undergraduate
    Non-Science Concentrator (1962 : Oakland University)
Oakland University.

FIGURE 3-7   Cover of a journal.

Description:
    Cataloging & classification quarterly. — Vol. 1, no. 1 (fall
1980)-   . — New York : Haworth Press, c1981-
    v. : ill. ; 26 cm.
    Quarterly.
    Title from cover.
    ISSN 0163-9374 = Cataloging & classification quarterly

Main entry:
Title

Added entry:
Title: Cataloging and classification quarterly.

PUNCTUATION

One of the unique features of the ISBD is a set of prescribed punctuation. The prescribed punctuation mark precedes each element in the description and signifies the nature of that element. The ISBD prescribed punctuation marks differ considerably from standard prose punctuation because they were selected to function as a device of recognition for both machine and human manipulation of bibliographic records. A person faced with a bibliographic record in an unknown language, for instance, can identify its statement of responsibility because it follows the slash.

Specific and detailed rules with regard to prescribed punctuation are given in each chapter in AACR2R. Following is a summary of the use of each mark of prescribed punctuation.

Brackets

See *Parentheses; Square brackets.*

Colon

A colon precedes

1. Each unit of other title information
2. The name of a publisher, distributor, printer, manufacturer, etc.
3. Other physical details (e.g., illustrations)
4. Terms of availability

A colon and a space separate introductory wording from the main content of a note.

Comma

A comma

1. Separates units within a statement, e.g., phrases within a title, names of authors within a statement of responsibility
2. Precedes each subsequent edition statement
3. Precedes the date of publication, distribution, printing, manufacture, etc.
4. Precedes the ISSN of a series or subseries in the series area

Dash

A full stop, space, dash, space (. —) precedes each area in the description, unless the area begins a new paragraph.

Diagonal Slash

A diagonal slash precedes the first statement of responsibility.

Ellipses

See *Mark of omission.*

Equals Sign

An equal sign precedes

1. A parallel title
2. A parallel edition statement
3. An alternative numbering in the numeric or chronological designation area of a serial publication
4. A key title in the standard number and terms of availability area

Full Stop

1. A full stop, space, dash, space (. —) precedes each area or repetition of an area. It is omitted if the area begins a new paragraph.
2. A full stop ends the last area in a paragraph.
3. A full stop is used as an abbreviation mark (e.g., 2nd ed.; 24 cm.). When the abbreviation mark occurs at the end of an area, the full stop which is a part of the prescribed punctuation is omitted (i.e., 2nd ed. —).
4. A full stop precedes the title of a supplement or section.
5. A full stop precedes the title of a subseries.

Hyphen

A hyphen follows the numeric or alphabetic designation, or both, and the date of the first issue of a serial publication.

Mark of Omission

A mark of omission (...) is used

1. To indicate an abridged title proper or other title information
2. To indicate an omission from the statement of responsibility
3. To replace the date or numbering that varies from issue to issue in the title proper of a serial publication

Minus Sign

A minus sign is used to indicate the Southern Hemisphere when giving the declination of the center of a celestial chart.

Parentheses

Parentheses are used

1. To enclose the details of printing or manufacture (place : name, date)
2. To enclose the full address of a publisher, distributor, etc. (if given) after the name of the place
3. To enclose physical details of accompanying material
4. To enclose each series statement
5. To enclose a qualification to the standard number or terms of availability
6. To enclose the continuous pagination of a multivolume monograph after the number of volumes
7. To enclose statement of tactile data for material for the visually impaired
8. To enclose the statement of coordinates and equinox in the mathematical data area for cartographic materials
9. To enclose the number of records, statements, etc. after the designation for a computer file; the number of statements and/or bytes after the designation for a program file; the number of records and/or bytes in each file after the designation for a multipart file
10. To enclose the number of frames of a microfiche or a filmstrip and the playing time of a film or recording
11. To enclose a date following a designation that is numeric, alphabetic, or both for a serial publication

Period

See *Full stop.*

Plus Sign

A plus sign

1. Precedes a statement of accompanying material
2. Is used to indicate the Northern Hemisphere when giving the declination of the center of a celestial chart

Question Mark

A question mark is used to indicate a conjectural interpolation.

Semicolon

A semicolon precedes

1. Each subsequent statement of responsibility
2. A second or subsequent named place of publication, distribution, etc.
3. Dimensions (e.g., size) in the physical description area
4. Subsequent statements of responsibility relating to a series or subseries
5. The numbering within a series or subseries
6. The projection statement for cartographic materials
7. A new sequence of numbering, etc., in the numeric, alphabetic, chronologic, or other designation area for a serial publication

Slash

See *Diagonal slash.*

Space

A space precedes and follows each mark of prescribed punctuation, except the comma, full stop, hyphen, and opening and closing parentheses and square brackets. The comma, full stop, hyphen, closing parenthesis, and square bracket are not preceded by a space; the hyphen, opening parenthesis, and square bracket are not followed by a space.

Square Brackets

Square brackets are used

1. To enclose information taken from outside the prescribed source or sources
2. To enclose the general material designation

3. To enclose a supplied statement of function of a publisher, distributor, etc.

When adjacent elements within one area are to be enclosed in square brackets, they are enclosed in one set of square brackets unless one of the elements is a general material designation, which is always enclosed in its own set of brackets. When adjacent elements are in different areas, each element is enclosed in a separate set of square brackets.

LEVELS OF DESCRIPTION

Cutter's Levels

Charles A. Cutter, in his *Rules for a Dictionary Catalog*,[3] first proposed the idea of three different levels of cataloging (short, medium, and full) to accommodate the different needs of libraries of different sizes and purposes. The first edition of the *Anglo-American Cataloging Rules* (1967) and the preceding ALA codes were each designed to respond to the needs of general research libraries and made only occasional alternative provisions for other types of libraries. On the whole, these codes prescribed a level of bibliographic description (i.e., the number and degree of bibliographic details) that was suitable for the catalog of a large general research library, a level not required by many libraries.

Levels of Description in AACR2R

To accommodate the needs of different types of libraries, the second edition of the *Anglo-American Cataloguing Rules* (1978) provided three levels of bibliographic description, reflecting Cutter's ideals of a flexible code. This provision continues in AACR2R.[4]

First level (rule 1.0D1)

This level contains minimal bibliographic information and is intended for minor items and for entries in catalogs with a policy of minimum description. The following schematic illustration shows the bibliographic elements to be included:

> Title proper / first statement of responsibility, if different from main entry heading in form or number or if there is no main entry heading. — Edition statement. — Material (or

---

[3]Charles Ammi Cutter. *Rules for a Dictionary Catalog.* 4th ed. Rewritten. Washington: Government Printing Office, 1904. P. 11.
[4]*Anglo-American Cataloguing Rules.* 2nd ed., 1988 revision. Pp. 14–15.

type of publication) specific details. — First publisher, etc., date of publication, etc. — Extent of item. — Note(s). — Standard number

Second level (rule 1.0D2)

This level is intended for the standard range of items found in the library and for entries in catalogs with a policy of standard description. The following elements are included:

Title proper [general material designation] = parallel title : other title information / first statement of responsibility ; each subsequent statement of responsibility. — Edition statement / first statement of responsibility relating to the edition. — Material (or type of publication) specific details. — First place of publication, etc. : first publisher, etc., date of publication, etc. — Extent of item : other physical details ; dimensions. — (Title proper of series / statement of responsibility relating to series, ISSN of series ; numbering within the series. Title of subseries, ISSN of subseries ; numbering within subseries). — Note(s). — Standard number

Third level (rule 1.0D3)

This level represents full description and is recommended for items which, in the context of the catalog, are considered to be important and rare. All elements set forth in the rules which are applicable to the item being described are included.

Policies on descriptive level

Each library should either choose a level of description for all items cataloged for that library or establish guidelines for the use of all three levels in the same catalog depending on the type of material being described. Since the level of description is essentially a policy matter, it is recommended that each cataloging record carry an indication of the level at which the item has been described. Library of Congress policies regarding levels of description lie somewhere between the second and the third level for fully cataloged materials.

Examples

The following examples show the first and second levels of description for the same item.

First level
Opportunities for education in urban and regional affairs at
Canadian universities and community colleges / Policy
Planning Division, Central Mortgage and Housing Corporation.
— 4th ed., 1973-74. — Central Mortgage and Housing
Corporation, [1973?]. — xvii, 465 p. — English and/or French.

Second level
Opportunities for education in urban and regional affairs at
Canadian universities and community colleges [text] =
Programmes de cours en affaires urbaines et regionales offerts
par les universités et collèges communautaires canadiens /
Policy Planning Division, Central Mortgage and Housing
Corporation. — 4th ed., 1973-74 / edited by Ollie Crain. —
Ottawa : Central Mortgage and Housing Corporation,
[1973?]. — xvii, 465 p. ; 28 cm. — English and/or French.

The cataloging records shown in Figures 3-1 to 3-12 are based on LC
cataloging. For illustrations of the first level of description of the same
items, see Appendix C.

EXERCISE A

Supply the missing punctuation marks in the following descriptions.

1. George Magoon and the down east game war   history,   folklore,
   and the law   Edward D. Ives   Urbana   University of Illinois
   Press   c1988   xiv 335 p   ill   24 cm   Publications of the
   American Folklore Society   New series

2. Baroque oboe concertos   sound recording   New York   N.Y.
   RCA Victor   p1990   1 sound disk   digital stereo 4¾ in.
   Red seal

3. Techniques of decision making   motion picture   United States
   Office of Education   Washington   The Office   Distributed by
   National Audiovisual Center   1977   1 film reel   28 min   sd
   col   16 mm   1 workbook   You in public service

AREAS OF DESCRIPTION

AACR2R provides detailed rules with regard to each area of description,
and numerous examples are included to illustrate the rules. The general
rules are presented in Chapter 1, and rules for specific types of materials

are given in Chapters 2 through 12. The major elements in bibliographic description are discussed below, with examples. For each area and element, the AACR2R rule number and corresponding MARC tags or subfield codes are given. Neither the discussion nor the examples are intended to be exhaustive. It is essential to consult the text of AACR2R and USMARC *Concise Formats* for details and further examples.

In presenting data in a bibliographic description, information taken from the chief source of information is preferred. If the information required is unavailable or insufficient from the chief source, other sources are used. In Chapters 2 through 12, which deal with specific types of materials, prescribed sources of information for each area are listed. Information taken from outside the prescribed source or sources is enclosed in brackets.

Title and Statement of Responsibility Area (Mnemonic Rule: *.1) [MARC Field 245]

This area contains the following elements: (1) title proper, (2) general material designation, (3) parallel titles, (4) other title information, and (5) statements of responsibility. Each of these is discussed in turn below.

1. Title proper (rule *.1B) [MARC field 245, subfield ‡a]

The title proper, which includes any alternative titles, is transcribed from the chief source of information exactly as to wording, order, and spelling, though not necessarily as to punctuation and capitalization. It is usually readily identifiable in book-form materials. For manuscripts and non-book materials, the title proper is often lacking, and one must be supplied. A supplied title is enclosed in brackets.

> Anglo-American cataloguing rules
> Carmen (fragments of acts 1 and 2)
> The common market for telecommunications and information services
> Grand Canyon geology
> Michael Morcombe's Birds of Australia
> Principles of public international law
> Women, equality, and the French Revolution
> [Design of a dormitory]
> [Drift globe]
> [Letters]
> [Map of the Counties of Sussex and Hants with the Isle of Wight]
> [Sea shells]

The rules for capitalization are presented in Appendix A in AACR2R. The first word of the title proper is always capitalized. Other words are capitalized according to the rules for the language involved. For English, proper names and proper adjectives in the title are capitalized. The word following an initial article is capitalized only if the main entry of the work is under the title, as shown in the following example:

> The Quantifying spirit in the 18th century
> The Olde daunce
> The Future south

A long title proper may be abridged if this can be done without losing essential information. The first five words of the title proper are never omitted. The omissions are indicated by the mark of omission.

> Members of the Ancient and Honorable Artillery Company in the colonial period, 1638-1774 ...

A title proper consisting of the title of a work and that of a part of the work not grammatically linked is recorded in two parts, separated by a period.

> Bibliography on Holocaust literature.   Supplement
> Journal of the Chemical Society.   Faraday transactions

2. General material designation (rule *.1C) [MARC field 245, subfield ‡h]

This is an *optional addition*. The general material designation (GMD), enclosed in square brackets, e.g., [slide], indicates the broad class of material to which the item being described belongs. For printed or book-form material, the term *text* is used as the GMD. Most libraries probably will choose to use the GMD for nonbook materials, but not otherwise. For example, the Library of Congress includes the GMD only when cataloging the following types of material: computer file, filmstrip, kit, microform, motion picture, slide, sound recording, transparency, and videorecording.

For certain forms of materials, British and North American cataloging agencies use different terms as the GMD. List 1 under rule 1.1C1 is designed for British use, and list 2 is for North American and Australian use. For details of the lists, see page 21 of AACR2R.

> *Examples*
> MS-DOS/BASIC [computer file]
> Orienteering, what's that? [filmstrip]
> Platonis Res publica [microform]
> Respirators [motion picture]

Leipziger Bach-Collegium [sound recording]
The Adventures of a two-minute werewolf [videorecording]
Dog days of Arthur Cane [videorecording]

3. Parallel titles (rule *.1D) [MARC field 245, subfield ‡b]

A parallel title is the title proper in *another* language or script. It should not be confused with an alternative title or other title information, which is not equivalent in meaning to the title proper.

The one hundred new tales = Les cent nouvelles nouvelles

4. Other title information (rule *.1E) [MARC field 245, subfield ‡b]

Other title information includes any title other than the title proper, the alternative title, the parallel or series title(s), and variations on the title proper such as spine title, sleeve title, etc. Subtitles, avant titres, and phrases appearing in conjunction with the title proper or any phrase indicative of the character, contents, etc. of the item or the motives for, or occasion of, its production or publication all fall into this category. Other title information is preceded by a space-colon-space (:) following the title proper or the general material designation.

City of Anoka, Minnesota : street index map with address system

Distributed algorithms : 4th international workshop, Bari, Italy, September 24-26, 1990 : proceedings

How the museum print collection grew : transcript of a lecture, November 26, 1989

Konzert in A-Dur für Oboe d'amore (Oboe), Streicher und Basso continuo : Rekonstruktion nach BWV 1055 = Concerto in A major for oboe d'amore (oboe), strings, and basso continuo : reconstructed from BWV 1055

Living standards measurement study : abstracts of working papers 1–59

Marbled paper : its history, techniques, and patterns : with special reference to the relationship of marbling to bookbinding in Europe and the Western world

Nicholas of Cusa : in search of God and wisdom : papers from the American Cusanus Society

Toxicology : a primer on toxicology principles and applications ...

The unfinished journey : American [sic] since World War II

Chemistry [computer file] : balancing equations

Growing up at the table [filmstrip] : teaching feeding skills to the mentally retarded child at home

Hidden alcoholics [motion picture] : why is Mommy sick?

The young Kiri [sound recording] : the early recordings, 1964-70

5. Statements of responsibility (rule *.1F) [MARC field 245, subfield ‡c]

The statement of responsibility names the person or persons responsible for the intellectual or artistic content of the item being described, the corporate body or bodies from which the content emanates, or the persons or corporate bodies responsible for the performance of the content. The persons named include writers, editors, compilers, adapters, translators, revisers, illustrators, reporters, composers, artists, photographers, cartographers, collectors, narrators, performers, producers, directors, and investigators. The statement or statements that appear prominently in the item are transcribed in the form in which they appear in the source of information. Words taken from sources other than those prescribed are enclosed in square brackets.

Annual report / Saskatchewan Parks, Recreation, and Culture

The Changing geography of the United Kingdom / edited for the Institute of British Geographers by R.J. Johnston and V. Gardiner

The complete works of Rather of Verona / translated with an introduction and notes by Peter L.D. Reid

Computerizing the corporation : the intimate link between people and machines / Vicki C. McConnell, Karl W. Koch

Freud on women : a reader / edited and with an introduction by Elisabeth Young-Bruehl

Nuclear weapons in the university classroom : an interdisciplinary teaching reference / Michael S. Hamilton, William A. Lindeke, John MacDougall

Oak Grove Cemetery, Nacogdoches, Texas / [compiled by Mrs. Roy Dean Burk]

Principles of ambulatory medicine / edited by L. Randol
Barker, John R. Burton, Philip D. Zieve

Sound and sentiment : birds, weeping, poetics, and song in
Kaluli expression / Steven Feld

Winslow Homer : a symposium / edited by Nicolai
Cikovsky, Jr.

When the statement of responsibility in the source of information contains names of more than three persons or corporate bodies, only the first
named, followed by ... [et al.], is included in the statement of responsibility in the cataloging record.

The age of reptiles : the great dinosaur mural at Yale / by
Vincent Scully ... [et al.]

Paradox programming / by Patricia A. Hartman ... [et al.]

When there are two or more statements of responsibility, each naming
one or more persons or corporate bodies performing different functions,
they are separated by a space-semicolon-space.

The Boss of the 8th / Broncho Motion Picture Co. ; [written]
by T.H. Ince and R.V. Spencer

Bungalow fungalow / by Pegi Deitz Shea ; illustrated by
Elizabeth Sayles

An introduction to the basic problems of moral philosophy /
Jacques Maritain ; [translated by Cornelia N. Borgerhoff]

International copyright and neighboring rights law :
commentary with special emphasis on the European
Community / Wilhelm Nordemann, Kai Vinck, Paul W.
Hertin ; English version by Gerald Meyer, based on the
translation by R. Livingston

Managing urban freeway maintenance / E. Nels Burns ;
topic panel, Richard A. Cunard ... [et al.]

Mexican celebrations / Eliot Porter and Ellen Auerbach ;
essays by Donna Pierce and Marsha Bol

New World Avenue and vicinity / Tadeusz Konwicki ;
translated by Walter Arndt ; with drawings by the author

The Odyssey of Homer : a new verse translation / by Allen
Mandelbaum ; with twelve engravings by Marialuisa de
Romans

A rich land, a poor people : politics and society in modern
Chiapas / Thomas Benjamin ; [drawings by Alberto Beltran]

Self-definition and self-discovery in early Christianity : a
study in changing horizons : essays in appreciation of Ben F.
Meyer / from former students ; edited by David J. Hawkin
& Tom Robinson

Setting national priorities : policy for the nineties / Henry J.
Aaron, editor ; John E. Chubb ... [et al.]

Sud / V. Tendriakov = The trial / V. Tendryakov ; edited
by Peter Doyle

With the exception of British titles of nobility or honor (e.g., Sir, Dame,
Lord, and Lady), titles and abbreviations of titles of nobility, address,
honor, and distinction are generally omitted from the statement of
responsibility; the same is true for initials of societies and for other
listings of qualifications. Exceptions are made when such a title is
necessary grammatically for identification of the person and when the
name consists of a given name or a surname only.

Human races / by Stanley M. Garn
[*On title page:* by Stanley M. Garn, Ph.D.]

Stories of Charlemagne and the twelve peers of France from
the old romances / by A.J. Church
[*On title page:* by Prof. A.J. Church, M.A.]

The cruise of the "Janet Nichol" among the South Sea Islands
: a diary / by Mrs. Robert Louis Stevenson

Oh, the places you'll go! / by Dr. Seuss

Edition Area (Rule *.2) [MARC Field 250]

This area contains four elements: (1) edition statement, (2) statements of
responsibility relating to the edition, (3) statement relating to a named
version of an edition, and (4) statements of responsibility relating to a
named revision of an edition. Each is discussed below.

1. Edition statement (rule *.2B) [MARC field 250, subfield ‡a]

An edition statement found in an item, including one for the first edition,
is transcribed. Standard abbreviations and numerals (in place of spelled-
out words) are used (see Appendixes B and C of AACR2R).

1989/90 ed.
2nd ed.
1st ed.
1st American ed.
[1st MIT Press ed.]
Conference ed.
Rev. ed.
Ed. of 1952
Release 1.0
Version 2.1.
Prelim. draft
[3rd draft]

2. Statements of responsibility relating to the edition (rule *.2C) [MARC field 250, subfield ‡b]

A statement of responsibility relating to one or more, but not all, editions is given after the edition statement instead of after the title.

Rev. ed. / Mrs. William Homer Watkins
3rd ed. / [edited by] William B. Pratt, Palmer Taylor
Updated ... June, 1981 / Ronning Cartography

3. Statement relating to a named revision of an edition (rule *.2D) [MARC field 250]

A statement designating the item as a revision of an edition (a named reissue of a particular edition containing changes from that edition) is given after the edition statement and its statements of responsibility.

2nd ed., 1988 revision
2nd ed., enl. and up to date

4. Statements of responsibility relating to a named revision of an edition (rule *.2E) [MARC field 250, subfield ‡b]

The statement relating to a named revision of an edition may be followed by its own statement or statements of responsibility, if there are any (rule *.2E).

Material (or Type of Publication) Specific Details Area (Rule *.3) [MARC Fields 254 (Music), 255 (Cartographic Material), 256 (Computer File), and 362 (Serials)]

This area is applicable only to the following types of material: (1) cartographic materials, (2) music, (3) computer files, (4) serials, and (5) cartographic materials, music, and serials in microform. For each type of material, this area is defined for specific details or unique characteristics, as shown below.

1. Cartographic materials (rule 3.3) [MARC field 255]

Called the *mathematical data area,* this area contains the statement of scale, the statement of projection, and the statement of coordinates and equinox (optional).

> Southern area, metropolitan Los Angeles / cartography by Joanne M. Sasao. — **Scale [ca. 1:44,000]**

> Metro system map : [Washington D.C. metropolitan area]. — **Not drawn to scale**

> Replogle 12 inch diameter globe world classic series / Leroy M. Tolman, cartographer. — **Scale 1:41,849,600 (W 180°— E 180°/N 90°—S 90°)**

2. Music (rule 5.3) [MARC field 254]

Called the *musical presentation statement area,* this optional area records a statement appearing in the chief source of information indicating the physical presentation of the music.

> Murder of a great chief of state : in memory of John Kennedy = Meurtre d'un grand chef d'état : a là mémoire de John Kennedy / Darius Milhaud — **Partition in 16.**

3. Computer files (rule 9.3) [MARC field 256]

Called the *file characteristics area,* this area gives information about the type of file [i.e., *computer data, computer program(s), computer data and program*], followed by number of records, statements, etc.

> Computer program (1 file : 300 statements)

4. Serials (rule 12.3) [MARC field 362]

For serial publications, this area, called the *numeric and/or alphabetic, chronological, or other designation area,* contains the numeric or alphabetic designation, or both, and/or the chronological designation relating to the first and last (if the serial is completed) issue.

> Acute toxicity data : journal of the American College of Toxicology, part B. — **Vol. 1, no. 1-**

Anniversary report / Harvard and Radcliffe, Class of 1984.
— 5th-

Annual planning information. Chico metropolitan statistical
area (Butte County). — **1985/1986-1988/1989**

Annual report / Saskatchewan Parks, Recreation, and
Culture. — **1987/1988-**

Culture. — **Vol. 1, no. 1-**

Journal of the American Society for Mass Spectrometry. —
Vol. 1, no. 1 (Jan./Feb. 1990)-

Journal of the Chemical Society. Faraday transactions /
Royal Society of Chemistry. — **Vol. 86, no. 1 (7th Jan. 1990)-**

Air repair. — **Vol. 1, no. 1 (July 1951)-v. 4, no. 4 (Feb. 1955)**

5. Cartographic materials, music, and serials in microform (rule 11.3)

When cataloging a cartographic item, music, or serial in microform, the
material (or type of publication) specific detail is given as in the case of
such materials in printed form. In other words, rules 3.3, 5.3, and 12.3
are applied.

Publication, Distribution, etc., Area (Rule *.4) [MARC Field 260]

This area records information about the place, name, and date of all types
of activities relating to the publishing, distributing, releasing, issuing,
and manufacturing of the item being described.

   If the item being described displays two or more places of publication, distribution, etc. or names of publishers, distributors, etc., the
first-named place of publication, distribution, etc. and the corresponding
publisher, distributor, etc. are recorded. However, if the first-named
place is in a foreign country and a place in the country of the cataloging
agency is named in a secondary position, with or without a corresponding publisher, etc., the latter is recorded also.

   The elements in this area are recorded in the following order: (1)
place of publication, distribution, etc., (2) name of publisher, distributor,
etc., (3) statement of function of publisher, distributor, etc. (optional), (4)
date of publication, distribution, etc., and (5) place of manufacture, name
of manufacturer, date of manufacture.

1. Place of publication, distribution, etc. (rule *.4C) [MARC field 260, subfield ‡a]

The place of publication, distribution, etc. is recorded in the form and the grammatical case in which it appears in the item. The name of the country, state, province, etc. (abbreviated according to Appendix B of AACR2R) is added to the name of a local place if it is considered necessary for identification, or if it is considered necessary to distinguish the place from others of the same name. The name of the country, state, province, etc. is enclosed in brackets if it does not appear in the pre-scribed sources of information.

> Philadelphia
> [Washington, D.C.]
> Albany, N.Y.
> Cambridge [England]
> Cambridge, Mass.
> Newbury Park, Calif.
> Oxonii
> Dordrecht, Netherlands
> Basel ; New York

If the place is not known, the abbreviation [S.l.], for *sine loco,* is given.

> [S.l.] : Lawson-Gould Music Publishers : Exclusively distributed by Alfred, c1990.

Optionally, the place of publication may be followed by the address of the publisher if it is not widely known.

> Portland, Me. **(P.O. Box 658, Portland 04104-0658)** : J. Weston Walch

This element is not applicable to the description of manuscripts or of naturally occurring objects.

2. Name of publisher, distributor, etc. (rule *.4D) [MARC field 260, subfield ‡b]

The name of the place is followed by the name of the publisher, distributor, etc., given in the shortest form in which it can be understood and identified.

> New York : **Doubleday**
>
> New York : **Praeger**
>
> [New York : **Garland**]

Providence, R.I. : **Published for the Conference Board of the Mathematical Sciences by the American Mathematical Society**

Boca Raton : **Florida Atlantic University Press** ; Gainesville, Fla. : **University Presses of Florida [distributor]**

Los Alamitos, Calif. : **IEEE Computer Society Press** ; Piscataway, N.J. : **Additional copies ordered from IEEE Service Center**

Cambridge [England] ; New York : **Cambridge University Press**

London ; New York : **Published by Routledge and the International Social Science Council with the cooperation of UNESCO and the Institute of Environmental Studies, Free University, Amsterdam**

Oxford [England] : **Clarendon Press** ; New York : **Oxford University Press**

Washington : **National Gallery of Art** ; Hanover, N.H. : **Distributed by the University Press of New England**

If the name of the publisher, distributor, etc. has appeared in the title and statement of responsibility area, a shortened form is used here.

Aerial survey, Manhattan Island, New York City / made by Fairchild Aerial Camera Corporation, New York City, Aug. 4, 1921. — [New York] : **The Corporation**

An outline of the history of the National Society Colonial Dames XVII Century, 1915-1962 : Miss Mary Florence Taney, founder / [Mrs. Ernest B. Waitt]. — [United States] : **The Society**

For a sound recording, if both the name of the publishing company and the name of a subdivision of that company or a trade name or brand name are displayed on the item, the latter is recorded.

For a motion picture or videorecording, this element contains the name of the publisher and optionally the name of the distributor, releasing agency, etc. and/or the name of a production agency or producer not named in the statements of responsibility.

If the name of the publisher, distributor, etc. is not known, the abbreviation [s.n.], for *sine nomine,* is given.

United States : **[s.n.]**, 1972

3. Date of publication, distribution, etc. (rule *.4F) [MARC field 260, subfield ‡c]

The year of publication, distribution, etc. of the edition, revision, etc. named in the edition area is recorded in western-style arabic numerals. If there is no edition statement, the year of the first publication of the edition to which the item belongs is recorded. If the date transcribed from the item is known to be incorrect, the correct date is added in square brackets.

Boulder, Colo. : Westview Press, **1990**

Chicago : [s.n.], **1964 [i.e., 1946]**

New York : Penguin Books, **1990**

The date of distribution, if it is different from the date of publication, is added.

It is optional to add the latest date of copyright following the date of publication, distribution, etc. if it is different.

If the dates of publication, etc. are not known, the copyright date or, lacking such, the date of manufacture is given in its place.

Urbana : University of Illinois Press, **c1990**

Zurich, Switzerland : Tudor, **p1987**

If none of the dates discussed above can be assigned to the item being described, an approximate date of publication is given.

[Chicago] : Replogle Globes, Inc., **[1989?]** *(probable date)*

[Nacogdoches, Tex.] : Nacogdoches Historical Commission, **[1963?]**

[ca. 1900] *(approximate date)*

If a multipart item contains more than one date, the earliest and the latest dates are recorded.

New York : Academic Press, **1969-1973**

If the multipart item is not yet complete, the earliest date followed by a hyphen (called an open entry) is given.

[Regina] : Saskatchewan Parks, Recreation, and Culture, **[1988]-**

For a manuscript, the date is given in this area unless it is already included in the title.

For an art original, unpublished photograph, or other unpublished graphic item (rule 8.4F2), the date of creation is recorded.

For a naturally occurring object (unless it has been mounted for viewing or packaged for presentation), no date is recorded. For artefacts not intended primarily for communication, the date of manufacture is recorded.

4. Place of manufacture, name of manufacturer, date of manufacture (rule *.4G) [MARC field 260, subfields ‡e, ‡f, ‡g]

If the name of the publisher is unknown, the place and name of the printer or manufacturer are recorded in parentheses and following the place, name, and date of publication and/or distribution if they are found on the item, its container or case, or accompanying printed material.

[S.l. : s.n.], c1987 **(Houston : Hart Graphics, Morin Division)**

The date of manufacture is included here if it has not been used in place of an unknown date of publication, distribution, etc.

Physical Description Area (Rule *.5) [MARC Field 300]

This area presents the physical characteristics of the item being cataloged. It contains the following basic elements: (1) extent of item (including specific material designation), (2) other physical details, (3) dimensions, and (4) accompanying material. The terms with which each type of material is described vary greatly. They are enumerated below.

1. Extent of item (including specific material designation) (rule *.5B) [MARC field 300, subfield ‡a]

The number of physical units and parts are recorded in arabic numerals followed by the specific material designation (abbreviated according to Appendix B of AACR2R). The more common kinds of specific material designations used for different types of material are listed below. In the description, each of these terms is preceded by the number of units (e.g., 436 p., 3 film cassettes, etc.). For a multipart item that is not yet complete, the specific material designation alone preceded by three spaces is given.

Books, pamphlets, and printed sheets
v. *(for volume or volumes)*
p. *(for page or pages)*
leaf
column
broadside

sheet
portfolio

Cartographic materials
atlas
diagram
globe
map
map section
profile
relief model
remote-sensing image
view

Manuscripts
leaf
p.
v.
item *(for a collection of manuscripts)*
box *(for a collection of manuscripts)*
ft. *(for a collection occupying more than 1 linear foot of shelf space)*

Music
score
condensed score
close score
miniature score
piano [violin, etc.] conductor part
vocal score
piano score
chorus score
part

Sound recordings (each designation followed by the playing time)
sound cartridge
sound cassette
sound disc
sound tape reel
sound track film reel [cassette, etc.]
piano [organ] roll, etc.

Motion pictures and videorecordings (each designation followed by the playing time)
film cartridge
film cassette
film loop

film reel
videocartridge
videocassette
videodisc
videoreel

Graphic materials
art original
art print
art reproduction
chart
filmslip
filmstrip
flash card
flip chart
photograph
picture
postcard
poster
radiograph
slide
stereograph
study print
technical drawing
transparency
wall chart

Computer files
computer cartridge
computer cassette
computer disk
computer reel

Three-dimensional artefacts and realia
art original
art reproduction
braille cassette
diorama
exhibit
game
microscope slide
mock-up
model
[*the specific name of the item or the names of the parts of the item*]

Microforms
aperture card
microfiche *or* microfiche cassette
microfilm *or* microfilm cartridge [cassette, reel]
microopaque

Serials
[*the appropriate specific material designation selected from the terms
listed above*]

2. Other physical details (rule *.5C) [MARC field 300, subfield ‡b]

Other physical details are added for the following types of materials:

Books, pamphlets, and printed sheets (rule 2.5C)
illustrative matter (use *ill.* for general illustrative matter and
specify one or more of the following if considered
important: coats of arms, facsimiles, forms, genealogical
tables, maps, music, plans, portraits, samples)

Cartographic materials (rule 3.5C)
number of maps in an atlas
color
material
mounting

Manuscripts (rule 4.5C)
name of material (if not paper) on which a single manuscript
is written (e.g., parchment, vellum)
illustrative matter (same as books, etc.)

Music (rule 5.5C)
illustrative matter (same as books, etc.)

Sound recordings (rule 6.5C)
type of recording
playing speed
groove characteristics (analog discs)
track configuration (sound track films)
number of tracks (tapes)
number of sound channels
recording and reproduction characteristics

Motion pictures and videorecordings (rule 7.5C)
aspect ratio and special projection characteristics (motion
pictures)
sound characteristics

color
projection speed if other than standard speed (motion pictures)

Graphic materials (rule 8.5C)
medium (chalk, oil, pastel, etc.) and the base (board, canvas, fabric, etc.) *(for art originals)*
process in general terms (engraving, lithograph, etc.) or specific terms (copper engraving, chromolithograph, etc.) *(for art prints)*
method of reproduction (photogravure, collotype, etc.) (for *art reproductions*
double sided *(for charts and flip charts)*
sound (if the sound is integral) *(for filmstrips, filmslips, and flash cards)*
transparency or negative print *(for photographs)*
sound (if integral) *(for slides)*
method of reproduction (blueprint, photocopy, etc.) *(for technical drawings)*
color (col., sepia, b&w, tinted, etc.) *(for all graphic media other than art originals, radiographs, and technical drawings)*

Computer files (rule 9.5C)
sound *(for a file encoded to produce sound)*
color *(for a file encoded to display in two or more colours)*

Three-dimensional artefacts and realia (rule 10.5C)
material (marble, glass, wood, plastic, etc.)
color

Microforms (rule 11.5C)
negative
illustrative matter (same as books, etc.)
color

Serials
[*physical details appropriate to the item being described as outlined above*]

3. Dimensions (rule *.5D) [MARC field 300, subfield ‡c]

The dimension of the item follows the extent of the item and/or other physical details. The part of the item to be measured varies according to type of material.

Books, pamphlets, and printed sheets (rule 2.5D) *(in centimeters, to the next whole centimeter up, and in millimeters if less than ten centimeters)* height of the volume or volumes

height × width (if width is less than half the height or greater than the height)

Cartographic materials (rule 3.5D) *(in centimeters, to the next whole centimeter up)*

height × width *(for two-dimensional cartographic items, relief models, and for atlases with the width less than half the height or greater than the height)*

height of the volume or volumes *(for atlases)*

diameter *(for globes)*

Manuscripts (rule 4.5D) *(in centimeters, to the next whole centimeter up)*

height

height × width (if width is less than half the height or greater than the height)

height × width × depth *(for collections of manuscripts in containers)*

Music (rule 5.5D)

[*same as for books, pamphlets, etc.*]

Sound recordings (rule 6.5D)

diameter of the disc in inches *(for sound discs)*

gauge (width) in millimeters *(for sound track films)*

dimensions of the cartridge and width of the tape (if other than the standard measurement) in inches *(for sound cartridges and sound cassettes)*

diameter of the reel in inches and width of the tape (if other than standard) in fractions of an inch *(for sound tape reels)*

Motion pictures and videorecordings (rule 7.5D)

gauge (width) in millimeters and (if 8 mm) whether single, standard, super, or Maurer *(for motion pictures)*

gauge (width) in inches or millimeters *(for videotapes)*

diameter in inches *(for videodiscs)*

Graphic materials (rule 8.5D)

height × width in centimeters *(for all graphic materials except filmstrips, filmslips, and stereographs)*

gauge (width) in millimeters *(for filmstrips and filmslips)*

Computer files (rule 9.5D)

diameter in inches, to the next ¼ inch up *(for disks)*

length of the side of the cartridge in inches to the next ¼ inch up

length × height of the face of the cassette in inches, to the next
⅛ inch up *(for computer cassettes)*

Three-dimensional artefacts and realia (rule 10.5D)
dimensions of the object in centimeters to the next centimeter
up
name and dimensions of container (if any)

Microforms (rule 11.5D)
height × width in centimeters to the next centimeter up *(for
aperture cards)*
height × width in centimeters to the next centimeter up (if
other than 10.5 × 14.8 cm. *(for microfiche)*
width in millimeters *(for microfilms)*
height × width in centimeters to the next centimeter up *(for
microopaques)*

Serials (rule 12.5D)
[*dimensions appropriate to the type of material of the serial being
described*]

4. Accompanying material (rule *.5E) [MARC field 300, subfield ‡e]

There are four ways of describing accompanying material:

1. Record the details in a separate entry.
2. Record the details in a multilevel description (i.e., as an analytic).
3. Record the details in a note.
4. Record the number of physical units in arabic numerals and the
   name of the accompanying material at the end of the physical
   description.

Examples of physical description are given below:

Books
xiii, 259 p. : ill. ; 23 cm.
xviii, 225 p. : map ; 23 cm.
xvi, 245 p., [38] p. of plates : ill. (some col.) ; 32 cm.
xv, 220 p., [1] leaf of plates ; ill., maps ; 24 cm.
vi, 43 p. : col. ill. ; 28 cm.
4 v. : maps ; 28 cm.
1 v. (unpaged) ; 28 cm.
ii, 248 p. : ill., ports. ; 28 cm.
347 p. (large print) : 23 cm.
14 p., 40 p. of plates : ports. ; 35 cm.

Cartographic materials
2 maps on 1 sheet : col. ; 45 × 84 cm., sheet 77 × 93 cm.
1 globe : col., plastic, mounted on plastic and wood base ;
    31 cm. in diam.
1 map : col. ; 55 × 76 cm., folded to 23 × 10 cm.

Microforms
246 microfilm reels ; 35 mm.

Music
1 score (19 p.) + 2 parts ; 30 cm.
1 score (3 v.) + 2 parts (3 v.) ; 28 cm.
1 vocal score (xxxix, 297 p.) ; 29 cm.

Sound recordings
1 sound disc : digital, stereo. ; 4¾ in.

Motion pictures and videorecordings
1 film reel (12 min., 30 sec.) : sd., col. ; 16 mm. + 1 release sheet
1 videocassette (200 min.) : sd., col.
5 videocassettes (140 min.) : sd., col. + 1 teacher's manual

Graphic materials
1 photoprint
1 filmstrip (92 fr.) : col. ; 35 mm. + 1 sound cassette (16
    min. : analog) + 1 guide
5 filmstrips (ca. 116 fr. each) : col. ; 35 mm. + 5 sound
    cassettes (98 min. : analog) + 5 teacher's guides

Computer files
5 computer disks ; 3½–5¼ in. + 1 manual (looseleaf) + 4
    guides + 3 quick answer cards + templates

In the description of different types of materials, the greatest variations occur in the physical description area. For more details and further examples, consult AACR2R.

Note: Multimedia items (rule *.10)
If an item consisting of two or more components belonging to two or more distinct material types has been described in terms of the predominant component in the preceding areas, the physical description is also presented in terms of the predominant component with details of the subsidiary component given as accompanying material (cf. rule 1.10).

1 filmstrip (127 fr.) : col. ; 35 mm + 1 sound cassette

A multimedia item that has no predominant component is described as a kit if it has a collective title. The term [kit] or [multimedia] may be used as the general material designation, and the physical description may be presented by one of the following methods:

1. Physical descriptions of all components are presented in the same statement.

> 45 flash cards, 50 worksheets, 12 duplicating masters, teacher's guide ; in container ; 16 × 24 × 18 cm.

2. Physical description of each component is presented separately.

> 1 filmstrip (74 fr.) : col ; 35 mm.
> 1 sound disc (17 min.) : 33⅓ rpm, mono ; 12 in.

3. A general statement, if the item consists of a large number of heterogeneous components, is used.

> various pieces
> 16 various pieces

Series Area (Rule *.6) [MARC Field 4XX][5]

This area contains the following elements. In recording these elements, the corresponding rules in the title and statement of responsibility area are followed.

1. Title proper of series (rule *.6B)
2. Parallel titles of series (rule *.6C)
3. Other title information of series (rule *.6D)
4. Statements of responsibility relating to series (rule *.6E)
5. ISSN (International Standard Serial Number) of series (rule *.6F)
6. Numbering within series (rule *.6G)
7. Subseries (rule *.6H)
8. More than one series statement (rule *.6J)

This area is not applicable to the description of manuscript texts. In describing a microform, the series to which the microform belongs is described in the series area, and the series to which the original belongs is recorded in a note.

Examples of series statements are shown below:

> (Brown Judaic studies ; no. 110, 178)

> (Coleridge's writings ; 1)

> (Commission on Ecology papers ; no. 9)

---

[5]The 4XX fields are used for different types of series statements, and different subfield codes are defined for each field.

(Contributions to the study of religion, ISSN 0196-7053 ; no. 27)

(The facts, feeling, and wonder of life)

(The Johns Hopkins University studies in historical and political science ; 106th ser., 1 (1988))

(Lecture notes in mathematics ; 1436)

(Monograph series / American Group Psychotherapy Association ; monograph 6)

(Occasional paper / International Monetary Fund, ISSN 0251-6365 ; 78)

(Publications of the Early Music Institute)

(Report / Human Sciences Research Council ; P-65)

(Research report / International Food Policy Research Institute ; 80)

(Safety gear series)

(Sci-mate software system)

(Studies in British history ; v. 23)

(Studies in the anthropology of North American Indians)

(University of North Carolina studies in the Germanic languages and literature ; no. 112)

If the item belongs to a subseries which is named in the item along with the main series, both series are recorded within the same set of parentheses and separated by a full stop.

(American university studies. Series II, Romance languages and literature ; v. 151)

(Monographs in international studies. Southeast Asia series ; no. 88)

(Publications of the American Folklore Society. New series)

(Studies in the history of art, ISSN 0091-7338 ; v. 40. Monograph series ; 2)

If the item belongs to two or more series, the series statements are enclosed in separate parentheses. In MARC records, each series is recorded in a separate 4XX field.

(Area handbook series) (DA pam ; 550-167)

(Russian Research Center studies ; 85) (Harvard historical studies ; v. 108)

(Studies in social and political theory ; v. 8) (Political and legal philosophy today ; no. 1)

(Studies in the history of art, ISSN 0091-7338 ; 26) (Symposium papers ; 11)

Note Area (Rule *.7) [MARC Fields 5XX][6]

Useful descriptive information which cannot be presented in the other areas is given in notes. Some notes supplement or clarify information given in the preceding areas; others provide additional bibliographic information. The notes may be based on information taken from any suitable source. In notes containing data relating to those in the preceding areas, prescribed punctuation is used, except that a full stop is used in place of a full stop-space-dash-space. When quotations from the item or from other sources are used as notes, they are enclosed in quotation marks.

The kinds of notes used are listed below, with examples.

1. Nature, scope, or artistic form:

    Catalogue of the exhibition held Nov. 11, 1990-Feb. 24, 1991

    Compact disc

    For 4 voices

2. Language of the item and/or translation or adaptation:

    English and Cuna

    Greek text; commentary in Latin

    Text in Russian; introduction and prefatory materials in English

    Translation of: L'ami lointain

    Translation of: Carnets, janvier 1942-mars 1951

3. Source of title proper:

    Title from cover

    Title from text on verso

---

[6]MARC codes in the 500 series are used with notes, depending on their type; and unique subfield codes are defined for each 5XX field.

4. Variations in title:

   Alternate title: Alexandria, Virginia metropolitan area

   Cover title: Genealogical data of Ancient and Honorable Artillery Company of Massachusetts, 1638-1774

   Cover title: The Riley manuscripts

   Spine title: Patterning science and technology

5. Parallel titles and other title information:

   Parallel titles on container: Arien = Airs

6. Statements of responsibility:

   Based on: The adventures of a two-minute werewolf / Gene DeWee

   Consultant, Julia M. Gottesman

   "In association with the Frank Lloyd Wright Foundation and the Phoenix Art Museum"

   Sponsored by the Neutron Scattering Group of the Institute of Physics and Royal Society of Chemistry

   "Written under the auspices of the Center for International Affairs, Harvard University"— P. [i]

7. Edition and history:

   "The bulk of this book is reprinted from The economic way of thinking, sixth edition ... c1991"—T.p. verso

   Reprint. Originally published: Boston, Mass. : P.R. Warren, 1905

   "Reprinted from Mining and metallurgy, March 1941"

   Reproduction of engraving by Paul Revere, drawn by Josh. Chadwick

   Rev. ed. of: Historical dictionary of Rhodesia/Zimbabwe

   Formed by the union of: Journal of the Chemical Society. Faraday transactions. I, Physical chemistry in condensed phases, and: Journal of the Chemical Society. Faraday transactions. II, Molecular and chemical physics

8. Material (or type of publication) specific details (used with types of materials listed in Table 3-3):

TABLE 3-3   Material-Specific Details

Type of Material	Note Regarding
Cartographic materials	Mathematical and other cartographic data
Manuscripts	Place of writing
Music	Notation
Computer files	File characteristics
Serials	Numbering and chronological designation

Examples of Material-Specific Details notes:

Vol. 3, no. 4 omitted

Number of routines: 102

Oriented with north to the right

Plainsong notation

9. Publication, distribution, etc.:

"Copyright 1952 city of Alexandria, Virginia"

The 1st work recorded at the Liszt Ferenc Music Academy, Budapest, 1985; the remainder recorded at Studio Cle d'Ut, Paris, 1985

Made in 1977

10. Physical description:

Duration: ca. 6:00

Durations: 22:00; 5:19; 10:44; 9:04; 6:29

Ill. on lining papers

One folded map in pocket

VHS

11. Accompanying material and supplements:

Accompanied by: Drift globe guide. 15 p. : ill., maps ; 28 cm.

Accompanied by graphs: Plate 1. Mineral production of the United States in 1938 — Plate 6. World production of metallic minerals in 1938, U.S. imports and exports

Notes by Ton Koopman and Anthony Hicks in English, French, and German; libretto in Italian with English, French, and German translations (83 p. : facsim.)

12. Series:

Cahiers II

Series statement from jacket

13. Dissertations:

Thesis (Ph.D.)—Harvard University, 1981

14. Audience:

Elementary grades through junior high school students

Senior high school students

15. Reference to published descriptions:

The Memoirs have been published in the Kentucky State Historical Society register

16. Other formats:

Issued also as videorecording

Issued as U-matic ¾ in. or Beta ½ in. or VHS ½ in.

17. Summary:

Summary: Fourteen-year-old Walt, discovering in himself a tendency to turn into a werewolf, puts his talent to constructive use to thwarting the activities of a gang of burglars

18. Contents:

Contents: Diary-journal — New endings — Problem solving — Mapping — Interviewing

Contents: 1. Libraries A–L — 2. Libraries M–Z. Index

Contents: pt. A. Methods of surface analysis — pt. B. Chemisorption of probe molecules

Includes index

Includes bibliographical references (p. [135]–149) and index

19. Numbers borne by the item (other than those presented in the standard number and terms of availability area):

"R-4004-NCRVE/UCB."

"R-3943-FMP, November 1990."

"ACM order number: 417890"—T.p. verso

20. Copy being described, library's holdings, and restrictions on use:

LC copy has handwritten attribution to Charles Burney

LC copy signed by author

21. "With" notes:

With: The Bostonian Ebenezer. Boston : Printed by B. Green & J. Allen, for Samuel Phillips, 1698 — The cure of sorrow. Boston : Printed by B. Green, 1709. Bound together subsequent to publication

22. Combined notes relating to the original:

Rev. ed. of: La Guardia Civil, 1844-1978. c1979

Standard Number and Terms of Availability Area (Rule *.8) [MARC Fields 020 (ISBN), 022 (ISSN)]

This area contains the following elements: (1) standard number, (2) key title, and (3) terms of availability (optional).

1. Standard number (rule *.8B) [MARC fields 020, 022, subfield code ‡a]

The number recorded is the International Standard Book Number (ISBN), International Standard Serial Number (ISSN), or any other internationally agreed standard number. This element does not apply to the description of manuscripts.

2. Key title (rule *.8C) [MARC field 222]

This element applies to serial publications only.

> *Example*
> Journal of the American Society for Mass Spectrometry

3. Terms of availability (rule *.8D) [MARC field 020, subfield ‡c]

This element is optional.

Examples

ISBN 1-557-75135-8 : $10.00 ($7.50 to university faculty and students)

ISBN 0-226-67544-0 (cloth : alk. paper) : $19.95. — ISBN 0-226-67545-9 (paper)

ISBN 0-444-88812-8 (set). — ISBN 0-444-88242-1 (v. 1). — ISBN 0-444-88243-X (v.2)

ISSN 1047-3289

ISSN 0229-009X = Culture (Québec. 1981)

For sale ($295.00)

SUPPLEMENTARY ITEMS (RULE *.9)

A *supplement*, which is an item that complements or adds to an existing publication, can be treated in one of two ways: (1) as a separate item or (2) as a dependent item.

As a Separate Item

A separate cataloging record is created for the supplement. The supplement is linked to the main item by means of an added entry for the latter and a note explaining the relationship between the two.

As a Dependent Item

The supplement is recorded in the description of the main item as accompanying material or in a note.

ANALYTICS

An *analytical entry* is a bibliographic record that describes a part or parts of a larger item. The part or parts being described may be a monograph within a monographic series, a volume in a multivolume set, or a part of a volume.

Analytics of Monographic Series and Multipart Monographs

An individual part of a monographic series or of a multipart monograph can be described in one of four ways:[7] (1) with analytical added
entries, (2) in a separate record, (3) in a contents note, or (4) using "in"
analytics.

Analytical added entries (rule 13.2)

An added entry (consisting of the part's main entry heading and/
or uniform title) is made to the comprehensive entry for the larger
work. In this case, the part should be named either in the title and
statement of responsibility area or in the note area of the record for the
main item.

In a separate record (rule 13.3)

If the part being described has a distinctive title, a complete record
describing the part may be created with details of the series or comprehensive item given in the series area.

In a contents note (rule 13.4)

The title or name and title of the part may be cited in a contents note in
the record of the comprehensive entry for the larger work.

"In" analytics (rule 13.5)

In this method, the part being analyzed is presented in the description,
and the citation of the larger item is given in a note beginning with the
word *In*.

The record contains the following elements which are applicable to
the item being described:

[7]AACR2R provides yet another method, called *multilevel description* (rule 13.6),
whereby the descriptive information is divided into two or more levels. The first level gives
only information relating to the item as a whole, and subsequent levels give information
relating to groups of parts or individual parts contained in the item. This method is
normally used by national bibliographies. Most libraries, including the Library of Congress, do not employ multilevel description.

Title and statement of responsibility area. — Edition area. — Numeric or other designation. — Publication, distribution, etc., area. — Extent and specific material designation of the part : other physical details ; dimensions. — Notes.

In [Main entry. Uniform title of whole item]. Title proper. — Edition statement. — Numeric or other designation of a serial, or publication details of a monographic item.

Example

Developing a national foreign newspaper microfilming program / John Y. Cole. — p. 5–17 ; 24 cm.

In Library resources & technical services. — Vol. 18, no. 1, Winter 1974

EXERCISE B

Prepare a bibliographic description for each of the following.

1. *The Poet's Poet and Other Essays* (See reproduction of title page, Fig. 3-8. Other physical details: the book has 352 pages and measures 20 centimeters in height.)

2. *The Contradictions of Leadership* (See reproduction of title page and verso, Fig. 3-9. Other physical details: the book has 8 preliminary pages numbered with Roman numerals and 161 pages of text and measures 22 centimeters in height.)

3. *The Short Prose Reader* (An anthology compiled by Muller and Wiener; see reproduction of title page and verso, Fig. 3-10. Other physical details: the book has 23 preliminary pages numbered with Roman numerals and 498 pages of text measures 22 centimeters in height, has a bibliography appearing on pages 494 through 498, and costs $15.95.)

4. *Symphonies 4 & 5* (A compact disc; see reproduction of disc and case, Fig. 3-11. Other physical details: the playing time is 67 minutes 50 seconds, and it is a digital, stereo recording, measuring 4¾ inches. The recording was made at Davies Symphony Hall, San Francisco, in May and June 1989.)

5. *Schaum's Outline of Theory and Problems of College Mathematics* (See Fig. 3-12, reproduction of cover, title page, and verso of the book. Other physical details: the book has 8 preliminary pages numbered with

Roman numerals and 459 pages of text and measures 28 centimeters in height. This edition is a revision of the first edition by the same author. The book is illustrated and includes an index. The title on the spine reads *College Mathematics.*)

6. Prepare bibliographic descriptions for books, serials, and nonprint materials of your choice, with items in hand.

THE POET'S POET

AND

Other Essays

WILLIAM A. QUAYLE

SECOND EDITION

CINCINNATI: CURTS & JENNINGS
NEW YORK: EATON & MAINS
1897.

FIGURE 3-8   Exercise B,1. On verso: Copyright, 1897, by Curts & Jennings.

The Contradictions
of Leadership

A Selection of Speeches by

James F. Oates, Jr.

Introduction by Blake T. Newton, Jr.

With an interpretative essay

by Robert K. Merton

Edited by Burton C. Billings

Appleton-Century-Crofts
Educational Division
Meredith Corporation
NEW YORK

Library of Congress Catalog Card Number: 76-119723

Printed in the United States of America

390-67490-7

FIGURE 3-9   Exercise B, 2.

THE SHORT PROSE READER

SIXTH EDITION

Gilbert H. Muller
The City University of New York
LaGuardia

Harvey S. Wiener
The City University of New York

McGRAW-HILL, INC.

New York St. Louis San Francisco Auckland Bogotá Caracas
Hamburg Lisbon London Madrid Mexico Milan Montreal New Delhi
Paris San Juan São Paulo Singapore Sydney Tokyo Toronto

This book was set in Goudy Old Style by the
College Composition Unit in cooperation with
General Graphics Services, Inc.
The editors were Lesley Denton and David Dunham;
the production supervisor was Friederich W. Schulte.
The cover was designed by Amy Becker.
R. R. Donnelley & Sons Company was printer and binder.
Cover painting: Young Girl Reading by Fragonard, courtesy of
Art Resource.

Acknowledgments appear on pages 494–498,
and on this page by reference.

THE SHORT PROSE READER

Copyright © 1991, 1989, 1987, 1985, 1982, 1979 by McGraw-Hill, Inc. All rights reserved. Printed in the United States of America. Except as permitted under the United States Copyright Act of 1976, no part of this publication may be reproduced or distributed in any form or by any means, or stored in a data base or retrieval system, without the prior written permission of the publisher.

2 3 4 5 6 7 8 9 0 DOC DOC 9 5 4 3 2 1

ISBN 0-07-044135-9

FIGURE 3-10 Exercise B, 3.

FIGURE 3-11   Exercise B, 4.

OUTLINE SERIES

THEORY AND PROBLEMS OF

COLLEGE MATHEMATICS
2/ed

ALGEBRA

DISCRETE MATHEMATICS

GEOMETRY • TRIGONOMETRY

INTRODUCTION TO CALCULUS

Frank Ayres, Jr.
Phillip A. Schmidt

Covers all course fundamentals and supplements any class text

■ Teaches effective problem-solving techniques

■ 1,583 Solved Problems with complete solutions

■ Also includes 1,470 additional problems with answers

SCHAUM'S OUTLINE OF

THEORY AND PROBLEMS

OF

COLLEGE MATHEMATICS
Second Edition

Algebra

Discrete Mathematics

Trigonometry

Geometry

Introduction to Calculus

FRANK AYRES, Jr., Ph.D.
Formerly Professor and Head
Department of Mathematics
Dickinson College

PHILIP A. SCHMIDT, Ph.D.
Dean of the School of Education
S.U.N.Y., The College at New Paltz

SCHAUM'S OUTLINE SERIES

McGRAW-HILL, INC.

New York St. Louis San Francisco Auckland Bogotá Caracas
Lisbon London Madrid Mexico Milan Montreal New Delhi
Paris San Juan Singapore Sydney Tokyo Toronto

FRANK AYRES, Jr., Ph.D., was formerly Professor and Head of the Department of Mathematics at Dickinson College, Carlisle, Pennsylvania. He is the author or coauthor of eight Schaum's Outlines, including *Calculus, Trigonometry, Differential Equations,* and *Modern Abstract Algebra.*

PHILIP A. SCHMIDT, Ph.D., has a B.S. from Brooklyn College (with a major in mathematics), an M.A. in mathematics, and a Ph.D. in mathematics education from Syracuse University. He is currently Dean of the School of Education at SUNY College at New Paltz. He is the author of *3000 Solved Problems in Precalculus* and *2500 Solved Problems in College Algebra and Trigonometry* as well as numerous journal articles. He has also completed a revision of the late Barnett Rich's *Geometry.*

2 3 4 5 6 7 8 9 10 11 12 13 14 15 16 17 18 19 20 SHP SHP 9 2

ISBN 0-07-002664-5

Sponsoring Editor: John Aliano
Production Supervisor: Leroy Young
Editing Supervisors: Meg Tobin, Maureen Walker
Cover design by Amy E. Becker.

FIGURE 3-12 Exercise B, 5.

CHAPTER FOUR
CHOICE OF ACCESS POINTS

Each bibliographic record is given one or more access points through which the record can be retrieved. An *access point* is defined as a name, term, or code under which a bibliographic description is entered or filed in a catalog. In a manual catalog and in the public display of many online catalogs, an access point is presented in the form of a heading added to the description in a cataloging record. In manual catalogs, each heading applied to a record results in a separate catalog entry. In online catalogs, each access point constitutes a key with which a cataloging record may be identified and retrieved. It also serves as a filing key in the display of records.

The basis for the access point may be the subject content of the work. In this case, it is called a *subject entry,* and the heading used is called a *subject heading* (to be discussed in Part Three). Or the basis for the access point may be a bibliographic identifier, such as the author or the title of the work. This kind of access point is determined by descriptive cataloging rules. The four types of bibliographic access points found in a catalog are

1. Names of persons who perform certain functions
   a. Authors
   b. Editors and compilers
   c. Translators
   d. Illustrators
   e. Other related persons (e.g., the addressee of a collection of letters; a person honored by a Festschrift)
2. Names of corporate bodies related to the item being described in a function other than solely as distributor or manufacturer
3. Titles
4. Names of series

Sometimes the access point or heading is in the form of a name-title combination, for example:

Johnson, Samuel, 1709-1784. Dictionary of the English language.

CONCEPTS

Main Entry

Among the access points assigned to a catalog record, one is designated as the *main entry* heading. The other access points are called *added entry* headings. In the traditional (e.g., card) catalog, the record that bears the main entry represents a complete catalog record of the item and is called the *main entry card* or *unit card*.

In recent years, the concept of main entry has been challenged. It is questioned whether, in a multiple-entry file, particularly in an online catalog or database, the main entry has any real significance.[1] Some feel that since the user can retrieve the catalog record through any of the entries (or access points), they should have equal value.

Nonetheless, in AACR2R, the concept of main entry is still maintained as being valid at least under the following circumstances:[2]

1. In making a single entry listing
2. In making a single citation for a work (as required for entries for related works and for some subject entries)
3. In assigning uniform titles and in promoting the standardization of bibliographic citation

Chapter 21 of AACR2R is devoted to the choice of access points and the designation of the main entry.

Authorship

The rules for entry in AACR2R are largely based on the Paris Principles. The key statement regarding choice of main entry in this document is that the functions of the catalog "are most effectively discharged by an entry for each book under a heading derived from the author's name or from the title."[3] The author's name is therefore the primary choice as main entry. The author as main entry represents a long cataloging tradition. A brief examination of the concept of authorship may be helpful in understanding this tradition.

[1]For an examination of this issue, see M. Nabil Hamdy. *The Concept of Main Entry as Represented in the Anglo-American Cataloging Rules: A Critical Appraisal with Some Suggestions: Author Main Entry vs. Title Main Entry.* Littleton, Colo.: Libraries Unlimited, 1973.
[2]*Anglo-American Cataloguing Rules.* 2nd ed., 1988 revision. Chicago: American Library Association, 1988. P. 2.
[3]International Conference on Cataloguing Principles, Paris, 1961. *Report of International Conference on Cataloguing Principles.* A. H. Chaplin and Dorothy Anderson, eds. London: Organizing Committee of ICCP, 1963. P. 92.

Definition of *author*

Because the rules for the choice of entry are centered on the concept of authorship, it would seem that a clear, unambiguous definition of it would be needed for the effective application of the rules. Ironically, such a definition is difficult to achieve. The difficulty is attested by various attempts at defining the term *author* throughout the evolution of cataloging codes.[4]

Cutter

> Author, in the narrower sense, is the person who writes a book; in a wider sense it may be applied to him who is the cause of the book's existence by putting together the writings of several authors (usually called *the editor,* more properly to be called *the collector*). Bodies of men (societies, cities, legislative bodies, countries) are to be considered the authors of their memoirs, transactions, journals, debates, reports, etc. [p. 14].

AA 1908

> 1. The writer of a book, as distinguished from translator, editor, etc. 2. In a broader sense, the maker of the book or the person or body immediately responsible for its existence. Thus, a person who collects and puts together the writings of several authors (compiler or editor) may be said to be the author of a collection. Corporate bodies may be considered the authors of publications issued in their name or by their authority [p. xiii].

ALA Draft 1941

Same as ALA 1908 except that "corporate bodies" is replaced by "a corporate body."

ALA 1949

> 1. The writer of a work, as distinguished from the translator, editor, etc. By extension, an artist, composer, photographer, cartographer, etc. 2. In the broader sense, the maker of the work or the person or body immediately responsible for its existence. Thus, a person who collects and puts together the writings of several authors (compiler or editor) may be said to be the author of a collection. A corporate body may be considered the author of publications issued in its name or by its authority [p. 230].

[4]Paul S. Dunkin. *Cataloging USA.* Chicago: American Library Association, 1969. Pp. 24–26. See also Julia Pettee. "The Development of Authorship Entry and the Formulation of Authorship Rules as Found in the Anglo-American Code." *Library Quarterly,* **6**:270–290, July 1936. Also in *Foundations of Cataloging: A Sourcebook.* Michael Carpenter and Elaine Svenonius, eds. Littleton, Colo.: Libraries Unlimited, 1985. Pp. 75–89.

AACR (1967)

The person or corporate body chiefly responsible for the creation of the intellectual or artistic content of a work, e.g., the writer of a book, the compiler of a bibliography, the composer of a musical work, the artist who paints a picture, the photographer who takes a photograph [p. 343].

AACR2 (1978)

A personal author is the person chiefly responsible for the creation of the intellectual or artistic content of a work [p. 284].

AACR2R (1988)

Same as in AACR2 (1978), (p. 312).

Personal authorship

The concept of authorship in cataloging is rooted in the tradition of scholarly practice in the western world. Although traditionally the title has been the main element of bibliographic identification in the orient, particularly in ancient times, the western tradition, probably derived from the classical Greco-Roman tradition, has emphasized the author as the chief element of identification of works.[5] Classical works have generally been identified by their authors—Homer, Plato, Herodotus, etc. On the other hand, the concept of authorship was not stressed in the Germanic tradition. Many of the Germanic sagas, Anglo-Saxon poems, and early epics and tales, for example, are anonymous, constituting the bulk of what is known as *anonymous classics.*

The concept of authorship remained somewhat vague and diffuse in the Middle Ages. However, since the Renaissance, the practice of identifying works by their authors, representing perhaps a revival of the Greco-Roman tradition, has prevailed in western scholarship. This concept of authorship was no doubt strengthened by the invention of printing, which led to the author's rights in literary property. Even in the orient, most modern works are now identified by their authors, perhaps as a result of the influence of western practice.

The practice of assigning main entry under the author in library catalogs can be thought of as conformity to the scholarly tradition.

Corporate authorship and responsibility

Until the middle of the nineteenth century, the concept of authorship was confined mainly to personal authors. Corporate authorship (i.e., attributing authorship of a work to a corporate body) as an element of

[5]Dunkin. Pp. 23–24.

bibliographic identification is a relatively recent concept. Early bibliographies and catalogs did not provide for entries under corporate bodies, nor did Germanic cataloging practice before the Paris Principles. In the Anglo-American cataloging tradition, the recognition of corporate authorship began in the nineteenth century. The rules for the British Museum Catalogue became the first major cataloging code to prescribe corporate author entries.[6]

As an entry element, corporate "authors" have always presented problems. Lubetzky's attack[7] on the "corporate complex" resulted in a thorough examination of the problem before the Paris Conference. Although the Paris Principles include specific guidelines relating to corporate authorship and corporate main entry, criticisms and discussions following the publication of AACR (1967) and other cataloging codes based on the Paris Principles have demonstrated that the rules for works of corporate authorship were open to diverse interpretations and were therefore unsatisfactory. This state of confusion prompted Eva Verona's study on corporate headings in the catalogs, national bibliographies, and cataloging codes of many countries. Her study reveals the chaotic state of corporate authorship: "Among the great number of cataloguing codes recognizing corporate authorship, it is scarcely possible to find even two which interpret the concept in the same way."[8] One major problem was the lack of even a general agreement among different codes as to the definition of corporate authorship. Efforts were made toward international consensus on the definition and treatment of corporate authorship.

Beginning with AACR (1967), a shift in the concept of corporate authorship took place. There was a redefinition of the role of corporate bodies mandating the term *corporate authorship* no longer be used. Instead, the rules in question are phrased in terms of works "emanating from one or more corporate bodies," i.e., works issued by, caused to be issued by, or originating with, one or more corporate bodies.[9] Although the rules still provide for entering certain works under a corporate body, the number of instances in which corporate bodies are assigned as main entries has been greatly reduced. This shift in the concept of corporate authorship brought the Anglo-American cataloging rules closer than

[6]Ake I. Koel. "Can the Problems of Corporate Authorship Be Solved?" *Library Resources & Technical Services*, **18**:349, Fall 1974.

[7]Seymour Lubetzky. *Cataloging Rules and Principles: A Critique of the A.L.A. Rules for Entry and a Proposed Design for Their Revision.* Washington: Library of Congress, 1953. Pp. 16–35.

[8]Eva Verona. *Corporate Headings: Their Use in Library Catalogues and National Bibliographies: A Comparative and Critical Study.* London: IFLA Committee on Cataloguing, 1975. Pp. 8–9.

[9]AACR2R (1988). P. 313.

their predecessors to the Paris Principles, which also avoid use of the term *corporate authorship* and replace it with the concept of "corporate responsibility."

CHOICE OF MAIN ENTRY

For works written by one person, the choice of main entry presents little problem. However, when more than one person is responsible for the existence of the work, particularly if these persons perform different functions, the choice becomes complicated. Throughout the evolution of the definition of the term *author*, an attempt has been made to exclude certain contributors to the existence of the work, such as translators, textual editors, illustrators, and publishers. On the other hand, corporate bodies are included, and until 1975, compilers and editorial directors of works also were given the status of author. In 1975, rules 4 and 5 in AACR (1967) which contained such provisions were revised to exclude compilers and editorial directors in the choice of main entry. This principle is continued in AACR2 (1978) and AACR2R (1988).

Types of Main Entry

The main entry of a work is always a personal name entry, a corporate name entry, or a title entry. Most book-form materials have main entry under personal authors, while many government publications are entered under corporate bodies. Serial publications and nonbook materials usually have title main entries.

Conditions of Authorship

The choice of main entry is based on the condition of authorship of each work. The rules for the choice of entry in AACR2R are organized according to these conditions of authorship:

> Works for which a single person or corporate body is responsible
> Works of unknown or uncertain authorship or by unnamed groups
> Works of shared responsibility (works resulting from collaboration
>   between two or more persons or corporate bodies performing the
>   same kind of activity in the creation of the content of an item)
> Collections and works produced under editorial direction
> Works of mixed responsibility (i.e., previously existing works that
>   have been modified, or collaborations between two or more per-
>   sons or corporate bodies performing different kinds of activities,
>   e.g., adapting or illustrating a work written by another person)

Rules for Choice of Entry

Following is a summary of the rules for the choice of entry grouped by types of main entry. In the MARC format, the 1*XX* fields are designated for main entry under personal authors, corporate bodies, and uniform titles. When the main entry is under the title proper, the indicator 0 in the first position in the 245 field is assigned.

Entry under personal author [MARC field 100]

1. Single personal authorship
For works of single personal authorship, entry is under the author (rule 21.4A).

> Islands in the stream / Ernest Hemingway *(main entry under the heading for Hemingway)*

> A Benjamin Britten discography / compiled by Charles H. Parsons *(main entry under the heading for Parsons)*

> The complete silky terrier / Peggy Smith *(main entry under the heading for Smith)*

> Job evaluation [transparency] / Herbert H. Oestreich *(main entry under the heading for Oestreich)*

> Carmen [sound recording] / George Bizet *(main entry under the heading for Bizet)*

2. Shared responsibility
For works of shared responsibility, i.e., works produced by the collaboration of two or more persons who performed the same kind of activity such as writing, adapting, or performing, entry is under (1) principal author if indicated (rule 21.6B):

> William S. Burroughs : a reference guide / Michael B. Goodman with Lemuel B. Coley *(main entry under heading for Goodman; added entry under the heading for Coley)*

> Beyond ambition : how driven managers can lead better and live better / Robert E. Kaplan with Wilfred H. Drath and Joan R. Kofodimos *(main entry under heading for Kaplan; added entries under the headings for Drath and Kofodimos)*

> Single market Europe : opportunities and challenges for business / Spyros G. Makridakis and associates *(main entry under the heading for Makridakis)*

or (2) author named first if responsibility is shared between two or three persons and no principal author is indicated (rule 21.6C):

The making of an economist / Arjo Klamer and David Colander *(main entry under the heading for Klamer; added entry under the heading for Colander)*

The intelligent design of computer-assisted instruction / Richard Venezky, Luis Osin *(main entry under the heading for Venezky; added entry under the heading for Osin)*

Taliesin West [slide] / Julius Shulman & Jeffrey Cook *(main entry under the heading for Shulman; added entry under the heading for Cook)*

Officially supported export credits : developments and prospects / G.G. Johnson, Matthew Fisher, and Elliot Harris *(main entry under the heading for Johnson; added entries under the headings for Fisher and Harris)*

3. Mixed responsibility
For works of mixed responsibility, i.e., previously existing works that have been modified (e.g., adaptations, revisions, translations) and new works in which different persons or bodies performing different kinds of activity (e.g., collaborative work by a writer and an artist, reports of interviews), entry is under

1. Adapter for a paraphrase, rewriting, adaptation for children, or version in a different literary form (e.g., novelization, dramatization) (rule 21.10):

Gone with the wind, the screenplay / Sidney Howard ; based on the novel by Margaret Mitchell *(main entry under the heading for Howard; added entry (name-title) under the heading for Mitchell)*

2. Writer of the text for a work that consists of a text for which an artist has provided illustrations (rule 21.11A):

Bungalow fungalo / by Pegi Deitz Shea ; illustrated by Elizabeth Sayles *(main entry under the heading for Shea; added entry under the heading for Sayles)*

3. Artist for separately published illustrations (rule 21.11B):

Blake's Grave : a prophetic book, being William Blake's illustrations for Robert Blair's The grave *(main entry under the heading for Blake; added entry (name-title) under the heading for Blair)*

4. Original author of an edition that has been revised, enlarged, updated, etc. by another person if the original author is still considered to be responsible for the work (rule 21.12A):

> Commonsense cataloging / Esther J. Piercy. — 2nd ed. / revised by Marian Sanner *(main entry under the heading for Piercy; added entry under the heading for Sanner)*

> Dewey decimal classification, 20th edition : a study manual / Jeanne Osborn ; revised and edited by John Phillip Comaromi *(main entry under the heading for Osborn; added entry under the heading for Comaromi, and name-title added entry under the uniform title for Dewey decimal classification and relative index)*

5. Reviser of an edition if the original author is no longer considered to be responsible for the work (rule 21.12B):

> Commonsense cataloging : a cataloger's manual / Rosalind E. Miller & Jane C. Terwillegar. — 4th ed. rev. *(main entry under the heading for Miller; added entry under the heading for Terwillegar)*

6. Commentator of a work consisting of a text and a commentary by a different person, if the latter is emphasized (rule 21.13B):

> Pylon / annotated by Susie Paul Johnson *(Contains also the text of Faulkner's Pylon) (main entry under the heading for Johnson; added entry (name-title) under the uniform title heading for Pylon)*

> The Theaetetus of Plato / Myles Burnyeat ; with a translation of Plato's Theaetetus by M.J. Levett, revised by Myles Burnyeat *(main entry under the heading for Burnyeat; added entry (name-title) under the uniform title heading for Theaetetus)*

7. Author of the text of a work consisting of a text and a commentary by a different person, if the text is emphasized (rule 21.13C):

> Antony and Cleopatra / edited by Marvin Spevack ; associate editors, Michael Steppat and Marga Munkelt *(A new variorum edition of Shakespeare; includes the text and commentaries on the play) (main entry under the heading for Shakespeare; added entry under the heading for Sevack)*

> The essential Wyndham Lewis : an introduction to his work / edited by Julian Symons *(main entry under the heading for Lewis; added entry under the heading for Symons)*

8. Original author of a translation (rule 21.14A):

> . The distant friend / Claude Roy ; translated by Hugh Harter *(main entry under the heading for Roy)*

9. Biographer-critic of a work by a writer accompanied by, or inter-woven with, biographical or critical material, if the latter is emphasized (rule 21.15A):

The life and letters of Frances Baroness Bunsen [microform] / by Augustus J.C. Hare *(main entry under the heading for Hare; added entry under the heading for Bunsen)*

10. Writer of a work accompanied by, or interwoven with, bio-graphical or critical material by another person who is presented as editor, compiler, etc. (rule 21.15B):

The life and letters of Frederic Shields / edited by Ernestine Mills *(main entry under the heading for Shields; added entry under the heading for Mills)*

Entry under corporate body [MARC fields 110 and 111]

Main entry under a corporate body[10] is restricted to those works which emanate from (i.e., are issued by or have been caused to be issued by or have originated with) a corporate body *and* fall into one or more of the following categories (rule 21.1B2):

1. Works of an administrative nature dealing with the corporate body itself or its internal policies, procedures, and/or operations; its finances; its officers and/or staff; or its resources (e.g., catalogues, inven-tories, membership directories):

A catalogue of the fifteenth-century printed books in the Harvard University Library / by James E. Walsh *(main entry under the heading for the library; added entry under the heading for Walsh)*

Annual report of the Director / University of Michigan, University Library *(main entry under the heading for the library)*

Directory of members & services / Turnaround Management Association *(main entry under the heading for the association)*

2. Some legal and governmental works of the following types: laws (rule 21.31), decrees of the chief executive that have the force of law (rule 21.31), administrative regulations (rule 21.32), constitutions (rule 21.33), court rules (rule 21.34), treaties, etc. (rule 21.35), court decisions (rule 21.36), legislative hearings, religious laws (e.g., canon law), liturgical works (rule 21.39):

---

[10]A *corporate body* is defined as "an organization or group of persons that is identified by a particular name and that acts, or may act, as an entity." AACR2R (1988). P. 617.

Regulations relating to the administration of the [Minnesota] Office of Liquor Control Commission *(main entry under the heading for the office)*

The constitution of the State of Hawaii *(main entry under the heading for Hawaii with uniform title for the constitution)*

3. Works that record the collective thought of the body (e.g., reports of commissions, committees, etc.; official statements of position on external policies):

Research strategies for the U.S. global change research program / Committee on Global Change (U.S. National Committee for the IGBP) of the Commission on Geosciences, Environment, and Resources, National Research Council *(main entry under the heading for the Committee)*

High interest easy reading : for junior and senior high school students / William G. McBride, editor, and the Committee to Revise High Interest–Easy Reading of the National Council of Teachers of English *(main entry under the heading for the committee; added entry under the heading for McBride)*

4. Works that report the collective activity of a conference (proceedings, collective papers, etc.), of an expedition (results of exploration, investigation, etc.), or of an event (an exhibition, fair, festival, etc.) falling within the definition of a corporate body (see 21.1B1), provided that the conference, expedition, or event is prominently named in the item being cataloged:

Software engineering environments : proceedings / International Workshop on Environments, Chinon, France, September 18-20, 1989 ; F.W. Long, ed. *(main entry under the heading for the workshop; added entry under the heading for Long)*

Heat transfer in combustion systems : presented at the Winter Annual Meeting of the American Society of Mechanical Engineers, San Francisco, California, December 10-15, 1989 / sponsored by the Heat Transfer Division, ASME ; edited by N. Ashgriz ... [et al.] *(main entry under the heading for the Meeting; added entries under the heading for Ashriz and the heading for the Heat Transfer Division)*

The formative period in the Cajamarca Basin, Peru : excavations at Huacaloma and Layzon, 1982 / Kazuo Terada, Yoshio Onuki [Report 3 of the Japanese Scientific Expedition to Nuclear America] *(main entry under the heading for the Expedition; added entries under the headings for Terada and Onuki)*

5. Sound recordings, films, videorecordings, and written records of performances resulting from the collective activity of a performing group as a whole, where the responsibility of the group goes beyond that of mere performance, execution, etc. (for corporate bodies that function solely as performers on sound recordings, see rule 21.23):

> The best of the Doors [sound recording] *(main entry under the heading for the musical group The Doors)*

6. Cartographic materials emanating from a corporate body other than a body merely responsible for their publication or distribution:

> National Geographic atlas of the world (issued by the National Geographic Society) *(main entry under the heading for the Society)*

> The Gulf war zone : a series of Hammond pull-out maps *(main entry under the heading for Hammond Incorporated)*

Official communications from heads of state, heads of government, heads of international bodies, popes, patriarchs, bishops, etc. are entered under their corporate headings (rule 21.4D1):

> Humanae vitae *(Pope Paul VI's encyclical) (main entry under the corporate heading for Pope Paul VI)*

> Urbanaid / proposed by Mayor John V. Lindsay, City of New York *(main entry under the corporate heading for the mayor)*

Entry under title [MARC field 245 with 0 as first indicator and field 130]

By way of elimination, works that do not fall into the categories of works which require main entry under a person or a corporate body are entered under the title. In other words, a work is entered under the title when

1. The personal authorship is unknown, diffuse (i.e., authorship being shared among four or more persons without indication of principal responsibility), or cannot be determined and the work does not emanate from a corporate body:

> The Role of national saving in the world economy : recent trends and prospects / by Bijan B. Aghevli ... [et al.] *(main entry under title; added entry under the heading for Aghevli)*

> Tetrahedron, asymmetry *(main entry under title)*

> The song of Roland / translated with an introduction and notes by Glyn Burgess *(an anonymous classic) (main entry under the uniform title for the song; added entry under the heading for Burgess)*

Lewis and Clark stayed home [computer file] *(main entry under title)*

2. It is a collection or a work produced under editorial direction that has a collective title:

Reading in the middle school / Gerald G. Duffy, editor *(main entry under title; added entry under the heading for Duffy)*

The Performance of power : theatrical discourse and politics / edited by Sue-Ellen Case and Janelle Reinelt *(main entry under title; added entries under the headings for Case and Reinelt)*

Small fires : letters from the Soviet people to Ogonyok Magazine, 1987-1990 / selected and edited by Christopher Cerf and Marina Albee with Lev Gushchin ; consulting editor, Lynn Visson ; translator, Hans Fenstermacher ; with an introduction by Vitaly Korotich *(main entry under title; added entries under Ogonek and under the headings for Cerf, Albee, Gushchin, and Visson)*

3. It emanates from a corporate body but does not fall into any of the categories listed under rule 21.1B2 and is not of personal authorship:

Journal of the Chemical Society. Faraday transactions / Royal Society of Chemistry *(main entry under title; added entry under the heading for the society)*

Nicholas of Cusa ; in search of God and wisdom : papers from the American Cusanus Society / edited by Gerald Christianson and Thomas M. Izbicki *(main entry under title; added entries under the headings for the society, Christianson, and Izbicki)*

Subject authorities in the online environment : papers from a conference program held in San Francisco, June 29, 1987 / sponsored by Resources and Technical Services Division, American Library Association ... [et al.] ; edited by Karen Markey Drabenstott *(main entry under title; added entries under the headings for Drabenstott and the Division)*

Winslow Homer : a symposium / edited by Nicolai Cikovsky, Jr. *(main entry under title because the symposium is not named; added entry under the heading for Cikovsky)*

4. It is accepted as sacred scripture by a religious group:

The Old Testament *(main entry under the uniform title for the Bible)*

Upanishads du yoga *(main entry under the uniform title for Upanishads)*

Changes in Title Proper (Rule 21.2)

Monographs in one physical part

If the title proper of a monograph in one physical part changes between one edition and another, a separate entry is made for each edition.

Monographs in more than one physical part

If the title proper of a monograph in more than one physical part, e.g., a multivolume set, changes between parts, the title proper of the first part is given as the title of the whole monograph. If another title proper appearing on later parts predominates, the later title proper is used as the title proper for the whole monograph.

Serials

If the title proper of a serial changes between one volume or issue and another, a separate cataloging record for each title is made.

> Air repair. — Vol. 1, no. 1 (July 1951)-v. 4, no. 4 (Feb. 1955)
> *(Continued by: Journal of the Air Pollution Control Association)*

> Journal of the Air Pollution Control Association. — Vol. 5, no. 1 (May 1955)-v. 36, no. 12 (Dec. 1986) *(Continues: Air repair)* *(Continued by: JAPCA)*

> JACPA. — Vol. 37, no. 1 (Jan. 1987)-v. 39, no. 12 (Dec. 1989) *(Continues: Journal of the Air Pollution Control Association)* *(Continued by: Journal of the Air & Waste Management Association)*

> Journal of the Air & Waste Management Association. — Vol. 40, no. 1 (Jan. 1990)- *(Continues: JACPA)*

Changes of Persons or Bodies Responsible for a Work (Rule 21.3)

Monographs

In the case of a change in responsibility between the parts of a multipart monograph, main entry is made under the person or corporate body that has predominant responsibility. If none is predominant, main entry is made under the heading appropriate to the first part. In the latter case, if more than three persons or corporate bodies are responsible for the completed work, main entry is made under the title.

Serials

A new entry is created for a serial even if the title proper remains the same and the numbering continues if (1) the heading for a corporate body under which a serial is entered changes or (2) the main entry for a serial is under a personal or corporate heading and the person or corporate body is no longer responsible for the serial.

ADDED ENTRIES (RULES 21.29–21.30)

In addition to the main entry heading, added entries are assigned to bibliographic records in order to provide additional access points through names and titles that are bibliographically significant. Added entries are generally made for potential access points not chosen as the main entry. They appear in the form of personal name headings, corporate name headings, titles, series, and name-title headings. A name-title heading consists of the name heading of a person or corporate body and the title of an item, for example:

Faulkner, William, 1897-1962.   Pylon.

Added Entries under Personal Names [MARC Field 700]

These are made for the following:

1. Collaborators (up to three). If there are four or more collaborators, added entry is made for the first named.
2. Writers.
3. Editors and compilers (rarely made for a serial publication).
4. Translators (made in certain cases only).
5. Illustrators (made in certain cases only).
6. Other related persons. These are persons related to the work in a way other than being responsible for the creation of the content of the work (e.g., the addressee of a collection of letters, a person honored by a Festschrift).

Added Entries under Corporate Names [MARC Fields 710 and 711]

An added entry is made under a corporate body that is prominently named in the work unless it functions solely as distributor or manufacturer. If four or more corporate bodies are involved in a particular work, an added entry is made under the first named.

Added Entries under Titles [MARC Field 245 with 1 as First Indicator and Fields 730 and 740]

An added entry is made under the title proper if it has not been used as the main entry, unless the title added entry is so similar as to duplicate the main entry heading, a reference to the main entry heading, or a subject heading (in a catalog in which name-title and subject entries are interfiled). An added entry is also made for any other title (cover title, caption title, running title, etc.) which differs significantly from the title proper.

Added Entries under Series [MARC Fields 440 and 8XX]

An added entry is made under the heading for a series to which the item belongs except in the following cases:

1. If the items in the series are related to one another only by common physical characteristics
2. If the items in the series have been numbered primarily for stock control or to benefit from lower postage rates

Analytical Added Entries

This is an added entry made for a work contained within the work being cataloged. The heading for the added entry is determined by the way the work contained would be entered, except that a name-title heading is used in cases requiring entry under a person or a corporate body.

Tracing

In library catalogs in the card or book form, the added entries are recorded in a paragraph called a *tracing* which appears on the main entry record. In the tracing, each added entry is preceded by a roman numeral. Subject entries are preceded by arabic numerals.

In the MARC record, added entries are denoted by field tags 7XX and 8XX or by indicators in the 2XX fields.

EXERCISE A

Determine the main and added entries for the items in Exercise B, Chapter 3.

CHAPTER FIVE
NAME AUTHORITY CONTROL
AND FORMS OF HEADINGS
AND UNIFORM TITLES

NAME AUTHORITY CONTROL

It was noted in Chapter 1 that most libraries and bibliographic databases maintain a *name authority file* consisting of *name authority records* and that the process of creating those records and maintaining the name authority file is called *name authority control*. Name authority control has three main purposes: (1) to ensure that all works written by a particular author are retrievable with the same access point (or under the same heading), (2) to ensure that only works by that author are entered under a particular heading, and (3) to save the time and effort of having to establish the heading each time a work by the same author is cataloged.

A name authority record is made when an author's heading is established, i.e., authorized for use as a heading, for the first time. This record generally contains the following information:

1. The heading, established according to cataloging rules, to be used in catalog entries
2. The sources upon which decisions were made in establishing the heading
3. Tracings for cross-references to this heading

Until a change of the heading is necessitated by changes in the author's name or upon additional information, this established heading is used in cataloging records whenever the author's heading is required as a catalog entry, whether as a main entry, an added entry, or a subject entry.

Frequently, a person changes his or her name or uses a different form of name, and the rules require that the new name or form be used in catalog entries with *see* references from the old. In such a case, ideally, the name authority record is updated, and all previously prepared catalog entries under the person's heading are recataloged. This is an important part of catalog maintenance.

In the MARC formats, the codes used vary depending on the type of headings and on whether the heading appears in the authority record or is used as a main or added entry or a subject entry in the bibliographic record. In *bibliographic* records:

100   Main entry—Personal name
110   Main entry—Corporate name
111   Main entry—Meeting name
130   Main entry—Uniform title

600   Subject added entry—Personal name
610   Subject added entry—Corporate name
611   Subject added entry—Meeting name
630   Subject added entry—Uniform title

700   Added entry—Personal name
710   Added entry—Corporate name
711   Added entry—Meeting name
730   Added entry—Uniform title

800   Series added entry—Personal name
810   Series added entry—Corporate name
811   Series added entry—Meeting name
830   Series added entry—Uniform title

In *authority* records:

100   Heading—Personal name
110   Heading—Corporate name
111   Heading—Meeting name
130   Heading—Uniform title

400   *See from* tracing—Personal name
410   *See from* tracing—Corporate name
411   *See from* tracing—Meeting name
430   *See from* tracing—Uniform title

500   *See also from* tracing—Personal name
510   *See also from* tracing—Corporate name
511   *See also from* tracing—Meeting name
530   *See also from* tracing—Uniform title

Examples of name authority records are shown in Figure 1-5, Figure 5-1 and Appendix B.

In recent years, the Library of Congress and many large research libraries have converted their name authority files into machine-readable form. In this way, name authority control becomes more efficient and effective than when maintained manually. Furthermore, in many automated systems, the name authority file is linked to the bibliographic file so that new or revised headings automatically replace old headings in all bibliographic records and appropriate cross-references are generated or revised.

```
ARN:       340244          Rec stat:    c
Entered:   19840819        Replaced:    19870805
Type:      z      Enc lvl:    n      Source:        Lang:
Roman:     ∎      Upd status: a      Mod rec:       Name use: a
Govt agn:  ∎      Ref status: a      Subj:     a    Subj use: a
Series:    n      Auth status: a     Geo subd: n    Ser use:  b
Ser num:   n      Auth/ref:   a      Name:     a    Rules:    c ¶
  1  010          n  79108313  ¶
  2  040          DLC ‡c DLC ‡d DLC ¶
  3  100 10       Lindbergh, Anne Morrow, ‡d 1906-  ¶
  4  400 10       Morrow, Anne Spencer, ‡d 1906-  ¶
  5  400 10       Lindbergh, Charles Augustus, ‡c Mrs., ‡d 1906- ¶
  6  400 10       Lindbergh, Anne Spencer, ‡d 1906- ¶
  7  670          Her North to the Orient ... c1935. ¶
  8  670          NUCMC data from Library of Congress, Manuscript div. for
·osvenor family. Papers, 1827-1968 ‡b (Anne Morrow Lindbergh) ¶
  9  670          NUCMC file ‡b (Lindbergh, Anne Morrow, 1906-; b. Anne Spencer
)rrow; Mrs. Charles Augustus Lindbergh) ¶
 10  670          Sapieyevski, J. Love songs, c1979: ‡b t.p. (poems by Anne
)encer Lindbergh) ¶
```

```
ARN:       448636          Rec stat:    c
Entered:   19840819        Replaced:    19900209
Type:      z      Enc lvl:    n      Source:        Lang:
Roman:     ∎      Upd status: a      Mod rec:       Name use: a
Govt agn:  ∎      Ref status: a      Subj:     a    Subj use: a
Series:    n      Auth status: a     Geo subd: n    Ser use:  b
Ser num:   n      Auth/ref:   a      Name:     a    Rules:    c ¶
  1  010          n  80067088  ¶
  2  040          DLC ‡c DLC ‡d DLC ¶
  3  053          PR6007.A95 ¶
  4  100 20       Day Lewis, C. ‡q (Cecil), ‡d 1904-1972. ¶
  5  400 10       Lewis, Cecil Day-, ‡d 1904-1972 ¶
  6  400 10       Lewis, C. Day ‡q (Cecil Day), ‡d 1904-1972 ¶
  7  400 20       Day-Lewis, Cecil, ‡d 1904-1972. ‡w nnaa ¶
  8  400 20       Day Lewis, Cecil, ‡d 1904-1972 ¶
  9  500 10       Blake, Nicholas, ‡d 1904-1972 ¶
 10  670          Oxford poetry ... 1927. ¶
 11  670          His A question of proof, 1990: ‡b CIP t.p. (Nicholas Blake) ¶
 12  670          Dic. of Irish lit., 1969 ‡b (Day-Lewis, Cecil, 1904-1972;
eud.: Nicholas Blake) ¶
```

```
▶ ARN:     2683056         Rec stat:    c
  Entered:   19900209      Replaced:    19900308
  Type:    z      Enc lvl:    n      Source:        Lang:
  Roman:   ∎      Upd status: a      Mod rec:       Name use: a
  Govt agn: ∎     Ref status: a      Subj:     a    Subj use: a
  Series:  n      Auth status: a     Geo subd: n    Ser use:  b
  Ser num: n      Auth/ref:   a      Name:     a    Rules:    c ¶
▶  1  010         n  90609288  ¶
▶  2  040         DLC ‡c DLC ‡d DLC ¶
▶  3  053         PR6007.A95 ¶
▶  4  100 10      Blake, Nicholas, ‡d 1904-1972 ¶
▶  5  500 20      Day Lewis, C. ‡q (Cecil), ‡d 1904-1972 ¶
▶  6  670         His A question of proof, 1990: ‡b CIP t.p. (Nicholas Blake) ¶
▶  7  670         Dic. of Irish lit., 1979 ‡b (Day-Lewis, Cecil, 1904-1972;
pseud.: Nicholas Blake) ¶
```

FIGURE 5-1 Name authority records.

FORMS OF HEADINGS

After the main entry and added entries for a work have been determined, the next step is to decide in what form these entries are to be presented. Chapters 22 through 25 of AACR2R are devoted to the forms of headings to be used in catalog entries.

Principles of Uniform and Unique Headings

One of the functions of the catalog, as stated in the Paris Principles,[1] is to ascertain which works by a particular author are in the library. This is achieved by entering all works by a particular author under a *uniform heading*, regardless of how many names or how many forms of a name an author has used. This principle, when implemented in a catalog, improves recall (i.e., the ratio of retrieved relevant items to all relevant items from a catalog) because no matter how many different names or different forms of a name have appeared in an author's works, all can be retrieved through the authorized heading established for the author.

The principle of uniform heading is observed with few exceptions in the case of personal name headings. However, the principle is somewhat modified in the case of headings for corporate bodies, many of which undergo frequent name changes. How the names of corporate bodies are handled is discussed later in this chapter.

The corollary of the principle of uniform heading (i.e., one heading for each author) is that of *unique heading*. The principle of unique heading requires that each heading represent only one author. In other words, if two or more authors have the same name, normally the name for each is modified by attaching additional elements; the most common modification is the addition of birth and death dates. The reason for using unique headings is to improve precision (i.e., the ratio of retrieved relevant items to all retrieved items). In the case of a personal heading, when the unique heading is used as the access point, only works by the author represented by that heading will be retrieved, excluding works by other authors who happen to have the same name.

This principle also applies to title entries. When a work has appeared under various titles, one is chosen as the *uniform title*. Uniform titles are discussed later in this chapter.

HEADINGS FOR PERSONS

The determination of a personal name heading is normally based on information obtained from the chief sources of information in works by that person issued in his or her language. If the author has written other works, it is important to take into consideration the information they contain. If most of the author's works are not accessible, reference sources, particularly bibliographic and biographic sources, will have to

---

[1]International Conference on Cataloguing Principles, Paris, 1961. "Statement of Principles." In A. H. Chaplin and Dorothy Anderson, eds., *Report of International Conference on Cataloguing Principles*. London: Organizing Committee of the International Conference on Cataloguing Principles, 1963. P. 91.

be consulted. For persons who work in a nonverbal context (as do painters and performers) or who are not known primarily as authors, the headings are determined from reference sources issued in their languages. The headings for persons not primarily known as authors are often established to be used as subject entries for works about them. Such headings are discussed under biography in Chapters 8 and 9.

In determining the uniform heading for a person, there are three basic aspects: (1) choice of name, (2) choice of form, and (3) choice of entry element.

Choice of Name (Rule 22.2)

A large number of people have had more than one name in their lifetimes. In many cases, an author uses a name which is different from his or her real name or uses more than one name in his or her writings. In some cases, a person changes his or her name for one or another reason. If the catalog is to show what works by a particular author are in the library, all his or her works must be listed under the same name. Therefore, the first question that must be answered is, Which name should be used?

Before this question can be answered, another, more basic question must be examined. Is a person who writes necessarily only one author? If a person writes under two names for different purposes, could he or she not be considered two authors? A scientist who uses his or her real name in scientific works may choose to use a pseudonym in writing science fiction. It is not unreasonable to treat these works as by two different authors. In this case, this person's works may be listed under two different names in the catalog. The basic question is then, Can a person be more than one author? Over the years, the answer has sometimes been no and sometimes been yes, at least in practice, if not officially sanctioned by cataloging rules.

In analyzing this problem in 1969, Paul S. Dunkin pointed out two basic approaches. He called the first the *rigid approach*. The person's real name is chosen as the heading, regardless of what other names or how many names the person has used. He called the second the *relaxed approach*. In this case, the heading is the author's name as it appears in the work being cataloged. If an author has used several names, his or her works would then be listed under several headings. In other words, "A uniform heading is not a uniform heading for an individual person. ... Instead, it is the uniform heading for an author. But a person may be as many authors as he [or she or it] wishes."[2]

---

[2] Paul S. Dunkin. *Cataloging U.S.A.* Chicago: American Library Association, 1969. P. 29.

Before 1967, the ALA codes followed the first approach. As a result, works by Mark Twain were listed under the heading **Clemens, Samuel Langhorne** and those by Novalis appeared in the catalog under **Hardenberg, Friedrich, Freiherr von.**

AACR (1967), based on the Paris Principles, adhered to neither approach strictly. It may be viewed as a modified rigid approach. Each person was allowed only one personal name heading, regardless of how many names the person may have used in his or her works. However, this name heading did not have to be the person's real name. The criterion for the choice of name rested on the principle of the most commonly known name, as evidenced in his or her works. The Paris Principles state that "the *uniform heading* should be the name by which the author is most frequently identified in editions of his works, in the fullest form commonly appearing there."[3]

AACR2 (1978) followed the same principle of choosing the predominant name as the heading. However, in the case of an author having used different pseudonyms without any one of them being predominant (see rule 22.2C3–4), the rules allowed as an option the use of the name appearing in each item as the heading for that item. As a result, when there is no predominant name, a person may have had more than one heading. This reflected the more relaxed approach mentioned by Dunkin and represented a softening of the principle of uniform heading.

In other words, in previous cataloging codes, the term *author* was more or less equated with the term *person.* Each person was recognized as capable of being one author only. An author who deliberately established different identities in writing different kinds of works, such as fiction and scientific or political works, was represented by one uniform heading. AACR2 (1978) did, however, allow multiple headings for the same person in limited cases.

By 1988, as reflected in AACR2R, there was a major change: The AACR2R rules fully recognize that the same person may have "separate bibliographic identities" (rule 22.2B2) for different types of works. These separate bibliographic identities are then treated as different authors represented by different headings but connected with cross-references. For example, C. Day Lewis used the pseudonym Nicholas Blake in writing mysteries and detective stories while using his real name in his other works. Accordingly, under AACR2R, two headings are established for him. Works such as *A Tangled Web, The Beast Must Die,* and *A Question of Proof* are entered under the heading for **Nicholas Blake,** and works such as *Notable Images of Virtue: Emily Brontë, George Meredith, W.B. Yeats* and *The Poetic Image* are entered under the heading for **C. Day Lewis.**

---

[3]International Conference on Cataloguing Principles. Op. cit. P. 93.

Furthermore, under AACR2R, multiple headings are established for contemporary authors who do not have separate bibliographic identities but who use one or more pseudonyms or use their real names and one or more pseudonyms. Thus, for a contemporary author, name headings are established on the basis of names on title pages whether or not the author in question also has published under another name.

On the other hand, the principle of uniform headings is observed for all authors who are not contemporary and who have not established separate bibliographic identities. For each author, the uniform heading is based on the name that is most commonly known.

For an author (other than one using a pseudonym or pseudonyms) who has changed his or her name, the heading is based on the latest name, unless an earlier name is better known.

Choice of Form of Name (Rule 22.3)

After a name has been chosen, the next step is to determine which form of that name (if it appears in more than one form) is to be used in the heading. This decision is needed because, on the title pages of works by a given author and in references sources, the form of name may vary according to (1) fullness, (2) language, or (3) spelling.

1. Fullness

A person's name may vary in fullness, in terms of the number of elements involved or in terms of abbreviations or initials. Again, the basis for choice is the predominant or most commonly known form, e.g., **Friedrich Schiller** instead of Johann Christoph Friedrich von Schiller and **D. H. Lawrence** instead of David Herbert Lawrence.

2. Language

A person's name may appear in different languages, particularly in the case of famous authors and internationally known persons, e.g., **Domingo de Guzman** or **Saint Dominic, Quintus Horatius Flaccus** or **Horace**, and **Karl V, Carlos I,** or **Charles V**. There is no one simple, clear-cut criterion for choice. The decision varies according to language, to type of name (given names or names containing surnames), and to chronologic period. In general, there is a strong preference for well-established English forms and for Latin and Greek forms over vernacular forms.

3. Spelling

The same name may be spelled in more than one way, and a decision must be made regarding which spelling should be used in the heading. The basis for choice is official orthography or predominant spelling.

Choice of Entry Element

Most names contain more than one element, a simple example being given name and surname. Thus, for any name under consideration, after it has been determined which form to use, it must then be decided which element in the name is to be used as the entry word. The names of the majority of people living in modern times are entered under surname. Certain surnames, such as compound surnames and those with separately written prefixes, contain more than one word. In such cases, one of the words in the surname is chosen as the entry word. Some people, particularly royalty and people of earlier times, do not have surnames or do not use them. Headings for these people reflect the given name. Again, if the given name contains more than one word, the entry element must be determined.

The general principle for choice of entry element of a personal name is the person's preference (if known) or the way the name would normally be listed in authoritative alphabetical lists in his or her language or country.

1. Entry under surname (rule 22.5)

A name containing a surname is entered under that surname, e.g., **Shakespeare, William**. If the surname consists of several elements, one of them is chosen as the entry element, as follows.

Compound surnames
A surname consisting of two or more proper names is entered according to the preferred or established form (if known), e.g., **Day Lewis, C.** In other cases, entry is under the first element except for names of married women. The name of a married woman that consists of a maiden name and husband's surname is entered under the husband's surname (except names in Czech, French, Hungarian, Italian, or Spanish), e.g., **Lindbergh, Anne Morrow**.

Surnames with separately written prefixes
Many surnames include an article or preposition or combination of the two. These names are entered according to the usage of the person's language or country of residence. Because usage varies among different

languages and countries, separate rules are provided based on languages or language groups. For American and British names, the entry element is the prefix, e.g., **Van Den Hoven, Adrian.**

2. Entry under title of nobility (rule 22.6)

For persons who use their titles rather than their personal surnames in their works or are listed under their titles in reference sources, the entry element is the proper name in the title of nobility. The elements in the name are arranged in the following order:

> Proper name in the title, personal name in direct order, the term of rank in the vernacular
> **Shaftesbury, Anthony Ashley Cooper, Earl of**

3. Entry under given name, etc. (rule 22.8)

A name that consists of a given name or given names only is entered under the part of name as listed in reference sources, e.g., **Thomas,** *of Sutton;* **Leonardo,** *da Vinci.*

4. Entry of Roman names (rule 22.9)

The name of a Roman active before A.D. 476 is entered according to the practice in reference sources, e.g., **Cicero, Marcus Tullius.**

5. Entry under initials, letters, or numerals (rule 22.10)

A name consisting of initials, separate letters, or numerals or consisting primarily of initials is entered under the first initial, letter, or numeral, e.g., **H. D.; A. E.; 110908.**

6. Entry under phrase (rule 22.11)

A name consisting of a phrase or other appellation that does not include a forename, as well as a name consisting of a forename or forenames preceded by words other than a term of address or a title of position or phrase, is entered under the first element, e.g., **Dr. X; Poor Richard;** but **Seuss,** *Dr.*

Additions to Names

The following elements are added to the headings for persons.

1. Titles of nobility and terms of honour (rule 22.12)

The title of nobility or a British term of honour is added after the name if the title or term appears commonly in association with the name in the person's works or reference sources.

> **Bismarck, Otto,** *Fürst von*
> **Scott,** *Sir* **Walter**[4]

2. Saints (rule 22.13)

The word *Saint* is added after the name of a Christian saint (excluding popes, emperors, empresses, kings, or queens).

> **Francis,** *of Assisi, Saint*
> **Gregory I,** *Pope*
>   (instead of Gregory, Saint, Pope)

3. Spirits (rule 22.14)

The word *(Spirit)* is added to a heading established for a spirit communication.

> **Twain, Mark** *(Spirit)*

4. Additions to names entered under surname only (rule 22.15)

The addition is in the form of a word or phrase associated with the name in works by the person or in reference sources.

> **Seuss,** *Dr.*

5. Additions to names entered under given name, etc. (rule 22.16)

(a) *Royalty.* A phrase consisting of the title and the name of the state or people governed is added.

> **Louis XVI,** *King of France*
> **Akihito,** *Emperor of Japan*
> **Rainier III,** *Prince of Monaco*

(b) *Popes.* The word *Pope* is added.

> **John Paul II,** *Pope*

---

[4]Note that rule 22.12B requires placement of the term before the forename, but the Library of Congress practice places it after the forename, i.e., **Scott, Walter,** *Sir.*

(c) *Bishops, etc.* The title or a phrase consisting of the title and the name of the latest see (if applicable) is added.

> **Anselm**, *Saint, Archbishop of Canterbury*
> **Giles**, *of Rome, Archbishop of Bourges*

Distinguishing Persons with the Same Name

As discussed earlier, the principle of unique headings requires that a particular heading should represent one person or author only. When two or more persons have the same name, additional elements normally are added to distinguish between them. The most common elements used for this purpose are the person's dates and/or fuller forms of the name. Optionally, these elements may be added to all personal names even when there is no need to distinguish between otherwise identical headings.

1. Dates (rule 22.17)

> **Shakespeare, William**, 1564-1616
> **Eliot, T. S. (Thomas Stearns)**, 1888-1965
> **Mumford, Lewis**, 1895-
> **Pann, Anton**, *ca.* 1797-1854

2. Fuller forms of the name (rule 22.18)

If a fuller form of a person's name is known, and if the heading as prescribed does not include all of that fuller form, the fuller form of the name is added in parentheses. The fuller form may consist of spelled out forenames for initials included in the heading or forenames, surnames, or initials which are not part of the heading.

> **Comaromi, John P. (John Phillip)**
> **Eliot, T. S. (Thomas Stearns)**
> **Johnson, Cathy (Cathy A.)**
> **Smith, G. E. Kidder (George Everard Kidder)**

If the dates and fuller forms of the name are not available to distinguish between two or more identical headings, another element is used for this purpose. This element may be a suitable brief term, a term of address, a title of position or office, initials of an academic degree, initials denoting membership in an organization, etc. (see rule 22.19B), e.g.,

> **Blair, William**, *Inspector of schools*

For headings in the form of given names only, see rule 22.19A. In rare cases when no suitable addition can be made, the heading in question is used without qualification.

GEOGRAPHIC NAMES IN HEADINGS

Geographic names are used in headings for various purposes: to distinguish between corporate bodies with the same name, as additions to other corporate names, and as headings for governments and nongovernmental communities. Chapter 23 of AACR2R is devoted to the forms in which geographic names are to be presented in headings. Its major provisions are summarized below.

Language (Rule 23.2)

The basic principle is to use the English form of the name of a place if there is one in general use. Otherwise, the vernacular form is used.

> *English form*
> **Germany**
> (*not* Deutschland)
> **Naples**
> (*not* Napoli)
> **Munich**
> (*not* München)
>
> *Vernacular form*
> **São Paulo**
> **Puerto Rico**
> **Rio de Janeiro**

Changes of Name

If the name of a place changes, both the former name and the current name may be used as appropriate (see rules 24.3E and 24.4C6).

Additions to Place Names (Rule 23.4)

The name of a larger place (abbreviated according to Appendix B in AACR2R) is added to the name of a place located within the larger place. Unless the place is located within one of the exceptional countries discussed below, this geographic qualifier normally consists of the name of the country.

Naples *(Italy)*
Rio de Janeiro *(Brazil)*
Paris *(France)*

If the name of the country fails to distinguish between two places with the same name, the name of a smaller geographic entity is also added.

Friedberg *(Bavaria, Germany)*
Friedberg *(Hesse, Germany)*

In the case of a number of countries, the name of a jurisdiction immediately below the country level is used as the geographic qualifier. These exceptional countries include Australia, Canada, Great Britain, and the United States.

A place in a state, province, or territory in **Australia, Canada,** or the **United States**	Add the name of the state, province, or territory
A place in the **British Isles**	Add *England, Ireland, Northern Ireland, Scotland, Wales, Isle of Man,* or *Channel Islands*

Examples
Lexington *(Mass.)*
London *(England)*
Tyrone *(Northern Ireland)*

Geographic qualifiers are not added to the states, provinces, territories, etc. within the exceptional countries.

England
Massachusetts
Northern Ireland
Ontario

HEADINGS FOR CORPORATE BODIES

Definition

A *corporate body* is defined as "an organization or group of persons that is identified by a particular name and that acts, or may act, as an entity."[5] By this definition, corporate bodies include associations, institutions, business firms, radio and television stations, nonprofit enterprises, governments, government agencies, religious bodies, local churches, confer-

[5]AACR2R (1988). P. 617.

ences, expeditions, projects and programs, exhibitions, fairs, festivals, etc.

The three aspects involved in the determination of a personal name heading—choice of name, choice of form, and choice of entry element—also pertain to corporate headings. These are discussed below.

Choice of Name (Rule 24.1)

Corporate bodies frequently undergo name changes. When a corporate body has been identified by more than one name, a decision must be made on which one will be represented in the heading. In dealing with corporate bodies that have undergone changes of name, the principle of uniform heading is suspended. While a personal author who has changed his or her name is normally represented by one heading only, a corporate body with a changed name is treated as a separate entity and represented by a different heading. In other words, each time a corporate body undergoes a name change, a new heading is established to be used in cataloging works issued by the body under that name. As a result, the former names as well as the current one may all be used as headings in the same catalog. This principle is called *successive entry*. The publications issued by the corporate body are entered under the name used at the time of publication, with *see also* or explanatory references connecting the successive entries.

> **Society for Horticultural Science (U.S.)**
>   see also the later heading:
> **American Society for Horticultural Science**
>
> **American Society for Horticultural Science**
>   see also the earlier heading:
> **Society for Horticultural Science (U.S.)**

Choice of Form

As in the case of personal names, a corporate name may exist in different forms. Here the principle of uniform heading generally applies, in that one of the variant forms is chosen to be used in the heading, with references from the other forms.

Fullness of name (rules 24.2–24.3)

If the name has appeared in various degrees of fullness, the criteria for choice (in the order of preference) are the form found in the chief sources of information, the predominant form, and a distinctive brief form (including an initialism or an acronym).

American Library Association
Henry E. Huntington Library and Art Gallery
Unesco

Also, a conventional form of name in common use is preferred to the fuller, official name.

> **Westminster Abbey**
> (*not* Collegiate Church of St. Peter in Westminster)

Spelling (rule 24.2C)

If the form of the name varies in spelling, the following criteria (in the order of preference) are used: the form resulting from an official change in orthography, the predominant spelling, and the spelling found in the first item cataloged.

Language (rule 24.3)

While the basic principle is to choose the form in the official language of the body in question, the rules reflect a strong preference for the English form. This is particularly evident in the cases of ancient and international bodies, religious orders and societies, and governments.

> **United Nations**
> **International Federation of Municipal Engineers**

Modifications (Rules 24.4–24.11)

In certain cases, modifications are made to the form chosen.

Additions

The following elements are sometimes added to the corporate name:

1. A general (or generic) designation is added if the name alone does not convey the idea of a corporate body, e.g., **Queen Elizabeth** *(Ship)* or **Spyro Gyra** *(Musical group)*, or if the following additions fail to distinguish between two or more bodies having the same name.
2. The name of the place in which the corporate body is located is added in order to distinguish two or more bodies having the same name, e.g., **National Research Council** *(U.S.)*, **Trinity College** *(Hartford, Conn.)*, or **Trinity College** *(Burlington, Vt.)*.
3. The name of an institution (with which the corporate body is commonly associated) instead of the local place name is

added to distinguish two or more bodies having the same name, e.g., **National Crime Prevention Institute** *(University of Louisville).*

4. The year of founding or the inclusive years of existence are added if the local place names fail to distinguish two or more bodies with the same name.

Omissions

Elements generally omitted from the heading are (1) initial articles, (2) citations of honors, and (3) terms indicating incorporation.

Other modifications

Names of certain types of corporate bodies require specific modifications (rules 24.6–24.11): governments; conferences; exhibitions, fairs, festivals, etc.; chapters, branches, etc.; local churches; and radio and television stations.

Choice of Entry Element

When a corporate body is entered under its own name, the entry element is generally the initial word in the name with a few exceptions such as initial articles, ordinal numbers, and terms denoting royal privileges. Previous cataloging codes often required the use of the name of the place in which the corporate body was located as the entry element, e.g.,

Pennsylvania. University.

This practice was discontinued in the Anglo-American Cataloguing Rules. Most names are now entered directly, e.g.,

University of Pennsylvania.

The principle of entering a corporate body directly under its name applies to most corporate bodies except certain subordinate or related bodies and government bodies and officials.

Subordinate and related bodies (rules 24.12–24.13)

In the case of a subordinate or affiliated body, selecting the entry element poses a more complex problem. A subordinate body may be entered under its own name or as a subheading under the name of a higher body, depending on various factors.

In general, a subordinate body or a related body is entered directly under its own name, with the exception of six types of subordinate and related bodies (see rule 24.13). These are subordinate bodies that are normally identified in close association with the names of their higher bodies or parent bodies, that have indistinctive names, or whose names contain a word implying subordination (e.g., *division, department, committee, commission,* etc.).

> **University of Illinois.** *Library*
> **Electrochemical Society.** *Electronics Division*
> **American Society of Mechanical Engineers.** *Vibrations and*
> *Sound Committee*

Direct or indirect subheading (rule 24.14)

Often a corporate body is subordinate to another body which is subordinate to yet another, higher body. In some cases, there may be several levels in the hierarchy. The general rule is to enter a subordinate body, after it has been decided that it should be treated as a subheading, under the lowest element in the hierarchy that is entered under its own name. In other words, all elements between the subheading and the higher element entered under its own name are omitted, unless the omission results, or is likely to result, in a conflict, i.e., two or more bodies with the same heading. Then the name of the lowest element in the hierarchy that will distinguish between the bodies is interposed. A heading is *direct* when an intervening element has been omitted. An *indirect* heading includes intervening elements. For example,

> *Direct subheading*
> **American Library Association.** *Reference Tools Advisory*
> *Committee.*
> *Hierarchy:* American Library Association
>   Reference and Adult Services Division
>   Reference Tools Advisory Committee

> *Indirect subheading*
> **American Library Association.** *Reference and Adult Services*
> *Division. History Section. Bibliography and Indexes Committee*
> *Hierarchy:* American Library Association
>   Reference and Adult Services Division
>   History Section
>   Bibliography and Indexes Committee

Conferences, Congresses, Meetings, etc. (Rule 24.7)

By definition, conferences, congresses, meetings, etc. are a type of corporate body. Headings for these are established in the form:

Name of conference *(number if any : date : place or institution).*

Conference on the Analysis of Census Data from Colonial Central Africa *(1986 : University of Wisconsin—Milwaukee)*

Symposium on Patterning Science and Technology *(1st : 1989 : Hollywood, Fla.)*

Governments and Government Bodies (Rules 24.3E, 24.6, 24.17–24.26)

Because of certain special characteristics of governments and government bodies, separate rules concerning the entry element of their names are provided.

The heading for a government is normally the conventional name, i.e., the geographic name of the area over which the government exercises jurisdiction, unless the official name is in common use.

United States
(not United States of America)

Kentucky
(not Commonwealth of Kentucky)

Greater London Council

The rules in Chapter 23 with regard to geographic names apply to headings of governments consisting of jurisdictional names, e.g., the rules requiring the addition of the name of a larger place and/or a type-of-jurisdiction qualifier.

Chicago (Ill.)
Toronto (Ont.)
Edinburgh (Scotland)
Veracruz (Mexico : State)

A body created or controlled by a government is normally entered under its own name, with the exception of eleven types (rule 24.18) of government bodies that are entered as subheadings under the headings for the governments. The government agencies that are entered subordinately are those with indistinctive names or with names implying administrative subordination and those serving an executive, legislative, or judicial function. The subordinate body is entered as a direct or indirect subheading (rule 24.19) based on similar principles for other corporate bodies.

National Research Council (U.S.)
University of North Dakota
Library of Congress
United States. *Internal Revenue Service*
California. *Bureau of Employment Agencies*
Cambridge (Mass.). *Division of Parks and Forestry*
Hierarchy: Cambridge, Massachusetts
            Dept. of Public Works
            Division of Parks and Forestry

Government Officials (Rule 24.20)

Certain government officials (heads of state, heads of governments and of international intergovernmental bodies, and governors of dependent or occupied territories) have corporate headings in the form of

Heading for government. Title of the office

e.g., **Chicago (Ill.).** *Mayor*

For heads of state, a separate heading is established for each incumbent in the form of

Heading for government. Title of the office (inclusive years of the reign or incumbency : name of person in brief form)

e.g., **United States.** *President (1961-1963 : Kennedy)*
New York. *Governor (1983-   : Cuomo)*
France. *Sovereign (1814-1824 : Louis XVIII)*

As a result of this provision, each head of state has a corporate heading in addition to his or her personal heading. The corporate heading is used as the main entry for official communications, with an added entry under the personal heading (see rule 21.4D1). The personal heading is used as the main entry for other works (see rule 21.4D2–D3). Works by popes, patriarchs, bishops, etc., are treated similarly.

Catholic Church. *Pope (1978-   : John Paul II)*

UNIFORM TITLES

A *uniform title* is "the particular title by which a work that has appeared under varying titles is to be identified for cataloguing purposes."[6] The uniform title brings together under one heading the various manifesta-

[6]AACR2R. P. 624.

tions (e.g., editions, translations) of a work regardless of how many different titles it has appeared under. This device is particularly useful when the main entry of the work is under title. Without the use of a uniform title, the various manifestations of a work bearing different titles would be scattered throughout the catalog. It serves also to distinguish works with like titles. It is particularly useful for famous authors, such as Shakespeare, whose works have been published by many publishers in different countries under various titles. For example, the uniform title for Albert Camus' *Notebooks* is **Camus, Albert, 1913-1960. Carnets.**

The rules for uniform title are not used for a manifestation of a work that is a revision or update in the same language as the original work. Revised and updated editions that have titles different from the original are treated as separate works with a note on the record to make the connection between the revision or update and the original.

Chapter 25 of AACR2R provides rules for uniform titles. When a uniform title is chosen among variant titles of a work, cross-references are made from titles, other than titles proper, not used as the uniform title (see rule 26.4).

Special rules are given for the use of uniform titles in cataloging special types of materials such as manuscripts, legal materials, sacred scriptures, liturgical works, and music. However, to what extent these rules are applied in cataloging is a policy matter to be decided by individual cataloging agencies. The decision is normally based on the extent of the collection and on the nature and purpose of the collection (e.g., whether it is part of a research library).

Anonymous Classics Written before 1501

Almost all libraries apply the rules of uniform titles to the cataloging of anonymous classics written before 1501. The rules pertaining to such works are summarized and discussed below.

Format

In bibliographic records in manual catalogs and in the public display of records in many online catalogs, the uniform title is given as the heading on the catalog entry, occupying the position normally taken by the main entry heading.

Choice of uniform title (rule 25.4)

The criteria in order of preference for choosing the title to be used as the uniform title are

1. Title by which the work is identified in modern reference sources
2. Title most frequently found in modern editions
3. Title most frequently found in early editions
4. Title most frequently found in manuscript copies

Language

The title in the original language is used except for a work originally written in classical Greek or in another language not in the roman script; for such works, an English title is preferred if there is one that is well-established. A list of uniform titles frequently found in library catalogs follows:

Arabian nights
Aucassin et Nicolette
Avicenna
Beowulf
Book of the dead
Chanson de Roland
Everyman
Gawain and the Grene Knight
Havelok the Dane
Mother Goose
Nibelungenlied

If the item being cataloged is in a language different from that of the original, the name of the language of the item is added to the uniform title.

Aucassin et Nicolette.   English

If two or more works bear the same title, or if the uniform title is identical or similar to the heading for a person or corporate body, an appropriate qualifier is added.

Pearl *(Middle English poem)*

Adoration of the shepherds *(Chester plays)*
Adoration of the shepherds *(Coventry plays)*

Genesis *(Anglo-Saxon poem)*
Genesis *(Middle High German poem)*

Special Rules for the Bible (Rules 25.17–25.18A)

Sacred scriptures are entered under uniform titles. For the Bible, because of the numerous manifestations, certain elements are added in the form of subheadings to the uniform title. These are set forth in special rules.

The general formula for the heading for a particular version of the Bible is given below. Elements that are not applicable in a particular case are omitted.

> **Bible.** [O.T. or N.T.]. [individual book or group of books]. [language]. [version]. [year].

e.g., **Bible.** *N.T. Luke. English. New English. 1965.*
Bible. *English. Living Bible. 1989.*

For selections and miscellaneous extracts from the Bible, the elements are arranged in the following manner:

> **Bible.** [language]. [version]. *Selections.* [date].

e.g., **Bible.** *English. Authorized. Selections. 1972.*

> **Bible.** [O.T. or N.T.]. [individual book or group of books]. [language]. [version]. *Selections.* [date].

e.g., **Bible.** *O.T. Psalms. English. New International. Selections. 1988.*
Bible. *O.T. Pentateuch. English. Rosenberg. Selections. 1990.*

Other Sacred Scriptures

Rules pertaining to the uniform titles for other sacred scriptures, such as the *Koran, Talmud,* and *Vedas,* are also provided (see rules 25.18B–25.18M).

> **Koran.** *Sūrat al-Baqarah*
> **Talmud.** *English. Selections*
> **Vedas.** *Atharvaveda*

CHAPTER SIX
REFERENCES

References, also called *cross-references*, are provided to connect related headings in the catalog and to give access to names, different forms of names, and uniform titles not used as headings. Chapter 26 of AACR2R contains rules for making references. Because references are directly associated with both the choice of names and the forms used for them in headings, Chapter 26 complements Chapters 22 through 25; conversely, the rules for headings in these chapters often contain instructions for references in specific situations. In addition, the rules in Chapter 26 provide general instructions covering all situations where references are appropriate.

There are four kinds of references.

1. *See* reference. A *see reference* directs the user from a name or a form of the name or a title not used as a heading to the one chosen as a name heading or uniform title heading.
2. *See also* reference. A *see also reference* connects related authorized headings.
3. Name-title reference. This is a *see* or *see also* reference in the form of [*name. title*], e.g.,

   Shakespeare, William, 1564-1616. Hamlet
   United States. Treaties, etc.

   This form is used when the reference is made from a title entered under a personal or corporate heading.
4. Explanatory reference. This is a *see* or *see also* reference containing an explanatory note giving more explicit guidance to the user.

In the MARC authority format, simple *see* references are recorded in the 4XX fields, simple *see also* references in the 5XX fields, and explanatory references in the 66X fields. Complete MARC authority records are shown in Appendix B of this book.

In making a reference, the name of a person, place, or corporate body from which reference is made is structured according to the rules for forms of headings in Chapters 22 through 24 of AACR2R.

Katz, Bill, 1924-
see*
Katz, William A., 1924-

* * *

Doolittle, Hilda, 1886-1961
see
H. D. (Hilda Doolittle), 1886-1961

* * *

D., H. (Hilda Doolittle), 1886-1961
see
H. D. (Hilda Doolittle), 1886-1961

* * *

Eliot, Thomas Stearns, 1888-1965
see
Eliot, T. S. (Thomas Stearns), 1888-1965

* * *

George, David Lloyd, 1863-1945
see
Lloyd George, David, 1863-1945

* * *

Lloyd George, David Lloyd George, Earl, 1863-1945
see
Lloyd George, David, 1863-1945

* * *

Day Lewis, Cecil 1904-1972
see
Day Lewis, C. (Cecil), 1904-1972

* * *

Lewis, C. Day (Cecil Day), 1904-1972
see
Day Lewis, C. (Cecil), 1904-1972

* * *

Day Lewis, C. (Cecil), 1904-1972
   see also**
Blake, Nicholas, 1904-1972

     * * *

   Blake, Nicholas, 1904-1972
      see also
Day Lewis, C. (Cecil), 1904-1972

     * * *

Plaidey, Jean, 1906-
     For works of this author entered under other names, see also
     Carr, Philippa, 1906-
     Ford, Elbur, 1906-
     Holt, Victoria, 1906-
     Kellow, Kathleen, 1906-
     Tate, Ellalice, 1906-

*Many libraries, including the Library of Congress, use "search under" rather than "see."
**Many libraries, including the Library of Congress, use "search also under" rather than "see also."

FIGURE 6-1   Personal name references.

Before a reference is made, it is generally recommended that at least one bibliographic record appear under the heading referred to; otherwise, the reference would be "blind." It is general practice to record (or trace) the terms *from* which references have been made on the name authority record for the heading *to* which they are made. In a manual name authority record, the symbol x on the name authority record means a *see* reference has been made from the term following, and the symbol xx means a *see also* reference has been made. In an automated system, identifying tags perform the same function.

    The most common kinds of references made to each type of heading are summarized below.

PERSONAL NAME HEADINGS (RULE 26.2)

See References [MARC Authority Fields 400, 664]

See references are made *from* the following:

1. Names not used as the heading: pseudonyms, real names, phrases used in lieu of names, secular names, names in religion, earlier names, and later names

2. Forms of the name not used as the heading: full name, initials, different language form, different spelling, and different romanization
3. Different entry elements: different elements of a compound name, prefix, part of surname following a prefix, first given name of person without surname, epithet or byname, last element not used as the entry element, person as saint, family name of saint or ruler, inverted form, and direct form

See also References [MARC Authority Fields 500, 663]

See also references are made between different headings for the same person when the person's works have been entered under more than one heading (cf. rule 26.2D1).

Examples of personal name references are shown in Figure 6-1 (pages 146-147). In addition, there are examples of personal name authority records, showing valid headings and references, in both Chapter 5 and Appendix B of this book.

NAMES OF CORPORATE BODIES AND GEOGRAPHIC NAMES (RULE 26.3)

1. *See* references are made from variant names and different forms (language, spelling, romanization, initials, acronyms, full names, etc.) of a name [MARC authority fields 410, 411, and 451].
2. *See also* references are made between independently entered but related corporate headings [MARC authority fields 510, 511, and 551].
3. Typically, explanatory references are made between earlier headings and the later heading of a corporate body [MARC authority fields 663, 664, 665, and 666].

Examples of corporate name references are shown in Figure 6-2 (pages 150-151). In addition, there are some examples of authority records for corporate and geographic names, showing valid headings and references, in Appendix B of this book.

UNIFORM TITLES (RULE 26.4)

1. *See* references are made from different titles and variants of the uniform title to the uniform title [MARC authority field 430].

2. *See also* references are made to connect uniform titles of related works [MARC authority field 530].

Examples of uniform titles are shown in Figure 6-3 (page 152). In addition, there are some examples of name authority records for uniform titles, showing valid headings and references, in Appendix B of this book.

EXERCISE A

Establish headings and cross-references for the following:

1. William A. Quayle (cf. Exercise B in Chap. 3)

2. James F. Oates, Jr. (cf. Exercise B in Chap. 3)

3. Jean Sibelius (cf. Exercise B in Chap. 3)

4. Mrs. John F. Kennedy

5. D. H. Lawrence

6. Internal Revenue Service of the U.S. government

7. Association for Library Collections and Technical Services

8. The First International Conference on Educational Measurement (held in 1967 in Berlin)

TOPICS FOR DISCUSSION

1. *Anglo-American Cataloguing Rules* (all editions) specify the bibliographic elements to be included in a cataloging record. From the user's point of view, evaluate the relative importance of each of these elements: title, statement of responsibility, edition statement, publisher, physical description, series statement, notes, ISBN, etc. As a user, have you made use of each of these elements at least on one occasion?

2. Discuss the concept of main entry in terms of different types of bibliographic records, e.g., catalogs, bibliographies, single- or multiple-entry listings.

3. In the definitions of *author* given in various codes, the descriptive phrase changed from "the *cause* of the book's existence" to "the person or body *immediately* responsible for its existence" to "the person or corporate body *chiefly* responsible for the creation of the

AALA
see
Alaska Association of Legal Assistants

* * *

ASHS
see
American Society for Horticultural Science

* * *

American Society for Horticulture Science
see
American Society for Horticultural Science

* * *

Society for Horticultural Science (U.S.)
see also the later heading
American Society for Horticultural Science

* * *

American Society for Horticultural Science
see also the earlier heading
Society for Horticultural Science (U.S.)

* * *

Galveston Chapter of the Red Cross
see
American National Red Cross.   Galveston Chapter

* * *

American Red Cross, Galveston Chapter
see
American National Red Cross.   Galveston Chapter

* * *

Maryland.   Dept. of Health, State
see
Maryland.   State Dept. of Health

* * *

Maryland.   Division of Community Assistance.   Maryland Codes Administration
see
Maryland Codes Administration

* * *

Corporation of the City of Glasgow (Scotland)
see
Glasgow (Scotland)

* * *

Glaschu (Scotland)
see
Glasgow (Scotland)

* * *

Austria
see also the earlier headings
Austro-Hungarian Monarchy
Holy Roman Empire

FIGURE 6-2   Corporate and geographic name references.

intellectual or artistic content of a work." Compare these phrases and discuss their implications in the rules for choice of access points.

4. Review the principle of uniform heading in terms of headings for persons and headings for corporate bodies. Discuss the impact of the softening of this principle in AACR2R in the treatment of persons with separate bibliographic identities and contemporary authors using more than one name in their works.

5. In establishing a heading for a personal author, two basic approaches were discussed (see p. 127). Consider the advantages and disadvantages of each approach, and consider how each approach would function in different types of libraries: academic, special, public, school, or research and nonresearch libraries.

Song of Roland
  see
Chanson de Roland

    * * *

Aucassin et Nicolete
  see
Aucassin et Nicolette

    * * *

Of Aucassin and Nicolette
  see
Aucassin et Nicolette

    * * *

Thousand and one nights
  see
Arabian nights

    * * *

Arabian nights
  For separately published parts of this collection, see
Ali Baba
Sindbad the sailor
[etc.]

FIGURE 6-3 Uniform title references.

PART III
SUBJECT ACCESS IN
LIBRARY CATALOGS

BASIC TOOLS

Library of Congress, Subject Cataloging Division. *Library of Congress Subject Headings.* 8th ed.– Washington: Cataloging Distribution Service, Library of Congress, 1975– . (Published annually, with weekly updates issued quarterly.) Also available on microfiche, in machine-readable form as *Subject Authorities* (MARC tapes) and on CD-ROM as *CDMARC Subjects.*

Library of Congress, Subject Cataloging Division. *Subject Cataloging Manual: Subject Headings.* 4th ed. Washington: Cataloging Distribution Service, Library of Congress, 1991.

Library of Congress, Subject Cataloging Division. *Subject Headings Used in the Dictionary Catalogs of the Library of Congress.* 1st ed.–7th ed. Washington: Library of Congress, 1914–1966.

National Library of Medicine (U.S.). *Medical Subject Headings.* Bethesda, Md.: National Library of Medicine; distributed by National Technical Information Service, U.S. Department of Commerce, 1975– . (Published annually.)

Sears List of Subject Headings. 14th ed. Martha T. Mooney, ed. New York: H. W. Wilson Company, 1991.

BACKGROUND READING

Chan, Lois Mai. *Library of Congress Subject Headings: Principles and Application.* 2nd ed. Littleton, Colo.: Libraries Unlimited, 1986. Pp. 3–45, 347–369.

Cutter, Charles A. *Rules for a Dictionary Catalog.* 4th ed. Rewritten. Washington: Government Printing Office, 1904. (Republished, London: The Library Association, 1953.) First published under the title

Rules for a Printed Dictionary Catalogue in 1876 as Part II of the U.S. Bureau of Education, *Public Libraries in the United States.*

Dunkin, Paul S. "What Is It About? Subject Entry." In *Cataloging U.S.A.* Chicago: American Library Association, 1969. Pp. 65–95.

Library of Congress Subject Headings: Principles of Structure and Policies for Application. Annotated version. Prepared by Lois Mai Chan for the Library of Congress. Washington: Library of Congress, 1990.

"Principles of the Sears List of Subject Headings." In *Sears List of Subject Headings.* 14th ed. New York: H. W. Wilson Company, 1991. Pp. 1–23.

Wilson, Patrick. *Two Kinds of Power: An Essay on Bibliographical Control.* Berkeley: University of California Press, 1968.

FURTHER READING

Aluri, Rao; Kemp, D. Alasdair; Boll, John J. *Subject Analysis in ONline Catalogs.* Englewood, CO: Libraries Unlimited, 1991.

Bates, Marcia J. "Rethinking Subject Cataloging in the Online Environment." *Library Resources & Technical Services* 33(4):400–12 (October 1989).

Chan, Lois Mai, and Theodora Hodges. "Subject Cataloguing and Classification: The Late 1980s and Beyond." In Michael Gorman et al., eds., *Technical Services Today and Tomorrow.* Englewood, Colo.: Libraries Unlimited, 1990. Pp. 74–85.

Dykstra, Mary. *PRECIS: A Primer.* Revised reprint. Metuchen, N.J., and London: Scarecrow Press, 1987.

Haykin, David Judson. *Subject Headings: A Practical Guide.* Washington: Government Printing Office, 1951.

Holley, Robert P. "Subject Cataloguing in the USA." *International Cataloguing* 14:43–45 (October 1985).

Markey, Karen. *Subject Searching in Library Catalogs Before and After the Introduction of Online Catalogs.* OCLC Library, Information and Computer Science Series, no. 4. Dublin, Ohio: OCLC, 1984.

Miksa, Francis. *The Subject in the Dictionary Catalog from Cutter to the Present.* Chicago: American Library Association, 1983.

Prevost, Marie Louise. "An Approach to Theory and Method in General Subject Heading." *Library Quarterly,* **16**:140–151, April 1946.

Studwell, William E. *Library of Congress Subject Headings: Philosophy, Practice, and Prospects.* New York: Haworth Press, 1990.

Subject Cataloging: Critiques and Innovations. Sanford Berman, ed. New York: Haworth Press, 1985.

CHAPTER SEVEN
SUBJECT CATALOGING

In addition to author and title entries, library catalogs and other bibliographic retrieval tools provide a topical approach to the records in their systems through access points that represent subject content. A user searches by subject for the following purposes: (1) to identify or retrieve specific items of which the subject is known (sometimes referred to as *known-item searching*) and (2) to search for information on a given subject. In this sense, subject entries, like author and title entries, serve the dual function of location and collocation. In addition, because the title of a work often does not clearly or completely indicate the subject content of the item, additional subject access points are used frequently to evaluate the relevancy of the retrieved items to the searcher's interest.

There are two ways of searching by subject: (1) through words in titles and/or notes (particularly contents notes) and (2) through words or phrases in specifically assigned index terms.

The first approach is also called *natural-language* or *free-text searching*. The available access points are words in the title or note areas of a bibliographic description. In card catalogs and many microform catalogs, title access is limited to the first word in the title, disregarding initial articles. In an online catalog that offers keyword searching, however, the user may use almost any of the words in a title or a note as an access point. The advantage is that information may be retrieved on the words authors used in titles, words which often reflect the most current terminology in a particular subject field. The drawback is that when a user wishes to retrieve all information, or as much information as possible, on a given subject, he or she must search on all the synonyms for that subject. A further problem arises when a title does not contain words that indicate subject content; this is the case for many titles in the humanities and social sciences.

The second approach is known as *controlled vocabulary access*. In this case, specific words or phrases designated as subject index terms are assigned to each record; each term normally represents only one subject, and a given subject is normally represented by only one term. In other words, among possible synonyms, one term is chosen as the subject index term. The searcher who uses a particular controlled term is then able to retrieve all records bearing that term. A controlled vocabulary also disambiguates homonyms by distinguishing between words with the same spelling but different meanings.

A controlled vocabulary system depends on a master list of the terms that can be assigned to documents. For most library catalogs, manual or online, these are called *subject headings;* for many abstracting and indexing systems, they are called *descriptors* or perhaps simply *preferred* or *authorized* terms. Preferred terms are maintained in a *subject headings list* or *thesaurus.* A subject headings list or thesaurus contains the subject access terms to be used in the cataloging or indexing operation at hand. When there are synonymous terms for a given subject, these terms are included in the list as *lead-in* terms, and references under them direct the searcher to the authorized term for the subject. Authorized terms that are related in meaning are also linked by references; in traditional subject cataloging terminology, the links from lead-in terms were called *see* references, and the links to related terms were called *see also* references; in the abstracting and indexing terminology, *see* references are called *use* references, and *see also* references are differentiated into types, such as *broader term* (BT), *narrower term* (NT), and *related term* (RT). The latter usage is rapidly becoming standard within subject cataloging as well.

Subject headings lists and thesauri require ongoing maintenance. This is accomplished through a control system, called a *subject authority system,* which, for each term, documents the basis for decisions on the term and on what links connect it with other terms. Subject authority systems are discussed in greater detail later in this chapter.

HISTORY OF SUBJECT ACCESS IN LIBRARY CATALOGS

Early library catalogs were primarily finding-lists providing author or catchword entries for each item along with a symbol indicating its location in the collection. The catchword entry played an important role in the evolution of subject headings. The catchword was usually the leading word in the title, but in cases where the leading word failed to express the subject content of a book, e.g., *An Introduction to Physics,* another word from the title more indicative of the subject content, in this example *Physics,* was used as the entry word, i.e., an access point. This practice represented a step between the catchword entry and the true subject entry. Thus, by the middle of the nineteenth century, librarians had begun to be aware of the significance of the subject approach to library material.[1]

---

[1]Julia Pettee. *Subject Headings: The History and Theory of the Alphabetical Subject Approach to Books.* New York: H. W. Wilson Company, 1947. P. 151.

Depending on the type of catalog, subject entries may appear in different forms and configurations. When a heading contains terms from different levels of a hierarchy of subjects, it is called a *classed* or *classified entry*. When a heading contains the most specific word or phrase describing the subject, it is called a *specific and direct entry*.

The Classed or Classified Catalog

The classed entry is probably the earliest form of subject entry. It begins with the term at the top of the hierarchy to which the subject being represented belongs, with each level in the hierarchy included in the subject heading. Thus a classed subject heading for "southern pines" would be.

Plants—Trees—Evergreens—Pines—Southern pines

When such entries are filed systematically or hierarchically, they are collocated according to their subject relationships.

A subject catalog made up of classed entries is called a *classed catalog*. The order of progression of subjects is from the general to the specific. For most searches, using such a catalog effectively requires an accompanying alphabetical index listing individual terms to allow the subject to be approached from any level of the hierarchy.

In American libraries, the classed catalog as a public tool was replaced in the late nineteenth century by the dictionary or alphabetical catalog. However, as a working tool, the classed catalog still exists in the form of shelflists which are arranged according to whatever classification system a given library uses. The main difference between a shelflist and a classed catalog is that a shelflist contains only one entry for each item, filed by its classification number. The classed catalog, on the other hand, includes added entries for documents that deal with more than one subject.

A variation on the classed catalog is the *alphabetico-classed catalog*, a hybrid of the classified approach and the alphabetical approach. In this form of catalog, the classed entries are arranged differently from those in the classified catalog. On each level of the hierarchy, the subject terms are arranged alphabetically rather than strictly by subject relationships. This form of catalog has all but disappeared from American libraries.

The Alphabetical Specific Catalog

The alphabetical specific entry is a controlled heading for a specific subject (without terms for the higher levels of its subject hierarchy), e.g., *Southern pines*. It was introduced in the late nineteenth century by Charles A. Cutter. Entries are arranged in alphabetical order without regard to their subject relationships or hierarchical status; thus subject collocation is sacrificed for quick and direct access. A later development than classed or alphabetico-classed catalogs, it quickly and almost completely replaced other catalog forms in U.S. libraries. Today this is the form of subject entry found in most card catalogs, in recent book catalogs, and in many microform or printed-book catalogs.

As mentioned in Chapter 1 of this book, in many libraries with card catalogs, alphabetical subject entries are interfiled with author and title entries to form a single alphabetical sequence. A catalog with this kind of arrangement is called a *dictionary catalog*. If catalog cards are arranged in more than one alphabetical sequence (say, authors and titles together and subjects separate), the result is called a *divided catalog*. The same patterns obtain in some printed and microform catalogs.

The Online Catalog

In the online catalog, the arrangement of subject entries is of no concern to users, since they cannot see how the records are arranged in computer memory. How subject entries are collocated in on-screen displays, however, is very important to users. Unfortunately, there is yet no standard display among different online systems. Users using different online catalogs often have to become accustomed to different display orders.

When the online library catalog was first developed, existing card catalog records were converted into machine-readable form and new records were created according to the same rules used in forming card catalog entries. As a result, the alphabetical specific headings that had been used in manual catalogs for a century were transferred to the online catalog with little structural change. Efforts to introduce changes that will render subject headings more amenable to the online environment have only been implemented gradually in order to avoid large-scale changes in existing records. Online capabilities offer many possibilities for improved subject access. Already, there are impressive benefits: keyword searching, selective search combinations through Boolean operations (X or Y, X and Y, X but not Y, for instance), and automatic switching from lead-in terms to controlled terms.

SUBJECT CATALOGING SYSTEMS

Before there was a standard list for subject headings, catalogers in individual libraries assigned subject headings as they saw fit. With the increase in interlibrary loan operations and the introduction of centralized cataloging through the distribution of Library of Congress (LC) printed cards, the advantages of having a standard list became apparent. Such a list would ensure consistency within the same library catalog as well as among catalogs of different libraries, thereby making retrieval easier for users who move from library to library as well as facilitating both interlibrary cooperation and the development of union catalogs.

In 1895, the first standard list for subject headings appeared. The *List of Subject Headings for Use in Dictionary Catalogs*, produced by an American Library Association (ALA) committee of which Cutter was a prominent member, was based on Cutter's principles. It went through three editions (1895, 1898, 1911). In 1910–1914, when LC began publishing its list under the title *Subject Headings Used in the Dictionary Catalogues of the Library of Congress*, it was found unnecessary to continue the ALA list.

Once LC began distributing printed cards at the beginning of the twentieth century, the library's practice soon became the de facto standard for cataloging in the United States. After LC began publishing its subject headings list in 1914, it became a standard tool for subject cataloging in American libraries.

The list has gone through many editions; beginning with the eighth, the title was changed to *Library of Congress Subject Headings* (LCSH). Since 1986, the list has been available in machine-readable form, called the *Subject Authority File*, from which other versions are published.

LCSH and its predecesors reflect the practice of a large research collection and neither were nor are always suited to medium-sized or small collections. Early on, the gap was filled by a list compiled by Minnie Earl Sears and published in 1923 under the title *Subject Headings for Small Libraries*. It was renamed *Sears List of Subject Headings* and has gone through fourteen editions so far, with the most recent appearing in 1991. Despite the relatively greater ease of using subject headings from LC cataloging copy, the Sears list is still favored for general collections in many small and medium-sized American libraries. Lists of subject headings also have been developed for special fields. The best known among these is *Medical Subject Headings* (MeSH). Chapters 8, 9, and 10 of this book discuss these standard lists and systems in detail.

Both LCSH and the Sears list adopted the principles of the alphabetical specific catalog first propounded by Cutter. However, LCSH and the Sears list differ in many respects. Details on each are given in Chapters 8 and 9, respectively.

GENERAL PRINCIPLES OF SUBJECT CATALOGING

The rules for subject headings in a dictionary catalog were first set forth by Charles Ammi Cutter in his *Rules for a Dictionary Catalog*.[2] These rules formed the basis of subject headings in American libraries for years to

[2]Charles Ammi Cutter. *Rules for a Dictionary Catalog.* 4th ed. Rewritten. Washington: Government Printing Office, 1904. (First published in 1876.)

come and are a strong force even today. Writing on the subject approach, Cutter stated two objectives: (1) to enable a person to find a book of which the subject is known and (2) to show what the library has on a given subject.[3] The first addresses the need to locate individual items; the second addresses the need to collocate materials on the same subject. It was on the basis of these needs that Cutter set forth his basic principles of subject entry. They are important because the impact of his principles on subject headings construction and maintenance is still discernible today. The basic principles of subject headings are described below.

The User and Usage

For Cutter, the most important consideration in the cataloging of library materials was the best interest of the user. He called this principle "the convenience of the public."[4] He felt that catalogers should be concerned with "the public's habitual way of looking at things" and that these habits should not be ignored, even if they occasionally demand a sacrifice of logic and simplicity. On this principle, the public's usage becomes an important determining factor in selecting the terms and the forms of subject headings.

The principle, though unassailable in intent, is the hardest of Cutter's recommendations to implement effectively in a system designed for wide general use. One cannot define *user* and *usage* because there is no such thing as a "typical library user." Patrons come into the library with different backgrounds and different purposes, and there has never been an objective way to determine how they approach the catalog or what their purposes are. As a result, in an attempt to follow Cutter's lead, catalogers have formed subject headings on the basis of what they assume to be the needs and habits of users.

Another approach to effective subject access is to attempt to develop a system that adheres to strictly formed principles, on the assumption that a logical and consistent system can be learned by its users. When one looks beyond Cutter's insistence on reflecting general usage, one finds that his early rules went a long way toward laying the groundwork for a logical and consistent subject access apparatus.

In current subject heading systems, the most important factors, evolved over the years, are (1) uniform and unique headings, (2) specific and direct entry, (3) consistency and currency in terminology, and (4) provision of cross-references.

[3]Ibid. P. 12
[4]Ibid. P. 6.

Uniform and Unique Headings

In order to show what a collection or a database has on a given subject, it must adopt a principle of *uniform headings;* that is, it must bring under one heading all the material dealing principally or exclusively with that particular subject. This principle is similar to that requiring a uniform heading for a given personal author. If a subject has more than one name (*ascorbic acid* and *vitamin C,* for instance), one must be chosen as the heading. In general, it is hoped that the term chosen is unambiguous and familiar to all users of the catalog. Similarly, if there are variant spellings of the same term (e.g., *marihuana* and *marijuana*) or different possible forms of the same heading, only one is used as the heading. Examples of variant heading forms might be *Air quality* versus *Air—Quality* or *Quality of air.* One must be chosen, with the others listed as lead-in terms. However, in a few cases, duplicate entries are made for certain headings; for example, headings such as *United States—Foreign relations—Japan* and *Japan—Foreign relations—United States* may both be used, although they are two forms of the same heading. The reason for duplicate entries is to provide access under both United States and Japan in manual catalogs. In online catalogs that provide searching on component parts of a heading, such duplicate entries have little value.

The converse of the principle of uniform headings is *unique headings;* that is, the same term should not be used for more than one subject. If the same term must be used in more than one sense, as is often the case when different disciplines or fields of knowledge are involved, some qualification or clarification must be added so that it will be clear to the user which meaning is intended, e.g., *Cold* and *Cold (Disease).*

Specific and Direct Entry

The principle of *specific entry* governs both how subject headings are formed (thesaurus construction and maintenance) and how they are assigned to documents (indexing or subject cataloging). Regarding formulation, the principle requires that a heading be as specific as (in other words no broader than) the topic it is intended to cover. In application, it requires that a work be assigned the most specific heading that represents its subject content. Ideally, the heading should be coextensive with (no broader or narrower than) the subject content of the work.

The rule for specific entry was set forth by Cutter in his *Rules for a Dictionary Catalog:*

> Enter a work under its subject headings, not under the heading of a class which includes that subject. ... Put Lady Cust's book on "The Cat" under

Cat, not under *Zoology* or *Mammals* or *Domestic animals;* and put Garnier's "Le fer" under *Iron,* not under *Metals* or *Metallurgy.*[5]

Cutter claimed that this rule is the main distinction between the dictionary catalog and the alphabetico-classed catalog. In an alphabetico-classed catalog, the subject "cats" would appear under a heading such as:

Zoology—Vertebrates—Mammals—Domestic animals—Cats

Actually, there is no difference in terms of specificity between this heading and the heading *Cats* used in an alphabetical specific catalog. The difference lies in the access point. In the classed catalog or the alphabetico-classed catalog, the heading contains a series, or chain, of hierarchical terms beginning with, and therefore listed under, the broadest term and leading to the most specific. In the alphabetical subject catalog, on the other hand, the subject is listed directly under its own name. In other words, the major characteristic of the alphabetical specific catalog is that its entries are both *specific* and *direct.*

Consistent and Current Terminology

It follows from what has been said above, particularly regarding the justifications for uniform headings, that the terminology in headings should be both consistent and current. Two elements are particularly important here: synonymy and changing usage.

Choices among synonymous terms may require difficult decisions. By principle, common usage prevails when it can be determined. For example, a popular term is preferred to a scientific one in a general library and in standard lists of headings designed for general collections. Of course, the more specialized a library's collection and clientele, the more specialized its indexing terminology should be; special libraries, therefore, often develop their own thesauri or make extensive modifications of standard lists.

Changes in usage present many practical difficulties. A term may be chosen on the basis of common usage at the time it is established but become obsolete later on. For emerging subjects, it often takes time for terminology to crystallize. For example, when computers first appeared, the Library of Congress subject heading chosen for them was *Electronic calculating machines;* this was later changed to *Computers.* Even when the revision of thesauri or subject heading lists keeps pace with needed changes, updating obsolete vocabulary in catalog entries poses a problem in workload because of the large number of items listed under

[5]Ibid. P. 66.

existing subject headings; this is one reason changes to more current terms are sometimes slow in implementation. In many online catalogs and databases where the bibliographic and authority files are linked, updating is easier; once a heading is changed, every record that was linked to the old heading can be linked to the new.

Cross-references

Three types of cross-references are used in the subject headings structure: (1) the *see* (or USE) reference, (2) the *see also* [or BT (broader term), NT (narrower term), or RT (related term)] reference, and (3) the *general* reference.

See (or USE) references

To make sure that users who happen to consult the catalog under different names for (or different forms of the name of) a given subject will be able to locate material on it, *see* or USE references are provided to lead them from the terms they have looked under to the authorized heading for the subject in question. These references guide users *from* terms that are not used as headings *to* the authorized headings.

See also (including BT, NT, and RT) references

This type of reference connects headings that are related in some way, either hierarchically or otherwise. Unlike the *see* reference, a *see also* reference relates headings that are all used as entries in the catalog. The headings involved may overlap in meaning but are not fully synonymous—if they were, they would not both be used in the catalog. By connecting related headings, the *see also* (RT, for *related term*) reference calls the user's attention to material related to his or her interest. By linking hierarchically related headings, *see also* (BT, for *broader term*, and NT, for *narrower term*) references restore some of the advantages of the classed catalog in an alphabetical specific catalog, in that the user is guided to specific branches or aspects of a subject. By linking headings related nonhierarchically, *see also* references provide users with additional access points for the subject being sought.

General reference

While a *specific* reference directs the user from the term being consulted to another individual heading, a *general* reference directs the user to a group or category of headings instead of to individual members of the group or category. It is sometimes called a *blanket reference;* an example is **Exhibitions—Awards** *see also* the subdivision Awards under names of individual exhibitions. An obvious advantage of using general references is economy of space; they obviate the need to make long lists of specific references.

SUBJECT AUTHORITY CONTROL

Any retrieval system offering both controlled terminology and a cross-reference apparatus must have a means of maintaining control over the vocabulary and the references. Librarians and other retrieval systems personnel have devised such a means, referred to as *authority control*. Name authority control devices were discussed in Chapter 5; subject authority control systems follow much the same pattern.

Subject authority systems have two main purposes: to ensure uniformity and consistency in subject heading terminology and cross-references. To these ends, headings are *established* when they are used for the first time, and *subject authority records* are set up for them.

In the *ALA Glossary*, a subject authority file is defined as

> A set of records indicating the authorized forms of terms used as subject headings in a particular set of bibliographic records; the references made to and from the authorized forms; and the information used, and its sources, in the establishment of the headings and the determination of the references to be made.[6]

Thus a subject authority record contains the following information: the established heading; scope notes, if any; cross-references made from it to other headings; and the sources or authorities on which the decision on the heading form was based. All authority records for a given system are kept in a *subject authority file,* which is either part of an online system or maintained manually on cards.

Levels of Subject Authority Control

There are at least two levels of subject authority control: central and local. On the first level, a central agency, such as the Library of Congress or the H. W. Wilson Company, maintains the subject authority file (in card or machine-readable form) or subject headings list (in print form), making changes to existing headings and cross-references as well as adding new ones.

On the local level, a library devises a subject authority apparatus that

[6]*ALA Glossary of Library and Information Sciences.* Hartsill Young et al., eds. Chicago: American Library Association, 1983. P. 220.

ensures conformity and currency of the subject headings and cross-references appearing in its own catalog. Most libraries rely on one of the standard subject headings lists, such as LCSH or the Sears list, and create local subject authority records only for headings not yet appearing in the standard list. In some libraries, newly established headings are simply recorded in a *subject headings list*, along with needed maintenance information. Local subject authority work then includes correcting erroneous headings and cross-references, updating obsolete headings, and adding or revising cross-references necessitated by new headings. Methods of local subject authority control vary according to the type of catalog, i.e., card or online. In online catalogs, subject authority control mechanisms vary according to the design and capabilities of the system.

Functions of a Subject Authority File[7]

In the library setting, a subject authority file serves a number of functions:

1. *Cataloging.* In subject cataloging, the subject authority file serves as the source of indexing vocabulary and as the means of verifying or validating headings assigned to individual cataloging records. With the subject authority file, a cataloger can ensure that the same heading is assigned to all works on the same subject and that each heading represents only that particular subject. Furthermore, by consulting the subject authority file, the cataloger can ensure that all headings assigned to cataloging records conform to the established forms.

2. *Catalog maintenance.* Even after cataloging records have been created, adjustments must be made from time to time as a result of heading changes. When existing headings are revised or new headings are added, cross-references are often affected and should be adjusted. The subject authority file, reflecting the most current status of headings and cross-references, serves as the source for verification and validation. The subject authority file is particularly useful when a library converts its catalog from the manual form to the online mode and wishes to have previously existing records reflect current practice.

3. *Retrieval.* Enhanced retrieval must be considered the ultimate function of subject authority control, because the purpose of normal-

[7]Lois Mai Chan. "Functions of a Subject Authority File." In *Subject Authorities in the Online Environment: Papers from a Conference Program Held in San Francisco, June 29, 1987.* Sponsored by Resources and Technical Services Division, American Library Association, Library and Information Technology Association, Association of College and Research Libraries, Public Library Association. Karen Markey Drabenstott, ed. ALCTS Papers on Library Technical Services and Collections, no. 1. Chicago and London: American Library Association, 1991.

izing subject access points is to enable the catalog user to retrieve relevant cataloging records. There are two ways in which the subject authority file can aid the user in retrieval. First, the subject headings displayed in the subject authority file show the user the terminology and form of subject access points in the catalog. Second, the cross-references guide the user to related headings when the user's input terms fail to retrieve useful records.

GENERAL METHODS OF SUBJECT ANALYSIS

No matter what the subject access system within which a subject cataloger is working, subject analysis of a particular work or document involves basically three steps: (1) determining the overall subject content of the item being cataloged, (2) identifying multiple subjects and/or subject aspects and interrelationships, and (3) representing both in the language of the subject headings list at hand.

1. The most reliable and certain way to determine the subject content is to read or examine the work in detail. Since this is not always practical for reasons of cost, catalogers usually have to use other means. Titles are sometimes but not always a fair indication of content. *An Introduction to Chemistry* is undoubtedly what its title implies, but *Tourist Attraction* is a novel rather than a travel book. It is always wise to look beyond the title for the subject content of the work. Other features of the work often provide information relating to content. These include abstracts if any, tables of contents, chapter headings, prefaces, introductions, indexes, book jackets, slipcases, or other accompanying descriptive material—the latter two being particularly helpful in the case of nonbook materials. When these elements fail to provide a clear picture of what the work is about, external sources, such as bibliographies, catalogs, review media, and other reference sources, may prove helpful. Occasionally, subject specialists may have to be consulted, particularly when the subject matter is unfamiliar to the cataloger.

2. The next step is to identify the main and subsidiary subjects, including different aspects of the subject, such as author's point of view, time, and place. A work may deal with several subjects separately or deal with two or more subjects in relation to each other. The interrelationships of subjects in a work are called *phase relations.* Some examples of phase relations follow:

> *Influence phase.* The influence of one thing, one concept, or one person on another is a very common approach in scholarly works.
> *Bias phase.* Some works on a particular subject have a bias toward, or aim at, a specific group of readers or audience, e.g., *Fundamentals of Physical Chemistry for Premedical Students.*

Tool or application phase. This relationship is particularly common among scientific or technical works, e.g., *Chemical Calculations: An Introduction to the Use of Mathematics in Chemistry.*
Comparison phase. This relationship is common in literary and social science studies.

3. The final step is to represent the content according to a particular system or scheme. The first two steps are the same in all subject analysis operations. The third step varies according to whether representation is through subject headings, indexing terms, or classification numbers. In many cases, the cataloger or indexer starts with a tentative wording or phrasing and tries to match it in the tool being used.

ASSIGNING SUBJECT HEADINGS: GENERAL GUIDELINES

Although policies regarding subject heading assignment may vary from library to library, certain general practices are followed by most libraries in this country. These are discussed below.[8]

Levels of Subject Cataloging

The levels of indexing, i.e., whether subject representation is provided for both parts and comprehensive whole, depends on the policy of the indexing agency. In some, indexing is primarily at the work-as-a-whole (such as a book or a journal) level; in others, it is at the level of chapter or article content. In catalogs in American libraries prepared according to the Library of Congress, Sears, or the National Library of Medicine systems, subject headings are assigned to each item to bring out the overall content of the work being cataloged. Occasionally, subject headings for parts of a work are assigned. These are called *analytical* entries (for a component part such as a short story, play, or chapter) or *partial contents* entries (for a substantial portion of a work).

Headings for individual persons, families, corporate bodies, places, etc., are assigned if they are considered significant to the work as a whole.

Specific (Coextensive) Entry

The heading that represents precisely the subject content of the work is assigned as the primary subject heading, unless such a heading does not exist and cannot be established. In the absence of a coextensive heading,

---

[8]For specific guidelines for assigning headings from a particular subject headings list, consult the following chapters in this book and the introduction to the list and/or cataloging manual of the system.

a broader or more general heading may be used. In such cases, the broader heading is the most *specific* authorized heading in the hierarchy that covers the content of the work. In many cases, several headings may be assigned in order to cover different aspects of a subject.

With a few exceptions, a general heading which comprehends the specific primary heading is not assigned as an additional heading to a work dealing with only the specific subject. For example, the subject heading **Science** is not assigned to a work on chemistry, which receives the heading **Chemistry**. In this case, headings representing subordinate concepts of **Chemistry** are not assigned either.

Number of Headings

The number of headings assigned to each work depends on the nature of its content, the structure of available headings, and the policies established by the cataloging agency. A recent policy of the Library of Congress, for example, allows up to ten subject headings for each item. The ideal situation is one in which one heading will suffice to express the subject of the work being cataloged. However, in many cases, more than one heading may be required because the subject content of a particular work cannot be totally expressed in a single heading. Furthermore, headings are sometimes assigned to bring out secondary topics or concepts treated in the work.

Certain categories of works, such as general periodicals and individual works of fiction, are often not assigned any subject headings.

Multitopical and Multielement Works

For a multitopical or multielement work, more than one heading may be required; what is done in a given library or cataloging agency depends on the policy of the agency in question. The following guidelines reflect Library of Congress practice and may be followed by libraries using LCSH or the Sears list.

A multitopical work (one that deals with two or three distinctive subjects or concepts separately) is assigned two or three separate headings, unless the two or three subjects constitute approximately the totality of a general subject; in the latter case, the heading for the general subject is used. For example, a book about Chinese and Japanese literature is assigned two headings, one for each literature, but a book about Greek and Latin literature is assigned the heading for classical literature. When a work deals with four or more subjects, all of which form parts of a larger subject, it is given the heading for the larger subject, e.g., **South America—Description and travel** for a book about traveling in Argentina, Brazil, Chile, and Ecuador. When individual subjects in a work do not belong to a particular broad subject, they are given separate headings if there are no more than four; for more than four topics, the practice is to use either several very general headings or a form heading only, e.g., **French essays**.

For a multielement work (one that features a single central topic considered from different aspects or containing various elements such as form, place, and time), the most desirable heading is one that brings out these aspects or elements. If such a heading is not available, a new heading may be established or several headings may be used as appropriate. Whether all the concepts, aspects, and elements identified in the subject of a work should be represented in the catalog depends on the types of users for whom the catalog is intended. The main criterion is the potential value or usefulness of the headings for the users.

The methods and procedures outlined above represent general approaches to subject cataloging. Individual systems often have special policies or guidelines. These are discussed in the following chapters.

CHAPTER EIGHT
LIBRARY OF CONGRESS
SUBJECT HEADINGS

Library of Congress Subject Headings (LCSH) is a list of subject headings originally developed by the Library of Congress for use on its cataloging records. The list was begun toward the end of the nineteenth century and first published in 1914. Since then, it has become the standard list used by most large general libraries in the United States, as well as by many special libraries and some smaller libraries; it is also used in many libraries abroad. LCSH is now available in three formats: print (now in its fifteenth edition and published annually), machine-readable (called the *Subject Authority File*, established in 1986), and microfiche (first issued in 1975). The machine-readable version is also available on CD-ROM, called *CDMARC Subjects*. LCSH is revised weekly, with new and changed headings incorporated into the Subject Authority File. The weekly updates are published every month in print; the microfiche and CD-ROM versions are issued every three months and represent a cumulation of recent additions and changes into the main list.

LCSH is essentially a subject authority list; in other words, it is a list of terms authorized by the Library of Congress for use in its own subject cataloging. Libraries using LCSH for subject authority control have relied on the list and follow Library of Congress policies and practices as de facto standards. Yet there is no code for subject cataloging comparable to *Anglo-American Cataloguing Rules* for descriptive cataloging. In 1984, in response to expressed need of the library community for a guide to subject cataloging, the Library of Congress began publishing its internal instructions for subject cataloging in *Subject Cataloging Manual: Subject Headings*.[1] This manual, now in its 4th edition (1991), contains detailed instructions for establishing and assigning subject headings but is not cast in the form of a subject cataloging code. In 1990, a document entitled *Library of Congress Subject Headings: Principles of Structure and Policies for Application*[2] was published. This document serves as a succinct

---

[1]Library of Congress, Subject Cataloging Division. *Subject Cataloging Manual: Subject Headings*. Preliminary ed. Washington: Library of Congress, 1984. 4th ed., 1991.

[2]*Library of Congress Subject Headings: Principles of Structure and Policies for Application.* Prepared by Lois Mai Chan. Washington: Library of Congress, 1990.

statement of the principles and policies governing LCSH with respect to both construction of subject headings and their application. The following discussion is based on the *Subject Cataloging Manual* and that statement of principles and policies.

To use LCSH effectively, it is important to realize its scope: what it contains and what it does not contain. Its most prominent feature is the set of headings authorized for use as subject access points in bibliographic records. It also contains many terms that are not authorized as headings but are included as lead-in (also called *referred-from*) terms to help users as well as catalogers find the applicable authorized term for a topic at issue. Cross-references under the lead-in terms give directions to the associated authorized headings. However, not all authorized subject headings appear in LCSH: catalogers may derive headings from the Name Authority File or (acting under established policies) construct suitable headings on their own. In other words, many subject headings appearing in LC's bibliographic records are not listed in LCSH. A list of the principal categories of headings omitted appears in the introduction to the printed version of the list. These omissions include (1) headings residing in the Name Authority File, (2) headings with free-floating subdivisions, and (3) headings containing free-floating phrases such as **... in art, ... in literature,** etc.

FORMAT OF HEADINGS AND MARC CODING

Subject headings appear in different formats in the print, microform, and machine-readable versions of LCSH and in manual and MARC bibliographic records. These are discussed below.

Subject Authority Records

In the print version of LCSH, authorized headings appear in boldface type, e.g., **Art, Berries, Illustration of books, Reference books,** etc. Each valid heading is followed by scope notes, cross-references, and subdivisions, if any.

Entries printed in lightface roman type are not to be used as subject headings; they are the lead-in terms discussed above (i.e., synonyms or variants of regular headings) followed by cross-references to the authorized headings. Examples of entries are shown below:

> **Berries** (*May Subd Geog*)
>   [*SB381-SB386 (Culture)*]
>   BT Fruit
>   Fruit-culture

RT Cookery (Berries)
SA *names of berries, e.g.,* Strawberries
NT Amelanchier
    Blueberries
    Canned berries
    Frozen berries
    Ornamental berries
    Rubus
    Salmonberry
—**Harvesting**
—**Varieties**

Economic conditions
    USE *subdivision* Economic conditions *under names of*
        countries, regions, cities, etc.
        Economic history

Fine arts
    USE **Art**
        Arts

Libraries—Reference books
    USE **Reference books**

Reference books
    [*Z711*]
    UF Bibliography—Reference books
        Books, Reference
        Libraries—Reference books
        Reference books, English
    BT Bibliography
        Books and reading
    NT Bibliography—Best books
        Children's reference books
        Encyclopedias and dictionaries
—**Bibliography**
    [*Z1035*]
    BT Bibliography—Best books
        Bibliography—Bibliography
—**Chemistry, [San Francisco (Calif.), Journalism,**
    Shakespeare, William, 1564-1616, etc.]

In the machine-readable Subject Authority File, each main heading
or main heading–subdivision combination is represented by a separate
authority record. The valid heading and the references are identified by
specific tags. Each subdivision within a heading is identified by a sub-

field code. The field tags and subfield codes used in subject authority records are shown below.

Heading fields
150   Heading—Topical term
151   Heading—Geographic name

Common subfield codes
‡x   General (i.e., topical and form) subdivision
‡y   Chronological subdivision
‡z   Geographic subdivision

Tracing fields
260   Complex see reference—Subject
360   Complex see also reference—Subject
450   See from tracing—Topical term
451   See from tracing—Geographic name
550   See also from tracing—Topical term
551   See also from tracing—Geographic name

Common subfield codes
‡i   Explanatory text

Note fields
667   Nonpublic general note
670   Source data found
675   Source data not found
680   Public general note
681   Subject example tracing note

Common subfield codes
‡a   Defined variously in each field
‡b   Information found
‡i   Explanatory text

Field 150 includes form headings as well as topical headings. The authority records related to the heading **Reference books** are shown in Figure 8-1.

Subject Headings in Bibliographic Records

In manual catalogs, the subject headings assigned to a particular bibliographic record are recorded, along with added entries, in a paragraph called *tracings*. In the tracings, subject headings are preceded by arabic numerals and added entries by Roman numerals. Each subject heading string appears in the form of **[Main heading]** or **[Main heading—Subdivision—Subdivision—]**. For an example of tracings on a catalog card, see Figure 1-1 in Chapter 1.

```
▶ ARN:      2037138          Rec stat:     n
  Entered:  19871218         Replaced:     19871218
   Type:        z       Enc lvl:     n      Source:           Lang:
   Roman:       ▮       Upd status:  a      Mod rec:          Name use: b
   Govt agn: ▮          Ref status:  b      Subj:        a    Subj use: a
   Series:      n       Auth status: a      Geo subd: ▮       Ser use:  b
   Ser num:     n       Auth/ref:    a      Name:        n    Rules:    n ¶
▶    1  010      sh 85112186  ¶
▶    2  040      DLC ‡c DLC ¶
▶    3  053      Z711 ¶
▶    4  150   0  Reference books ¶
▶    5  450   0  Bibliography ‡x Reference books ¶
▶    6  450   0  Books, Reference ¶
▶    7  450   0  Libraries ‡x Reference books ¶
▶    8  450   0  Reference books, English ¶
▶    9  550   0  Bibliography ‡w g ¶
▶   10  550   0  Books and reading ‡w g ¶


▶ ARN:      2037160          Rec stat:     n
  Entered:  19871218         Replaced:     19871218
   Type:        z       Enc lvl:     n      Source:           Lang:
   Roman:       ▮       Upd status:  n      Mod rec:          Name use: b
   Govt agn: ▮          Ref status:  n      Subj:        a    Subj use: a
   Series:      n       Auth status: a      Geo subd: ▮       Ser use:  b
   Ser num:     n       Auth/ref:    a      Name:        n    Rules:    n ¶
▶    1  010      sh 85112188  ¶
▶    2  040      DLC ‡c DLC ¶
▶    3  150   0  Reference books ‡x Chemistry, [San Francisco (Calif.),
  Journalism, Shakespeare, William, 1564-1616, etc.] ¶
```

```
▶ ARN:      2037151          Rec stat:     n
  Entered:  19871218         Replaced:     19871218
   Type:      z       Enc 1v1:     n      Source:           Lang:
   Roman:     ▮       Upd status:  a      Mod rec:          Name use:  b
   Govt agn:  ▮       Ref status:  b      Subj:        a    Subj use:  a
   Series:    n       Auth status: a      Geo subd: ▮       Ser use:   b
   Ser num:   n       Auth/ref:    a      Name:        n    Rules      n ¶
▶    1  010      sh 85112187 ¶
▶    2  040      DLC ‡c DLC ¶
▶    3  053      Z1035 ¶
▶    4  150   0  Reference books ‡x Bibliography ¶
▶    5  550   0  Bibliography ‡x Best books ‡w g ¶
▶    6  550   0  Bibliography ‡x Bibliography ‡w g ¶
```

FIGURE 8-1   Subject authority records for **Reference books.**

In the MARC bibliographic record, subject headings are identified by field tags, which include the following:

600   Personal name heading
610   Corporate name heading
630   Uniform title
650   Topical heading
651   Geographic name heading

Subfield codes for fields 600, 610, and 630 are similar to those in fields 100, 110, and 130 in a name authority record. Subfield codes for fields 650 and 651 are similar to those in fields 150 and 151 in a subject authority record.

In recent years, the Library of Congress also has made occasional use of field 653, Index term—Uncontrolled, for additional subject entries that are not taken from LCSH nor constructed from established subject/thesaurus-building rules.

For examples of coded subject headings in bibliographic records, see Figure 1-1 and Appendix A of this book.

MAIN HEADINGS: FUNCTIONS, TYPES, SYNTAX, AND SEMANTICS

Subject headings may be categorized into various types according to their functions. A *topical heading* represents a concept or object dealt with in a work. It reflects what the work is *about*. When headings are used to represent the physical or bibliographic form of the item being cataloged, they are called *form headings*. A form heading reflects what the work *is* rather than what it is *about*. Proper names also may be used as subject headings for works focusing on individual persons, corporate bodies, places, and other named entities. These are called *headings for named entities.*

Topical and Form Headings [MARC Authority Field 150; Bibliographic Field 650]

A topical or form heading may contain one or more words. A one-word heading represents a single object or concept, while a multiple-word heading may represent a single concept or object or multiple concepts or objects. A heading also may carry a subdivision or subdivisions that bring out one or more aspects of the main subject. When a heading contains more than one concept, either in the form of a phrase heading or a heading with subdivisions, it is called a *pre-coordinated heading.*

Syntax

On the basis of their syntactical structure, topical and form headings may be divided into two main categories: single-noun headings and phrase headings.

Single-noun headings
The simplest form of main heading consists of a noun or substantive, e.g., **Cabbage, Cats, Economics, Poetry, Locomotion, Cataloging, Aged, Poor**, etc. Some single-noun headings are followed by a qualifier, which is discussed on page 178.

Phrase headings
When a subject or concept cannot be properly expressed by a single noun, a phrase is used. There are several patterns of phrase headings: adjectival, conjunctive, prepositional, inverted, and free-floating. These are discussed individually below.

Adjectival Phrase Headings   These are the most common type of phrase heading; they consist of a noun or noun phrase with an adjectival modifier. The adjectival modifier can be in one of several forms: a common adjective, a proper adjective, a geographic name, a noun modifier, or a noun in the possessive case, e.g., **Agricultural credit, Teenage automobile drivers, Abelian varieties, English literature, California sea lion, Library science, Cowper's glands, Carpenters' square**, etc.

Conjunctive Phrase Headings   These headings consist of two or more nouns, noun phrases, or both, with or without modifiers, connected by the word *and*. This form serves two purposes: (1) to express a reciprocal relationship between two general topics discussed at a broad level from the perspectives of both topics, e.g., **Literature and science, Church and social problems**, etc., or (2) to connect subjects that are often treated together in works because they are similar, opposite, or closely associated, e.g., **Emigration and immigration, Open and closed shelves, Debtor and creditor, Skis and skiing, Children's encyclopedias and dictionaries, Bolts and nuts**, etc.

Prepositional Phrase Headings   These headings consist of nouns, noun phrases, or both, with or without modifiers, connected by a preposition, e.g., **Breach of contract**. Such phrase headings usually serve one of two purposes: (1) to express complex relationships between topics which cannot be represented by a single noun or a conjunctive phrase, e.g., **Children in motion pictures, Costume in art, Electric discharges through gases, Federal aid to youth services**, etc., or (2) to represent a concept or object that cannot be stated in English in any other way than by using a prepositional phrase, e.g., **Boards of trade, Figures of speech, Fathers of the church**, etc.

Inverted Phrase Headings   In many cases, a phrase heading is inverted in order to bring a significant word into a prominent position as the entry element, e.g., **Chemistry, Organic; Maps, Statistical; Bridges, Steel plate deck; Knowledge, Sociology of;** etc. In a manual catalog or a single-entry listing or display, the inverted form brings together headings containing the same initial word for the purpose of subject collocation.

Free-floating Phrase Headings   A number of phrases are designated as free-floating components which may be combined with any existing heading or with any heading within designated categories to form new phrase headings, e.g.,

[Personal name] in fiction, drama, poetry, etc.
[Topic or place] in literature
[Topic or place] in art
[Name of river] Watershed

The resulting combinations are usually not listed in LCSH.

> **Nixon, Richard M. (Richard Milhous), 1913-   , in fiction, drama, poetry, etc.**
> **Culture in literature**
> **New Zealand in art**

Semantics

Respecting semantics, LCSH is a controlled-vocabulary list, a list that is designed to offer uniform and unique subject terminology. A main heading represents a topic: a thing, a concept, a process, an activity, a person, an organization, a geographic or jurisdictional entity, an event, a fictional construct. As is the case with the design of any controlled-vocabulary list, one consideration is to avoid terms that have the same meaning as other terms in the list; in LCSH, this is done by authorizing only one term from a set of synonyms. A second design consideration in such lists is to avoid headings that have more than one meaning; LCSH solves the problem of multiple meaning in part by using *qualifiers.*

Many English words or phrases have more than one meaning. In thesaurus construction, the first approach to solving the problem of multiple meaning is to find an acceptable synonym that is not ambiguous. Often, however, the most appropriate term for a topic has multiple meanings. When this is the case, a second term enclosed in parentheses (called a *qualifier*) is added to resolve the ambiguity. Examples are **Chairs (Sella), Cold (Disease)**, and **Pool (Game)**.

A qualifier also may be used to provide context for obscure or technical terms, in which case it usually takes the form of the name of a discipline or of a category or type of things, e.g., **Charge transfer devices (Electronics), Chlorosis (Plants)**, and **Correlation (Statistics)**.

Semantic confusion also arises with authorized terms that are close or overlapping in meaning to other authorized terms. This problem is resolved through the use of scope notes. Many headings in LCSH are provided with scope notes that (1) define the heading's scope, (2) specify the range of subject matter to which it is applied in LC cataloging records, (3) distinguish between related headings, or (4) state which of several meanings of a term is the one to which its use in LC catalogs is limited. The following examples are illustrative.

> **College graduates**
> Here are entered works on college graduates as a socioeconomic group. Works on college graduates in relation to their alma maters are entered under Universities and colleges—Alumni.

Drafts
>Here are entered works dealing in general with orders for the payment of money drawn by one party on another, and including nonnegotiable instruments such as postal money orders, cashier's checks, "Anweisungen," etc. Works on bills of exchange both foreign and domestic are entered under the heading Bills of exchange.

Growth factors
>Here are entered works on a group of polypeptides that control cellular responses such as cell multiplication by mechanisms analogous to classical endocrine hormones.

Headings for Named Entities [MARC Authority Fields 100, 110, 111, 130; Bibliographic Fields 600, 610, 611, 630]

Proper names are often needed as subject headings, and very few are listed in LCSH. The Name Authority File gives the established form for a large number of proper names, including names for persons, corporate bodies, and jurisdictions. Qualifiers are added as prescribed by *Anglo-American Cataloguing Rules (2nd edition, 1988 revision)* (AACR2R). Names not covered by AACR2R (e.g., names of geographic features and fictitious characters) are established by the Library of Congress according to principles and policies compatible with those in AACR2R. These headings are listed in LCSH.

The sections that follow discuss three categories of name headings: personal names, corporate names, and geographic or jurisdictional names.

Personal names [MARC authority field 100; bibliographic field 600]

In order to group together in the catalog works written by and about the same person, the same form of personal heading used as main or added entry is used as subject entry. Personal name headings serving as main and added entries as well as subject entries are established according to AACR2R and stored in the Name Authority File. On the other hand, personal name headings used only as subject entries are established and included in LCSH and the Subject Authority File. These include family name headings, headings for gods and goddesses, and headings for legendary and fictitious characters. Examples are given below.

Bakewell family
Kennedy family
Lincoln family

Aphrodite (Greek deity)
Baal (Deity)
Venus (Roman deity)
Robin Hood (Legendary character)
Snoopy (Fictitious character)

Corporate names [MARC authority field 110; bibliographic field 610]

Names of corporate bodies are used as subject headings for works that describe their origin and development and analyze and discuss their organization and function. Corporate name headings, established and stored in the Name Authority File, are used for this purpose. Thus a corporate subject heading conforms to the main or added entry heading for the same entity. The most common types of corporate bodies are associations and firms, governments and their agencies, institutions, committees, and commissions.

American Library Association
United States. Food and Drug Administration
Germany. Luftwaffe
Johns Hopkins University
Joint Commission on Rural Reconstruction. Rural
    Economics Division

Geographic names[3] [MARC authority field 151; bibliographic field 651]

Names of places and geographic features may appear as main headings or as subdivisions under topical or form headings. For a given place, the form of the geographic name should be the same when used in either position. There are two types of geographic names: jurisdictional and nonjurisdictional.

Jurisdictional names
Geographic headings that serve also as main or added entries in descriptive cataloging, also called *jurisdictional headings*, are established according to AACR2R and stored in the Name Authority File. For example,

Madrid (Spain)
New Jersey
Seattle (Wash.)

---

[3]Library of Congress, Subject Cataloging Division. *Subject Cataloging Manual: Subject Headings*. 4th ed. Washington: Library of Congress, 1991. H690.

Nonjurisdictional names
Nonjurisdictional geographic names, including names of natural geographic features, can be used as subject headings even though they are not used as main or added entries. Such names, established according to the policies discussed below, are listed in LCSH. If the name exists in more than one language form, English is generally preferred. Furthermore, in many cases, qualifiers are added in order to make the headings unique or compatible with jurisdictional headings. Two types of qualifiers are used with geographic names: geographic and generic.

Geographic Qualifiers   The term *geographic qualifier* refers to the addition of the name of a larger geographic entity (normally the name of the country) to a place name. The AACR2R rules governing jurisdictional names are followed for nonjurisdictional names as far as applicable. For places in certain countries, including Canada, Great Britain, and the United States, the name of the appropriate first-order political subdivision (i.e., state, province, constituent country, etc.) is used as the geographic qualifier, e.g., **Ben Nevis (Scotland), Sheep River (Alta.), Albany (N.Y.)**, etc.

The name of a natural feature generally does not require a geographic qualifier unless it is wholly contained within one or two jurisdictions or when there are two or more entities bearing the same name.

> **Amazon River**
> **Ohio River Valley**
> **Berkel River (Germany and Netherlands)**
> **Table Rock Lake (Mo. and Ark.)**
> **Ventana Wilderness (Calif.)**
>
> **San Juan River (Colo.-Utah)**
> **San Juan River (Colombia)**
> **San Juan River (Nicaragua and Costa Rica)**
> **Golden Triangle (Pittsburgh, Pa.)**
> **Golden Triangle (Southeastern Asia)**

Generic Qualifiers   The names of many natural features contain a generic term, e.g., **Ohio River, Baltic Sea**. If it is necessary to distinguish between headings and/or cross-references that have the same name and geographic qualifier, a generic qualifier is added to the nonjurisdictional name.

> **Big Bear Lake (Calif.)** (heading for the city)
>
> **Big Bear Lake (San Bernardino County, Calif. : Lake)**
> (heading for the lake in San Bernardino County. There are four other Big Bear Lakes.)

Marco Island (Fla.) USE **Marco (Fla.)**
(heading and reference for the city)

Marco Island (Fla. : Island)

Entry Element[4]   When a geographic name consists of more than one element, the elements are rearranged so that the distinctive portion of the name occurs in the initial position. Two situations account for the majority of inverted geographic names.

1. The inverted form is used when the name of a natural geographic feature consists of a specific and a generic term, and the generic term precedes the specific term.

> **Fuji, Mount (Japan)**
> **Superior, Lake**
> **Mexico, Valley of (Mexico)**

but **Rocky Mountains**
   Beaver Creek (Ky.)
   Indian Lake (Ohio)

2. The inverted form is often used when the geographic heading consists of a geographic name preceded by a directional adjective which is not an integral part of the proper name.

> **Africa, Southern**
> **California, Northern**
> **Texas, East**

but **South Africa**
   North Dakota
   East China Sea

SUBDIVISIONS [MARC SUBFIELDS ‡x, ‡y, ‡z]

A main heading may be subdivided by one or more of four kinds of subdivisions: form, topical, period, and geographic. In many cases, there may be several subdivisions following a main heading. The result is a string of elements, e.g., **United States—History—Civil War, 1861-1865—Naval operations—Submarine**.

Most heading/subdivision combinations are specifically authorized by the Library of Congress as allowable subject strings. However, some commonly used form and topical subdivisions have been given a differ-

[4]Ibid. P. 6.

ent status; they are of general application (under stated conditions) and are known as *free-floating subdivisions*. These are discussed on pages 184 to 188.

In the print and microfiche versions of LCSH, under a main heading, period subdivisions (arranged chronologically) appear first, followed by form and topical subdivisions (arranged alphabetically), and then by geographic subdivisions (in a separate alphabetical sequence).

Although, in appearance, a main heading with one or more subdivisions resembles an entry in a classed catalog, a subdivision used with a main heading in LCSH, with few exceptions, represents a form or aspect of the main subject, instead of a subordinate class of the main subject.

Form Subdivisions [MARC Subfield ‡x]

Form subdivision has been defined as an extension of a subject heading based on the bibliographic or physical form or literary or artistic genre in which the material in a work is organized and/or presented.[5] While a main heading normally expresses what the work is *about,* a form subdivision represents what it *is,* i.e., what form the treatment of the subject takes.[6] Different works may deal with the same subject but not be the same kind of work; in other words, they are in different bibliographic forms.

> **Engineering—Examinations, questions, etc.**
> **—Indexes**
> **—Periodicals**
> **Gardens—Pictorial works**
> **—Poetry**

Topical Subdivisions [MARC Subfield ‡x]

In general, LCSH does not authorize any topical heading/subdivision combination that constitutes a species, part, or kind of the subject represented by the main heading; in other words, by policy, there should be no authorized headings of the type *Biology—Botany*. Such a heading is characteristic of the alphabetico-classed catalog and is against the principle of specific entry, which excludes genus-species or class-inclusion relationships. (There are, however, a small number of exceptions, such as **Wages—Minimum wage**.) Typically, a *topical subdivision* limits the

---

[5]*Library of Congress Subject Headings: Principles of Structure and Policies for Application.* Prepared by Lois Mai Chan. Washington: Library of Congress, 1990. P. 17.
[6]Ibid. P. 17. And David Judson Haykin. *Subject Headings: A Practical Guide.* Washington: Government Printing Office, 1951. P. 27.

concept expressed by a main heading to a special subtopic; very often, a subdivision represents an activity or operation applied to or associated with the subject denoted by the main heading. For example, the heading **Agriculture—Accounting** means accounting as applied to the field of agriculture and does not mean accounting as a kind or division of the subject agriculture. This type of topical subdivision is used extensively in LCSH.

Free-Floating Form and Topical Subdivisions

In order to ensure consistency and better control of subject strings, subdivisions and main headings are not combined randomly or at will by each cataloger at the Library of Congress. As a rule, each new combination of a subdivision with a main heading must be approved by an editorial committee at the library before its use becomes authorized.

An exception to the rule stated above is a group of widely used subdivisions called *free-floating subdivisions*. The term refers to those form or topical subdivisions which subject catalogers at the Library of Congress are authorized to use under a particular subject or name heading, where applicable and appropriate, without prior authorization. Consequently, these main heading/subdivision combinations may appear on LC bibliographic records without being listed in LCSH.

Free-floating subdivisions are listed either separately (apart from main headings) or under representative main headings called *pattern headings*, with the intention that they may be combined with appropriate main headings at the time of application. There are four categories of free-floating subdivisions: those of general application, those to be used only under specific categories of headings, those controlled by pattern headings, and those indicated by "multiples."

Free-floating subdivisions of general application

Form and topical subdivisions that are applicable to a large number of headings are designated as *free-floating subdivisions of general application*. A list of these subdivisions appears in *Subject Cataloging Manual: Subject Headings*.[7] Following are some examples of general free-floating subdivisions.

　　—**Abstracts**
　　—**Cost effectiveness**
　　—**Library resources**
　　—**Lighting**

[7]Library of Congress, Subject Cataloging Division. Op. cit. H1095.

—Periodicals—Indexes
—Software
—Study and teaching

Under each subdivision in this list, instruction is given as to the types of headings to which the particular subdivision is applicable. For example the subdivision —**Lighting** is applicable only under main headings representing vehicles, structures, buildings, rooms, installations, etc.

Free-floating subdivisions under specific types of headings

Many subdivisions are only applicable to, and only authorized for use as free-floating subdivisions under, specific categories of main headings. Separate lists of free-floating subdivisions have been established and published in *Subject Cataloging Manual: Subject Headings*[8] for use with the following categories of main headings: classes of persons, ethnic groups, names of corporate bodies, names of persons, names of places, and names of bodies of water, streams, etc. The following headings, although not listed in LCSH, are valid headings that were constructed using these free-floating subdivisions.

Actors—Political activity
Asian-Americans—Race identity
American Library Association—Employees
Illinois—Governors—Election
Kant, Immanuel, 1724-1804—Ontology
Milton, John, 1608-1674—Political social views
Carter, Jimmy, 1924-   —Inauguration

Free-floating subdivisions controlled by pattern headings

Certain form or topical subdivisions are common in a particular subject field or applicable to headings in a particular category. Instead of authorizing them heading by heading and repeating them under each heading within the category, they are listed under a chosen heading in the category. This chosen heading then serves as a *pattern heading* of subdivisions for headings in that category. The applicable subdivisions are displayed under the pattern heading in LCSH and in the Subject Authority File. Topical and form subdivisions listed under a pattern heading may be transferred and used with another heading in the same category even though the combination does not appear in LCSH. For example, under **English language**, the pattern heading for languages, the subdi-

---

[8]Library of Congress, Subject Cataloging Division. Op. cit. H1100, H1103, H1105, H1110, H1140, and H1145.5.

TABLE 8-1   Pattern Headings in LCSH

Category	Pattern Heading
Animals (General)	Fishes
Animals, Domestic	Cattle
Chemicals	Copper
	Insulin
Colonies	Great Britain—Colonies
Diseases	Cancer
	Tuberculosis
Educational institutions	
Individual	Harvard University
Type	Universities and colleges
Indians	Indians of North America
Industries	Construction industry
	Retail trade
Languages and groups of	English language
languages	French language
	Romance languages
Legal topics	Labor laws and legislation
Legislative bodies	United States. Congress
Literary authors	
Groups of literary authors	Authors, English
Individual literary authors	Shakespeare, William, 1564-1616
Literary works entered under	Shakespeare, William, 1564-1616. Hamlet
author	
Literary works entered under title	Beowulf
Literatures (including individual	English literature
genres)	
Materials	Concrete
	Metals
Military services	United States—Armed Forces
	United States. Air Force
	United States. Army
	United States. Marine Corps
	United States. Navy
Music compositions	Operas
Musical instruments	Piano
Organs and regions of the body	Heart
	Foot
Plants and crops	Corn
Religious bodies	
Religious and monastic orders	Jesuits
Religions	Buddhism
Christian denominations	Catholic Church
Sacred works	Bible

TABLE 8-1   (Continued)

Category	Pattern Heading
Sports	Soccer
Theological topics	Salvation
Vehicles, Land	Automobiles
Wars	World War, 1939-1945
	United States—History—Civil War, 1861-1865

SOURCE: Library of Congress, Subject Cataloging Division, *Subject Cataloging Manual: Subject Headings*, 4th ed. Washington: Library of Congress, 1991. H1146. Pp. 3–5.

vision —**Pronoun** is listed. Therefore, the combination **Japanese language—Pronoun** may be used, even though the combination does not appear in the list as such.

Table 8-1 shows the pattern headings designated for each subject category. For example, headings for individual corporate bodies may be subdivided according to the patterns listed in the table.

Catholic Church (as model for Christian denominations)
United States. Congress (for legislative bodies)
United States. Army (for armies of other countries)
United States. Navy (for navies of other countries)
Harvard University (for higher education institutions)

As are other elements of LCSH, the provisions under pattern headings are under continual review. Therefore, the latest edition of LCSH plus its weekly updates, the Subject Authority File, or the latest edition of *Subject Cataloging Manual: Subject Headings* should be consulted for complete and current lists of subdivisions under pattern headings.

Free-floating subdivisions indicated by "multiples"

Certain subject headings carry *multiple subdivisions,* a device naming a few examples as suggestions for analogous subdivisions.

Birth control—Religious aspects—Buddhism [Christianity, etc.]

Vietnamese Conflict, 1961-1975—Foreign public opinion—British [German, Russian, etc.]

In both these examples, the subdivision and the terms given in square brackets serve as examples of similar subdivisions that may be used without prior authorization, e.g.,

Vietnamese Conflict, 1961-1975—Foreign public
opinion—French

Chronological Subdivisions [MARC Subfield ‡y]

Chronological (also called *period* or *time) subdivisions* are used with headings for the history of a place or subject. Certain subject areas—such
as history, politics and government of individual countries, music, art,
and national literatures—lend themselves particularly to historical or
chronological treatment. Chronological subdivisions are also used in
other subject areas, such as science and technology, although to a lesser
extent.

Chronological subdivisions are listed individually under the appropriate headings in LCSH. They are not free-floating, with the exception
of the following combinations:

> —History—16th century
> —History—17th century
> —History—18th century
> —History—19th century
> —History—20th century

These subdivisions may be used under individual corporate name headings or topical headings to which the free-floating subdivisions —History can be assigned appropriately, e.g., **Friendship—History—18th
century**. However, they are not used with headings that begin with the
name of a region, country, etc. For example, *America—History—19th
century* is not a valid heading because chronological subdivisions under
names of places are enumerated in the list.

Chronological subdivisions in LCSH appear in various forms. Examples are given below.

1. The name of a monarch, an historical period, or an event followed
   by dates:

   France—History—Louis XIV, 1643-1715
   American literature—Revolutionary period, 1775-1783
   United States—History—Civil War, 1861-1865

2. The preposition *to* followed by a date:

   French literature—To 1500

3. Dates alone:

   English language—Grammar—1870-1949
   English language—Grammar—1950-
   Greece—History—1453-1821

4. The name of the century:

Japanese fiction—19th century
United States—History—20th century

5. An inverted noun, adjective heading:

Sculpture, Ancient
Sculpture, Baroque
Sculpture, Medieval
Sculpture, Renaissance
Sculpture, Rococo
Sculpture, Romanesque

The modifiers in these noun, adjective headings in fact denote both period and subject characteristics. They are generally not considered to be true chronological subdivisions and therefore are interfiled alphabetically with other subdivisions that have no period connotation.

Frequently, both a broad period subdivision and period subdivisions covering events or lesser epochs falling within the broad period are listed under the same main heading. However, they are not usually used together for the same work; the heading closest to the period treated in the work being cataloged is the one chosen.

Great Britain—History—Norman period, 1066-1154
—History—Medieval period, 1066-1485
—History—1066-1687
—History—Angevin period, 1154-1216
—History—Plantagenets, 1154-1399
—History—13th century
—History—14th century
—History—Wars of the Roses, 1455-1485

For example, the heading **Great Britain—History—Norman period, 1066-1154** is assigned to a work such as *The Reign of William Rufus and the Accession of Henry the First,* while the heading **Great Britain—History—1066-1687** is used with a work covering the history of England from 1200 to 1640.

EXERCISE A

Assign Library of Congress subject headings to the following topics: main headings and headings with topical and/or form subdivisions.

1. Papers on surface-enhanced raman scattering

2. Geometric function theory in several complex variables

3. The communicative ethics controversy

4. Dictionary of concepts in recreation and leisure studies

5. Geography in the curriculum

6. Proceedings of a conference on condensed matter, particle physics, and cosmology

7. A handbook for counseling the troubled and defiant child

8. Construction materials: types, uses, and applications

9. Control theory of distributed parameter and applications: proceedings of a conference

10. An introduction to urban geographic information systems

11. Paleontology of vertebrates

12. The adolescent in the family

13. The rhythm and intonation of spoken English

14. The biblical doctrine of salvation

15. An English-Swedish, Swedish-English dictionary

16. An historical study of the doctrine of the Trinity

17. ABC: A child's first book

18. Twenty-three days with the Viet Cong: a personal narrative

19. The principal voyages and discoveries of the English nation to 1600

20. Public attitudes toward life insurance

Geographic Subdivisions[9] [MARC Subfield ‡z]

A *geographic subdivision* indicates the origin or the locality of the main subject and may be used after subjects that lend themselves to geographic treatment (i.e., that show variations when treated in or with regard to different places). Headings that may be subdivided by place carry the designation (*May Subd Geog*) immediately after their listing in LCSH. This information also appears in the machine-readable name and subject authority records.

Geographic subdivision is essentially accomplished by inserting the name of a place, e.g., a city, a province, a country or other political entity,

[9]Library of Congress, Subject Cataloging Division. Op. cit. H807, H830.

a region, or a geographic feature, into a subject string; there are, however, established conventions governing form of geographic name and citation order within the string.

A main heading or a main heading/subdivision combination may be subdivided by place either directly or indirectly, depending on the place in question.

Direct geographic subdivision

With *direct* geographic subdivision, the name of the place follows the heading or another subdivision immediately without the interposition of the name of a larger geographic entity.

> **Education, Elementary—United States**
> **Music—Africa**
> **Art—Great Britain**
> **Education—Demographic aspects—Japan**

Indirect geographic subdivision

With *indirect* geographic subdivision, the name of a larger geographic entity, normally the name of the country, is interposed between the main heading and the place in question (e.g., **Music—Austria—Vienna**). Indirect subdivision has the effect of gathering material on a particular subject under the name of the larger geographic entity. With a few exceptions, geographic names are entered indirectly after a heading when the place in question falls wholly within a country.

> **Charities—Italy—Florence**
> **Cities and towns—France—Brittany**
> **Municipal government—Spain—Castilla y León**
> **Rural development projects—Kenya—Coast Province**
> **Wool industry—Government policy—Italy—Naples**
> **(Kingdom)**

Exceptions
The larger divisions of certain countries are entered directly without the name of the country as an intervening element. Among these exceptional countries are

Country	*Divisions*
Canada	Provinces
Great Britain	Constituent countries
United States	States

For example,

> Education—British Columbia
> Music—Scotland
> Agriculture—Florida

In addition, the names of the following cities are assigned directly: Berlin, Jerusalem, New York, and Washington, e.g.,

> Rabbis—New York (N.Y.)

When the place in question falls within a division (called a *first-order political division*) in one of the exceptional countries, the name of the first-order political division is used as the intervening element in an indirect geographic subdivision.

> Music—Québec (Province)—Montréal
> Geology—Scotland—Highlands
> Minorities—Missouri—Saint Louis

No more than two levels of geographic subdivision are used within a given heading, e.g.,

> Horse breeders—Kentucky—Lexington
> (*not* Horse breeders—Kentucky—Fayette
> County—Lexington)

In local subdivision, the latest name of any entity whose name has changed during the course of its existence is always used, regardless of the form of the name appearing in the work cataloged. For example, the heading **Banks and banking—Zaire—Kinshasa** is assigned to a work about banks in Leopoldville, Belgian Congo.

Similarly, local subdivision reflects the present territorial sovereignties of existing nations, regardless of whatever past territorial division is described in the work cataloged. For a region or jurisdiction that existed in the past under various sovereignties, it is the name of the country now in possession (as long as the region or jurisdiction is located wholly within that country) that is used. For instance, the heading **Education—France—Alsace** is assigned to a work about the status of education in Alsace in 1910.

When subdividing indirectly, if the geographic qualifier of the subordinate entity is identical to the name of the country or the name of the first-order political subdivision of an exceptional country, the geographic qualifier is omitted to avoid redundancy.

> **Sill River** (*Austria*) (as a main heading)
> *but* **Stream measurements—Austria—Sill River**

> **Guadalajara** (*Spain : Province*) (as a main heading)
> *but* **Transportation—Spain—Guadalajara** (*Province*)

When the qualifier and the country subdivision are not identical, the qualifier is retained.

> **Great Lake** (*Tas.*) (as a main heading)
> **Boats and boating—Australia—Great Lake** (*Tas.*)

In summary, the following places are entered *indirectly:*

1. Places below the level of the first-order political divisions of the exceptional countries noted above
2. Places of the following types when they fall wholly within one of the other countries:
   a. Subordinate political jurisdictions, such as provinces, districts, counties, cities, etc., with the exceptions noted below
   b. Historic kingdoms, principalities, etc.
   c. Geographic features and regions, such as mountain ranges, bodies of water, lake regions, watersheds, metropolitan areas, etc.
   d. Islands situated within the territorial limits of the country in question

The following places are entered *directly:*

1. Countries or larger geographic entities
2. The first-order political divisions of the exceptional countries
3. Any jurisdiction or region which does not lie wholly within a single existing country or first-order political subdivision of an exceptional country, including:
   a. Historic kingdoms, empires, etc.
   b. Geographic features and regions, such as continents and other major regions, bodies of water, mountain ranges, and so on, e.g., **Europe; Sahara; Great Lakes; Mexico, Gulf of; Rocky Mountains; Nile River Valley;** e.g., **Slave-trade—Africa.**
4. Islands or groups of islands situated some distance from land masses, even if they do not represent autonomous political rules, e.g., **Geology—Bermuda Islands.**
5. The cities of Berlin, Jerusalem, New York, and Washington, e.g., **Museums—New York (N.Y.).**

Order of Subdivisions

The citation order (i.e., the order in which elements are strung together in a heading) normally follows the pattern [**Main heading—Topical subdivision—Geographic subdivision—Chronologic subdivision—Form subdivision**]. However, there are variations to this pattern, particularly with regard to geographic subdivision, which may be used before or after a topical subdivision. It is the designation (*May Subd Geog*) in LCSH that determines the pattern. When (*May Subd Geog*) follows the main heading but not the topical, period, or form subdivision, the geographic subdivision is interposed between the main heading and the other subdivision.

> **Farm buildings—Kentucky—Fayette County—Heating and ventilation**
> **Geology—United States—Maps**
> **Art—Italy—Naples—Exhibitions**

When the designation (*May Subd Geog*) follows the topical, period, or form subdivision, the geographic subdivision follows the other subdivision.

> **Art—Conservation and restoration—Italy—Naples**
> **Farm buildings—Specifications—Kentucky—Fayette County**
> **Teachers—Training of—United States—Bibliography**
> **Visual aids—Collectors and collecting—Standards—North America**

When a place name is the main heading, the citation order is usually **[Geographic main heading—Topical subdivision—Chronologic subdivision—Form subdivision]**. For example,

> **France—Intellectual life—20th century—Historiography**

EXERCISE B

Assign Library of Congress subject headings to the following topics: geographic headings and headings with geographic and/or chronological subdivisions.

1. **a.** Assign subject headings on the social conditions of the following places:
    Athens, Georgia
    Athens, Greece
    Brittany, France
    Cambridge, Great Britain
    Munich, Germany
    New York (the city)
    Ottawa, Canada
    Tennessee
    Rio de Janeiro (the state), Brazil
    Mississippi Valley
   b. Assign subject headings on the art from places listed under **a.**

2. Assign subject headings to the following topics:
   a. Events leading to the American Civil War, 1837–1861
   b. A history of slavery and slave trades in Sub-Saharan Africa
   c. Profile of Ontario's provincial electoral districts based on statistics collected in the 1986 census
   d. Popular culture in the United States during the cold war
   e. Lobbying for social changes in the United States
   f. Christian life and the church in the Holy Roman Empire during the tenth century
   g. Essays on the Hungarian Protestant Reformation in the sixteenth century
   h. Violence in American families
   i. Managing social services in the United States: designing, measuring, and financing
   j. U.S.–Yugoslav economic relations since World War II
   k. Social relations in Elizabethan London
   l. Public school choice in American education
   m. The Gypsies of Eastern Europe
   n. The Taiwan uprising of February 28, 1947
   o. Working women look at their home lives
   p. Norman illumination of manuscripts at Mont St. Michel, 966–1100
   q. Life in a Japanese Zen Buddhist monastery
   r. The German community in Cincinnati
   s. A pictorial guide to San Francisco
   t. A catalog of Great Britain railway letter stamps

CROSS-REFERENCES

As discussed in Chapter 7, cross-references are provided in the catalog for two purposes: (1) to guide users from their search terms to valid headings, and (2) to link related headings. In LCSH, the main types of relationships expressed by cross-references are equivalence, hierarchy, and association.

Equivalence Relationships [MARC Authority field 45X]

USE references direct library users making subject searches from the unauthorized or nonpreferred terms they may have entered to the authorized or valid headings for the subject in question. USE terms include synonyms in direct and inverted word order, alternative spellings (including singular and plural forms), alternative endings, changed or canceled headings, abbreviations and acronyms, phrases in different word order, and occasionally, opposite terms that are often treated together in works. Examples of USE references are shown below.

Emancipation
USE **Liberty**

English hymns
USE **Hymns, English**

Illiteracy
USE **Literacy**

Machine-readable Catalog System
USE **MARC System**

Resemblance, Protective
USE **Mimicry (Biology)**

Unconventional warfare
USE **Guerrilla warfare**

In the print and microfiche versions of LCSH, reciprocal entries appear under the valid headings with the symbol UF (used for) preceding the nonpreferred terms. For example:

Liberty
UF Emancipation

Hymns, English
UF English hymns

Literacy
UF Illiteracy

MARC System
UF Machine-readable Catalog System

Mimicry (Biology)
UF Resemblance, Protective

Guerrilla warfare
UF Unconventional warfare

Hierarchical Relationships [MARC Authority Field 55X]

Previously included under what were called *see also* references, hierarchical references indicate topics that are either broader or narrower in scope than the one in question. Two symbols are used for these purposes: BT (broader topics) and NT (narrower topics). For example:

Poetry
BT Literature
NT Children's poetry
Classical poetry
Lyric poetry
Odes

Lyric poetry
  BT Poetry
  NT Ballads
        Dithyramb
        Odes
        Sonnets

Sonnets
  BT Lyric poetry

Headings connected by the BT or NT references are all valid headings. Each heading is connected to the heading or headings on the level immediately above or below it in the appropriate hierarchy or hierarchies. Therefore, there is no direct link between the heading **Poetry** and the heading **Sonnets** or **Dithyramb**. However, this policy may be relaxed where the hierarchies are not well or clearly defined. For instance, the heading **Odes** is linked to both **Poetry** and **Lyric poetry**. In MARC authority records, the broader topics are traced in field $55X$ in the record for the narrower topic.

Associative Relationships [MARC Authority Field 55*X*]

The symbol RT (related topic) is used to link headings that are related in concept but not in a hierarchical sense. Such references are usually made for the following types of relationships: headings with meanings that overlap to some extent, headings representing a discipline and the object studied, and headings representing persons and their fields of endeavor. Examples are shown below.

  Aliens
    RT Citizenship
        Immigrants
        Naturalization

  Entomology
    RT Insects

  God
    RT Theism

  Law
    RT Jurisprudence
        Legislation

  Physicians
    RT Medicine

    In the print and microfiche versions of the subject headings list, instructions for RT references are provided under both terms involved.

Theism	God
RT God	RT Theism

Medicine	Physicians
RT Physicians	RT Medicine

In MARC authority records, RT references are traced in records for both headings.

The following entry, taken from LCSH, illustrates the different types of cross-references associated with the heading **Inter-library loans**.

> **Inter-library loans**
> UF Book lending
>   Books, Lending of
>   Loans, Inter-library
> BT Libraries—Circulation, loans
>   Library cooperation
> RT Exchanges, Literary and scientific
> NT Document delivery

In explanation, the cross-references mean that *Book lending; Books, Lending of;* and *Loans, Inter-library* are synonymous terms not used as headings for the concept represented by the subject heading **Inter-library loans**, that **Libraries—Circulation, loans** and **Library cooperation**—both valid headings—represent broader concepts, that **Document delivery** represents a narrower topic, and that **Exchanges, Literary and scientific** represents a concept related to the heading **Inter-library loans**, but not in a hierarchical sense.

Figure 8-2 shows the MARC authority records for the heading **Inter-library loans**.

General References

In addition to the references discussed above, there is a type of general or blanket reference, represented by the symbol SA (see also), which refers from one heading to a group of headings or to subdivisions used under other headings. For example:

> **Courts of last resort**
> SA *names of individual supreme courts*

> **Cranberries**
> **—Diseases and pests**
> SA *names of pests, e.g.,* Cranberry root-worm

> **Atlases**
> SA *subdivision* Maps *under names of countries, cities, etc., and under topics*

```
▶ ARN:        2115640           Rec stat:    n
  Entered:     19871218          Replaced:    19871218
  Type:      z      Enc lvl:     n       Source:          Lang:
  Roman:     ▮      Upd status:  a       Mod rec:         Name use: b
  Govt agn:  ▮      Ref status:  b       Subj:       a    Subj use: a
  Series:    n      Auth status: a       Geo subd: i      Ser use:  b
  Ser num:   n      Auth/ref:    a       Name:     n      Rules:    n ¶
▶   1   010         sh 85067196  ¶
▶   2   040         DLC ‡c DLC ¶
▶   3   053         Z713 ¶
▶   4   150   0     Inter-library loans ¶
▶   5   450   0     Book lending ¶
▶   6   450   0     Books, Lending of ¶
▶   7   450   0     Loans, Inter-library ¶
▶   8   550   0     Exchanges, Literary and scientific ¶
▶   9   550   0     Libraries ‡x Circulation, loans ‡w g ¶
▶  10   550   0     Library cooperation ‡w g ¶
```

```
▶ ARN:        3035505           Rec stat:    n
  Entered:     19911005          Replaced:    19911005
  Type:      z      Enc lvl:     n       Source:          Lang:
  Roman:     ▮      Upd status:  a       Mod rec:         Name use: b
  Govt agn:  ▮      Ref status:  a       Subj:       a    Subj use: a
  Series:    n      Auth status: a       Geo subd: ▮      Ser use:  b
  Ser num:   n      Auth/ref:    a       Name:     n      Rules:    n ¶
▶   1   010         sh 91004122  ¶
▶   2   040         DLC ‡c DLC ¶
▶   3   150   0     Inter-library loans ‡x Policy statements ¶
▶   4   450   0     Policy statements for inter-library loans ¶
▶   5   670         Work cat.: Morris, L.R. Interlibrary loan policies directory,
  1991. ¶
```

FIGURE 8-2   Subject authority records for **Inter-library loans.**

ASSIGNING SUBJECT HEADINGS—SPECIAL MATERIALS

General guidelines for assigning subject headings are discussed in Chapter 7. The Library of Congress also has established policies regarding subject heading assignment for specific types of works. Some of the most common types are discussed below. The examples shown follow the format of the print version of LCSH, where the subdivisions are preceded by the symbol dash (—) rather than by the MARC codes.

Subject Headings for Literary Works[10]

There are two main types of works in the field of literature: (1) literary works and (2) works *about* literature. A literary work may consist of an individual work or a collection of works by one or more authors. A work about literature may focus on literature in general, in a particular language or from a particular nationality, on a particular period and/or genre of literature, on a particular author, or on a particular work. Subject headings are assigned to bring out various aspects, including language, nationality, genre or form, theme, character, authorship, etc.

---

[10]*Library of Congress Subject Headings: Principles of Structure and Policies for Application.* Op. cit. Pp. 60–63. And Library of Congress, Subject Cataloging Division. Op. cit. H1155.2, H1155.4, H1155.6, H1155.8

Works about literature in general

Works about literature in general are assigned appropriate headings regarding the approach, type, or form of literature treated in the work.

> **Literature—History and criticism**
> (for a history and/or discussion of literature in general)
>
> **Criticism**
> (for a work on the principles of literary criticism, not used with a work of criticism)
>
> **Poetics**
>
> **American fiction—20th century—History and criticism**
>
> **Drama—20th century—Congresses**
>
> **Poetry, Modern—19th century—Bibliography**

Works discussing the relationship between literature and other subjects are given headings such as **Literature and technology, Literature and history, Music and literature,** and **Politics and literature.**

Discussions about particular themes in literature are assigned **[Subject or theme] in literature** in addition to other appropriate literature headings.

> **Politics in literature**
> (For a study of political themes in twentieth-century American fiction, assign this heading in addition to **American fiction—20th century—History and criticism.**)
>
> **Soldiers in literature**
>
> **War in literature**

The phrase **in literature** is free-floating; in other words, any valid heading may be combined with this phrase to form a new heading, such as **Prophecy in literature,** even though the combination is not listed in LCSH or the Subject Authority File.

A discussion about a particular individual as a theme or character in literature, fiction, drama, poetry, etc. is given the heading **[name of person** (in AACR2R form)] **in fiction, drama, poetry, etc.** For instance:

> **Shakespeare, William, 1564-1616, in fiction, drama, poetry, etc.**
>
> **Nixon, Richard M. (Richard Milhous), 1913-   , in fiction, drama, poetry, etc.**

Anthologies and collections of literary works by more than one author

In addition to other appropriate topical headings, a literary form heading is assigned as a main heading.

Literature—Collections
(for an anthology of world literature not limited to any language or genre)

Drama, Medieval
(for an anthology or collection of medieval drama not limited to a particular language or nationality; note that the subdivision —**Collections** is not used.)

American drama—20th century
(for a collection of twentieth-century American plays)

In each of these cases, the literature heading represents the form rather than the subject content of the work. The subdivision —**Collections** is not free-floating and may be used with a given heading only when so listed in LCSH or the Subject Authority File. The distinction between a collection of and a discussion of literature is indicated by adding to the latter the subdivision —**History and criticism**, e.g., **French literature—20th century—History and criticism.**

If a collection is organized around a particular theme, an additional topical heading with an appropriate literary form subdivision is also assigned. For example:

Mother, I will always love you / edited by Susan Polis Schutz
1. **Mothers—Poetry.**
2. **American poetry—Women authors.**
3. **American poetry—20th century.**

New plays for the black theatre / edited by Woodie King, Jr.
1. **American drama—Afro-American authors.**
2. **American drama—20th century.**
3. **Afro-Americans—Drama.**

The praise of Lincoln : an anthology of poems
1. **American poetry—19th century.**
2. **Lincoln, Abraham, 1809-1865—Poetry.**

Late harvest: a gathering of rural American writing / edited by David R. Pichaske
1. **Country life—United States—Literary collections.**
2. **Wilderness areas—United States—Literary collections.**
3. **American literature.**

Works written by individual authors

Headings representing major literary genres, e.g., **American drama** or **German fiction**, are *not* assigned to individual literary works except in the case of literary works for children, which do receive form headings. In other words, the heading **American fiction—19th century** is not assigned to Mark Twain's *The Adventures of Tom Sawyer* nor the heading **English poetry—19th century** to Tennyson's *In Memoriam*. In the case of collected works by one author, a literary form heading is assigned only when the form is highly specific, e.g., **Allegories; Fables; Fairy tales; Radio stories; Amateur theater; Carnival plays; Children's plays; College and school drama; Didactic drama; Radio plays; Sonnets, American;** and **Concrete poetry.**

If a literary work to be cataloged is a drama or poem featuring a specific theme or is based on the life of a real person, a topical heading in the form of the topic or the personal name with the subdivision **—Drama** or **—Poetry** is used.

> *Henry IV, part 2 ; Henry V* / by William Shakespeare
> 1. **Henry IV, King of England, 1367-1413—Drama.**
> 2. **Henry V, King of England, 1387-1422—Drama.**

It is easy to confuse the situations in which the heading **[Name]—Drama** or **[Name]—Poetry** is used with those in which the heading **[Name] in fiction, drama, poetry, etc.** is appropriate. The former is used for a drama or poem featuring the person named as a character, while the latter is used for a discussion of (i.e., a work about) the person as a character in literature.

If a collection of works in various forms by an individual author centers around a particular theme, a topical heading with the subdivision **—Literary collections** is used. For example:

> *Selected works of Angelina Weld Grimke* / edited by Carolivia Herron
> 1. **Afro-Americans—Literary collections.**

For a collection of novels or stories by an individual author, the form subdivision **—Fiction** is assigned only under an identifiable topic, e.g., **Automobile racing—Fiction.** For an individual novel or story, a topical heading with the subdivision **—Fiction** is assigned only if the work is biographic fiction, historical fiction, or an animal story.

> *King Leopold's soliloquy* / Mark Twain
> 1. **Léopold II, King of the Belgians, 1835-1909—Fiction.**
> 2. **Zaire—History—To 1908—Fiction.**

Gate of rage / C.Y. Lee
  1. **China—History—Tiananmen Square Incident, 1989—Fiction.**

Works about individual authors: Biography and criticism

A work about an individual author is assigned a personal name heading in AACR2R form with or without a subdivision. For subdivisions, those which may be used are the ones listed under the pattern heading **Shakespeare.**

> **Kafka, Franz, 1883-1924**
> **Defoe, Daniel, 1661?-1731—Political and social views**
> **Goethe, Johann Wolfgang von, 1749-1832—Dramatic works**[11]

The subdivision **—Biography** or a subdivision denoting a biographic approach is used only when the work in hand is a true biography of the author. In this case, a second heading representing the class of persons to which the author belongs is also assigned.

Dostoyevsky : dreamer and prophet / Judith Gunn
  1. **Dostoyevsky, Fyodor, 1821-1881—Biography.**
  2. **Novelists, Russian—19th century—Biography.**

Conversations with Mary McCarthy / edited by Carol Gelderman
  1. **McCarthy, Mary, 1912-   —Interviews.**
  2. **Authors, American—20th century—Interviews.**

If the work contains both biographic information and criticism of the author's works, the personal name heading without subdivision is assigned.

Kafka / Pietro Citati
  1. **Kafka, Franz, 1883-1924.**
  2. **Authors, Austrian—20th century—Biography.**

Critical works without biographic information are assigned the personal name heading with the subdivision **—Criticism and interpretation** or another more specific subdivision designating criticism.

---

[11]Note that this heading, assigned to works about Goethe's plays, is different from the heading **Goethe, Johann Wolfgang von, 1749-1832—Drama**, which is assigned to plays featuring Goethe as a character.

Understanding Graham Greene / by R.H. Miller
1. **Greene, Graham, 1904-   —Criticism and interpretation.**

Works about Individual Works

For a work that contains criticisms or commentaries on another work, the uniform title for the work commented on is assigned in addition to other appropriate headings. If the work commented on is of known authorship, a [**Name. Title**] subject heading is used, as shown in the asterisked heading in the following example:

Defoe's politics : Parliament, power, kingship, and Robinson Crusoe / Manuel Schonhorn
1. **Defoe, Daniel, 1661?-1731—Political and social views.**
*2. **Defoe, Daniel, 1661?-1731. Robinson Crusoe.**
3. **Politics and literature—Great Britain—History—18th century.**
4. **Political fiction, English—History and criticism.**
5. **Great Britain—Politics and government—1660-1714.**

For a work about a foreign title, the uniform title consists of the author's name and the title in the original language regardless of the language in which the criticism is written.

Crime and punishment : a mind to murder / Gary Cox
1. **Dostoyevsky, Fyodor, 1821-1881. Prestuplenie i nakazanie.**

Oxford readings in Vergil's Aeneid / edited by S.J. Harrison
1. **Virgil. Aeneis.**

If the original work is entered under its title, the subject entry consists of the title alone.

Atlantic monthly

For an anonymous classic or a sacred work, the subject heading is in the AACR2R form of the uniform title.

Arabian nights
Beowulf
Bible. N.T. John
Chanson de Roland
Nibelungenlied
Pearl (Middle English poem)

Subject Headings for Biography[12]

Collective biography

When a work consists of four or more life histories, it is generally considered a *collective biography*. The heading **Biography** is assigned to a collective biography not limited to a place or a specific class of persons. When the persons treated in a collective biography belong to a specific period, a period subdivision is added, e.g., **Biography—20th century**. When the persons are from a particular place, the subject heading consists of the name of the place with the subdivision **—Biography**, e.g., **Illinois—Biography**. Two examples of general collective biography are given below.

> *Webster's American biographies* / Charles Van Doren, editor
> 1. **United States—Biography.**

> *The Biographical roll of honor*
> 1. **Biography—20th century—Dictionaries.**
> 2. **United States—Biography—Dictionaries.**

When the persons belong to a particular ethnic group or a particular profession or subject field, the appropriate term for the members of that group with the subdivision **—Biography** is used as the subject heading.

> **Arabs—Biography**
> **Chinese Americans—Biography**
> **Artists—Biography**
> **Authors, English—19th century—Biography**
> **Baseball—Coaches—Biography**
> **Dentists—Biography**
> **Physicists—Biography**

The subdivision **—Biography** is also used under names of corporate bodies and historical events, periods, etc.

> **United States. Army—Biography**
> **United States—History—Revolution, 1775-1783—Biography**

When the required term referring to a special class of persons is not available in LCSH, the subject heading consists of the name of the relevant subject or discipline with the subdivision **—Biography** (not free-floating in this case).

> **Art—Biography**
> (for all kinds of people associated with art, including artists, dealers, collectors, museum personnel, etc.)

[12]Library of Congress, Subject Cataloging Division. Op. cit. H1330.

If the work contains lists of works of authors active in particular fields as well as biographic information about those authors, the subdivision —**Bio-bibliography** is used under names of countries, cities, etc. and under subjects.

>California—Bio-bibliography
>American literature—Bio-bibliography
>Franciscans—Bio-bibliography

This subdivision is not used with names of individual persons.

Individual biography

For the biography (including autobiographic writings such as diaries and correspondence) of an individual, three types of headings may be assigned: (1) the name of the biographee, (2) a biographical heading, and (3) other appropriate headings.

1. The name of the biographee in AACR2R form is assigned. If the biography focuses on a specific aspect of the person's life, an appropriate subdivision taken from the list, "Free Floating Subdivisions Used under Names of Persons"[13] or from the pattern heading **Shakespeare, William, 1564-1616** (for literary authors) is added. Note that the subdivision —**Biography** is not used under names of individual persons except literary authors.

>**Freud, Sigmund, 1856-1939—Correspondence**
>**Reagan, Ronald**
>**Twain, Mark, 1835-1910—Biography**

2. In addition to the personal name heading, a *biographical* heading in the form of **[Class of persons]—[Place]—[Subdivision indicating type of biographic work]** is assigned. This practice in effect violates the general principle of *not* assigning a general heading and a specific heading encompassed in the general heading to the same work. The doubling (i.e., assigning both a specific heading and a general heading to the same work) is done for the purpose of collocating biographies of persons in the same field or with similar characteristics. For example, a biography of the basketball player Michael Jordan is assigned the following headings:

>*Michael Jordan* / by Phil Berger with John Rolfe
> 1. **Jordan, Michael, 1963-   —Juvenile literature.**
> 2. **Basketball players—United States—Biography—Juvenile literature.**

[13]Library of Congress, Subject Cataloging Division. Op. cit. H1110.

A biography of Nancy Reagan is assigned the following headings:

My turn : the memoirs of Nancy Reagan
1. **Reagan, Nancy, 1923-** .
2. **Reagan, Ronald.**
3. **Presidents—United States—Wives—Biography.**

3. For a partial biography or a biography which includes material about the field in which the biographee was involved, an additional topical heading or headings may be assigned to bring out the subject.

Franz Boas, social activist : the dynamics of ethnicity / Marshall Hyatt
1. **Boas, Franz, 1858-1942.**
2. **Anthropologists—United States—Biography.**
3. **Anthropology—History.**
4. **Anthropologists—Germany—Biography.**
5. **United States—Ethnic relations.**

To a work about a statesman, ruler, or head of state which contains information about his or her personal life, three types of headings are assigned: (1) the personal name heading with applicable subdivision(s), (2) a biographical heading, i.e., the class-of-persons heading with appropriate subdivision(s), and (3) a heading for the event or period of the country's history in which the person was involved.

The presidency of Theodore Roosevelt / Lewis L. Gould
1. **United States—Politics and government—1901-1909.**
2. **Roosevelt, Theodore, 1858-1919.**
3. **Presidents—United States—Biography.**

If the work contains mainly biographic material, the first two types of headings are assigned.

Woodrow Wilson / August Heckscher
1. **Wilson, Woodrow, 1856-1924.**
2. **Presidents—United States—Biography.**

If the work presents the history of the jurisdiction for the period or events in which a statesman or ruler participated but contains less than 20 percent biographic material, the biographical heading is omitted.

H.C. Bankole-Bright and politics in colonial Sierra Leone, 1919-1958 / Akintola J.G. Wyse
1. **Sierra Leone—Politics and government—1896-1961.**
2. **Bankole-Bright, H. C., d. 1958.**

Corporate headings, such as **Great Britain**. *Sovereign (1660-1685 : Charles II)*, which are used in descriptive cataloging as main or added entries, are not used as subject entries. Instead, the personal name heading and the appropriate heading for the history of the period are used.

EXERCISE C

Assign subject headings to the following topics: literature and biography.

1. A history of modern German literature

2. Essays on American and British fiction

3. A study of the themes of order and restraint in the poetry of Philip Larkin, a British author

4. Women and literature in France

5. Irony in Rabelais

6. Memoirs of Richard Nixon

7. Columbus and the age of discovery

8. Bibliographies of studies in Victorian literature for the years 1975–1984

9. A critical study of characterization in Jacobean tragedies

10. A commentary on the epistles of Peter and Jude

11. A study of the theme of friendship in fifteenth-century Chinese literature

12. Mary Stuart in sixteenth- and seventeenth-century literature: a critical study

13. A reader's guide to Walt Whitman

14. A journal of twentieth-century Spanish literature

SUBJECT HEADINGS FOR CHILDREN'S LITERATURE
Library of Congress List of Juvenile Headings

A special list of subject headings for children's literature also was developed by the Library of Congress. In 1965, the library initiated the Annotated Card (AC) Program for children's materials, with the purpose of providing more appropriate and extensive subject cataloging for juvenile titles through more liberal application of subject headings and through the use of headings more appropriate to juvenile users. In some cases, existing Library of Congress subject headings were reinterpreted or modified in order to achieve these purposes; in other cases, new headings were added. The result is a separate list of subject headings which represent exceptions to the master list of LC headings. It was first published in 1969 as *Subject Headings for Children's Literature*, and it has been kept current ever since. Beginning with the eighth edition of LCSH, the list, now entitled *AC Subject Headings*, has been included in LCSH, where it precedes the master list. In application, this list must be used in conjunction with the master list.

Subject Cataloging of Children's Materials

In LC cataloging records for materials intended for children up through age fifteen or the ninth grade, two sets of subject headings are assigned: (1) regular headings implying juvenile nature or with juvenile subdivisions and (2) alternative headings (called *AC headings*) for children's materials. These are discussed below.

Regular headings implying juvenile nature or with juvenile subdivisions

Topical or nonfictional juvenile materials are assigned appropriate topical headings with juvenile subdivisions such as **—Dictionaries, Juvenile; —Juvenile drama; —Juvenile fiction; —Juvenile films; —Juvenile literature** (for nonliterary works); **—Juvenile sound recordings** (not used with musical sound recordings); and **—Juvenile poetry.** Juvenile belles lettres are assigned juvenile literary form headings such as **Children's plays** and **Children's poetry** and/or regular literary form headings without juvenile subdivisions, e.g., **Ballads, Germanic.** In many cases, topical headings with juvenile literary form subdivisions are assigned to bring out themes, places, etc. This method is usually used when children's materials are integrated into the general collection of the library.

Alternative headings for children's materials

For libraries that maintain separate collections and/or catalogs for children, alternative headings consisting of regular subject headings without juvenile subdivisions supplemented by headings from *AC Subject Headings* (which may contain additional headings or variant forms of headings designed for use with children's materials) are provided on LC cataloging records. For juvenile belles lettres, topical headings with literary form subdivisions are assigned more liberally than in the case of adult materials in order to provide topical access to such materials. Many topical headings, which are not generally used with adult literature, are assigned to juvenile fiction and drama.

Examples of subject headings assigned to children's materials are shown below. On annotated cards and CIP (cataloging-in-publication) information for children's materials prepared by the Library of Congress, the AC subject headings, which may or may not differ from the regular headings, are enclosed in brackets. In MARC records, AC headings are identified by the second indicator 1 in 6XX fields.

Laura loves horses / by Joan Hewett
  [1. **Horsemanship—Fiction.**]

Charlotte's web / E.B. White
  [1. **Animals—Fiction.**
  2. **Fantasy.**]

Something big has been here / poems by Jack Prelutsky ; drawings by James Stevenson
  1. **Children's poetry, American.**
  [1. **American poetry.**
  2. **Humorous poetry.**]

Polaroid and other poems of view / Betsy Hearne
  1. **Young adult poetry, American.**
  [1. **American poetry.**]

Macmillan first dictionary / Judith S. Levey, editor in chief
  1. **English language—Dictionaries, Juvenile.**
  [1. **English language—Dictionaries.**]

Under the sea from A to Z / by Anne Doubilet ; photographs by David Doubilet
  1. **Marine fauna—Juvenile literature.**
  2. **Marine flora—Juvenile literature.**
  3. **English language—Alphabet—Juvenile literature.**
  [1. **Marine animals.**
  2. **Marine plants.**
  3. **Alphabet.**]

Mars / by James A. Corrick
  1. **Mars (Planet)—Juvenile literature.**
  2. **Mars (Planet)—Exploration—Juvenile literature.**
  [1. **Mars (Planet)**
  2. **Outer space—Exploration.**]

CHAPTER NINE
SEARS LIST OF SUBJECT
HEADINGS

Neither *Library of Congress Subject Headings* nor the earlier ALA list (described in Chap. 7) was judged suitable for the access needs of small and medium-sized general libraries. Accordingly, Minnie Earl Sears developed a new list with smaller libraries in mind. Recognizing the advantages of uniformity, in working out her list she decided to follow the general principles that underlie the Library of Congress list, with certain exceptions to meet the particular needs of small libraries. Therefore, although the Sears list is not an abridgment of the Library of Congress list, it is very similar in format and structure.

Sears' list was titled *List of Subject Headings for Small Libraries;* the first edition appeared in 1923. Since then, the list has gone through many editions, the most recent being the fourteenth. Sears was responsible for the first three (1923, 1926, and 1933). With the sixth edition, the title was changed to *Sears List of Subject Headings.* The editor of the fourteenth edition, which appeared in 1991, is Martha T. Mooney.[1]

Today, the Sears list is used widely by school libraries and small public libraries in the United States. Thus the Sears and the Library of Congress lists together serve as the two standard lists for subject headings for general libraries in this country.

Throughout the history of the Sears list, its editors have followed the general policy set forth by Minnie Earl Sears: close parallels with *Library of Congress Subject Headings* (LCSH) with variations and modifications as appropriate for smaller libraries. Recent editions of the Sears list also have incorporated headings from the Library of Congress's *Subject Headings for Children's Literature,* with a few exceptions where Sears headings are in a slightly different form. The variations, however, do not affect basic structure and principles. These are principles of alphabetical specific headings first enunciated by Charles A. Cutter: specific and direct entry, common usage, uniformity (i.e., uniform headings), and

---

[1]Other editors of the Sears list have been fourth (1939) and fifth (1944), Isabel Stevenson Munro; sixth (1950) through eighth (1959), Bertha M. Frick; ninth (1965) through twelfth (1982), Barbara M. Westby; and thirteenth (1986), Carmen Rovira and Caroline Reyes.

syndetic devices.² Such variations as there are usually occur in the following areas: terminology, e.g., **Social work** instead of **Social service;** spelling, e.g., **Marijuana** instead of **Marihuana;** word order, e.g., **Colleges and universities** instead of **Universities and colleges;** and a lower degree of specificity, e.g., combining closely related headings such as **Art, French** and **Art—France** into **Art, French** only.

In format, the Sears list resembles the print version of LCSH. Headings and their subdivisions used as subject entries in a catalog are printed in boldface type. Those printed in lightface roman are not to be used as subject entries; they are synonymous terms or variant forms of authorized headings and are followed by *see* references to the terms that are used as headings. Sample entries are shown below.

> Agricultural pests—Biological control. *See* **Pests—Biological control**
>
> **Biological rhythms   574.1**
> *See also* **Jet lag**
> *x*   Biological clocks; Biology—Periodicity; Biorhythms
> *xx*   **Periodicity**
>
> Conundrums. *See* **Riddles**
>
> Cookery, Microwave. *See* **Microwave cookery**
>
> **Electric heating   621.402; 644; 697**
> *x*   Electricity in the home
> *xx*   **Heating**

Except for very general subject headings, each valid heading in the Sears list is followed by one or more classification numbers taken from the *Abridged Dewey Decimal Classification.* Since the list is designed for use in small libraries, the corresponding DDC numbers are seldom carried out more than four places beyond the decimal point. The symbols *x* and *xx*, indicating cross-references, are explained on pages 214 and 215.

The following sections of this chapter discuss and explain the basic technical features of the Sears list. The topics covered are main headings, cross-references, subdivisions, classes of headings omitted from the list, and subject headings for biography and literature. Readers should note that because the Sears list is a close parallel to LCSH, much of what is said about it repeats what was said in the preceding chapter about LCSH. This repetition is unavoidable, given the purposes of a book on library

²For a discussion of these principles, see "Principles of the Sears List of Subject Headings." In Martha T. Mooney, ed., *Sears List of Subject Headings.* 14th ed. New York: H. W. Wilson Company, 1991. Pp. 1–23.

cataloging and classification; many readers will need all pertinent information on the Sears list gathered into one chapter.

Sears headings consist of single nouns, compounds, adjective-noun phrases, and prepositional phrases. The list contains cross-references and provides for subdivisions of headings. Many terms that can be used in subject cataloging according to the Sears list do not appear explicitly in the list but must be supplied by catalogers. All these topics are discussed and explained below.

MAIN HEADINGS
Single-Noun Headings

Most of the broad fields of knowledge, and concrete objects, are represented by headings consisting of a single noun, e.g., **Chemistry, Education, Law, Books, Rocks, Water,** etc. When a noun has more than one meaning, a qualifier is added in parentheses to limit the heading to one subject or concept, e.g., **Bridge (Game)** or **Masks (Sculpture).** The choice of the singular or the plural form depends on the term involved. In general, abstract concepts are represented by the singular noun, e.g., **Credit,** while concrete objects are represented by the plural, e.g., **Books.** Sometimes both the singular and the plural forms of a noun are used as headings. In such cases, they carry different meanings, e.g., **Essay** (the technique) and **Essays** (the works) or **Symphony** (as a musical form) and **Symphonies** (musical scores).

Phrase Headings

Compound headings

Compound headings consist of two nouns or noun phrases connected by the word *and.* They are mainly used for the following purposes: (1) to connect topics or concepts which are usually treated together in books, e.g., **Skis and skiing, Clothing and dress,** or **Cliff dwellers and cliff dwellings,** (2) to connect opposite subjects that are usually treated together in books, e.g., **Debtor and creditor** or **Open and closed shop,** and (3) to express a relationship between two concepts or things, e.g., **Church and education** or **Medicine and religion.**

Adjectival headings

Adjectival headings are used when a subject or concept cannot be properly expressed by a single noun. The most common type of adjectival heading consists of a noun or noun phrase with one or more adjectival modifiers, e.g., **English language, Space flight, Ground effect machines, College students, Children's songs,** etc. In many cases, the heading is inverted in order to bring the noun forward as the entry element, e.g., **Chemistry, Physical and theoretical** or **Trusts, Industrial.**

Prepositional phrase headings

Some concepts are expressed by nouns or noun phrases connected by prepositions that express their relationships, e.g., **Cookery for the sick, Electricity in agriculture, Religion in the public schools,** or **Detergent pollution of rivers, lakes,** etc.

CROSS-REFERENCES

Cross-references are used to guide users who consult the catalog under terms that are not used as subject headings to those which are and to call users' attention to materials related to the topics being consulted. While a heading may appear many times in the catalog, each reference is made only once regardless of how many times the heading involved has been assigned to bibliographic records. Cross-references appear in three forms for different purposes: specific *see* references, specific *see also* references, and general references. When any heading in the Sears list has cross-references associated with it, there are coded instructions under the heading to indicate what should be done. These instructions are described and explained in the following sections.

Specific *See* References

Specific *see* references appear under unauthorized terms and indicate that another term should be used. In the Sears list, instruction for making *see* references is given after the authorized heading and indicated by a preceding *x*. The symbol *x* indicates that *see* references are to be made *from* the terms that follow *to* the heading immediately above it. For example:

> **Physicians**
> *x* Doctors

> **Art, Modern**
> *x* Modern art

This means that in the printed Sears list there will be the lead-in terms *Doctors* and *Modern art* followed by *see* references to **Physicians** and **Art, Modern,** respectively.

> Doctors. *See* **Physicians**
> Modern art. *See* **Art, Modern**

It also means that if a cataloger is adding a record to the catalog using the subject heading **Physicians,** he or she should check to see that the catalog includes a *see* reference to **Physicians** from the lead-in term *Doctors.*

In general, *see* references are made from synonymous or near-synonymous terms and from inverted forms that are not used as subject headings. Occasionally, a *see* reference is made from a more specific term that is not used as a heading to the more general term that is used.

> Cooking utensils *See* **Household equipment and supplies**

Specific *See also* References

A *see also* reference connects a heading to a related heading or headings; such a reference is made only when the library has material listed under both headings. A *see also* reference is made for one of two purposes: to refer from a general subject to more specific parts of it (a downward hierarchical reference) or to refer from a subject to a related subject of more or less equal specificity (a same-level reference). A *see also* reference is *not* made from a given heading to one that is more general (an upward reference).

See also references are listed directly under many headings. In addition, reverse instructions are given under the headings referred from, indicated by the symbol *xx* (meaning *see also from*). This means that a cross-reference is to be made *from* the heading preceded by *xx* *to* the heading under which the *xx* listing appears. For instance, for the headings **Bees,** Sears shows the following:

Bees	**Honey**
See also **Honey**	*See also* **Bees**
xx **Honey; Insects**	*xx* **Bees**

This tells users who look under **Bees** that they might want to look under **Honey** as well. It also tells catalogers that under **Honey** and **Insects** there should be *see also* references to **Bees.** Thus users looking under either **Honey** or **Insects** will find a cross-reference to **Bees.** The two instructions given above result in the following references in the catalog:

Bees
See also
Honey

Honey
See also
Bees

Insects
See also
Bees

Users looking under **Bees** will not find a cross-reference to **Insects** because that would be an upward reference.

General References

A *general reference,* in either the *see* or the *see also* form, covers an entire category or class of headings rather than an individual heading. This device is used to save space in both the subject headings list and the library catalog. A general explanation or direction is given instead of a long list of individual headings.

Dogs
See also classes of dogs, e.g., **Guide dogs; Hearing ear dogs;** etc.; also names of specific breeds, e.g., **Collies;** etc.

Rivers
See also **Dams, Floods;** ... also names of rivers

Rocket planes
See also names of rocket planes, e.g., **X-15 (Rocket aircraft);** etc.

Army.   *See* **Armies; Military art and science;** and names of countries with the subhead *Army,* e.g., **United States. Army;** etc.

Examples of Cross-References

Following is an example of the different types of cross-references required for a particular heading.

Automobiles   388.3; 629.222
See also **Buses; Sports cars; Trucks;** also names of specific makes and models of automobiles, e.g., **Ford automobile;** etc.
x   Cars (Automobiles); Locomotion; Motor cars
xx   **Transportation, Highway; Vehicles**

Based on these instructions, the following references would be made in connection with the authorized heading **Automobiles**:

Automobiles
See also
Buses
Sports cars
Trucks
also names of specific makes and models of automobiles, e.g., **Ford automobile;** etc.

Cars (Automobiles)
See
Automobiles

Locomotion
See
Automobiles

Motor cars
See
Automobiles

Transportation, Highway
See also
Automobiles

Vehicles
See also
Automobiles

SUBDIVISIONS

In the Sears list, many general subjects are subdivided to indicate their specific aspects or to provide a subarrangement for a large number of works on the same subject. There are several types of subdivisions: subject or topical, form, period or chronologic, and place, local, or geographic.

Subject or Topical Subdivisions

A subject or topical subdivision added to a main heading brings out a specific aspect or characteristic of the general subject.

English language—Business English
English language—Dialects
English language—Etymology

Education—Curricula
Education—Finance

Form Subdivisions

A form subdivision expresses the physical or bibliographic form of the work being cataloged.

Chemistry—Dictionaries
Library science—Bibliography
Railroads—Maps
Space sciences—Periodicals

Some of the so-called form subdivisions actually represent the author's point of view or approach to the subject.

Economics—History
Gold—Law and legislation
Medicine—Study and teaching
Science—Philosophy

Form subdivisions are comparable with standard subdivisions in the Dewey Decimal Classification, which is treated in Chapter 12 of this text. Because many form subdivisions and some topical subdivisions are so common that they are applicable to many subjects, they are not enumerated under each heading with which they may be used but instead are listed together in the Sears introduction (pp. 29–31, 14th edition). Because they may be used under subject headings where applicable, the following combinations may be made by the cataloger even though they are not actually so listed:

Librarians—Directories
Music—Bibliography
Television—Law and legislation
Chemistry—Terminology

In addition to the list of common subdivisions mentioned above, instructions for the use of these subdivisions are also provided in the list itself under the appropriate terms.

Bibliography
  also names of persons, places, and subjects with the subdivision *Bibliography*, e.g., **Shakespeare, William, 1564-1616—Bibliography; United States— Bibliography; Agriculture—Bibliography;** etc.

Terminology. *See* **Names;** and subjects with the subdivision *Terminology*, e.g., **Botany—Terminology;** etc.

In addition, many subdivisions are applicable to headings in a particular category. Instead of enumerating these subdivisions under each heading in the category, one heading is chosen as the *key* heading under which typical subdivisions are listed. The following headings serve as the key patterns for subdivisions; in other words, they are analogous to pattern headings in LCSH.

Category	*Key heading*
Authors	**Shakespeare, William, 1564-1616**
Presidents	**Presidents—United States**
Peoples	**Indians of North America**
Countries	**United States**
States	**Ohio**
Cities	**Chicago (Ill.)**
Languages	**English language**
Literatures	**English literature**
Wars	**World War, 1939-1945**

The subdivisions listed under them may be used whenever appropriate with other headings in the same categories. For example, the subdivisions listed under **World War, 1939-1945** may be used with the heading for another war, e.g., **Korean War, 1950-1953—Causes.**

EXERCISE A

Assign subject headings from the Sears list to the following topics.

1. Reading habits of adolescents

2. Advertising and selling by mail

3. Encyclopedia of science and technology

4. *Library Journal*

5. Handbook of chemistry and physics

6. History of the First World War

7. *Journal of Plant Pathology*

8. A list of scientific journals

9. *Time* (magazine)

10. A Russian-English dictionary of medical terms

11. A bibliography of library and information science

12. Opportunities in textile careers

13. An amateur photographer's handbook

14. *Sears List of Subject Headings*

Period or Chronological Subdivisions

National history lends itself to chronological treatment. In the Sears list, chronological or period subdivisions are provided under the history of the United States and other countries about which American libraries are likely to have sizeable collections. Period subdivisions appear as further subdivisions under the subdivision —**History.**

>   **United States—History—1600-1775, Colonial period**
>   **—1689-1697, King William's War**
>   **—1775-1783, Revolution**
>   **—1861-1865, Civil War**
>
>   **Japan—History—0-1868**
>   **—1868-1945**
>   **—1945-1952, Allied occupation**
>   **—1952-**

Even though **United States** is a key heading, the period subdivisions listed under it may not be used under headings of other countries, because each country has a unique history and the period subdivisions appropriate to one country may not apply to other countries.

Place, Local, or Geographic Subdivisions

Many works deal with a subject with regard to a specific locality. For a subject that lends itself to such treatment, the Sears list authorizes geographic subdivisions; such authorization is indicated by a parenthetical statement following the main heading. For example, a heading such as **Flowers** (May subdiv. geog.) indicates that the following headings, though not listed, may be used as subject entries:

>   **Flowers—United States**
>   **Flowers—Hawaii**
>   **Flowers—Honolulu**

Some geographic subdivisions appear in the adjectival form.

>   **Folk art** (May subdiv. geog. or ethnic adjective form, e.g.,
>   **Folk art, American;** etc.)

EXERCISE B

Assign subject headings from the Sears list to the following.

1. Museums in New York City

2. Popular songs in the United States

3. History of Flemish painting

4. Canadian foreign policy, 1945–1954

5. *The Eisenhower Years: A Historical Assessment*

6. Party politics in Australia

7. Directory of hospitals in Athens, Georgia

8. The reign of Elizabeth, 1558–1603

9. A pictorial guide to San Francisco

10. *Famous American Military Leaders*

11. *Norwegian Folk Tales: A Collection*

12. *Getting to Know Iran and Iraq*

13. *The Land and People of Switzerland*

CLASSES OF HEADINGS OMITTED

Personal names, corporate names, and other proper names are potential subject headings because many works are written about individual persons, institutions, places, events, and so on. It is not practical or even possible to include in the subject headings list all names that may become subjects of works. Therefore, any catalog using Sears subject headings will show many subject entries that do not appear in the Sears list. When new names are needed for subject entries, the cataloger must derive the appropriate form. Most names that do not appear in the subject list are proper names, for persons, families, places, or corporate bodies. Some, however, are common or generic names for objects or activities.

In the arrays given below, the leading generic terms (those preceding *e.g.*) appear in the main list, with instructions for providing the headings that are to be supplied by the cataloger.

Proper Names

1. *Names of persons.* The form of a personal heading and its cross-references is established according to the *Anglo-American Cataloguing Rules* in order that works written by and about the same person can be collocated in the catalog. The name authority record (explained in Chap. 5) established for a person as an author serves to determine the form of both author and subject entries for that person. If a person whose name is required as a subject heading has not appeared as an author in the catalog, a name authority record should be established according to the same procedure as in descriptive cataloging. Examples of names of persons as subject headings are as follows:

> **Boone, Daniel, 1734-1820**
> **Bush, George, 1924-**

By way of exception, a few personal headings are included in the list. For example, **Jesus Christ** is included because of unique subdivisions; **Shakespeare, William, 1564-1616** is included to show subdivisions that may be used under names of other voluminous authors (in other words, it serves as a *key* heading); and **Napoleon I, Emperor of the French, 1769-1821—Drama** is included because it is used as an example under the heading **Drama**.

2. *Names of families.* The heading for the name of a family consists of the family name followed by the word **family,** e.g., **Kennedy family, Brontë family,** etc.

3. *Names of places.* Very few geographic or place names are listed as such in Sears. Those which are included serve as key headings for treatment of analogous headings. Geographic or place names fall into several different categories, as described below.

    a. Political units
        (1) Countries (e.g., **India, Belgium,** etc.). A number of countries are included to show their unique period subdivisions. **United States** serves as a key heading. The subdivisions (except period subdivisions which are not transferable) under **United States** may be used with names of other countries, e.g.,

> **India—Geography**
> **Belgium—Population**

        (2) States (e.g., **Colorado, Wyoming,** etc.). **Ohio,** as a key state, is listed with subdivisions which can be used under names of other states.

(3) Provinces, etc. (e.g., **Scotland, Ontario, British Columbia,** etc.).

(4) Counties (e.g., **Cook County (Ill.)**)

(5) Cities (e.g., **San Francisco (Calif.), Athens (Ga.), Dijon (France),** etc.). The name of the country or the state (if in the United States) is added to the name of a local place in accordance with AACR2R (1988) rules for geographic names. For subdivisions, **Chicago (Ill.)** serves as the key city.

b. Groups of states or countries (e.g., **Gulf States, Baltic States)**

c. Geographic features

(1) Mountain ranges and individual mountains (e.g., **Smokey Mountains, Mont Blanc,** etc.)

(2) Island groups and individual islands (e.g., **Virgin Islands, Jamaica,** etc.)

(3) River valleys and individual rivers (e.g., **Ohio Valley, Mississippi River,** etc.)

(4) Regions, oceans, lakes, etc. **(Indian Ocean, Kentucky Lake,** etc.)

4. *Names of nationalities* (e.g., **Belgians, Germans,** etc.).

5. *Names of national languages and literatures* (e.g., **Turkish language, Austrian literature,** etc.). **English language** and **English literature** are the key headings.

6. *Names of battles* (e.g., **Waterloo, Battle of, 1815).**

7. *Names of treaties* (e.g., **Portsmouth, Treaty of, 1905).**

8. *Names of Indian peoples* (e.g., **Navaho Indians, Oneida Indians,** etc.).

9. *Corporate Names.* Works about individual corporate bodies are assigned subject entries in the form of corporate name headings established according to AACR2R (1988) that are compatible with headings used as main and added entries. Among the types of corporate names that may figure as subject headings are the following:

a. Names of associations, societies, clubs, etc. (e.g., **American Chemical Society, American Library Association,** etc.)

b. Names of institutions: colleges, libraries, hospitals, etc. (e.g., **Smith College, Florida State University, New York Public Library, Massachusetts General Hospital,** etc.)

c. Names of religious denominations (e.g., **Methodist Church,** etc.)

d. Names of government bodies (e.g., **United States. Navy; California. Legislature;** etc.)

e. Names of hotels, retail stores, ships, etc. (e.g., **Christina (Ship),** etc.)

Common Names

In addition to the proper names mentioned above, there are a large number of generic names, mostly in scientific fields, that may be used as subject headings even though they are not listed. In each category, the more common species are named in the list.

1. Names of
   a. Animals (e.g., **Invertebrates, Amphibians, Kangaroos,** etc.)
   b. Birds (e.g., **Swallows**)
   c. Fishes (e.g., **Perch, Trout,** etc.)
   d. Flowers (e.g., **Carnations**)
   e. Foods (e.g., **Pork**)
   f. Fruits (e.g., **Grapefruit**)
   g. Games (e.g., **Badminton, Backgammon,** etc.)
   h. Musical instruments (e.g., **Harpsichord**)
   i. Nuts (e.g., **Chestnut**)—use the singular form because the same heading is used for the tree
   j. Sports (e.g., **Ice fishing**)
   k. Tools (e.g., **Hammers**)
   l. Trees (e.g., **Pine, Maple, Peach,** etc.)—use the singular form
   m. Vegetables (e.g., **Carrots, Spinach,** etc.)
2. Names of diseases (e.g., **Measles**)
3. Names of organs and regions of the body (e.g., **Kidney, Leg,** etc.).

4. Names of chemicals (e.g., **Glycine, Potassium chloride,** etc.)
5. Names of minerals (e.g., **Chlorite, Topaz,** etc.)

In the Sears list, instructions for providing the headings mentioned above are included under the broad terms. For example:

> **Tools**
> *See also* **Agricultural machinery;** ... also names of specific tools, e.g., **Saws;** etc.

> **Trees** (May subdiv. geog.)
> Names of all trees are not included in this list but are to be added as needed, in the singular form, e.g., **Oak;** etc.

EXERCISE C

Assign subject headings from the Sears list to the following.

1. Swedish word origins

2. *Poems for Thanksgiving* (by various authors)

3. Russian grammar

4. *The Peace Corps in Action*

5. *Chemicals of Life: Enzymes, Vitamins, Hormones*

6. A history of the American Medical Association

7. NATO and Europe

8. The German community in Cincinnati

9. *Wonders of the Himalayas*

10. *Eastern Europe: Czechoslovakia, Hungary, Poland*

11. *The Department of Defense: A History*

12. Sparrows of Asia

SUBJECT HEADINGS FOR SPECIAL TYPES OF MATERIALS

Certain types of library materials require special treatment; of these, the most common are biography and literature.

Subject Headings for Biography

Individual biography

For a biography of one, two, or three individuals, the name of each individual is used as a subject heading; the form of the heading should agree with the author entry for the same person. A biography of Robert F. Kennedy, for example, is assigned the heading

Kennedy, Robert F., 1925-1968.

A biography of two or three of the Kennedy brothers would be assigned headings under the name of each.

Frequently, when the biography of a person also contains material about the field in which the person is concerned, a second subject heading representing the subject field is added. For example, if the biography of President John F. Kennedy contains a substantial amount of material on his administration, a second heading **United States—History—1961-1974** is assigned in addition to the personal heading.

For persons about whom there is a large amount of material, subdivisions are used for subarrangement. The heading **Shakespeare, William, 1564-1616** serves as the key for subdivisions to be used under other voluminous authors when there is a large amount of material. The subdivisions listed under the heading **Presidents—United States** may be used under headings for individual presidents, prime ministers, and other rulers. In small libraries, for most individual biographies, the personal name alone without any subdivision is sufficient as the heading.

For autobiographic writings, including journals, memoirs, and letters, in addition to autobiographies, a subject heading identical to the author entry is often assigned. This is important in catalogs in which subject entries are in a separate file from other entries or that allow searching in subject fields only. The additional heading is unnecessary in catalogs that interfile personal names regardless of whether they are author or subject entries or in automated systems that allow searching in both name and subject fields at the same time.

Collective biography

For a biography of more than three persons, a subject heading covering the entire group is assigned, instead of individual personal headings. Various kinds of collective biographies are discussed below:

General biography
If a collective biography is not limited to any geographic area or subject field or a particular class of people, the general form heading **Biography** is assigned, e.g., for Van Loon's *Lives*. For a book *about* biography, the heading **Biography (as a literary form)** is used. For biographic reference works that are arranged in dictionary form, e.g., *Webster's Biographical Dictionary* or *International Who's Who*, the heading **Biography—Dictionaries** is used.

Local biography
When a collective biography contains lives of people from a particular geographic area or a specific ethnic group, e.g., *Who's Who in Australia* and *Canadian Who's Who*, the subject heading is in the form of the geographic or ethnic name with the subdivision **—Biography** or **—Biography—Dictionaries.**

> **Australia—Biography—Dictionaries**
> **Canada—Biography—Dictionaries**
> **Blacks—Biography**

Classes of persons
When a collective biography contains lives of persons of a particular subject field or a class, a subject heading is assigned in the form of the term representing the members of the field or the class, e.g., **Chemists,**

Explorers, Philosophers, Sailors, etc. In some cases, the heading may be divided geographically, using the adjective form, e.g., **Actors, American; Composers, German; Statesmen, British;** etc.

When there is no appropriate term to represent the members of a field, or when the name of the class or group refers to the subject in general rather than to individuals, the heading assigned is in the form of the name of the field or group with the subdivision —**Biography.**

> **Baseball—Biography**
> **France—History—Revolution, 1789-1799—Biography**
> **Women—Biography**

The headings used with collective biographies are not assigned to individual biographies. For example, the heading **Musicians** or **Musicians, American** is not used with a biography of Billy Joel. However, a reference should be made from the collective heading to the individual headings, e.g.,

> **Musicians.** *See also* ... names of musicians.

Subject Headings for Literature

There are two distinctive categories of works in the field of literature: (1) works *about* literature and (2) literary works or specimens. These receive different treatment in subject cataloging.

Works about literature

These works, in which literature *is* the subject, are treated like other works with subject headings representing the content and the scope of the works.

> **Literature**
> (with or without subdivisions depending on the scope)

> **American literature**
> (use **English literature** as the key for subdivisions)

> **Drama**

> **German drama—History and criticism**

> **Essay**

> **English essays—History and criticism**

Many of the more general literature headings are subdivided for special aspects. These may be used when appropriate. In addition, the general subdivisions listed in the Sears introduction (pages 29–31) also may be used. Note that the subdivision —**History and criticism,** instead of —**History,** is used with literature headings.

The headings discussed above do not apply to works about individual authors or about works written by them. A work about an individual author or about his or her work is assigned a heading in the form of the author's name, e.g., **Dickens, Charles, 1812-1870.** The heading for Shakespeare serves as a key for subdivisions used with voluminous authors.

Literary works or specimens of literature

In these works, literature is the *form* rather than the *subject*. There are two categories of literary works: collections of works of more than one author and single or collected works by individual authors.

Collections of works of more than one author
A literary form heading, e.g., **Essays; American drama—Collections,** is assigned to a collection of works of more then one author. To differentiate a topical heading from a form heading containing the same term, the singular form is used as the topical heading (for a work *about* the literary form), and the plural form, when there is one, is used as the form heading (for the specimens). When there is no acceptable plural form of a noun, the subdivision —**Collections** is added.

Subject heading	Form heading for collections
Essay	Essays
Short story	Short stories
Literature	Literature—Collections
Spanish literature	Spanish literature—Collections
Poetry	Poetry—Collections
German poetry	German poetry—Collections

Works by individual authors
For an individual literary work, no form heading is assigned. In other words, **English drama** is not assigned to a play written by Shakespeare, nor **American fiction** to Hemingway's novel *The Old Man and the Sea.*

For collected works by an individual author, no literary form heading is assigned if the works are in one of the major forms such as drama, fiction, and poetry. However, for collected works in a minor form such as parodies, satire, and short stories by an individual author, headings similar to those used with collections by more than one author are assigned. For example, E. A. Poe's *Selected Tales* is assigned the heading **Short stories, American.** Minor literary forms are not listed under the national adjectives. However, the introduction to Sears (p. 13) indicates that the national adjective may be added after the name of the form if national treatment is needed.

Literary forms used as subdivisions

Subject entries are often assigned to novels, poems, and plays based on lives of individuals or historical events. The subdivisions —**Fiction,** —**Poetry,** or —**Drama** is added to the topical heading to distinguish these works from factual accounts on the subjects.

> **United States—History—1861-1865, Civil War—Fiction**
> (for a work such as *Gone with the Wind* by Margaret Mitchell)

> **Lincoln, Abraham, 1809-1865—Drama**
> (for a work such as *Abe Lincoln in Illinois* by Robert E. Sherwood)

EXERCISE D

Assign subject headings from the Sears list to each of the following.

1. *Lives of Famous French Dramatists*

2. *American Men and Women of Science*

3. *French Short Stories: A Collection*

4. *Stories of Maupassant*

5. *Commentaries on the New Testament*

6. *Life of Pablo Picasso*

7. *Modern American Secret Agents*

8. *Famous New Yorkers*

9. *Life of Daniel Boone*

10. *The Agony and the Ecstasy* (an American novel based on the life of Michelangelo)

11. *Best Sports Stories*

12. *A Day in the Life of President Johnson* (Lyndon B.)

13. *The Combat Nurses of World War II*

14. *Book of Poetry for Children*

15. *A Man for All Seasons* (an English drama based on the life of Sir Thomas More)

16. *A Study of Mark Twain's Novels*

CHAPTER TEN
MEDICAL SUBJECT HEADINGS
AND OTHER SUBJECT
CATALOGING SYSTEMS

In addition to *Library of Congress Subject Headings* and *Sears List of Subject Headings*, there are other systems of subject cataloging, some for special libraries and others for general collections. This chapter discusses *Medical Subject Headings* (MeSH) as an example of a specialized vocabulary and two other subject cataloging systems, PRECIS and COMPASS, developed in Great Britain.

MEDICAL SUBJECT HEADINGS

Medical Subject Headings (MeSH) is the system designed and used by the National Library of Medicine (NLM) for assigning subject headings to books and journal articles in the medical sciences. It has gained wide acceptance outside NLM and is now widely used by both health sciences libraries and abstracting and indexing services in the health sciences. Since it was based on *Library of Congress Subject Headings* (LCSH) but has departed considerably from it, it serves as a good example of how an existing system can be adapted to serve a special purpose.

Brief History[1]

In the 1940s, a subject authority card file was established at NLM for use by its own catalogers. The headings followed the patterns set by LCSH but were not the same. A decade later, NLM decided to integrate access to citations to medical books and journal articles by constructing a thesaurus of *Medical Subject Headings* (MeSH) to be used both by catalogers of books, journals, audiovisuals, etc. and by indexers of journal article literature in *Index Medicus* and its online version MEDLINE. MeSH now exists in two versions: (1) *Index Medicus* MeSH, intended for use by searchers, published annually as Part 2 of the January issue of *Index*

[1]"The National Library of Medicine." In Allen Kent, ed., *Encyclopedia of Library and Information Science.* New York: Marcel Dekker, 1986. Vol. 41 (Suppl. 6), pp. 231–256.

Medicus, a comprehensive index to medical literature of the world, and (2) Annotated MeSH, an expanded version of MeSH, adapted to the needs of indexers and catalogers, as well as searchers. The following discussion is based on the Annotated MeSH.

Format

The Annotated MeSH appears in three volumes, each representing a different arrangement of the headings:

1. *Medical Subject Headings—Annotated Alphabetic List*[2] contains main headings and topical and form subheadings with notes and cross-references. Subheadings and instructions on their use are listed separately rather than under the main headings with which they may be used. Examples of main headings, subheadings, and cross-references are shown below.

> **NURSES**
> M1.526.485.650+   N2.350.630+
> /educ = EDUCATION, NURSING;/hist = HISTORY OF NURSING; do not use/man/methods; relation to nurs specialties;   Manual 34.17
> CATALOG:/geog /form
> 67(65)
>
> **NURSES' AIDES**
> M1.526.485.67.652+   N2.350.84.611
> do not use /hist /man /methods
>
> NURSES, HEAD see NURSING, SUPERVISORY
> N4.452.758.377.750
>
> **/nurses' instruction**
> catalogers' form subhead only; for materials prepared for a nursing audience; do not confuse with the topical subhead /nursing which is used for nursing care of diseases; see Appendix A for double-form subheads; DF; NURS INST 84
> search policy: CATLINE, AVLINE only; Online Manual; use: main heading AND NURSES' INSTRUCTION (SH)

Explanations of individual elements in each entry are shown in Figure 10-1 taken from the introduction to MeSH.[3]

In addition to their presence in the main list, topical subheadings also

[2]National Library of Medicine (U.S.). *Medical Subject Headings—Annotated Alphabetic List.* Bethesda, Md.: National Library of Medicine, distributed by National Technical Information Service, U.S. Department of Commerce, 1975– .
[3]Ibid., 1991. P. I-5.

SAMPLE ENTRIES

Below are sample entries for two MeSH Headings and one Topical Subheading. Further explanation may be found in the following introductory sections.

DESCRIPTOR

PRE-EXPLOSION SYMBOL

CONSIDER ALSO
CROSS-REFERENCE
TO OTHER TERMS

TREE NUMBER
(+INDICATES INDENTED
HEADINGS IN MESH TREE
STRUCTURES AT
THIS NUMBER)

INDEXING
ANNOTATION

CATALOGING
ANNOTATION

•NEOPLASMS
consider also terms at CANCER, CARCINO-, ONCO-, and TUMOR
C4+
avoid: too general; prefer specifics; policy: Manual section 24; /chem ind permitted but consider also CARCINOGENS; /class: consider also NEOPLASM STAGING (see note there) but "grading" =/pathol; /etiol: consider also ONCOGENIC VIRUSES; /vet: Manual 24.32-.36 or TN 136; TN 135: MeSH terms for neoplasms classed by tissue; /drug ther: consider also ANTINEOPLASTIC AGENTS & its specifics; /genet: consider also GENES, SUPPRESSOR, TUMOR;/immunol: consider also ANTIGENS, NEOPLASM & ANTIBODIES, NEOPLASM;/microbiol: consider also ONCOGENIC VIRUSES;/radiother: consider also BRACHYTHERAPY; do not use/second (= NEOPLASM METASTASIS); familial: consider also NEOPLASTIC SYNDROMES, HEREDITARY; metastatic cancer of unknown origin: index under NEOPLASM METASTASIS; Tumor Key: TN Suppl ___ CATALOG: form qualif permitted

HISTORY
NOTE

/diagnosis was NEOPLASM DIAGNOSIS 1964–65; /etiology was NEOPLASM ETIOLOGY 1964–65; /immunology was NEOPLASM IMMUNOLOGY 1964–65; /radiotherapy was NEOPLASM RADIOTHERAPY 1964–65; /therapy was NEOPLASM THERAPY 1964–65; NEOPLASM STATISTICS was heading 1964–65; CARCINOGENESIS was heading 1977

use NEOPLASMS /CI or NEOPLASMS/ET to search CARCINOGENESIS 1977 ——— ONLINE NOTE

see related
DNA, NEOPLASM
ONCOGENIC VIRUSES
PLEURAL EFFUSION, MALIGNANT
PRECANCEROUS CONDITIONS
RNA, NEOPLASM

BACKWARD SEE
CROSS-REFERENCES
FROM ENTRY TERMS

FORWARD SEE RELATED
CROSS-REFERENCES
TO OTHER DESCRIPTORS

X CANCER
X TUMORS

XR MEDICAL ONCOLOGY

BACKWARD SEE RELATED
CROSS-REFERENCE
FROM OTHER DESCRIPTOR

DESCRIPTOR

INDEXING ANNOTATION

MACACA MULATTA
B2649.801.201.468.660.540

HISTORY NOTE
(note: former
minor descriptor)

usually NIM: no qualif; when IM, only likely qualif are /abnorm /anat /blood-csf-urine /class /embryol /genet /growth /immunol /inj /metab /microbiol /parasitol /physiol /psychol /surg

91(81); was see under MACACA 1981–90; was RHESUS MONKEYS see under MACACA 1975–80

use MACACA MULATTA to search RHESUS MONKEYS 1975–80 ———
ONLINE NOTE

X MONKEY, RHESUS

PRE-EXPOSION SYMBOL

INDEXING ANNOTATION

TOPICAL SUBHEADING

HISTORY NOTE

ONLINE NOTE

➤/etiology
subhead only; includes "pathogenesis" & "causes"; see MeSH scope note in Introduction; indexing policy: Manual 19.4.28; DF:/etiol or/ET

66

search policy: Online Manual; use: main heading/ET or ET (SH) or SUBS APPLY ET

I-5

FIGURE 10-1 Sample entries in MeSH.

appear in two other separate lists: an alphabetical list with scope notes, abbreviations, and allowable categories, and a classified list with subheadings arranged under more than sixty subject categories. Form, geographic, and language subheadings used in cataloging are listed separately in Appendices A to C. This volume also contains instructions to indexers and catalogers. The notes accompanying the main headings and subheadings state the restrictions and proper application in each case.

2. *Medical Subject Headings—Tree Structures*[4] consists of a categorical arrangement placing headings in relationship to other headings that represent similar areas and concepts. A system of *tree numbers* (capital letters followed by one or more strings of numbers) is used to reflect the hierarchies.

The display of the tree structures is relatively self-explanatory, and there are no notes or cross-references. The tree structures themselves fall into fifteen categories:

A   Anatomy
B   Organisms
C   Diseases
D   Chemicals and Drugs
E   Analytical, Diagnostic, and Therapeutic Techniques and Equipment
F   Psychiatry and Psychology
G   Biological Sciences
H   Physical Sciences
I   Anthropology, Education, Sociology and Social Phenomena
J   Technology, Industry, Agriculture
K   Humanities
L   Information Sciences
M   Named Groups
N   Health Care
Z   Geographicals

Each category is subdivided into one or more subcategories, with headings arranged hierarchically in each. A heading may appear in several places in the tree structures if the topic belongs in more than one subcategory. Each heading is accompanied by the *full* tree number giving the location of the heading in the tree. When a topic appears in more than one hierarchy, additional numbers are given in each case for the locations of the heading elsewhere in the trees. The following excerpt serves as an example:

[4]National Library of Medicine (U.S.). *Medical Subject Headings—Tree Structures.* Bethesda, Md.: National Library of Medicine, distributed by National Technical Information Service, U.S. Department of Commerce, 1975– .

RESPIRATORY TRACT DIS-EASES	C8	
BRONCHIAL DISEASES	C8.127	
ASTHMA	C8.127.108	C8.381.495
		C8.674.95
		C20.543.480
ASTHMA, EXERCISE-INDUCED	C8.127.108.110	
STATUS ASTHMATICUS	C8.127.108.880	
BRONCHIAL FISTULA	C8.127.196	C8.702.196
		C23.439.687
BRONCHIAL SPASM	C8.127.321	

****

LUNG DISEASES	C8.381	

****

LUNG DISEASES, OBSTRUCTIVE	C8.381.495	
ASTHMA	C8.381.495.108	C8.127.108
		C8.674.95
		C8.20.543.480

The tree structures provide a classificatory approach to medical subject headings,[5] manifesting the hierarchical structure of the subject headings and providing a logical basis for the cross-references. In online systems, the tree numbers, also called *descriptor codes*, can be used to retrieve related subjects.

3. *Permuted Medical Subject Headings*[6] is a keyword index listing each significant word in a subject heading phrase or cross-reference regardless of its position in the phrase. An example is shown below.

REST

ADRENAL CORTICAL REST TUMOR see ADRENAL REST TUMOR
ADRENAL REST TUMOR
BED REST
MANDIBULAR REST POSITION see VERTICAL DIMENSION
REST
REST VERTICAL DIMENSION see VERTICAL DIMENSION

[5]Susan L. Gullion. "Cataloging and Classification: Classification and Subject Cataloging." In Louise Darling, David Bishop, Lois Ann Colaianni, eds., *Handbook of Medical Library Practice*. 4th ed. Chicago: Medical Library Association, 1983. P. 269.
[6]National Library of Medicine (U.S.). *Permuted Medical Subject Headings*. Bethesda, Md.: National Library of Medicine, distributed by U.S. Department of Commerce, National Technical Information Service, 1976– .

Structure of Headings

Major descriptors

Major descriptors, also called *main headings,* represent main topics. Most major descriptors are topical, in the form of single words or phrases. Examples are

NURSING ADMINISTRATION RESEARCH
NURSING
RESINS
RESPIRATORY CIRCULATION
THERAPEUTICS
THERMAL CONDUCTIVITY
VINYL COMPOUNDS

Some phrase headings are inverted in order to collocate significant terms, for example,

NURSES, MALE
RESPIRATION, ARTIFICIAL
RESPIRATORY THERAPY DEPARTMENT, HOSPITAL
THERAPY, COMPUTER-ASSISTED

There are also other types of major descriptors: publication types, check tags, and geographics. Publication types descriptors (previously called *citation types*) include such terms as **ABSTRACT, BIBLIOG-RAPHY, CLINICAL TRIAL, CONGRESS, MEETING REPORT,** and **MONOGRAPH;** they represent the nature of the information in an item or the manner in which it is conveyed. Thus, like a form heading, a publication-types descriptor characterizes what a publication *is* rather than what it is *about.* Check tags include such headings as **ANIMAL; HUMAN; IN VITRO;** and **SUPPORT, U.S. GOVT, NON-P.H.S.** They are used in indexing only and never in cataloging. Geographics include continents, countries, states, and certain cities, such as **ASIA, FRANCE, ILLINOIS,** and **NEW YORK CITY,** and other geographic entities, such as **ATLANTIC OCEAN, GREAT LAKES REGION,** and **PACIFIC IS-LANDS.**

Sometimes a major descriptor is coded **Non-MeSH.** This means that it is not used in indexing or cataloging but serves to group headings in the MeSH *Tree Structures.*

Subheadings

A subheading, also called a *qualifier,* is used to qualify a main heading by specifying one of its aspects. There are four types of subheading: topical, form, geographic, and language. The latter three are used only in cataloging and not in indexing. Examples of subheadings are shown below.

Topical subheadings (appearing in the main list and in two separate lists)
/administration & dosage
/analysis
/diagnosis
/embryology
/standards
/therapeutic use

Form subheadings (appearing in Appendix A of MeSH[7])
abbreviations
abstracts
abstracts—audiocassettes
abstracts—microfiche
atlases—videodiscs
congress
directories
handbooks
indexes
models
periodicals—directories
popular works—motion pictures
yearbooks

Geographic subheadings (appearing in Appendix B of MeSH)
Afghanistan
Africa
Africa, British East
Africa, Central
*****
Hawaii
Hebrides
Honduras
Hong Kong
*****
New South Wales
New York
New York City
New Zealand
*****

[7]Single-form subheadings also appear in the main list.

Pacific Islands
Pacific Ocean
*****
Rhodesia, Southern
Romania
Rome

Language subheadings (appearing in Appendix C of MeSH)
Afrikaans
Danish
Gaelic (Scots)
Hebrew
Japanese
multilingual
Swedish
undetermined
Zulu

Cross-references

There are two categories of references in MeSH: *see* references and *related concept indicators*. *See* references lead from a user's entry vocabulary to valid headings. They are made from synonyms, near-synonyms, abbreviations, alternate spellings, and other alternate forms. For example,

COMPUTER-ASSISTED THERAPY see THERAPY, COMPUTER-ASSISTED
NURSERY SCHOOLS see SCHOOLS, NURSERY
RESPIRATORS see VENTILATORS, MECHANICAL
VIDINE see CHOLINE
VILLAGE HEALTH WORKER see COMMUNITY HEALTH AIDES

Reciprocal entries, indicated by the symbol X, are found under the valid heading, as shown below.

COMMUNITY HEALTH AIDS
X BAREFOOT DOCTORS
X VILLAGE HEALTH WORKER

SCHOOLS, NURSERY
X NURSERY SCHOOLS

THERAPY, COMPUTER-ASSISTED
X COMPUTER-ASSISTED THERAPY
X PROTOCOL-DIRECTED THERAPY, COMPUTER-ASSISTED

There are two types of related concept indicators: *see related* and *consider also* references. The *see related* references are used to indicate the presence of other headings that relate to the topic conceptually. For example,

CHILD DAY CARE CENTERS
see related
NURSERIES

RESPIRATION
see related
APNEA
BREATH TESTS
BREATHING EXERCISES
DYSPNEA

Reciprocals are printed under the related headings, indicated by the symbol *XR* ("see related reference from"). For example,

NURSERIES
XR   CHILD DAY CARE CENTERS

BREATHING EXERCISES
XR   RESPIRATION

The *consider also* references, instituted in 1991, indicate the presence of other headings that relate to the topic linguistically. They are used primarily with anatomic headings. A *consider also* reference refers to groups of headings beginning with a common word stem. For example,

HEART
consider also terms at CARDI- and MYOCARDI-

KIDNEY
consider also terms at GLOMERUL-, NEPHR-, PYEL-, and RENAL

Cataloging Instructions

In bibliographic records, MARC codes used with MeSH are similar to those used with LCSH:

600   Personal name heading
610   Corporate name heading
630   Uniform title
650   Topical heading
651   Geographic name heading

The second indicator in each field distinguishes between LC subject headings and MeSH headings: 0 indicates LC headings, and 2 indicates MeSH headings.

The introduction to the MeSH *Alphabetic List*[8] sets out specific instructions regarding cataloging practices, i.e., assigning subject headings to books, journals, and audiovisuals, at the National Library of Medicine. These are summarized below.

Assigning main headings

Main headings are used to represent the primary topic(s) of the publication. In general, the most specific heading or headings available are assigned to bring out the main subject of the item. Two types of headings listed in the *Annotated Alphabetic List* are not used in cataloging: those carrying notation *check tags only* and those listed as non-MeSH headings.

If the topic in question contains more than one concept, catalogers may apply one or more of the three following methods:

1. Using two or more main headings
2. Using a precoordinated main heading
3. Using a main heading and a subheading, including topical, geographic, form, or language subheadings

These methods are discussed below.

Assigning two or more main headings

If a publication deals with two or more subjects that are subordinate to a broad heading, up to three separate, specific headings are assigned. If more than three subjects are involved, the broad heading encompassing the individual specific topics in the tree structure is assigned. If the specific subjects are not within a tree, as many specific headings as necessary are assigned.

Assigning pre-coordinated headings

A pre-coordinated main heading (i.e., a heading that combines two or more concepts), if available, is used instead of two or more separate headings, e.g., the phrase heading **NURSING RESEARCH** rather than two separate headings, **NURSING** and **RESEARCH**; and the heading with subdivision **SURGERY—in infancy & childhood** rather than two separate headings, **INFANT** and **SURGERY.**

Assigning subheadings

A main heading may be subdivided by topical, geographic, form, and/ or language subheadings.

[8]National Library of Medicine (U.S.). Op. cit., 1991. Pp. I-126–I-134.

Topical subheadings
No more than three topical subheadings are assigned under a given main heading. When more than three topical subheadings are applicable, the main heading is assigned without topical subheading. Restrictions regarding specific topical subheadings are stated under the main heading or the topical subheading.

Geographic subheadings
The list of Geographic Subheadings for Catalogers appears in Appendix B in the Annotated MeSH. It contains subheadings for continents, oceans, large regions, countries, states and provinces, and a few large cities.

All headings in the G2 tree for health occupations, such as **DENTISTRY, MEDICINE**, etc., and any main heading listed with the annotation **SPEC** (a specialty heading) may be subdivided geographically. Otherwise, geographic subheadings are used only when the usage is indicated under the main heading in the list as *specify geog* or **CATALOG: /geog /form.** Unlike LC subject headings, geographic subheadings always appear directly in MeSH, for example, **COMMUNITY HEALTH SERVICES—Boston** rather than *COMMUNITY HEALTH SERVICES—Massachusetts—Boston.* Furthermore, only one geographic subheading is allowed in a subject heading string. When two distinct geographic areas are applicable, two separate headings are assigned, for example,

> **DENTAL CARE—Michigan**
> **DENTAL CARE—Ohio**

If more than three geographic areas, all of which are within a larger area, are involved, the subheading for the larger area is used, for example,

> **DENTAL CARE—Midwestern United States**

Form subheadings
Form subheadings are used to indicate the form of the overall publication and are generally assigned to all subject headings for a particular publication. Form subheadings have fewer restrictions and are used whenever appropriate. The scope notes under form subheadings indicate the types of works with which form subheadings are used.

Each heading string carries no more than one form subheading, except in precombined subheadings listed in Appendix A of the Annotated MeSH, for example, **abstracts—microfiche** and **popular works—motion pictures.** If more than two form subheadings which are not pre-coordinated in the list apply to a particular publication, the main heading is repeated with individual form subheadings, for example,

> **EDUCATION, PHARMACY—United States—directories**
> **EDUCATION, PHARMACY—United States—handbooks**

Language subheadings

Language subheadings are used to indicate the language, other than English, in which the content of certain types of publications is presented. They are used only with dictionary, philology, or literature main headings and with the form subheadings **/dictionaries, /nomenclature, /phrases,** and **/terminology,** for example,

> DICTIONARIES, CHEMICAL—French
> LITERATURE, MODERN—German
> SURGERY—dictionaries—Spanish

When more than one type of subheading is applied to a main heading, the citation order of the subject string is established as follows: **Main heading/Topical subheading/Geographic subheading/Form subheading/Language subheading.** Few headings contain all four types of subheadings, since language subheadings are extremely limited in application.

Examples

The following examples illustrate the cataloging of medical publications using MeSH headings. The Library of Congress subject headings are shown for the purposes of comparison.

> *Difficult diagnosis in pediatrics /* [edited by] James A. Stockman III. 1990
> 1. **Pediatrics.**
>
> [LC subject heading:
> 1. **Children—Diseases—Diagnosis.**]
>
> *Respiratory physiology : an analytical approach /* edited by H.K. Chang, Manuel Paiva. c1989
> 1. **Respiration.**
> 2. **Respiratory System—physiology.**
>
> [LC subject headings:
> 1. **Respiration.**
> 2. **Lungs—Physiology.**]
>
> *Ethical dilemmas in pediatrics : a case study approach /* Edwin N. Forman, Rosalind Ekman Ladd. c1991
> 1. **Ethics, Medical.**
> 2. **Pediatrics—case studies.**
>
> [LC subject headings:
> 1. **Pediatrics—Moral and ethical aspects—Case studies.**]

Essentials of human anatomy & physiology / Elaine N. Marieb.
3rd ed. c1991
   1. **Anatomy.**
   2. **Physiology.**

[LC subject headings:
   1. **Human physiology.**
   2. **Human anatomy.**]

Medical use of snake venom proteins / editor, Kurt F. Stocker.
c1990
   1. **Snake Venoms—therapeutic use.**

[LC subject headings:
   1. **Poisonous snakes—Venom—Therapeutic
      use—Testing.**
   2. **Poisonous snakes—Venom.**]

Medical Spanish : the instant survival guide / Cynthia J. Wilber,
Susan Lister. c1990
   1. **Medicine—phrases—Spanish.**

[LC subject headings:
   1. **Spanish language—Conversation and phrase books
      (for medical personnel)**
   2. **Spanish language—Textbooks for foreign
      speakers—English.**
   3. **Medicine—Terminology.**]

*Medicaid spending in the 1980s : the access-cost containment
trade-off revisited* / Deborah Chang and John Holahan.
c1990.
   1. **Health Services Accessibility—economics—United
      States.**
   2. **Medical Assistance, Title 19—economics.**

[LC subject headings:
   1. **Medicaid.**
   2. **Poor—Medical care—United States—Cost control.**]

*Recovering from addiction : guided steps through the healing
process* / James R. Baugh. c1990
   1. **Compulsive Behavior—rehabilitation**

[LC subject heading:
   1. **Compulsive behavior—Patients—Rehabilitation.**]

The clinical child interview / Jan N. Hughes, David B. Baker. 1991
   1. **Child Behavior Disorders—diagnosis.**
   2. **Interview, Psychological—in infancy & childhood.**
   3. **Interview, Psychological—methods.**
   4. **Mental disorders—diagnosis.**
   5. **Mental disorders—in infancy & childhood.**

   [LC subject heading:
   1. **Interviewing in child psychiatry.**]

PRECIS

PRECIS (Preserved Context Index System),[9] an indexing system, was developed and used by the British National Bibliography for producing entries in the subject index in the weekly and cumulative issues of the bibliography that lists new British books. As a system primarily (though not exclusively) applied to the subject analysis of books, its function is similar to that of the subject headings systems used in the United States.

   In 1968, the British National Bibliography (BNB) became involved in the UK/MARC (Machine-Readable Cataloguing) Project. A new indexing system capable of providing coextensive subject indexing for each document in the MARC database and amenable to computer manipulation was needed. A project, under the direction of Derek Austin, was undertaken to develop such a system. After initial experiments and trials, a prototype version of a new indexing system called *PRECIS* was adopted by BNB from January 1971 to the end of 1973. In the meantime, further research was conducted. In January 1974, a new and improved version of PRECIS became operational.

   PRECIS was originally developed as a system for producing alphabetical subject indexes in a page format (including paper, microform, or display on a computer terminal). In addition to the procedures for formulating the index strings, a complex system of coding for the purpose of producing an accurately laid out and typographically correct hard-copy index also was developed. In an online environment, the complex coding has become unnecessary, and the application of PRECIS

[9]This discussion is based on the following documents:
   Derek Austin. "The Development of PRECIS, and Introduction to Its Syntax" and "The Semantics of PRECIS: Vocabulary Control and the RIN System." In Hans H. Wellisch, ed., *The PRECIS Index System: Principles, Applications, and Prospects, Proceedings of the International PRECIS Workshop.* Sponsored by the College of Library and Information Services of the University of Maryland, October 15–17, 1976. New York: H. W. Wilson Company, 1977. Pp. 3–28, 29–53.
   Derek Austin and Jeremy A. Digger. "PRECIS: The Preserved Context Index System." *Library Resources & Technical Services,* 21:13–10, Winter, 1977.
   Mary Dykstra. *PRECIS: A Primer.* Revised reprint. Metuchen, N.J.: Scarecrow Press, 1987.

was discontinued by the British Library in favor of a new subject system called *COMPASS*. Today, PRECIS remains of interest to students of subject analysis because of its sound grounding in classification theory and linguistic principles.

In developing PRECIS, Austin applied modern theory of classification as well as linguistic principles. Many of the theories and ideas developed in the 1960s by the Classification Research Group in Britain in search of a general classification scheme were adopted in the development of PRECIS by Austin, who was an active member of the group.

Underlying PRECIS is the theory of facet analysis and synthesis. The subject of a document is broken down into individual concepts, which are then recombined into a meaningful and logical string that summarizes the content of the document. This string serves as the source from which index entries are generated.

When PRECIS began, it was based on modern indexing and classification theory, but it then moved gradually toward a linguistic analysis approach. Breaking down a subject into its component parts and providing a hierarchical structure to them were based on modern indexing and classification theory. Reordering the parts into a meaningful string, on the other hand, drew on linguistic principles.

A basic principle of PRECIS is that each entry should represent the complete theme or topic of a document in summary form. This is called the *principle of coextensivity.*

The basic criteria for useful index entries were outlined as follows:

1. An entry can be made under any term likely to be sought in a string.
2. Each entry should be intelligible, and it should state the subject unambiguously.
3. Entries should be consistent in structure so that they collocate with those produced from other strings on similar themes.[10]

These criteria led to the development of the principle of *context dependency.* This principle requires that the individual concepts in an entry be organized in a one-to-one relationship in context-dependent order. In other words, each term in the entry should be related to the one immediately preceding and the one immediately following it. Each term sets the next term into its obvious context.

This can be illustrated by an example of a string summarizing the content of a document on "the training of skilled personnel in textile industries in France":

FRANCE—TEXTILE INDUSTRIES—SKILLED
PERSONNEL—TRAINING

[10]Derek Austin and Jeremy A. Digger. Op. cit. P. 17.

The four concepts which together summarize the total content of the document are arranged in a context-dependent order. The concept "France" establishes the environment in which the concept of "textile industries" is considered; the concept "textile industries" identifies the contextual whole of which "skilled personnel" forms a part; while the act of "training" is performed on the entity "skilled personnel." Once the concepts are arranged in this order, each is placed in closest proximity to the concept or concepts most closely related to it. These two notions—context dependency and one-to-one relations—are basic to this indexing system.

In order to preserve the one-to-one relationships in context-dependent order, each PRECIS entry is presented in a two-line and three-position format:

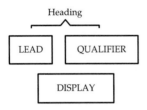

Following is an example of a PRECIS input string with the entries generated from it:

Input string assigned by the indexer (the blank boxes indicate that no entry has yet been generated):

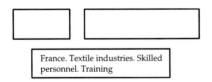

Entries generated by the computer:

France
Textile industries. Skilled personnel. Training

Textile industries. France
Skilled personnel. Training

Skilled personnel. Textile industries. France
Training

Training. Skilled personnel. Textile industries. France

A separate entry is generated with each significant term in the lead position. The lead that contains the entry element, printed in boldface type, must be occupied. The qualifier may contain any number of terms, which are of successively broader context to the right of the line. The terms in the display are of progressively narrower context to the right of the line.

The device of bringing each significant term to the lead position while maintaining the context-dependent order is called *shunting*. The two-line/three-position format and the established procedure of shunting ensure that each concept is placed immediately next to those most closely related to it, whatever position this particular concept may occupy in a particular entry. In the second entry in the example above, the concept "textile industries," when it is moved to the lead position, remains next to both "France" and "skilled personnel."

The index string is written according to a *schema of operators*, which sets the string in an established citation order that ensures context dependency. A summary of the primary operators is given below.[11]

0 Location   → Environment

1 Key system
2 Action or effect of action   } Core concepts
3 Agent of transitive action

4 Viewpoint-as-form
5 Selected instance,
     e.g., study region,   } Extra-core
     sample population   concepts
6 Form of document; target user

A string assigned to a document may contain any number of terms. Each string must begin with a primary operator in the range from 0 to 2 and must contain at least one term coded either (1) or (2). Examples:

a. *Subject*
    Marketing of cars

    String
    (1) cǎrs (the check mark √ indicates a lead term under
         which an entry is to be made)
         √
    (2) mǎrketing

[11]Mary Dykstra. Op. cit. P. 239.

b. *Subject*
Car production in Germany

String

(0) Germany

(1) cars

(2) production

c. *Subject*
Birth control (a Roman Catholic viewpoint)

String

(2) birth control

(4) Roman Catholic viewpoints

d. *Subject*
Bibliography on U.S. trade unions

String

(0) United States

(1) trade unions

(6) bibliographies

There is a direct connection between the primary operators, 0, 1, 2, and 3, and certain grammatical structures in everyday speech. The operator 0 corresponds to the locative case in grammar. The operators 1, 2, and 3 are used with terms that generally correspond to the object, verb (in the case of a transitive verb), and subject of a sentence. In the case of an intransitive verb, the operators 1 and 2 are used with terms that function as the subject and verb of a sentence. The role operators are devices for constructing the input strings and serve as instruction to the computer. They do not appear in the index entries.

Used in conjunction with the primary operators are a set of secondary operators for coordinate and dependent elements. These follow immediately the term with which they are associated.

f "Bound" coordinate concept
g Standard coordinate concept
p Part, property
q Member of quasi-generic group
r Assembly
s Role definer, directional property
t Author-attributed association

Examples of use of secondary operators:

Subject
A comparison between Christianity and Judaism

String

(1) Christianity
(*t*) compared with
(1) Judaism

Examples of operators for dependent elements:

(1) aircraft
(*p*) noise

(2) advertising
(*p*) costs

(1) pests
(*q*) birds

(1) schools
(*p*) curriculum subjects
(*q*) geography

(1) skilled personnel
(*r*) trade unions

(1) fish
(2) physiology
(5) study examples
(*q*) mackerel
(5) study regions
(*q*) South China sea

Example of a complicated string and the entries generated from it:

Subject
Teaching English to immigrant children in London's primary schools

String

(0) Lon√don

(1) prim√ary schools

(*p*) stud√ents

(*q*) immi√grants

(3) curriculum subjects

(*q*) Engli√sh language

(sub 4 ↑) (*p*) English language to immigrants [substitutes four
terms above]

(2) tea√ching

Entries

London
Primary schools. Students: Immigrants. Curriculum
subjects: English language. Teaching

Primary schools. London
Students: Immigrants. Curriculum subjects: English
language. Teaching

Students. Primary schools. London
Immigrants. Curriculum subjects: English language.
Teaching

Immigrants. Students. Primary schools. London
Curriculum subjects: English language. Teaching

English language. Curriculum subjects. Immigrants.
Students. Primary schools. London
Teaching

Teaching. English language to immigrants. Primary schools.
London

As a means of vocabulary control, PRECIS maintained a thesaurus
of individual index terms showing their relationship to other terms.
Three types of relationships are shown: equivalence relationship (indicated by *see* or *SEARCH UNDER*), hierarchical relationship (indicated
by *see also* or *RELATED TERMS*), and associative relationship (also
indicated by *see also* or *RELATED TERMS*), for example:

Industries
See also
Textile industries

Employees *See* **Personnel**

Staff *See* **Personnel**

Manpower
  See also
    Personnel

Education
  See also
    Training

COMPASS

Because the PRECIS system was developed for the purpose of generating multiple subject strings in a printed index, its complex coding and system of role operators are unnecessary in an online system. Since January 1991, in an effort to reduce the unit costs of cataloging, the British Library has used a subject system called *COMPASS* (Computer-Aided Subject System).[12] COMPASS is a simplified restructuring of PRECIS. It maintains an open-ended vocabulary allowing the introduction of new index terms as required. The index string is organized by the PRECIS principles of context dependency and role operators. As in the case of PRECIS, a subject string, once assigned, may be reused for indexing documents on the same subject.

On records created by the British Library, the MARC fields 650, 651, 690, 691, and 692 were eliminated, and in their place, two new fields are added:

660 Subject topical descriptors
661 Subject geographical descriptors

This system separates geographic terms from subject topical terms (i.e., names as subjects and topical terms and strings); for example, the following descriptors are assigned to a guide to French hotels and restaurants:

660 Hotels
660 Restaurants
661 France

---

[12]"The New British Library Subject System." *Select: National Bibliographic Service Newsletter*, **1**:3–4, June–July 1990. "COMPASS: A Rose by Any Other Name." *Select*, **2**:3, Winter 1990. Neil Wilson. "COMPASS: News from the Front," *Select*, **4**:6–7, Summer 1991.

MARC field 600 is retained for personal name subject entries, e.g.,

245   Van Gogh
600   Gogh, Vincent van, 1853-1890
660   Paintings
661   Netherlands

COMPASS retains from PRECIS its basic components: (1) an authority file of controlled terms and subject statements for use in bibliographic records and (2) a thesaurus containing a network of related terms, from broader to narrower and between used and non-used terms.

COMPASS headings appear in two forms:

1. Terms: unitary (single-word) or compound (multiple-word) expressions of simple subject concepts.
2. Strings: combinations of two or more terms expressing complex subject concepts or relationships.

Thus **Drug** and **Drug abuse** are *term* headings, and **Drug abuse. Prevention** is a *string* heading.

The arrangement of the terms in a string follows the PRECIS citation order based on core concepts (key systems, actions/effects, agents) and dependent elements (parts/properties, aggregates, and quasi-generics). The extracore concepts (viewpoints, study examples, target users, forms of documents) are not used.

The subject authority file contains two types of records: terms and strings. Term authority records contain terms representing simple concepts, topical or geographic, in the form of unitary (single-word) or compound expressions (more than one word), for example,

> **Poetry** (unitary topical term)
> **English fiction** (compound topical term)
> **Australia** (unitary geographic term)
> **New South Wales** (compound geographic term)

All geographic descriptors are single-concept terms. String authority records contain one type of string only: topical. Each string consists of a combination of two or more terms, for example,

> **Motor vehicles. Design. Applications of. Computers**

The 660 field may contain topical terms or strings. With the capability of keyword searching in online systems, it is no longer necessary to rotate the individual terms to the initial position as in the case of PRECIS strings.

COMPASS simplifies subject cataloging and authority maintenance operations at the expense of precision. Because topical and geographic concepts are entered in separate fields to be post-coordinated at the point of searching, the probability of false coordination increases. While such a system may decrease precision, the designers aimed at increasing recall of material, with the rationale that "the emphasis on recall rather than precision reflects the fact that in an automated catalogue environment the whole bibliographic record is available for searching and not just the traditional subject fields for subject headings or index terms."[13]

TOPICS FOR DISCUSSION

1. Compare subject access in manual and online catalogs in terms of points of access, browsing, and retrieval.

2. Because most of the currently used systems of subject cataloging were developed for manual catalogs, many of the features were introduced because of the unique demands of manual retrieval. Nevertheless, they contain features that are amenable to online retrieval. Identify these features in each of the systems studied.

3. Since some phrase headings in LCSH and in Sears are inverted and others appear in the direct form, discuss the problem in maintaining consistency in form. Examine the following groups of LC headings or similar headings in Sears and determine whether there are any consistent patterns.

Church music	Bessel's functions
Music, African	Functions, Abelian
African languages	Abelian groups
Languages, Universal	Groups, Continuous
English drama	Epic poetry, English
English poetry	Folk-drama, English
English fiction	Short stories, English

    (Compare also parallel headings for literature in other languages.) Discuss the implications of these variant forms for users and the adequacy of the device used to connect the variant forms. Furthermore, is the rationale for inverted headings still valid in online catalogs?

4. The phrases *Stability of ships, Ships' stability,* and *Ships—Stability* all express the same concept; so do *Chemical research* and *Chemistry—Research.* Because of the principle of uniform heading, only one form is used in LCSH with *see* references from the others. Examine the variations in forms of headings in LCSH and in Sears to see whether there is any consistent pattern for determining which type of phrase is to be used as the heading.

[13]"The New British Library Subject System." *Select,* 1:3, June-July 1990.

5. In LCSH, by interpolating the name of the larger geographic area between the subject heading and the local subdivision, the indirect form is a violation of the principle of specific entry. The reason given for this form is that "indirect subdivision assumes that the interest and significance of certain subjects are inseparable from the larger area—the country or state—or that the study of subordinate geographic areas is best considered as contributing to the study of the larger area."[14] Examine headings in LCSH to see whether materials on a particular subject treated from the point of view of subordinate geographic areas (e.g., states, counties, or cities) are grouped together with those treated from larger areas (e.g., continents, countries, states) which encompass the local area.

6. When free-text searching was first available in online systems, many assumed that there was no longer a need for controlled vocabulary. Do you agree? Discuss the advantages and disadvantages of these two approaches to information retrieval.

[14]David Judson Haykin. *Subject Headings: A Practical Guide.* Washington: U.S. Government Printing Office, 1951.

PART IV
CLASSIFICATION

BASIC TOOLS

Cutter, C. A. *C.A. Cutter's Three-Figure Author Table.* Swanson-Swift revision. Chicopee, Mass.: H. R. Huntting Company, 1969.

Cutter, C. A. *C.A. Cutter's Two-Figure Author Table.* Swanson-Swift revision. Chicopee, Mass.: H. R. Huntting Company, 1969.

Cutter, C. A. *Cutter-Sanborn Three-Figure Author Table.* Swanson-Swift revision. Chicopee, Mass.: H. R. Huntting Company, 1969.

Dewey, Melvil. *Abridged Dewey Decimal Classification and Relative Index.* Ed. 12. John P. Comaromi, ed.; Julianne Beall, Winton E. Matthews, Jr., and Gregory R. New, assistant eds. Albany, N.Y.: Forest Press, A Division of OCLC Online Computer Library Center, Inc., 1990.

Dewey, Melvil. *Dewey Decimal Classification and Relative Index.* Ed. 20. John P. Comaromi, ed.; Julianne Beall, Winton E. Matthews, Jr., and Gregory R. New, assistant eds. Albany, N.Y.: Forest Press, A Division of OCLC Online Computer Library Center, Inc., 1989.

Library of Congress. Subject Cataloging Division. *Classification.* Washington: Library of Congress. 1901– .

Library of Congress. Subject Cataloging Division. *LC Classification— Additions and Changes.* Washington: Library of Congress. List 1– . March/May 1928– .

Library of Congress. Subject Cataloging Division. *Subject Cataloging Manual: Shelflisting.* Washington: Library of Congress, 1987.

National Library of Medicine (U.S.). *National Library of Medicine Classification: A Scheme for the Shelf Arrangement of Books in the Field of Medicine and Its Related Sciences.* 4th ed. revised. NIH Publication no. 81-1535. Bethesda, Md.: U.S. Department of Health and Human Services, Public Health Service, National Institutes of Health, National Library of Medicine, 1981.

BACKGROUND READING

Chan, Lois Mai. *Immroth's Guide to the Library of Congress Classification.* 4th ed. Englewood, Colo.: Libraries Unlimited, 1990.

Comaromi, John P. *Book Numbers: A Historical Study and Practical Guide to Their Use.* Littleton, Colo.: Libraries Unlimited, 1981.

Comaromi, John P. "Conception and Development of the Dewey Decimal Classification." *International Classification,* 3:11–15, 1976.

Dunkin, Paul S. "Where Does It Go? Call Numbers." In *Cataloging U.S.A.* Chicago: American Library Association, 1969. Pp. 96–137.

Foskett, A. C. *The Subject Approach to Information.* 4th ed. Hamden, Conn.: Linnet Books; London: Clive Bingley, 1982.

"Introduction to the Dewey Decimal Classification." In *Dewey Decimal Classification and Relative Index.* Ed. 20. Vol. 1, pp. xxv–1.

"Introduction to the Dewey Decimal Classification." In *Abridged Dewey Decimal Classification and Relative Index.* Ed. 12. Pp. 5–25.

Lehnus, Donald J. *Book Numbers: History, Principles, and Application.* Chicago: American Library Association, 1980.

Maltby, Arthur. *Sayers' Manual of Classification for Librarians.* 5th ed. London: Andre Deutsch, 1975. Pp. 143–158, 174–189.

FURTHER READING

Chan, Lois Mai. "Library of Congress Classification as an Online Retrieval Tool: Potentials and Limitations." *Information Technology and Libraries,* 5:181–92, September 1986.

Comaromi, John P. *The Eighteen Editions of the Dewey Decimal Classification.* Albany, N.Y.: Forest Press Division, Lake Placid Education Foundation, 1976.

LaMontagne, Leo E. *American Library Classification with Special Reference to the Library of Congress.* Hamden, Conn.: Shoe String Press, 1961.

Osborn, Jeanne. *Dewey Decimal Classification, 20th Edition: A Study Manual.* Revised and edited by John P. Comaromi. Englewood, Colo.: Libraries Unlimited, 1991.

Palmer, Bernard I. *Itself an Education: Six Lectures on Classification.* 2nd ed. London: Library Association, 1971.

Ranganathan, S. R. *Elements of Classification; Based on Lectures Delivered at the University of Bombay in December 1944 and in the School of Librarianship in Great Britain in December 1956.* 2nd ed., revised and rewritten. B. I. Palmer, ed. London: Association of Assistant Librarians, Section of the Library Association, 1959.

Satija, M. P. "A Critical Introduction to the 7th Edition (1987) of the Colon Classification." *Cataloging & Classification Quarterly*, **12**(2):125–38, 1990.

Williamson, Nancy J. "The Library of Congress Classification: Problems and Prospects in Online Retrieval." *International Cataloguing*, **15**:45–48, October 1986.

CHAPTER ELEVEN
GENERAL PRINCIPLES OF
CLASSIFICATION

DEFINITION

Classification, broadly defined, is the act of organizing the universe of knowledge into some systematic order. It has been considered the most fundamental activity of the human mind. The essential act of classification is the multistage process of deciding on a property or characteristic of interest, distinguishing things or objects that possess that property from those which lack it, and grouping things or objects that have the property or characteristic in common into a class. Other essential aspects of classification are establishing relationships among classes and making distinctions within classes to arrive at subclasses and finer divisions. The classification of library materials follows the same pattern; it is thus a special application of a much more general human intellectual activity.

Library classification in particular has been defined as "the systematic arrangement by subject of books and other material on shelves or of catalogue and index entries in the manner which is most useful to those who read or who seek a definite piece of information."[1] In other words, library classification serves a dual function: to arrange items in a logical order on library shelves and to provide a systematic display of bibliographic entries in printed catalogs, bibliographies, and indexes. Examples of the latter use are the British National Bibliography and the Wilson Standard Catalogs for libraries, which are organized according to the Dewey Decimal Classification. Today, in some online catalogs, classification also serves a direct retrieval function.

As a shelving device, library classification has two objectives: to help the user identify and locate a work through a call number and to group all works of a kind together. In order to fulfill the first objective, any method of numbering or marking would be sufficient as long as there is a correspondence between the number or mark on the document and that on the cataloging entry. The second objective, on the other hand, represents a collocating function and requires the grouping of like materials together on the basis of chosen characteristics. Thus, in its

---

[1]Arthur Maltby. *Sayers' Manual of Classification for Librarians.* 5th ed. London: Andre Deutsch, 1975. P. 15.

function as a retrieval tool, classification may help to identify and retrieve a group of related items as well as a specific known item.

In any collection, the most appropriate basis for determining groups varies according to the needs of the collection. For example, library materials may be grouped by author, physical form, size, date of publication, or subject. In modern library classification systems, subject is the predominant characteristic for grouping.

In the library context, *classification* as a term refers both to the development of schemes for the systematic display of all aspects of the various fields of knowledge and to the art of arranging books or other objects in conformity with such schemes. In other words, it is used both for the creation of a classification scheme and for its application. For clarity in discourse, the people who are involved in these two processes are given different names. The inventor or creator of a classification scheme or a person who is engaged in the theory of classification is called a *classificationist*, while the person who applies such a scheme is referred to as a *classifier*.

BASIC CONCEPTS

The traditional ideas of library classification were borrowed from the logical or philosophical principles of classification. Classification begins with the universe of knowledge as a whole and divides it into successive stages of classes and subclasses, with a chosen characteristic as the basis for each stage. On the whole, the progression is from the general to the specific, forming a hierarchical, or "tree," structure, each class being a *species* of the class on the preceding level and a *genus* to the one below it. The classes on each level, usually mutually exclusive and totally exhaustive categories, form a coordinate relationship to one another and are collocated according to the affinity of their relationships. Classification according to hierarchical principles, with biologic taxonomy the prevailing model, was in a particularly active stage of development during the latter part of the nineteenth century. The Dewey Decimal Classification and the Library of Congress Classification, the most widely used library classification systems today, both originated at that time and reflect the general intellectual climate of the era.

With a particular hierarchy, the basis for division within a class into subclasses and sub-subclasses may vary considerably from subject to subject. For example, architecture can be classified according to schools and styles, periods, or types of buildings. Literature can be divided by language, genre/form, or period. Each characteristic is called a *facet*. Figure 11-1 illustrates the division of literature in the Dewey Decimal Classification based on the three facets named above.

FIGURE 11-1   Division of literature in the Dewey Decimal Classification.

The coordinate elements on each level or stage of division form an *array*, e.g., **American literature, English literature, German literature,** etc. The term *chain* refers to a string of subjects, each of which represents a different level in the hierarchy, e.g., **Literature—English literature—English poetry—Elizabethan poetry.** There is not always a built-in or natural order of the characteristics or facets in each class. For example, although language is a natural first-order division for literature, the next divisions could be first by form and then by period or equally reasonably the other way around; as many readers, presumably, would like to see Victorian novels, drama, poetry, and so on in close array as would like to see English poetry arranged chronologically. The original designers of classification systems made what they considered appropriate decisions on principles of division, class by class, and then they and their successors tried to maintain consistency within each class on how facets were determined and developed. Order of facets is called *citation order.*

Traditional library classification schemes tend to list all subjects and their subdivisions and provide ready-made symbols for them. Such a scheme is referred to as *enumerative* classification. Among existing library classification schemes, the Library of Congress Classification is considered to be the most enumerative.

Modern classification theory, on the other hand, places emphasis on *facet analysis* and *synthesis*—the analysis (or breaking up) of a subject into its component parts and the synthesis (or reassembling) of those parts as required by the document to be represented. Instead of enumerating all subjects in a hierarchical structure, modern theory argues that a classification scheme should identify the basic components of subjects and list under each discipline, or main class, the elements or aspects that are topically important within that class. Each class has its own class-specific *facets*. For instance, the class Education might have a facet for Persons Taught, a facet for Subjects Taught, a facet for Educators, a facet for Methods of Instruction, a facet for Educational Institutions, and so on. In addition, recurring or common facets, such as form, geographic divisions, and chronological divisions, are listed separately for application to all classes. In applying such a scheme, the act of classification essentially consists of identifying appropriate component facets and synthesizing (i.e., combining) them according to a predetermined *citation formula*. A system based on these principles is called a *faceted* or *analytico-synthetic classification*. An example is the Colon Classification.

Some classification systems provide minute details under each class or subject, while others provide broad subject divisions only. The former are referred to as *close classification* and the latter as *broad classification*.

NOTATION

Each classification scheme adopts a system of symbols to represent its classes and divisions. The purpose of such a device, called *notation*, is to furnish a brief designation of subjects (and sometimes their relationships as well) and to provide a sequential order for arrangement.

In some classification systems, the notation consists of all letters; in others, all numbers; and in still others, a combination of both. A *pure notation* is one in which only one type of symbol is used; an example is the notation of the Dewey Decimal Classification, which consists of arabic numerals. A system that employs more than one type of symbol is called a *mixed notation*; an example is the combined letters and arabic numerals in the notation of the Library of Congress Classification.

A *hierarchical notation* is one that reflects the structural order, or hierarchy, of the classification, and an *expressive notation* is one that expresses relationships among coordinate subjects. The notation used with the Dewey Decimal Classification is hierarchical, and that of the Universal Decimal Classification is both hierarchical and expressive. The notation of the Library of Congress Classification is neither.

Another feature of some notation schemes is internal *mnemonics*, or aids to memory. In this context, the term means that when a given topic recurs in the scheme, it is represented consistently by the same symbol. For example, in the Dewey Decimal Classification, poetry is represented by the number 1, hence 811 (American poetry), 831 (German poetry), 841 (French poetry), and so on. Correspondingly, 3 often pertains to Germany and 4 to France.

HOW TO CLASSIFY

Classifying and assigning subject headings both begin with the same intellectual process: determining the subject content and identifying the principal concepts in the work under consideration. This process was described in Chapter 7. Much of what was said in that chapter applies here, but the two processes are not fully parallel. One difference, of course, is that while in subject cataloging the content of a work is represented by verbal terms, it is notation that carries the meaning in classification. A more important difference is that because in American libraries classification is used mainly as a shelving or location device, only one class number is chosen for each work; in subject cataloging, on the other hand, any number of subject headings may be assigned to a work. Of course, where classification is considered a major retrieval device, as in libraries with a classed catalog or bibliographies arranged by classification numbers, two or more different classification numbers also may be assigned a given work.

Choosing a Number: General Guidelines

If the work is on a clearly defined subject, classifying it is a relatively simple operation. One needs simply to choose the appropriate number from the scheme being used. However, a work may deal with more than one subject or more than one aspect of a subject: different subjects may be treated together as parts of a broader subject; they may be brought together by the author because they are affinitive subjects considered separately; they may be treated in terms of their relationship to each other; or finally, a given subject may be treated from interdisciplinary points of view. Faceted classification schemes such as the Universal Decimal Classification or Colon Classification provide for combining class numbers to bring out every subject or aspect treated in a multisubject work. However, such combinations are not always possible with traditional schemes such as the Dewey Decimal or Library of Congress classifications; classifiers often have to choose one number from two or more numbers that represent the different subjects or aspects treated in the work.

The use of each classification system involves certain unique procedures, and for the Dewey Decimal, Library of Congress, and National Library of Medicine systems, these are discussed in detail in later chapters. The following discussion focuses on some of the general principles and guidelines that apply to the classification of library material in general.

1. Consider usefulness

When a work can be classed in more than one number in a scheme, consider where it will be most useful to the users.

2. Make subject the primary consideration

When the classification scheme allows alternatives, class by subject, then by form, except in literature, where language and literary form are what matter most.

3. Use the most specific number available

Class the work in the most specific number that will contain it. There may not be an exact number for every subject encountered, however. When there is no specific number for the work, place it in the next most specific category above it, depending on which scheme is used. For example, classify a history of Chicago in the number for Chicago, if available, instead of with the history of a larger geographic unit, such as Cook County, the state of Illinois, or the United States; if the system does not provide a specific number for Chicago, place it in the number for the next larger geographic unit for which the scheme makes provision.

4. Do not classify from the index alone

The index or indexes that accompany each classification scheme provide help in locating specific class numbers. However, the chosen number should always be checked in the schedules to ensure that the subject of the work being classified has been placed properly in the overall structure and that the instructions in the schedules restricting or elaborating the use of the number have been observed.

Choosing a Number: Multitopical Works

There is no hard and fast rule for the choice of a number for a multitopical work. The following guidelines, which are based on the works of classificationists,[2] are generally applicable.

1. Determine the dominant subject or the phase relations

Dominant subject
Classify under the dominant subject, if one can be determined. If the subjects are treated separately, a ready indication of preponderance may be the amount of space devoted to each. Another gauge is the author's apparent intention or purpose.

Phase relations
More complicated is a work in which the different subjects are viewed in relationship to each other. In such a case, an analysis of the relationship may help to determine the emphasis of the work. *Phase relations*, in

[2]"Introduction to the Dewey Decimal Classification." In *Dewey Decimal Classification and Relative Index.* Ed. 20. John P. Comaromi, ed. Julianne Beall, Winton E. Matthews, Jr., and Gregory R. New, assistant eds. Albany, N.Y.: Forest Press, a Division of OCLC Online Computer Library Center, Inc., 1989. Vol. 1, pp. xxxi–xxxiii. Paul S. Dunkin. *Cataloging U.S.A.* Chicago: American Library Association, 1969. Pp. 116–22. William Stetson Merrill. *Code for Classifiers.* 2nd ed. Chicago: American Library Association, 1939. Pp. 3–7.

other words the interrelationships of subjects treated in a work, were discussed earlier, in Chapter 7. In classification, the following considerations apply.

Influence Phase   Classify a work about the influence of one thing or author on another under the subject or author being influenced.

Bias Phase   Classify a work on a particular subject written with a bias toward, or aiming at, a specific group of readers (e.g., *Fundamentals of Physical Chemistry for Premedical Students*), under the subject (physical chemistry), not the element toward which it is biased (premedical or medical sciences).

Tool or Application Phase   Classify a work such as *Chemical Calculations: An Introduction to the Use of Mathematics in Chemistry* under the subject (chemistry) instead of the tool (mathematics).

Comparison Phase   Class under the subject emphasized or under the first subject.

Note   It should be stressed that the preceding are only *general* guidelines. If a work on the influence of one subject or one author on another clearly places emphasis on the subject or author exerting the influence, it should be classed with that subject or author. Similarly, if a work on a subject written for a specific group of readers is of little value to other readers, it should be classed under the number reflecting the intended readers.

2. Class under first subject

If the dominant subject cannot be ascertained—e.g., in works treating two or three subjects separately or in comparison without any indication of preponderance—class under the first subject. In the Dewey Decimal Classification, *first* means the one coming first in the schedules. For example, a work dealing equally with Judaism (296) and Islam (297) would be placed in 296. Lacking such specific instruction, *first* may mean the subject treated first in the work.

3. Class under broader subject

Class under the broader subject a work dealing with two or three subjects that are subdivisions of a broader subject and that together constitute the major portion of that subject, e.g., choosing the number for classical languages for a work about Greek and Latin. Likewise, for a work dealing with four or more subjects, all of which are divisions of a broader subject, class under the number that covers them all; for example, use the number for chemistry (540) for a work about physical (541), analytical (543), inorganic (546), and organic (547) chemistry.

CALL NUMBERS

To distinguish individual bibliographic items on the same subject, a book or item number is added to the class number to form a *call number* as a location symbol for the item in the library's collection. The term *call number* probably originated from the fact that in the earlier days most libraries had closed stacks, and a library user would have to "call" for a book from the collection by means of its unique number.

Many libraries adopt the principle of unique call numbers. Each item in the library is assigned a number different from any other call number in the collection. In this sense, the call number serves as the true address of the item. The call number consists of one or more elements based on the bibliographic characteristics of the item, such as the author's name, the title, the edition, the date of publication, the volume number, etc.

There are various ways of composing a call number, depending on the size of the collection and the classification system used. The procedures for assigning call numbers are discussed in the following chapters on individual classification schemes.

MARC CODING FOR CLASSIFICATION AND ITEM NUMBERS

In *USMARC Format for Bibliographic Data*, the following fields contain data relating to call numbers based on classification systems discussed in this book:

> 050   Library of Congress call number
>   Indicators:
>   First—existence in LC collection
>   0 = Item is in LC
>   1 = Item is not in LC
>   Second—source of call number
>   0 = Assigned by the Library of Congress (LC)
>   4 = Assigned by agency other than LC
>   Subfield codes:
>   ‡a = Classification number
>   ‡b = Item number

060   National Library of Medicine (NLM) call number
    Indicators:
      First—existence in NLM collection
        0 = Item is in NLM
        1 = Item is not in NLM
      Second—source of call number
        0 = Assigned by NLM
        4 = Assigned by agency other than NLM
    Subfield codes:
      ‡a = Classification number
      ‡b = Item number
080   Universal Decimal Classification number
082   Dewey Decimal call number
    Indicators:
      First—type of edition
        0 = Full edition
        1 = Abridged edition
      Second—source of call number
        0 = Assigned by LC
        4 = Assigned by agency other than LC
    Subfield codes:
      ‡a = Classification number
      ‡b = Item number
      ‡2 = Edition number
090–099 Local call numbers

MODERN LIBRARY CLASSIFICATION SYSTEMS

Many library classification systems have been developed in modern times, some for general collections and others for specialized subject collections. The following chapters discuss in detail the major systems used by American libraries and present briefly the salient characteristics of a number of other classification systems, along with information on their conception and development.

CHAPTER TWELVE
DEWEY DECIMAL
CLASSIFICATION

HISTORY
The Beginning

The publication in 1876 of a pamphlet entitled *A Classification and Subject Index for Cataloguing and Arranging the Books and Pamphlets of a Library* marked the beginning of the Dewey Decimal Classification (DDC), which was soon adopted by many libraries in the United States and later by libraries around the world. Today, in its twentieth edition, the Dewey Decimal Classification is the most widely used library classification system in the world.[1] The scheme, used in more than 135 countries, has been translated into many languages. In the United States, it is used in 95 percent of public and school libraries, 25 percent of college and university libraries, and 20 percent of special libraries.

DDC was conceived as a classification of knowledge for the purpose of organizing a library. Melvil Dewey (1851–1931), the founder of the system which was named after him, was assistant librarian at Amherst College when he developed the scheme. In the preface to the first edition (1876), Dewey states that the system was developed early in 1873 as a result of several months' study of some hundreds of books and pamphlets and of over fifty personal visits to various American libraries.

The 1876 edition, consisting of merely forty-four pages and published anonymously, contains a brief preface outlining Dewey's principles, the schedules for ten main classes subdivided decimally to form a total of 1000 categories numbered 000 to 999, and an alphabetical subject index. The division of main classes was based on an earlier classification system (1870) devised by W. T. Harris, who, in turn, based his scheme on an inverted order of Francis Bacon's classification of knowledge.[2]

[1]Melvil Dewey. *Dewey Decimal Classification and Relative Index.* Ed. 20. John P. Comaromi, ed., Julianne Beall, Winton E. Matthews, Jr., and Gregory R. New, assistant eds. Albany, N.Y.: Forest Press, A Division of OCLC Online Computer Library Center, Inc., 1989. Vol. 1, p. xxvi.

[2]Arthur Maltby. *Sayers' Manual of Classification for Libraries.* 5th ed. London: Andre Deutsch, 1975. P. 121. John Phillip Comaromi, on the other hand, argues that Hegel provided the philosophic underpinnings of Harris's and Dewey's classification systems (cf. his *The Eighteen Editions of the Dewey Decimal Classification.* Albany, N.Y.: Forest Press Division, Lake Placid Education Foundation, 1976. P. 29).

Bacon divides knowledge into three basic categories—history, poesy, and philosophy—corresponding to the three basic faculties of the human mind—memory, imagination, and reason. The classifications of Bacon, Harris, and Dewey are compared in Table 12-1.

In his new classification scheme, Dewey introduced two new features: relative location and relative index. Prior to Dewey, books in libraries were numbered according to their locations on the shelves. In other words, each book had a fixed location. The Dewey system, on the other hand, numbers books in terms of their relationship to one another without regard to the shelves or rooms where they are placed. Relative location allows indefinite intercalation; books can be moved about in the library without altering their call numbers. In the relative index, Dewey brings together under one term the locations in the scheme of a subject which, in many cases, falls in several fields of study.

Early Editions

The second edition of DDC, a considerable expansion from the 1876 edition, appeared in 1885, making a number of relocations—i.e., shifts of subjects from certain numbers to other numbers. This edition set the

TABLE 12-1   Classification Systems of Bacon, Harris, and Dewey

Bacon		Harris	Dewey
[Original]	[Inverted]		
		Science	
History	Philosophy	Philosophy	General works
(Memory)		Religion	Philosophy
		Social and political	Religion
		science	Sociology
		Natural sciences	Philology
		and useful arts	Science
			Useful arts
		Art	
Poesy	Poesy	Fine arts	Fine arts
(Imagination)		Poetry	Literature
		Pure fiction	
		Literary miscellany	
		History	
Philosophy	History	Geography and	History
(Reason)		travel	Biography
		Civil history	Geography and
		Biography	travel
		Appendix	
		Miscellany	

notational pattern for all subsequent editions. It was also in this edition that Dewey laid down his famous injunction of the "integrity of numbers." Being a pragmatist and a realist, Dewey was fully aware that a system that changed substantially from edition to edition would not be acceptable to librarians, because changes, particularly relocations, necessitate reclassification. Therefore, in the preface to the second edition, Dewey declared that the numbers may be considered "settled," and henceforth there would be expansions, when necessary, but few relocations. This policy had a stabilizing effect on subsequent revisions of DDC, particularly in the early editions; expansions were made as appropriate, but relocations were kept to a minimum. Nonetheless, in order to cope with new developments in knowledge, certain major changes could not be avoided.

Dewey himself supervised DDC revision through its thirteenth edition, working until his death in 1931. His interest in simplified spelling was reflected in the early schedules, e.g., Filosofy and Geografy.

Fifteenth Edition

The fourteenth edition followed the editorial policies that had governed work on earlier editions: expansion in detail as required, but little change in basic structure. The expansion, however, had not always been balanced, and there were many underdeveloped areas. With the fifteenth edition, it was decided that a new approach was necessary in order to give the scheme a more even structure and to keep up with new developments in knowledge, particularly in science and technology. Several innovations were introduced: details were cut back until all subjects reflected more or less equal degrees of subdivision; a large number of subjects were relocated; the index was pruned drastically; and the simplified spelling used in earlier editions was discontinued. The magnitude of the changes was considerable; for instance, some 31,000 entries in the fourteenth edition were reduced to 4700 in the fifteenth edition.

After the publication of the fifteenth edition in 1951, it soon became clear that the changes were too much for practicing librarians, most of whom refused to accept the new edition and continued to use the fourteenth. Criticism of the fifteenth edition was fierce and vehement. Many critics even pronounced the system dead.

Sixteenth Edition and Later Editions

The sixteenth edition, under the editorship of Benjamin A. Custer, appeared in 1958. This edition reflected a return to the former policy of detailed enumeration but incorporated some of the innovative features of the fifteenth edition, such as standard spelling, current terminology, and a pleasing typographic presentation.

The seventeenth through nineteenth editions, also under the editorship of Custer, continued to develop along similar lines. Attempts were made to keep pace with knowledge while maintaining "integrity of numbers" to the greatest reasonable extent.

The twentieth edition, under the editorship of John P. Comaromi, assisted by Julianne Beall, Winton E. Matthews, Jr., and Gregory R. New, appeared in 1989. The classification, by now, has grown into a four-volume set. A classifiers' manual, which was first issued as a separate publication after the appearance of the nineteenth edition, was incorporated into the twentieth edition, following the index.

Abridged Dewey Decimal Classification

Fairly early on it became obvious that a short form of the classification would be better suited to the needs of small and slowly growing libraries. Accordingly, an abridged edition of the scheme, about two-fifths the size of the full edition, was issued in 1894. In the beginning, the abridged edition was revised when the need arose; later, it was considered desirable to follow each full edition with an abridged edition. The present twelfth abridged edition accompanied the full twentieth edition.

From its first appearance, the abridged edition has been designed specifically for elementary and secondary school libraries, small public libraries with collections not expected to grow beyond 20,000 titles, and other collections of a general nature. It is used by most of the school libraries and many small libraries in this country and is also widely used in other countries, particularly Great Britain.

Through the ninth abridged edition, the numbers, on the whole, represented a true abridgment of those in the full edition. In the tenth, there was a basic change. Some numbers represented an adaptation rather than an abridgment of those in the full edition; in other words, many subjects were represented by numbers that were different instead of just shorter than those found in the full edition. In this sense, the tenth edition was in part an adaptation and in part an abridgment. In response to requests from users, the eleventh and twelfth abridged editions returned to being true abridgments of the full edition.

REVISION
Current Procedures for Revision

An editorial team consisting of the editor-in-chief and three assistant editors oversees and is responsible for DDC revision. The editorial office is a part of Collection Services at the Library of Congress; Forest Press, a division of OCLC Online Computer Library Center and the publisher of DDC, has a contractual arrangement with the Library of Congress for the editorial work. Between these two organizations is a group called the *Decimal Classification Editorial Policy Committee,* composed of practicing librarians and library educators, which advises both the editors and Forest Press concerning matters related to the revision of DDC; the committee examines proposed revisions and makes appropriate recommendations. The editors of DDC are also staff members of the Decimal Classification Division of the Library of Congress, which is responsible for assigning DDC numbers to LC cataloging records. The joint appointments ensure consistency and a great degree of coordination between the revision and the application of the system.

Presently, DDC is being revised at approximately seven- to ten-year intervals. Between editions, the schedules and tables are regularly reexamined; revisions of existing numbers and index entries, and provisions for new subjects, are made as required. This policy, called *continuous revision,* was adopted after publication of the nineteenth edition in order to ensure currency of the scheme. As a result, substantial revisions and new developments in the schedules may be published separately between editions.

Forms of Revision

Revisions usually take the following forms.

Expansion

This method is used to introduce new subjects as well as to provide more minute and specific subdivisions under existing subjects. The numerical notational system of DDC is such that new subjects can only be introduced as subdivisions under existing subjects. This is a reasonable approach, since new subjects seldom emerge totally independent of existing knowledge but usually appear as an offspring or outgrowth of an existing field. For existing knowledge, as library material proliferates, more minute subdivisions of existing topics are also required.

Reduction

Occasionally, existing subdivisions that are rarely used are discontinued and the subtopics are classed with the more general topic. In general, reductions are far outnumbered by expansions.

Relocation

In each edition, a number of existing topics are moved to different locations (i.e., numbers) in the scheme. Relocation is usually an attempt to meet one of the following goals:

1. To eliminate dual provisions when two or more numbers have the same meaning or overlap to a large extent. For example, before the twentieth edition, Waste technology was represented by both 604.6 (Waste technology) and 628.4 (Public sanitation). In the twentieth edition, 604.6 was eliminated so that all material on Waste technology is now classed in 628.4 (Waste technology, public toilets, street cleaning).
2. To make room for new subjects when there is no available number. For example, in the eighteenth edition, Antarctica was moved from the areas notation -99 to -989 in order that -99 could be used for Extraterrestrial worlds. In general, a number vacated as a result of relocation is not reused until a later edition. However, in this case, the urgency to accommodate the Extraterrestrial worlds outweighed this policy of *starvation.*
3. To provide uniformity of development for parallel subjects.
4. To reflect realignment of fields of knowledge. A new subject, which had been introduced as a subdivision under an existing subject, may turn out to belong more properly in a different field of knowledge. For example, Astronautics, which was originally placed in 629.1388 (as a subdivision under Aeronautics) was moved to 629.4 (as one of the "other branches" of engineering).
5. To rectify an improper placement by moving the topic to where it really belongs. For example, in the eighteenth edition, Yiddish language and literature, formerly in 492.49 and 892.49 (as subdivisions of Hebraic languages and literature) were relocated to 437.947 and 839.09 (as branches of Germanic languages and literatures).

Completely revised schedules

A completely revised schedule, previously called a *phoenix schedule,* represents the most drastic form of revision. With this method, an entire schedule, such as 780 (Music) in the twentieth edition and 340 (Law) in the eighteenth edition, is reconstructed without regard to previous divisions. The policy of integrity of numbers is suspended, and the editors are not hampered by the notational constriction in rearranging existing subjects and inserting new subjects. As a result, massive relocations occur within that schedule. In recent editions, the following schedules have been revised completely:

546 (Inorganic chemistry) and 547 (Organic chemistry) in edition 16
130 (Pseudopsychology, parapsychology, occultism) and 150 (psychology) in edition 17
340 (Law) and 510 (Mathematics) in edition 18

301–307 (Sociology), 324 (The political process), and -41 and -42 (areas notations for Great Britain in Table 2) in edition 19
780 (Music) and -711 (areas notation for British Columbia in Table 2) in edition 20

New schedules

Occasionally, the schedule for a particular subject is completely re-worked and moved to a new location so that there is no conflict with the old schedule. An example of a new schedule is the 004–006 (Data processing and Computer science) revision developed and published separately between the nineteenth and twentieth editions. The new schedule was eventually incorporated into the twentieth edition.

BASIC PRINCIPLES
Classification by Discipline

To say that classification groups together materials on the same subject is an oversimplification. In fact, both the Dewey Decimal Classification and the Library of Congress Classification, the major systems in use in this country, are classifications by discipline. The division of main classes and subclasses is based on academic disciplines, or fields of study, rather than on subject. Such division means that the same subject may be classed in more than one place in the scheme. For example, the subject "family," depending on the author's approach and perspective, may be classed in ethics, religion, sociology, social customs, family planning, home economics, or genealogy.

In Dewey Decimal Classification, knowledge was initially divided into ten main classes that mirrored the recognized academic divisions of Dewey's time: General works, Philosophy, Theology, Sociology (later Social sciences), Philology, Natural science, Useful arts, Fine arts, Literature, and History (see Table 12-2). Some of these are not considered disciplines today, but rather areas of study, each of which includes several academic disciplines. Based on the curriculum of a modern university, one would group such fields as Philosophy, Languages, Fine arts, and Literature as disciplines under the area of Humanities, in parallel with other areas of study such as Social sciences and Physical sciences, each of which also contains various disciplines. In DDC, however, Philosophy, Languages, Literature, etc. remain as coordinate subjects with Social sciences, Pure sciences, and Technology/Applied sciences. This fact alone makes the scheme somewhat uneven in the extent to which its basic organization of knowledge matches what prevails in the world today. Furthermore, over the last hundred years, the advance-

TABLE 12-2   Outline of Dewey Decimal Classification

000 Generalities	**500 Natural sciences & mathematics**
010 Bibliography	510 Mathematics
020 Library & information sciences	520 Astronomy & allied sciences
030 General encyclopedic works	530 Physics
040	540 Chemistry & allied sciences
050 General serials & their indexes	550 Earth sciences
060 General organizations & museology	560 Paleontology Paleozoology
070 News media, journalism, publishing	570 Life sciences
080 General collections	580 Botanical sciences
090 Manuscripts & rare books	590 Zoological sciences
100 Philosophy & psychology	**600 Technology (Applied sciences)**
110 Metaphysics	610 Medical sciences Medicine
120 Epistemology, causation, humankind	620 Engineering & allied operations
130 Paranormal phenomena	630 Agriculture
140 Specific philosophical schools	640 Home economics & family living
150 Psychology	650 Management & auxiliary services
160 Logic	660 Chemical engineering
170 Ethics (Moral philosophy)	670 Manufacturing
180 Ancient, medieval, Oriental philosophy	680 Manufacture for specific uses
190 Modern Western philosophy	690 Buildings
200 Religion	**700 The arts**
210 Natural theology	710 Civic & landscape art
220 Bible	720 Architecture
230 Christian theology	730 Plastic arts Sculpture
240 Christian moral & devotional theology	740 Drawing & decorative arts
250 Christian orders & local church	750 Painting & paintings
260 Christian social theology	760 Graphic arts Printmaking & prints
270 Christian church history	770 Photography & photographs
280 Christian denominations & sects	780 Music
290 Other & comparative religions	790 Recreational & performing arts
300 Social sciences	**800 Literature & rhetoric**
310 General statistics	810 American literature in English
320 Political science	820 English & Old English literatures
330 Economics	830 Literatures of Germanic languages
340 Law	840 Literatures of Romance languages
350 Public administration	850 Italian, Romanian, Rhaeto-Romanic
360 Social services; association	860 Spanish & Portuguese literatures
370 Education	870 Italic literatures Latin
380 Commerce, communications, transport	880 Hellenic literatures Classical Greek
390 Customs, etiquette, folklore	890 Literatures of other languages
400 Language	**900 Geography & history**
410 Linguistics	910 Geography & travel
420 English & Old English	920 Biography, genealogy, insignia
430 Germanic languages German	930 History of ancient world
440 Romance languages French	940 General history of Europe
450 Italian, Romanian, Rhaeto-Romanic	950 General history of Asia Far East
460 Spanish & Portuguese languages	960 General history of Africa
470 Italic languages Latin	970 General history of North America
480 Hellenic languages Classical Greek	980 General history of South America
490 Other languages	990 General history of other areas

SOURCE: Melvil Dewey. *Dewey Decimal Classification and Relative Index.* Ed. 20. John P. Comaromi, ed. Julianne Beall, Winton E. Matthews, Jr., and Gregory R. New, assistant eds. Albany, N.Y.: Forest Press, A Division of OCLC Online Computer Library Center, Inc., 1989, Vol. 2, p. x.

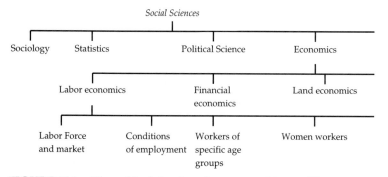

FIGURE 12-1   Hierarchical structure from general to specific.

ment of knowledge in different fields has varied considerably in both quantity and velocity so that some classes have remained fairly stable throughout successive editions, while others have undergone tremendous development and expansion. Thus disparity in treatment from class to class has been compounded.

Table 12-2 shows the current distribution of topics over the system.

Structural Hierarchy

Each of the ten *main classes* is divided into ten *divisions*, and each division is divided into ten *sections*, with further subdivisions made as required. Each level, divided on a base of ten because of the notational system, is subordinate to the level above it, thus forming a hierarchical structure that progresses from the general to the specific (Fig. 12-1). Each level of the hierarchy is called a *class*.[3]

In general, arrangement is first by discipline, then by subject with various levels of subject subdivisions, then by geographic and/or period specification, and then by form of presentation. Exceptions to this pattern are found in the Literature (800) and Generalia (000) classes. In the Literature class, arrangement of belles lettres is first by the discipline (literature), then by original language, then by literary form, and then by period of composition. In the Generalia class, certain categories of materials, including general encyclopedias (030), periodicals (050), newspapers (071–079), and general collections (080), are arranged first by form and then by language or place as provided by the schedules. Since these general materials do not deal with any specific subject and therefore do not belong to any specific discipline, there is no subject specification. The 800 class and these portions of the 000 class are sometimes called *form* classes.

[3]"Introduction." In *Dewey Decimal Classification and Relative Index.* Ed. 20. Op. cit. Vol. 1, p. xxviii.

NOTATION

Symbols

Dewey adopted a pure notation based on arabic numerals. Each topic in the scheme is represented by a number expressed in arabic numerals only, with decimal expansion as needed, e.g., 030, 150, 346.7304695, etc. Such a notation has the advantage of being widely recognized and transcending most language barriers.

Main classes and divisions in DDC are organized around a base of ten, a characteristic of the arabic numeral system. Main classes are numbered 0 through 9, as shown in Table 12-2. Further divisions and subdivisions follow the decimal principle, e.g.,

5 Natural sciences and mathematics
  51 Mathematics
  52 Astronomy and allied sciences
  53 Physics
  etc.

For such numbers to be considered sequential, there must be a leading decimal. However, to make its notation easier to grasp, DDC uses three-digit numbers for its main classes, for the divisions of main classes, and for major sections of those divisions; zeros are put in as fillers in the numbers for main classes and their branches. Thus we have 500 for the main class Natural sciences and 510 for one of its major branches, Mathematics. When more than three digits are needed to specify a topic, a decimal point is placed after the third digit, giving numbers such as 512.56 and 512.546. As decimal numbers, 512.546 precedes 512.56.

Notational Hierarchy

The DDC notation reflects the hierarchical order of the classification, showing the relationship between each level of knowledge and its superordinate and subordinate elements. Each of the ten main classes is divided into ten divisions represented by the second position in the notation. Thus, in 500 (general works on Natural sciences), 510 through 590 are used for the major branches of science, e.g., 510 (Mathematics), 520 (Astronomy and allied sciences), 530 (Physics), 540 (Chemistry and allied sciences), etc.

Each branch, in turn, is divided into ten sections, represented by the number in the third position of the notation, e.g.,

510 Mathematics
  511 General principles
  512 Algebra and number theory

513 Arithmetic
514 Topology

540 Chemistry and allied sciences
541 Physical and theoretical chemistry
542 Techniques, procedures, apparatus, equipment, materials
543 Analytical chemistry

The system allows further subdivision into various degrees of specificity by means of a continued decimal notation. The decimal point is always placed after the third digit, followed by as many digits as required by the subject matter. The notation never ends with a zero after the decimal point, since a terminal zero after a decimal point has no value.

As the classification progresses from the general to the specific, each level of division is indicated by the addition of one new digit. The following example illustrates the hierarchical structure present in both the notation and the classificatory categories, carried to three digits beyond the decimal point:

500 Natural sciences and mathematics
  510 Mathematics
    516 Geometry
      516.3 Analytic geometries
        516.37 Metric differential geometries
        516.372 Euclidean geometry

There are, however, a few exceptions to the hierarchical structure, as is the case for Biology (574), Botanical sciences (580), and Zoological sciences (590); most scientists would consider it more reasonable to make botany and zoology subtopics under biology rather than coordinate topics. The intention of the DDC classificationists is that, in general, the classificatory structure be hierarchical and, as such, be reflected in the notation.

Mnemonics

In assigning numbers to subjects, Dewey frequently used consistent numbers for recurring subjects. For example, Italy is regularly represented by the notation 5, which recurs in numbers related to that country: 945 (history of Italy), 914.5 (Description of Italy), 450 (Italian language), 554.5 (Geology of Italy), 195 (Italian philosophy), and 035 (General encyclopedic works in the Italian language). In literature, the number 1 represents poetry, thus 811 (American poetry), 821 (English poetry), 851 (Italian poetry), etc. This device helps readers to memorize or recognize class numbers more easily. Furthermore, it has enabled the system to develop from an enumerative system to a more nearly analytico-synthetic scheme in which many elements in a class number can be readily isolated and identified.

In the earlier editions, the mnemonic device was used most prominently in the following areas: form divisions, geographic divisions, languages, and literature. As the analytico-synthetic nature of the system increased, the mnemonic device has become standard practice for some aspects of the system.

DDC began as a basically enumerative system, in that the numbers for individual subjects, including compound and complex subjects, are enumerated in the scheme. In the second edition, however, the table for form divisions was introduced; also, certain numbers in the scheme were to be divided like certain other numbers, particularly those pertaining to geographic subdivision. Thus a limited amount of synthesis, or number building, existed from the early editions.

In the seventeenth edition, an areas table for geographic subdivisions was introduced. Then, in the eighteenth edition, five more auxiliary tables appeared; these enhance greatly the analytico-synthetic nature of the system.

EVALUATION

A great deal has been written about the merits and weaknesses of the Dewey Decimal Classification. Following is a brief summary of some of the opinions.

Merits

1. It is a practical system. The fact that it has survived many storms in the past hundred and twenty years and is still the most widely used classification scheme in the world today attests to its practical value.

2. Relative location was an innovation introduced by Dewey, even though it is now taken for granted.

3. The relative index brings together different aspects of the same subject scattered in different disciplines.

4. The pure notation of arabic numerals is universally recognizable. People from any cultural or language background can adapt to the system easily.

5. The self-evident numerical sequence facilitates filing and shelving.

6. The hierarchical nature of the notation expresses the relationships between and among the class numbers. This characteristic particularly facilitates online searching. The searcher can broaden or narrow a search by reducing or adding a digit to the class number.

7. Use of the decimal system enables infinite expansion and subdivision.

8. The mnemonic nature of the notation helps library users to navigate within the system.

9. The continuous revision and publication of the schedules at regular intervals ensure the currency of the scheme.

Weaknesses

1. The Anglo-American bias is obvious, particularly in 900 (Geography and history) and 800 (Literature). A heavy bias toward American protestantism is especially evident in 200 (Religion).

2. Related disciplines are often separated, e.g., 300 (Social sciences) from 900 (Geography and history) and 400 (Languages) from 800 (Literature).

3. The proper placements of certain subjects also have been questioned, e.g., Library science in general works (000s), Psychology as a subdivision under Philosophy (100s), and Sports and Amusements in The arts (700s).

4. In 800, literary works by the same author are scattered according to literary form when most scholars would prefer to have them grouped together.

5. The base of ten limits the hospitality of the notational system by restricting the capacity for accommodating subjects on the same level of a hierarchy to nine divisions.

6. The different rate of growth in various disciplines has resulted in an uneven structure. Some classes, such as 300 (Social sciences), 500 (Natural sciences), and 600 (Technology), have become overcrowded.

7. Even though an existing subject can be expanded indefinitely by virtue of the decimal system, no new numbers can be inserted between coordinate numbers—e.g., between 610 and 620—even when required for the accommodation of new subjects. The present method of introducing a new subject is to include it as a subdivision under an existing subject.

8. While the capacity for expansion is infinite, it also results in lengthy numbers for specific and minute subjects. The long numbers have been found inconvenient, particularly when the system is used as a shelving device.

9. Relocations and completely revised (i.e., phoenix) schedules, while necessary to keep up with knowledge, create practical problems in terms of reclassification for libraries using the scheme.

ASSIGNING CALL NUMBERS

A call number based on the Dewey Decimal Classification consists of two parts: the class number and the book or item number. The book or item number consists of one or more elements based on the bibliographic characteristics of the item. The construction of the DDC call number is discussed below.

CLASS NUMBERS [MARC FIELDS 082, 09X SUBFIELD ‡a][4]

The class number may be derived from the full edition or the abridged edition.

NUMBER BUILDING: FULL EDITION[5]

As a result of the influence of modern classification theory, DDC has become less enumerative and increasingly analytico-synthetic in recent editions. Many numbers that can be used in classifying works are not enumerated in the schedules. Instead, they must be built up from base numbers, by analogy, or according to the provisions of auxiliary tables. The discussion below illustrates how class numbers enumerated in the schedules are expanded as needed through notational synthesis—in other words, by what is called *number building*.

The main or base number is always taken from the schedules. The additional elements may come from either the schedules or the auxiliary tables, or both, and are added to the base number. (In this context, *added* means "tacked onto," not added in the arithmetical sense.) The order of the elements in each case is determined by instruction in the schedules or tables. In building numbers, decimal points are removed. After the process of synthesis is completed, a decimal point is inserted after the third digit.

[4]In bibliographic records prepared by the Library of Congress, field 082 carries the class number in subfield ‡a and an edition (i.e., edition of DDC on which the class number is based) number in subfield ‡2, e.g., 523.6 ‡2 20. In records that do not show the delimiter ‡, the subfield code 2 can be easily mistaken as part of the class number.
[5]Instruction in the use of the abridged edition follows on pages 303–314.

Combining Schedule Numbers

Adding an entire number to a base number

A bibliography of physics	016.53
1. The main number for bibliographies and catalogs of works on specific subjects or in specific disciplines with a note to "add to base number 016 notation 001–999" the number for the specific subject	016
2. The number for Physics	530
3. The subject number added to the base number	016 530
4. The resulting number with a decimal point after the third digit and the removal of the terminal 0 after the decimal point	016.53

Paper industry	338.47 676 2
1. Base number for Secondary industries of specific goods and services, with instruction to add 001–999	338.47
2. Number for Paper production	676 2
3. Add (2) to (1)	338 47 676 2
4. With decimal point inserted	338.47 676 2

Adding a fraction of a number or fractions of numbers to a base number

A general Russian periodical	057.1
1. Number for all serial publications as indicated in the index	050
2. Number in schedule for serial publications in Slavic languages, with instruction: "Add to base number 057, the numbers following 037 in 037.1–037.9."	057
3. The number in the sequence for Russian	037.1
4. Add the number following 037 to (2)	057 1
5. With decimal point inserted	057.1

A Presbyterian guide to Christian life	248.485
1. Base number for Guides to Christian life with instruction: "Add to base number 248.48 the numbers following 28 in 280.2–289.9."	248.48

2. The number for the Presbyterian Church
   in the sequence   285
3. Add the number following 28 to (1)   248 485
4. With decimal point inserted   248.485

Photographs of scientific subjects   779.95
1. Base number for photographs with
   instruction: "Add to base number 779
   the numbers following 704.94 in
   704.942–704.949."   779
2. The most appropriate number in the
   sequence Iconography of other specific
   subjects, with instructions: "Add to base
   number 704.949 notation 001–999."   704.949
3. The number for Science   500
4. Add (3) to (2)   704 949500
5. Add the number following 704.94 to (1)   779 9500
6. With decimal point inserted and
   terminal 0s removed   779.95

EXERCISE A

Assign Dewey Decimal Classification numbers to the following topics.

1. India under the British rule

2. Discipline of students through punishments in the public schools

3. Television commercials

4. A thesaurus of water resources terms

5. Planning public library buildings

6. A bibliography on diagnostic x-ray techniques

7. Inbreeding in relation to human eugenics

8. Commentaries on the Gospel of John

9. Colligative properties of electrolytic solutions

10. Unemployment in library services

11. Embryology of vertebrates

12. Curriculum design in schools

13. *Dear Comrades: Menshevik Reports on the Bolshevik Revolution and the Civil War*

Adding Notation(s) from the Auxiliary Tables to a Base Number

In the twentieth edition of DDC, there are seven auxiliary tables:

Table 1: Standard subdivisions
Table 2: Geographic areas, historical periods, persons
Table 3: Subdivisions for individual literatures, for specific literary forms
(handwritten: 800's)
(handwritten: Some) Table 3-A. Subdivisions for works by or about individual authors
(handwritten: 700's) Table 3-B. Subdivisions for works by or about more than one author
Table 3-C. Notation to be added where instructed in Table 3-B and in 808–809
Table 4: Subdivisions of individual languages *(handwritten: 420-490)*
Table 5: Racial, ethnic, national groups
Table 6: Languages
Table 7: Groups of persons

Notations from all tables, except those in Tables 3 and 4, are applicable throughout the entire schedules. Notations from Table 1 may be used wherever applicable. Notations from Tables 2, 5, 6, and 7 are used only when instructed.[6] Tables 3 and 4 apply only to certain schedules, Table 3 to the 800s and parts of 700s and Table 4 to 420–490; these, too, are used only when specifically instructed.

All notations from the auxiliary tables are preceded by a dash, indicating that these are not complete class numbers but must be used in conjunction with main numbers from the schedules. In some cases, a notation from one table may be added to one found in another table, and the combination is then attached to the appropriate main number from the schedules to form a complete class number.

Table 1. Standard subdivisions

After a specific class number has been chosen for a work, the classifier should then consider whether further specification concerning the bibliographic form or the author's approach is desirable, i.e., whether any of the standard subdivisions is applicable. Table 1 lists nine categories of standard subdivisions which are further subdivided into more detailed specifications. All notations for standard subdivisions begin with a 0, e.g., -01, -07154.

Notations from auxiliary tables are never used alone or as main

[6]However, notations from Tables 2, 5, and 7 may be added, according to instructions, to -09, 089, and -88, respectively, in Table 1, and the results are then used as standard subdivisions, i.e., may be used whenever appropriate.

numbers. With the exception of -04, the classifier does not need any specific instruction in the schedules in order to add the notations for standard subdivisions. Appropriateness and applicability are the general guides. For example, for a journal of inorganic chemistry, the standard subdivision -05 (for serial publications) is added to the base number 546 to form the number 546.05.

Standard subdivision notations and their meanings are given in Table 1. However, under certain numbers in the schedules, a few standard subdivisions may be listed when these subdivisions have special meanings or when extended notation is provided for the subject in question. For example under 610 (Medical sciences; Medicine), the standard subdivisions -06 (i.e., 610.6) and -07 (i.e., 610.7) have extended meanings, such as 610.696 (Medical relationships) and 610.73 (Nursing and services of medical technicians and assistants).

The standard subdivision -04 is reserved for special topics which have general application throughout the regular subdivisions of certain specific subjects. Therefore, it varies from subject to subject and is to be used only when the special topics are spelled out in the schedules, e.g., the subdivisions .04–.049 found under 331 (Labor economics).

Before adding a standard subdivision to a base number, the classifier should remove all the terminal zeros which are used as fillers in the base number, a requirement that is referred to as the *single-zero rule*. Therefore, standard subdivision -03 added to the base number 100 results in 103, not 100.03. A journal of library science is classed in 020.5, not 020.05.

However, there are exceptions to the single-zero rule. In many cases, notations beginning with -0, -00, or even -000 have been assigned meanings other than those for standard subdivisions. In these cases, the classifier is instructed to use more than one zero for standard subdivisions, e.g.,

320 Political science
  .01   Philosophy and theory
  .02–.08 Standard subdivisions
(Hence, 320.05 for a journal of political science)

352 Administration of local governments
  352.0001–352.0009 Standard subdivisions
(Hence 352.0009 for a history of the administration of local governments)

350 Public administration and military science
  350.0001–350.0009 Standard subdivisions
(Hence 350.0005 for a journal of public administration and military science)

When a standard subdivision (e.g., 507) or a span of standard subdivisions (e.g., 516.001–.009) is specifically named in the schedules, it is understood that the sub-subdivisions to these standard subdivisions may be used (e.g., 507.4 for science museums or 516.0076 for review and exercises in geometry) unless there are contrary instructions in the schedules.

Certain standard subdivision concepts, particularly for geographic treatment, are displaced to nonzero numbers. For example, insurance in France is represented by the number 368.944 (Insurance in France) instead of 368.00944. When zeros are to be removed, there are clear indications and/or directions in the schedules.

Although standard subdivisions may be applied whenever they are appropriate, there are certain restrictions on their use. In addition to specific restrictions appearing in the schedules relating to individual numbers (e.g., 362.[09] Do not use; class in 362.9), certain general restrictions are set forth in the manual for DDC:[7]

1. The classifier should not add standard subdivisions when they are redundant. In other words, for a history of the United States, do not add -09 to 973, which already means history. Likewise, it is redundant to add -03 to 423, which already means a dictionary of the English language.
2. Standard subdivisions should be added to the number chosen for a work only when the content of the work is equivalent to the whole, or approximately the whole, meaning of the number. In other words, standard subdivisions are not used when the work in hand deals with a subject more specific than the content of the number, i.e., when the subject represented in the work does not have its own specific number. For example, a history of classification systems is classed 025.4309, but a history of the Russian Library-Bibliographical Classification, which does not have its own number, is classed in 025.43, instead of 025.4309. In other words, the standard subdivision is not added unless the content of the work being classified covers the whole, or approximately the whole, of the subject represented by the main number. This is called the *approximate-the-whole rule.*
3. With a few exceptions noted below, the classifier should not add one standard subdivision to another standard subdivision unless there are specific instructions to do so. When two or more standard subdivisions are applicable to a work, choose one. In choosing a standard subdivision, observe the table of precedence found at the beginning of Table 1 (Vol. 1, p. 3), e.g., 020.7 for *Journal of Education for Librarianship* rather than 020.5 or 020.705. On the other hand, the use of more than one standard subdivision is allowed in the following cases:

[7]"Manual." In Melvil Dewey. *Dewey Decimal Classification and Relative Index.* Ed. 20. Op. cit. Vol. 4, pp. 735–41.

a. With standard subdivision -04 because of its unusual nature as a *standard* subdivision
b. With standard subdivisions which have extended meanings, e.g., 610.7305 for a journal of nursing, although both -073 and -05 appear to be standard subdivisions[8]
c. With standard subdivision concepts which have been displaced to nonzero numbers, e.g., 368.944068 (Management of insurance in France).

The following examples show the application of standard subdivisions:

The use of computers in education worldwide	370.285
1. Education	370
2. Standard subdivision for computer applications from Table 1	-0 285
3. Add (2) to (1) (without terminal zero) with decimal point inserted.	370.285
Skills for effective human services management	361.0068
1. Social problems and services with indication of an extra zero for standard subdivisions	361.0
2. Standard subdivision for management from Table 1	-068
3. Add (2) to (1) with decimal point inserted.	361.0068

Table 2: Geographic areas, historical periods, persons

Notations from Table 2, providing representation of geographic areas, historical periods, and persons relating to the main subject, may be used with numbers throughout the schedules as instructed. It is used in the following ways:

Used directly when so noted with numbers from schedules

Geology of Finland	554.897
1. Geology of Europe, with instruction to add area notation -41 to -49 to base number 55	554
2. Area notation for Finland from Table 2	-4 897
3. Add (2) to (1) with decimal point inserted.	554.897

[8]The subdivision -073 under the number 610 has been given an extended meaning, and there is a specific instruction in the schedule to add further standard subdivisions.

Social welfare services in New York City	362.97471
1. Social welfare problems and services: Historical, geographic, persons treatment with instruction: "Add to base number 362.9 notation 01-9 from Table 2."	362.9
2. Area notation for New York City	-7471
3. Add (2) to (1) with decimal point inserted.	362.97471
Emigration from Italy to New York City	325.245097471
1. Base number for emigration from specific continents, countries, localities	325.2
2. Area notation for Italy	-45
3. Add (2) to (1) as instructed.	325.245
4. Standard subdivision for New York City	-097471
5. Add (4) to (3).	325.245097471
North Dakota century school code	344.7840702632
1. Social, labor, welfare, health, safety, education, cultural law in specific jurisdictions and areas	344.3-.9
2. Area notation for North Dakota added to base number 344	344.784
3. School law	344.07
4. Combine (2) and (3) as instructed under 344.3-.9.	344.78407
5. Special form division for collected laws as listed under 342–347	-02632
6. Add (5) to (4).	344.7840702632

Used through interposition of notation -09 from Table 1
In Table 1, under -093 to -099, there is an instruction to add area notation 3–9 from Table 2 to base number -09, e.g., -0973, for historical, geographic, and persons treatment of a subject with regard to the United States. Once an area number is added to -09, the entire combination (e.g., -0973) becomes a standard subdivision. Since -09 is a standard subdivision and can be added to any number from the schedules as desired, virtually every number in the DDC system can be subdivided geographically. However, when direct geographic subdivision is provided as illustrated above, it takes precedence over the use of -09 and its subdivisions.

Commercial policy of the United States	380.130973
1. Number for Commercial policy, with no direct provision for geographic subdivision	380.13
2. Standard subdivision for United States	-0973
3. Add (2) to (1).	380.130973

Paper industry in England	338.4767620942
1. Number for Paper industry as constructed under Paper industry on p. 283	338.476762
2. Standard subdivision for England	-0942
3. Add (2) to (1).	338.4767620942

Used when so noted with numbers from other tables

American Chemical Society	540.6073
1. Number for Chemistry	540
2. Standard subdivision from Table 1 for national organizations	-0 60
3. Add area notation from Table 2 to (2) as instructed.	-0 6073
4. Add (3) to (1).	540.6073

American Physical Society	530.06073
Similar to the example above, except that the number 530 requires two 0s for standard subdivisions	

A history of descriptive research in Library Science	020.723
1. Number for library science	020
2. Standard subdivision for descriptive research	-0 723
3. Standard subdivision for historical treatment	-09
4. Add (2) to (1). (Since the classifier has been advised not to add one standard subdivision to another one, (2) is chosen over (3) according to the order of precedence for standard subdivisions.)	020.723

Used with another number from Table 2

Foreign relations between Japan and Great Britain	327.41052
1. Base number for foreign relations between specific nations as listed under 327.3–327.9	327
2. Area notation for Japan	-52
3. Area notation for Great Britain	-41
4. As instructed, add area notation for one nation to the base number, add 0, and to the result add area notation for the other nation. The order of the area notations is determined by the emphasis of the work. If Japan is emphasized.	327.52041
5. If Great Britain is emphasized.	327.41052
6. "If the emphasis is equal, give priority to the one coming first in the sequence of area notations."	327.41052

EXERCISE B

1. Assign Dewey Decimal Classification numbers to the subjects listed in Table 12-3.

2. Assign Dewey Decimal Classification numbers to the following topics.
   a. Financial management of special education in Ohio
   b. Brooklyn Public Library
   c. History of classical languages
   d. A dictionary of modern music and musicians
   e. Popular music in the United States
   f. *American Libraries* (official journal of the American Library Association)
   g. The government of American cities
   h. *Journal of Physical Oceanography*
   i. Foreign relations between Russia and Japan
   j. The Nazi spy network in Switzerland during World War II
   k. Social conditions in Japan after World War II
   l. Masterpieces of painting in the Metropolitan Museum of Art: An exhibition catalog
   m. Life and health insurance laws (United States)

TABLE 12-3 Exercise B.1: Area Notation

	United States	Tennessee	Scotland	Egypt
Area table notation				
History of				
Tourist guide to				
Newspapers from				
Folk songs from				
Political condition in				
Geology of				

n. Illinois rules and regulations for fire prevention and safety, as amended 1968
o. Arizona library laws (a compilation)
p. Tourist trade of Romagna, Italy, after World War II
q. Statistical methods used in social sciences
r. European immigrants in the United States during the 1930s
s. Computer-aided proofs in numerical analysis
t. An exhibition of twentieth-century American art from a Long Island collection

Table 3: Subdivisions for individual literatures, specific literary forms

Notations from Table 3 are used when applicable with the base numbers for individual literatures identified by an asterisk (*) under 810 to 890, with specific instructions under 808 to 809 and certain numbers in the 700s in the schedules. Syntheses of the notation for literature and music represent the most complex procedures in the DDC system. The application of Table 3 is discussed under "Classification of Literature" (pp. 296–302).

Table 4: Subdivisions of individual languages

Notations from Table 4 are used with base numbers for individual languages identified by an asterisk (*) under 420–490 in the schedules. The classifier's first task is to identify the language in hand.

Intonation of the German language	431.6
1. Base number for German language	43
2. Subdivision for intonation from Table 4	-1 6
3. Add (2) to (1) with decimal point inserted.	431.6

Bilingual dictionaries are a special case. Since a bilingual dictionary involves two languages, the classifier must first determine which language is to be used as the base number. Instructions for choosing the base number are given under -32 to -39 in Table 4. If the entry words are given in only one language with equivalent words in the second language, the number for the first language is used as the base number.

A German-French dictionary	433.41
1. Base number for the German language	43
2. Subdivisions for bilingual dictionaries	-32-39
3. Language notation for the French language from Table 6	-41
4. Add (3) to (2) and (1).	433.41

A bilingual dictionary containing entry words in both languages is classed as instructed, usually with the number for the language lesser known to the users as the base number.

An English-Spanish, Spanish-English dictionary	463.21
1. Base number for Spanish as the "more useful" for English-speaking users	46
2. Subdivision for bilingual dictionaries	-32-39
3. Add languages notation (-21) for English from Table 6 to the subdivision for dictionaries (-3) in Table 4.	-3 21
4. Add (3) to (1) with decimal point inserted.	463.21

As instructed under -32 to -39 in Table 4 (vol. 1, p. 418), "If classification with either language is equally useful, class with the language coming later in the sequence."

A German-French, French-German dictionary	443.31
1. Base number for French, since it is greater than the number for German, i.e., 43	44
2. Subdivision for bilingual dictionaries	-32-39
3. Add language notation (-31) for German from Table 6 to the subdivision for dictionaries (-3) in Table 4.	-3 31
4. Add (3) to (1) with decimal point inserted.	443.31

Table 5: Racial, ethnic, national groups

Notations from Table 5 are used with those numbers from the schedules and other tables to which the classifier is instructed to add racial, ethnic, national groups notation.

Social groups among the Hindis	305.89143
1. Base number for racial, ethnic, national groups with instruction to add notation from Table 5	305.8
2. Notation for Hindis from Table 5	-9143
Decorative arts of the Chinese	745.089951
1. Base number for Decorative and minor arts	745

2. Standard subdivision for treatment
among specific racial, ethnic, national
groups with instruction to add notation
from Table 5   -089
3. Notation for Chinese from Table 5   -951

Table 6: Languages

Notations from Table 6 represent the language aspect, or facet, of a
subject and are used with base numbers from the schedules. They are
added as instructed, a procedure similar to that employed with Tables
2 and 5.

A French Bible	220.541
A Swahili Bible	220.596392
The Old Testament in French	221.541
The Old Testament in Swahili	221.596392
The Book of Job in French	223.10541
The Book of Job in Swahili	223.10596392
A general Japanese periodical	059.9 56

Table 7: Persons

The procedure for using notations from Table 7 is similar to that employed for Tables 2, 5, and 6.

Children as artists	704.054
Paintings by athletes	750.88796

EXERCISE C

Assign Dewey Decimal Classification numbers to the following subjects
or titles.

1. Swahili grammar

2. A bibliography of anonymous works in German

3. A Chinese-English, English-Chinese dictionary

4. Islamic painting

5. Babylonian and Assyrian religion

6. *La Raza: The Mexican-Americans*

7. Mennonite Colonization in Mexico

8. The great Jewish families of New York

9. A German version of the New Testament

10. World War II letters of Barbara Wooddall Taylor and Charles E. Taylor

11. The Arabic linguistic tradition

12. Teaching English reading in the secondary school

13. The Spanish-speaking people from Mexico in the United States

14. *Farewell, My Nation: The American Indian and the United States, 1820–1890*

15. Italian-American women in Nassau County, New York, 1925–1981

16. The Jewish minority in the Netherlands

Classification of Literature

In the classification of literature, the subject or topical aspect is secondary to language, literary form, and period, which are the main facets of literature. Other facets include style, mood, themes, and subjects. In general, in DDC, the numbers for works by or about individual authors reflect primary facets, while those for collection and criticism of more than one author bring out other facets as well.

Citation order

With few exceptions, the citation order for the different facets in a class number for literature is

1. Main class literature is represented by the base number 8.
2. Language is the second element in the number, e.g., 82- for English literature, 895.1- for Chinese literature, and so on. When the work is not limited to any language, a zero is used to fill the second digit, e.g., 80- for world literature.
3. Literary form is the third element. Mnemonics are employed, e.g., -1 for poetry, -2 for drama, etc. Hence 821 is used for (English poetry, 895.12 for Chinese drama, and 820 for English literature not limited to a particular form.
4. Period, if applicable, follows literary form, e.g., 811.1 (colonial American poetry).
5. For literature written by more than one author and works about such literature, standard subdivisions with rather elaborate sub-

subdivisions for feature and theme are represented as further subdivisions under -08 (collections) and -09 (history and criticism).

The citation order varies when a collection by more than one author is not limited to a particular language/nationality or a literary form.

Examples

In DDC, classification of literature, particularly literature of specific languages, represents one of the most complex processes of number building. Table 3 is devised for use with the 800 class. It contains three parts:

1. Table 3-A: Subdivisions for works by or about individual authors
2. Table 3-B: Subdivisions for works by or about more than one author
3. Table 3-C: Notation to be added where instructed in Table 3-B and in 808–809

Because of the complexity, very detailed instructions are provided in the DDC manual (vol. 4, pp. 771–786), with a brief step-by-step instruction printed at the beginning of Table 3 (vol. 1, pp. 389–390). These should be studied carefully. The following examples show the many possible combinations of facets in the classification of literature. The examples are divided by various types of literary works and works about literature: (1) collections of literature by more than one author, (2) works about literature, (3) works written by individual authors, (4) works about individual authors, and (5) works about individual works.

1. Collections of literature by more than one author

An anthology of world literature	808.8
A Collection of nineteenth-century literature (Facet: Period)	808.80034
1. Base number for a collection of literature from specific periods	808.800
2. Standard subdivision for early nineteenth century from Table 1	-09034
A collection of Christmas literature (Facet: Feature/theme)	808.8033
1. Base number for a collection of literature displaying specific features	808.80
2. Notation from Table 3-C for themes relating to times (seasons, holidays, etc.)	-33

A collection of nineteenth-century poetry
(Facets: Form, period)   808.81034
1. Base number for a collection of poetry
   from a specific period   808.810
2. Period notation from Table 1   -09034

A collection of Christmas poetry
(Facets: Form plus Feature/theme)   808.81933
1. Base number for a collection of poetry
   displaying specific features   808.819
2. Notation from Table 3-C for holidays   -33

An anthology of Spanish literature
(Facet: Language)   860.8
1. Base number for Spanish literature   86
2. Subdivision for collections from Table
   3-B   -0 8

A collection of eighteenth-century Spanish
literature (Facets: Language plus period)   860.8004
1. Base number for Spanish literature   86
2. Notation from Table 3-B for collections
   of literary texts in more than one form,
   with instruction to add from Table 3-C   -0 80
3. Notation from Table 3-C for specific
   periods   -01-09
4. Notation for the eighteenth century
   from the period table for Spanish
   literature in the schedule (Vol. 3,
   p. 859)   4

A collection of Spanish poetry
(Facets: Language plus Form)   861.008
1. Base number for Spanish literature   86
2. Notation from Table 3-B for a collection
   of poetry   -1 008

A collection of eighteenth-century Spanish
drama (Facets: Language plus Form plus
Period)   862.408
1. Base number for Spanish literature   86
2. Notation from Table 3-B for drama of
   specific periods   -21-29
3. Notation for the eighteenth century
   from period table for Spanish literature   4
4. Notation for collections of literary texts   08

A collection of American Christmas poetry
(Facets: Language plus Form plus Feature/
theme)   <u>811</u>.008033
1. Base number for American literature   <u>81</u>
2. Collections of poetry featuring holidays
     (Tables 3-B and 3-C)   <u>-1</u> <u>008033</u>

A collection of nineteenth-century
American Christmas poetry (Facets:
Language plus Form plus Period plus
Feature/theme)   <u>811</u>.308033
1. Base number for American literature   <u>81</u>
2. Poetry (Table 3-B)   <u>11</u>-19
3. Nineteenth century (period table for
     American literature)   <u>3</u>
4. Collections featuring holidays (Tables
     3-B and 3-C)   <u>-08033</u>

2. Works about literature
Using examples similar to those listed above, one may synthesize the
following numbers for works about literature:

A history of world literature	<u>809</u>
A study of nineteenth-century literature	<u>809.034</u>
A study of Christmas literature	<u>809.9333</u>
A study of nineteenth-century poetry	<u>809.1034</u>
A study of Christmas poetry	<u>809.1933</u>
A history of Spanish literature	<u>860.9</u>
A study of eighteenth-century Spanish literature	<u>860.9004</u>
A study of Spanish poetry	<u>861.009</u>
A study of eighteenth-century Spanish drama	<u>862.409</u>
A study of American Christmas poetry	<u>811.00933</u>
A study of nineteenth-century American Christmas poetry	<u>811.30933</u>

3. Works written by individual authors
Because DDC classes literature by form, the works of an individual
author may be classed in different numbers if the author wrote in
different literary forms.
    The notation for works written by individual authors contains the
following facets: Literature (<u>8</u>), language, form, and period.

The Adventures of Huckleberry Finn by Mark Twain (novel)	813.4
The Celebrated Jumping Frog of Calaveras County by Mark Twain (humorous stories)	813.4
Essays by G. K. Chesterton	824.912
The Heart of Midlothian by Sir Walter Scott (novel)	823.7
The Lady of the Lake by Sir Walter Scott (poems)	821.7

Selected and collected works by individual authors are classed according to literary forms in the same numbers as individual works without the use of -08, the subdivision notation for collections by more than one author.

Short Stories by Sir Walter Scott	823.7
Selected Tales by Edgar Allen Poe	813.3

When the collected works are in different forms, the problem is then which number to use. In general, the number for the predominant form is chosen.

The Writings of Mark Twain	813.4
The Complete Poems and Plays of T.S. Eliot	821.912
Selected Prose and Poetry by Ralph Waldo Emerson	814.3

When no predominant form can be determined, or when the collection includes works in a variety of forms, the number -8 for Miscellaneous writings further subdivided by period and the sub-subdivision -09 is used.

Selected Prose, Poetry, and Eureka by Edgar Allen Poe	818.309
The Wisdom of Sir Walter: Criticisms and Opinions Collected from the Waverley Novels and Lockhart's Life of Sir Walter Scott	828.709
Selections from Voltaire	848.509
The Works of Oscar Wilde	828.809

   In DDC, literary authors do not receive individual unique class numbers as in the Library of Congress Classification. Authors writing in the same form and the same period share the same number. For example, all late-nineteenth-century American novelists are assigned the number 813.4. The only exception to this rule is Shakespeare as a dramatist, to whom the unique number 822.33 has been assigned.

In many libraries, fiction in English is not classified. Instead, it is assigned the letter F and subarranged alphabetically by author.

4. Works about individual authors
Works *about* an individual author are classed in the same number as assigned to the author's works, as instructed in Table 3-A (vol. 1, pp. 389–390).

Ezra Pound: A Collection of Critical Essays, edited by Walter Sutton	811.52
A Study of the Sonnets of Shakespeare	821.3
Aldous Huxley: A Study	823.912
An Essay on the Genius and Writings of Pope	821.5

In literature, it is often difficult to separate biography and criticism of an author. Therefore, they are usually both classed in the 800s.

The Letters of Sir Walter Scott	828.709
Romain Rolland and a World at War	848.91209

Note that the standard subdivision -0924 for individual biography is not used.

5. Works about individual works
Individual works and works about them are classed in the same numbers, as instructed in Table 3-A. The subdivision -09 is not used.

A critical study of Thackeray's *Vanity Fair*	823.8
A study of Marlowe's *Doctor Faustus*	822.3

EXERCISE D

Assign Dewey Decimal Classification numbers to the following.

1. A collection of German literature for and by Jews

2. Characterization in Jacobean tragedies, a critical study

3. A collection of devotional poetry from colonial America

4. A collection of seventeenth-century French drama

5. A history of science fiction in the United States

6. A study of the theme of friendship in fifteenth-century Chinese literature.

7. Abraham Lincoln in American literature, a critical study

8. A study of the theme of alienation in twentieth-century American fiction.

9. The diaries of Mark Twain

10. A history of Irish Gaelic poetry in the early period

11. A study of the theme of death in twentieth-century American poetry

12. A study of the characters in seventeenth-century French drama

13. A study of Shakespeare's tragedies by Clifford Leech

14. Collected poems of Byron

15. The art of writing short stories

16. An anthology of American short stories

17. Literary history of the United States: twentieth century

18. Women writers of contemporary Spain

19. A study of feminine fiction in England, 1713–1799

20. Study of literary criticism in Finnish universities

21. Essays on Russian and Polish literature

22. A study of French Renaissance tragedy

23. Interpret the following decimal classification numbers:
    a. 338.4769009421
    b. 338.926091724
    c. 551.2109989
    d. 782.4215520941
    e. 917.92003

Segmentation

As the preceding examples indicate, DDC class numbers can be rather long and unwieldy. The examples show the maximum specificity permitted by the system. In practice, some of these long numbers are found to be undesirable (particularly in smaller collections) or infeasible because of online system limitations. Since the notational structure is hierarchical, it allows various degrees of specificity through reduction of the length of the numbers. However, it is not desirable to cut the numbers arbitrarily; in each case, there are logical points at which the number can be shortened. To help librarians determine the appropriate places to cut, and to ensure consistency, these points are indicated on Library of Congress cataloging copy by means of prime marks (') or slash marks (/), a practice called *segmentation*, e.g., 342.73'029, 808'.042'07, 231.7'6'09031, or 363.73'94526'091638. Segmentation is particularly useful in handling numbers such as 812'.54'080352036872073.

DDC numbers on Library of Congress cataloging records are presented in one to three segments. A segmentation mark can indicate the end of an abridged number (as provided in the abridged edition) or the beginning of a standard subdivision.[9] A class number that is printed in one segment, e.g., 629.2, should not be shortened. When a number appears in two segments, it is recommended that small libraries consider using only the first segment. When a number is printed in three segments, the first segment is recommended for use by small libraries, the first two segments by medium-sized libraries, and the entire number by large libraries. In the case of a very long number, one or more synthesized elements from the last segment may be omitted, e.g., 812 or 812.54 based on the long example given at the end of the last paragraph.

NUMBER BUILDING: ABRIDGED EDITION[10]

It is a characteristic of the abridged edition to provide a broad classification without minute details. Thus, in many cases, the classifier will find that the abridged edition does not supply a number for a subject as specific as the content of the work being classified. When this is the case, the classifier should choose the most specific base number that the edition provides.

The abridged edition does, however, provide for a certain degree of notational synthesis, or *number building*, since it, like the unabridged DDC, is a partially analytico-synthetic scheme. For number building in the abridged edition, the main or base number is always taken from the schedules. To begin with, all decimal points are removed. The additional elements may come from either the schedules or the auxiliary tables, or both. The order of the elements in each case is determined by instructions in the schedules or tables. After the process of number building is completed, insert a decimal point after the third digit.

[9]Melvil Dewey. Op. cit. Ed. 20. Vol. 4, p. 959.
[10]The author assumes that readers who use the abridged DDC edition and have little interest in the full edition may turn directly to this section without studying what was said above about notational synthesis. This section has therefore been written to stand more or less alone, and so, necessarily, much of what was said above is repeated here.

Combining Schedule Numbers

Adding an entire number to a base number

Bibliography of Adult Education	016.374
1. The number for a subject bibliography with the instruction under 016.1–016.9: "Add to base number 016 notation 001–999," meaning any class number can be added to 016 to obtain the number for a bibliography of that subject	016
2. Adult education	374
3. (2) added to (1) with decimal point inserted	016.374

Adding a fraction of a number to a base number

An Interpretation of the Old Testament	221.6
1. Number for the Old Testament with note under 221.1–221.9: "Add to base number 221 the numbers following 220 in 220.1–220.9"	221
2. The number in that range meaning an interpretation	220.6
3. Add the number following 220 to (1).	221.6

EXERCISE E

Assign Dewey Decimal Classification numbers (abridged edition) to the following topics or titles.

1. Magnetism of the earth

2. Guidance and counseling in schools

3. Cataloging and classification of books in libraries

4. *Séance: A Book of Spiritual Communications*

5. A bibliography of bacteriology

6. Landscaping for homes

7. Acquisition of audiovisual materials in libraries

8. The causes of the Civil War

9. A bibliography of local transportation

10. The kinesiology of weight lifting

11. Designing dormitories

12. *Kentuckiana: A Bibliography of Books about Kentucky*

13. A concordance to modern versions of the New Testament

14. A critique of Marx's *Das Kapital*

15. Smallpox vaccination

16. Newspapers in Russia

17. Position of women in Old Testament

18. Paintings from the United States

19. An atlas of the moon

20. Public library administration

21. Greek mythology

22. *How to Prepare for College Entrance Examinations*

Adding Notation(s) from the Auxiliary Tables to a Base Number

In the abridged edition, there are four auxiliary tables:

Table 1: Standard subdivisions
Table 2: Geographic areas and persons
Table 3: Subdivisions for individual literatures, for specific literary forms
Table 4: Subdivisions of individual languages

Notations from Table 1 are applicable throughout the schedules wherever appropriate. Those from Table 2 also apply to all classes but can be used only when instructed. Table 3 applies only to the numbers 810 to 890 and is used only when specifically instructed. Table 4 applies to the numbers 420 to 490 and is also used with specific instructions.

All notations from the auxiliary tables are preceded by a dash, indicating that these are not complete class numbers but must be used in conjunction with numbers from the schedules. In some cases, a notation from one table may be added to one from another table, and the combination is then used with the appropriate number from the schedules.

Table 1: Standard subdivisions

After a specific number has been chosen for a work, the classifier should then consider whether further specification concerning the bibliographic form or the author's approach is desirable, i.e., whether any of the standard subdivisions is applicable. Table 1 lists nine categories of standard subdivisions, which are further subdivided into more detailed specifications. All notations for standard subdivisions begin with a 0, e.g., -01 and -075.

Notations from auxiliary tables are never used alone or as main numbers. With the exception of -04, the classifier does not need any specific instruction in the schedules in order to add the notations for standard subdivisions. Appropriateness and applicability are the general guides. For a journal of inorganic chemistry, the standard subdivision -05 (for serial publications) is added to the base number 546 to form the number 546.05. The standard subdivision -04 is reserved for special topics which have general application throughout the regular subdivisions of certain specific subjects, e.g., 604, and its subdivisions. Therefore, it varies from subject to subject and is to be used only when the special topics are spelled out in the schedules.

In adding a standard subdivision to a base number, the classifier should first remove all the zeros which are used as fillers. When this is done, standard subdivision -03 added to the base number 100 results in 103, not 100.03. A journal of library science is classed in 020.5, not 020.05.

However, there are exceptions to the single-zero rule. In many cases, notations beginning with 0 have been assigned meanings other than those for standard subdivisions. In these cases, the classifier is instructed to use more than one zero for standard subdivisions.

> 300 Social sciences
> Use 300.1–300.9 for standard subdivisions
> (Hence 300.3 for an encyclopedia of social sciences)

> 543 Analytical chemistry
> .001–.009 Standard subdivisions
> (Hence 543.005 for a journal of analytical chemistry)

When a standard subdivision (e.g., 507) or a span of standard subdivisions (e.g., 516.001-.009) is specifically named in the schedules, it is understood that the sub-subdivisions to these standard subdivisions may be used (e.g., 507.4 for science museums or 516.0076 for review and exercises in geometry) unless there are contrary instructions in the schedules.

Although standard subdivisions may be applied wherever they are appropriate, there are certain restrictions on their use. In addition to restrictions appearing in the schedules relating to specific numbers (e.g., do not use 362.09; class in 362.9), certain general restrictions are set forth in the manual:[11]

1. Unless there are instructions in the schedules permitting their use, the classifier should be cautious about adding a standard subdivision to the number chosen for a work that deals with a subject more specific than the content of the number, i.e., when the subject represented in the work does not have its own specific number. For example, a history of special libraries is classed in 026.0009, but a history of medical libraries, which does not have its own number, is classed in 026 instead of 026.0009. In other words, the standard subdivision is not added unless the content of the work being classified covers the whole, or approximately the whole, of the subject represented by the main number. This is called the *approximate-the-whole rule.*

2. The classifier should not add one standard subdivision to another standard subdivision unless there are specific instructions to do so. When two or more standard subdivisions are applicable to a work, choose one according to the table of precedence, which is found at the head of Table 1, e.g., choosing -068 over -09 and choosing -09 over -05.

Furthermore, the classifier should not add standard subdivisions when they are redundant. Therefore, for a history of the United States, do not add -09 to 973, which already means history. Likewise, it is redundant to add -03 to 423, which already means a dictionary of the English language.

Certain standard subdivision concepts, particularly for geographic treatment, are displaced to nonzero numbers. For example, political campaigns in the United States are classed in 324.973 instead of 324.0973. In such cases, the full range of standard subdivisions may be added further, e.g., maps of American political campaigns, 324.973022.

Table 2: Geographic areas and persons

Areas notation specifies the historical or geographic treatment of a subject and may be used with numbers throughout the schedules as instructed. Such notation is used in the following ways:

[11]Melvil Dewey. *Abridged Dewey Decimal Classification and Relative Index.* Ed. 12. Pp. 39–42.

Used directly when so noted with numbers from the schedules

Geology of Romania	554.98
1. Base number for regional geology	55
2. Areas notation for Romania from Table 2	-4 98
3. Add (2) to (1) with decimal point inserted.	554.98

Postage stamps from Japan	769.56952
1. Base number for postage stamps: historical, geographic, persons treatment	769.569
2. Area notation from Table 2 for Japan	-52
3. Add (2) to (1) with decimal point inserted.	769.56952

A History of Bulgaria	949.77
1. Base number for general history of specific countries. Cf. note under 930–990	9
2. Areas notation for Bulgaria from Table 2	-49 77
3. Add (2) to (1) with decimal point inserted.	949.77

Used through the interposition of notation -09 from Table 1
In Table 1, under -093 to -099, there is an instruction to add areas notation 3 to 9 from Table 2 to base number -09, e.g., -0973 for historical and geographic treatment of a subject with regard to the United States. The combination is then treated as one standard subdivision. Since -09 is a standard subdivision and therefore can be added to any number from the schedules when appropriate, virtually every number in the DDC system can be subdivided geographically, unless there is specific instruction in the schedules not to use the standard subdivision under the particular number.

Economic Geology of Germany	553.0943
1. Base number for economic geology	553
2. Standard subdivision for geographic treatment for Germany	-0943
3. Add (2) to (1) with decimal point inserted.	553.0943

When direct geographic subdivision as explained above is provided, it takes precedence over the use of -09 and its subdivisions.

EXERCISE F

Assign Dewey Decimal Classification numbers (abridged edition) to the following topics or titles.

1. How to teach cooking

2. *Is There Life on Mars? A Scientist's View*

3. Labor union discrimination against black American textile workers

4. Rocks from the moon

5. Flora and fauna of Alaska

6. Nursing education

7. A history of Kentucky during the Civil War

8. Monetary policy of France

9. History of political parties in Australia

10. An encyclopedia of engineering

11. A travel guide to Florida

12. A bibliography of Ohio imprints

13. A history of Christian churches in Iowa

14. *Journal of Political Science*

15. Farming in Iowa

16. A history of New Orleans

17. Interior decoration in Sweden

18. Social conditions in the United States

19. A history of Singapore

20. A collection of fairy tales

21. A gardener's handbook on diseases of flowers

22. Political conditions in the United States

23. Geology of Iran

24. *American Restaurants Then and Now*

25. United States policy toward Latin America

26. Kentucky folklore

27. Macroeconomic policy in Britain, 1974–1987

28. *Early Education in the Public Schools: Lessons from a Comprehensive Birth-to-Kindergarten Program in Brookline, Massachusetts*

Table 3: Subdivisions for individual literatures, for specific literary forms

Notations from Table 3 are used when applicable with the base numbers for individual literatures that are identified by an asterisk (*) under 810 to 890 in the schedules.

A number for literature usually contains the following elements:

1. The main class *Literature* is represented by the base number 8.
2. *Language* is the second element, e.g., 82- for English literature, 891.7 for Russian literature, etc. When the work is not limited to any language, the 0 is used to fill the second digit, e.g., 80- for world literature.
3. *Literary form* is the third element. Mnemonics are employed, e.g., -1 for poetry, -2 for drama, etc. Hence 821 is used for English poetry, 891.72 for Russian drama, etc. When the work covers more than one form, the -0 is used, e.g., 820 for English literature not limited to any particular form.
4. Standard subdivision when applicable, e.g., 830.5 (a journal of German literature).

Different types of literary works are handled in the following ways.

Collections of literature by more than one author

An Anthology of World Literature	808.8
An Anthology of World Drama	808.82
1. Base number for a collection of literary texts in specific forms from more than one literature	808.8
2. The number following 808 meaning drama	-2
3. Add (2) to (1).	808.82
An Anthology of English Literature	820.8
1. Base number for English literature	82
2. Notation for collections of literary texts from Table 3	-0 8

An Anthology of French Poetry	841.008
1. Base number for French literature	84
2. Notation from Table 3 for a collection of poetry by more than one author	-1 008

Works about literature

A History of World Literature	809
A Study of World Drama	809.2
1. Base number for a critical appraisal of literature in specific forms	809
2. Number following 808 in 808.1–808.7 meaning drama, i.e., 808.2	-2
A History of English Literature	820.9
1. Base number for English literature.	82
2. Notation from Table 3 for a history of more than one form by more than one author	-0 9
A Teacher's Handbook for French Literature	840.7
1. Base number for French literature	84
2. Standard subdivision notation from Table 1 for study and teaching	-0 7
An Outline of French Literary History	840.90002
1. Base number for French literature	84
2. Notation from Table 3 for history, description, appraisal of literature in more than one form by more than one author	-0 9
3. Standard subdivision from Table 1 for an outline, with two extra zeros as instructed under -09 in Table 3	0002

Works written by individual authors
The Dewey Decimal Classification classes literature by form; works by a given author who writes in different literary forms are classed in different numbers according to their forms. Standard subdivisions are not used with works by individual authors.

Poems by Henry Wadsworth Longfellow	811
Ivanhoe by Sir Walter Scott	823
Charles Lamb's *Essays*	824

In many libraries, all fiction is grouped together without regard to language and is assigned a simple notation F with the author's name or a Cutter number (see discussion on pages 315–317).

Selected and collected works by individual authors are classed in the same numbers as individual works.

Selected Poems by Edgar Allen Poe	811
Plays by Christopher Marlowe	822

When the collection contains works in various forms, the number for the predominant form or the form by which the author is best known is chosen.

The Writings of Mark Twain	813
Selected Prose and Poetry by Ralph Waldo Emerson	814

Works about individual authors

Works about individual authors are classed in the same numbers as the works written by them, as instructed in Table 3. The standard subdivision -09 is not used.

A Study of Longfellow's Poems	811
Commentary on Homer's Iliad	883
A Critical Appraisal of Sir Walter Scott's Novels	823

Table 4: Subdivisions of individual languages

Notations from Table 4 are used with base numbers for individual languages identified by an asterisk (*) in 420 to 490 in the schedules.

A Dictionary of the Russian Language	491.73
1. Base number for Russian	491.7
2. Notation for dictionaries from Table 4	-3
English Word Origins	422
1. Base number for English	42
2. Notation for etymology from Table 4	-2

Classification of Biography

Under 920 in the schedules, several methods of classing biography are presented. The preferred treatment is to class both individual and collected biography of persons associated with a specific subject with the subject, using standard subdivisions notation -092 from Table 1.

A Biography of Melvil Dewey	020.92
Biographical Directory of Libraries in the United States and Canada	020.92
A Biography of Abraham Lincoln	973.7092
Presidents of the United States	973.092

Note that biographies of heads of states are classed in the numbers for the history of their periods instead of in the number for political science.

Some libraries may find it desirable to use one of the optional methods:

1. Class both individual and collected biography of persons associated with a specific subject in 920.1 to 928.

A Biography of Melvil Dewey	920.2
Biographical Directory of Librarians in the United States and Canada	920.2
A Biography of Abraham Lincoln	923
Presidents of the United States	923

2. Class all individual biography, regardless of subject orientation, in 92 or B and all collected biography, regardless of subject orientation, in 92 or 920 without subdivision.

A Biography of Melvil Dewey	92 or B
Biographical Directory of Librarians in the United States and Canada	92 or 920
A Biography of Abraham Lincoln	92 or B
Presidents of the United States	92 or 920

3. Class individual biography of men in 920.71 and of women in 920.72.

EXERCISE G

Assign Dewey Decimal Classification numbers (abridged edition) to the following topics.

1. A history of American literature

2. An encyclopedia of Austrian literature

3. A biography of President Lyndon Baines Johnson

4. A biography of Walter Cronkite

5. A teacher's handbook of Latin literature

6. A critical study of twentieth-century drama

7. An English-Japanese, Japanese-English dictionary

8. A critical study of Russian novels

9. A history of Chinese poetry

10. The collected works of Henry Fielding

11. A handbook for sign language teachers

12. A critical study of the Afro-American as a character in American fiction

13. Remedial reading for French

14. A collection of Portuguese essays (by various authors)

15. A study of political themes in twentieth-century British literature

BOOK OR ITEM NUMBERS [MARC FIELDS 082, 09X, SUBFIELD ‡b][12]

Several kinds of book or item numbers, often referred to as *author notation* (or number), may be employed with DDC class numbers. The simplest form, used by many small school, public, and church libraries, is the initial based on the main entry, in most cases the author's last name. For example:

512	822.3
D	M

For slightly larger collections, more letters from the main entry or author's last name may be used. Hence:

512	822.3
Dic	Mar

[12]In bibliographic records prepared by the Library of Congress, the item number is not assigned. In other words, field 082 carries the class number in subfield ‡a and the DDC edition number in subfield ‡2.

An extreme of this method is to use the author's complete surname. For example:

512	822.3
Dickenson	Marlowe

However, this device is clumsy and is used by very few libraries, despite its ability to distinguish between authors' names that begin with the same letters.

Cutter Numbers

Most libraries use a device called *Cutter numbers,* named after its designer, Charles Ammi Cutter. Developed originally for use with the Cutter Expansive Classification, it is now used widely with the Dewey Decimal Classification. A simplified form is used with the Library of Congress Classification and is described in Chapter 13.

In this system, the author number is derived by combining the initial letter or letters of the author's last name with numbers from a numerical table that was designed to ensure an alphabetical arrangement of names, e.g., D556 (Dickens), D557 (Dickenson), and D558 (Dickerson). This device provides a shorter author number which is also easier to arrange and to read on the shelves.

There are now three Cutter tables: *Two-Figure Author Table,*[13] *Three-Figure Author Table,*[14] and the *Cutter-Sanborn Table,*[15] listed in the order of increasing details. The following instruction is based on the *Three-Figure Author Table.*

The Cutter number is formed according to the following procedures:

1. Locate on the Cutter table the first few letters of the author's surname or corporate name which is the *main entry* of the work. Use only the boldface letters shown in the combination and the arabic numbers next to it.

Dewes	514
Dewey	515
Dewil	516

Based on the preceding figures, the Cutter number for Melvil Dewey is D515.

[13]C. A. Cutter. *C. A. Cutter's Two-Figure Author Table.* Swanson-Swift revision. Chicopee, Mass.: H. R. Huntting Company, 1969.
[14]C. A. Cutter. *C. A. Cutter's Three-Figure Author Table.* Swanson-Swift revision. Chicopee, Mass.: H. R. Huntting Company, 1969.
[15]C. A. Cutter. *Cutter-Sanborn Three-Figure Author Table.* Swanson-Swift revision. Chicopee, Mass.: H. R. Huntting Company, 1969.

Certain letters in the alphabet appear more frequently as initial letters of names. In order to keep the Cutter numbers short, two letters are used in a combination for names beginning with a vowel or the letter S, and three letters are used for names beginning with the letters Sc.

813.54	813.54	813.54	813.54
Ed98	Sch56	Sm64	V896

2. Where there is no Cutter number that fits a name exactly, use the first of the two numbers closest to the name, e.g., T325 for Thackeray, based on

Thacher	325
Thad	326

3. Cutter numbers are treated decimally. Therefore, when required, any number can be extended by adding extra digits at its end. For example, if Sm52 has been assigned to Benjamin Smith and Sm53 has been assigned to Charles Smith and a Cutter number must be provided for Brian Smith, the number Sm525 can then be used. The filing order is Sm52, Sm525, Sm53. The number 5 or 6 is often chosen as the extra digit in order to leave room on both sides for future interpolation.

For the same reason, although the tables provide many numbers ending in the numeral 1, it is advisable to add a digit and not to use a Cutter number ending in 1 because it places a limit on expansion. For example, use L5115 instead of L511 for David Lee. Furthermore, avoid using zero because it is easily confused with the letter o, and if possible, use some means to distinguish the number 1 from the letter l, such as substituting the lower-case script form (*l*) for the latter.

4. When two authors classified in the same number share the same Cutter number in the table, assign a different number for the second author by adding a digit, e.g., M315 for Heinrich Mann and M3155 for Thomas Mann. If Thomas Mann has been assigned the number M315 before a number for Heinrich Mann is required, the number M3145 then can be used for the latter.

5. Names beginning with Mc, M', and Mac are treated as though they were all spelled Mac. The apostrophe is ignored, i.e., O'Hara being treated as Ohara.

6. When the main entry is under title, the Cutter number is taken from the first word (disregarding initial articles) of the title. *Encyclopaedia Britannica* is assigned En19. Therefore, it is more accurate to state that the Cutter number is derived from the main entry of the work, which may or may not be a personal author.

7. An exception is made for biographies. In order to group all biographies of a person together, the Cutter number is taken from the name of the biographee instead of the main entry. For example, all biographies of Napoleon are grouped in the Cutter number <u>N162</u>. In many libraries, this practice is extended to include works about corporate bodies, particularly firms and institutions.

Unique Call Numbers

When two or more authors with the same last name write on the same subject, they are assigned different author or Cutter numbers, e.g., <u>D557</u> for David Dickenson and <u>D558</u> or <u>D5575</u> for Robert Dickenson. When the same author has written more than one work on a particular subject, further devices—work marks, edition marks or date of publication, and copy and volume numbers—are added to create unique call numbers. These are discussed below.

Work mark

A *work mark* (sometimes called a *work letter*) is added to the author or Cutter number to distinguish different titles on the same subject by the same author. Work marks usually follow the Cutter number directly and consist of the first letter or letters (in lowercase) from the first word (disregarding articles) in the title. The following examples show the pattern.

512
D557i   *Introduction to Algebra* by D. Dickenson

512
D557p   *Principles of Algebra* by D. Dickenson

512
D557pr   *Progress in Algebra* by D. Dickenson

813.4
J233a   *The Ambassadors* by Henry James

813.4
J233am   *The American* by Henry James

813.4
J233p   *The Portrait of a Lady* by Henry James

In some cases, when books in a series by the same author on the same subject all begin with the same word, it is customary to use the first letter from each key word in the titles.

738.2
H324ce   Hayden's *Chats on English China*

738.2
H324co   Hayden's *Chats on Old China*

738.2
H324cr   Hayden's *Chats on Royal Copenhagen Porcelain*

Practices in assigning work marks vary slightly from library to library, since there are no definitive rules concerning this aspect of cataloging. The examples presented here should be understood as one of various alternatives and should not be taken as the *only* method.[16] Nonetheless, they illustrate the basic function of the call number, which is to provide a unique symbol for each item of library material and to ensure a logical arrangement of works that share the same class number.

EXERCISE H

Assign Cutter numbers and work marks to the following titles.

1. 973   Adams, Henry. *History of the United States of America.* 1962

2. 973   Adams, Henry. *The Formative Years: a History of the United States during the Administration of Jefferson and Madison.* 1948

3. 973   Adams, James Truslow. *The March of Democracy.* 1932–33

4. 973   Adams, Randolph G. *The Gateway to American History.* 1927

5. 973   Adams, Randolph G. *Pilgrims, Indians and Patriots: The Pictorial History of America from the Colonial Age to the Revolution.* 1928

6. 973   Baldwin, Leland Dewitt, 1897–   . *The Stream of American History.* 1965

7. 973   Bancroft, George. *History of the United States of America, from the Discovery of the Continent to 1789.* 1883–85

8. 973   Beals, Carleton. *American Earth: the Biography of a Nation.* 1939

9. 973   Schlesinger, Arthur Meier. *New Viewpoints in American History.* 1922

10. 973   Schlesinger, Arthur Meier. *Political and Social History of the United States, 1829–1925.* 1925

---

[16]See John P. Comaromi. *Book Numbers: A Historical Study and Practical Guide to Their Use.* Littleton, Colo.: Libraries Unlimited, 1981. Also see Donald J. Lehnus. *Book Numbers: History, Principles, and Application.* Chicago: American Library Association, 1980.

11. 973   Schouler, James. *History of the United States of America under the Constitution.* 1880–1913

12. 973   Sellers, Charles G. *A Synopsis of American History.* 1963

13. 973   Shaler, Nathaniel S. *The United States of America.* 1894

14. 973   Sheehan, Donald H. *The Making of American History.* 1950

15. 973   Sherwood, James. *The Comic History of the United States.* 1870

16. 973   *Six Presidents from the Empire State.* 1974

17. 973   Smith, Dale O. *U.S. Military Doctrine: A Study and Appraisal.* 1955

18. 973   Smith, Goldwin. *The United States: An Outline of Political History, 1492–1871.* 1893

Work marks are particularly important in cases where many books are classed under the same number, for example, B̲ (Biography) and F̲ (Fiction). Work marks for biographies and literary works therefore merit special consideration.

Biography
In order to group all biographies of the same person together on the shelf, the Cutter number is taken from the name of the biographee instead of the author. All biographies of Washington are cuttered under W277, and the work mark is then taken from the first letter of the main entry—which is usually the author's surname. The work mark a̲ is used for all autobiographic writings in order to place such works before biographies written by other people. A biography written by an author whose surname begins with the letter a̲ is then assigned two letters as the work mark, e.g., W277ad (for Adams, etc.). When there is more than one autobiographic work, an arbitrary arabic number may be added to the work mark.

> W277a   Washington, George. *Autograph Letters and Documents of George Washington Now in Rhode Island Collections*
>
> W277a1   Washington, George. *Affectionately Yours, George Washington: A Self-Portrait in Letters of Friendship,* edited by T. J. Fleming
>
> W277a2   Washington, George. *Last Will and Testament of George Washington of Mount Vernon*

W277ad   Adams, R. G. *Five Radio Addresses on George Washington*

W277b   Bellamy, F. R. *The Private Life of George Washington*

W277d   Delaware. Public Archives Commission. *George Washington and Delaware*

W277h   *Honor to George Washington and Reading about George Washington*

Literary works[17]

In the Dewey Decimal Classification, critical appraisals and biographies of individual authors are classed in the same numbers assigned to their works; thus they share the same class number and Cutter number. It is then the function of the work mark to distinguish the works written *by* and those written *about* an author. In this area particularly, libraries vary in their practices. For example, some libraries use an additional Cutter number for works about individual authors. There are as yet no standards or rules in this regard. The following is presented as an example of a workable mechanism.

Works by Individual Authors   These are assigned work marks taken from the titles.

821.5   Pope, Alexander

P8115d   *The Dunciad*

P8115ep   *An Epistle from Mr. Pope to Dr. Arbuthnot*

P8115es   *An Essay on Criticism*

P8115ess
or
P8115esm   *An Essay on Man*

P8115r   *The Rape of the Lock*

Biography and Criticism of Individual Authors   Since critical appraisals and biographies of an individual author share the same class number and Cutter number with the author's works, they require special work marks if the library does not wish to interfile these two categories of works. The most common device is to insert the letter z̲ between the Cutter number and the work mark.

---

[17]In many libraries, the practice outlined in this section also applies to philosophers and artists when works written by and about them are classed in the same numbers.

P8115zc   Clark, D. B. *Alexander Pope*

P8115zr   Russell, J. P. *Alexander Pope: Tradition and Identity*

With the use of the letter z̲, works *about* Pope will be filed after works written *by* him. The letter z̲ in this case is followed by the regular work mark based on the main entry. In this way, the letter z̲ alone is reserved for any title by the author with the first word beginning with the letter z̲.

833.912
M315z   Mann, Thomas. *Der Zauberberg*

M315z̲   Lehnert, Herbert. *Thomas-Mann-Forschung*

In some libraries, serial publications devoted to the study of an individual author are assigned the work mark z̲z̲ so that these publications will be filed after other critical works about the author, e.g., M̲3̲1̲5̲z̲z̲ for *Blätter der Thomas Mann Gesellschaft.*

As an alternative of using the letter z̲ as a work mark for works about an author, a second Cutter number based on the main entry of the work may be used.

821.5
P8115   Clark, D. B.
C547   *Alexander Pope*

821.5
P8115   Russell, J. P.
R914   *Alexander Pope: Tradition and Identity*

Works about Individual Works   If the library wishes to have individual works and critical works about them stand together on the shelf, a device may be used in the work mark for such an arrangement. The capital letter Z̲ is inserted between the work mark for the work criticized and the work mark taken from the critic's surname.

821.5
P8115dZs   Sitter, J. E. *The Poetry of Pope's Dunciad*

P8115dZw   Williams, A. L. *Pope's Dunciad: A Study of Its Meaning*

This practice may be extended to include translations of literary works if one wishes to have the original work and the translations stand together.

833.912	Mann, Thomas
M315b	*Bekenntnisse des Hochstaplers Felix Krull*
M315bE	*Confessions of Felix Krull, Confidence Man*

The letter E stands for an English translation.

In some libraries, the letter x is used as a work mark for an author's collected works, and the letter y is used for works such as bibliographies and concordances of individual authors.

821.5	Pope, Alexander
P8115xb	*Complete Poetical Works,* edited by H. W. Boynton
P8115xd	*Poetical Works,* edited by H. Davis
P8115ya	Abbott, E., comp. *A Concordance to the Works of Alexander Pope*

The only problem in this practice is that an individual work with a title beginning with the letter z would then be separated from other individual works. An alternative is to use the letter a as a work mark for collected works, similar to the treatment of autobiographies. In this case, collected works of an author would precede individual works, an arrangement preferred by many libraries. Bibliographies and concordances would then be treated like other works about the author.

The works written *by* and *about* an individual author are therefore arranged in the following order:

Collected works (arranged by date or by editor)

Individual works (arranged alphabetically by title)
Original text
Translations (subarranged alphabetically by language and then by translators' names)
Critical appraisals (subarranged alphabetically by the critics' names)

General critical appraisals not limited to a single work (subarranged by the critics' names)

Serial publications devoted to the study of the author

For example,

833.912	Mann, Thomas
M315a	*Gesammelte Werke*
M315t	*Der Tod in Venedig*
M315tE	*Death in Venice*

M315z	*Der Zauberberg*
M315zE	*The Magic Mountain*
M315zZm	Miller, R. D. *The Two Faces of Hermes: A Study of Thomas Mann's Novel, "The Magic Mountain"*
M315ze	Eichner, H. *Thomas Mann*
M315zs	Schroter, K. *Thomas Mann*
M315zz	*Blätter der Thomas Mann Gesellschaft*

It should be noted that in filing, capital letters precede lowercase letters.

Shakespeare constitutes a special case because of the large number of editions and translations of his works and of works about him. In DDC, he has been given a special class number, 822.33. Since no other author shares this class number, it would be redundant to take the Cutter number from his name. Therefore, a special scheme of Cutter numbers has been developed. It appears in the DDC schedules following the class number 822.33.

In the case of anonymous classics, the Cutter number is based on the uniform title, and the work mark may be taken either from the title of the version being cataloged or from the editor, translator, or the person most closely associated with the edition.

821.1	Pearl (Middle English poem)
P316c	*The Pearl;* with an introductory essay by S. P. Chase
P316g	*Pearl;* edited by E. V. Gordon
P316zk	Kean, P. M. *The Pearl: An Interpretation*

For various versions of the Bible, since the class number already represents the Bible, its parts (i.e., the Old and New Testaments), or individual books, it would be redundant to cutter under title. The Cutter number is then taken from the name of the version, the name of the editor, or, lacking such, from the name of the publisher.[18]

Edition mark

Many works appear in different editions, which share the same class and Cutter numbers. In order to create a unique call number for each edition, an edition mark in the form of a number added after the work mark or a date under the Cutter number is usually used.

[18]For libraries with a large collection of other sacred scriptures, a similar arrangement may be used.

025.431	025.431	025.431	025.431
D515d17	D515d18	D515d19	D515d20

or

025.431	025.431	025.431	025.431
D515d	D515d	D515d	D515d
1965	1971	1979	1989

Some libraries use dates as edition marks for all works; others use both methods in the catalog. The choice of method in each case depends on appropriateness; for instance, dates are usually used when editions are not numbered. When there is more than one edition of a work within a year—as is often the case with literary works—a letter is added arbitrarily to the date, e.g., 1976a, 1976b, 1976c, etc.

Copy and volume number

When a work is published in more than one volume, or when the library has more than one copy of a work, a volume or copy number, or in some cases both, is added to the call number on the physical volume in order to provide a unique address in the collection.

025.431	025.431
D515d19	D515d20
v.2	v.1
	copy 2

The copy designation does not appear on the bibliographic record, since the record represents the entire work rather than an individual copy. The volume number may or may not appear there depending on whether the record has been created for that particular volume or for the entire work.

Prefixes to Call Numbers

When a particular work is to be shelved in a special location or out of its ordinary place, a prefix is added to the call number. The most commonly used prefix is the letter R̲ for books in the reference collection.

R
031
En19

Prefixes are also used for large-size books, books in special collections, and nonbook materials.

EXERCISE I

1. Complete the call numbers for the following titles.

  a. 92   Arthur, Sir G. *Concerning Winston Spencer Churchill* [1874–1965]

  b. 92   Ashley, M. P. *Churchill as Historian* [W. S. Churchill, 1874–1965]

  c. 92   Bullock, A. L. C. *Hitler: A Study in Tyranny*

  d. 92   Churchill, Jennie Jerome, 1854–1921. *The Reminiscences of Lady Randolph Churchill*

  e. 92   Churchill, Randolph S., 1911–1968. *Winston S. Churchill* [1874–1965]

  f. 92   Churchill, Winston, Sir. 1874–1965. *A Roving Commission: My Early Life*

  g. 92   Churchill, Winston, Sir. 1874–1965. *Lord Randolph Churchill* [1849–1895]

  h. 92   Fishman, J. *My Darling Clementine* [wife of W. S. Churchill]

  i. 92   Gardner, B. *Churchill in Power* [W. S. Churchill, 1874–1965]

  j. 92   Graebner, W. *My Dear Mr. Churchill* [W. S. Churchill, 1874–1965]

  k. 92   Hackett, Francis. *What Mein Kampf Means to America*

  l. 92   Hitler, Adolph. *Mein Kampf*

  m. 92   Hitler, Adolph. *My Battle*

  n. 92   James, R. R. *Lord Randolph Churchill* [1849–1895]

  o. 92   Kraus, R. *Young Lady Randolph* [Churchill, 1854–1921]

  p. 92   Leslie, Anita. *Jennie: The Life of Lady Randolph Churchill* [1854–1921]

  q. 92   Leslie, Anita. *Lady Randolph Churchill: The Story of Jennie Jerome* [1854–1921]

  r. 92   Martin, R. G. *Jennie: The Life of Lady Randolph Churchill* [1854–1921]

  s. 92   Smith, B. F. *Adolph Hitler: His Family, Childhood and Youth*

2. Complete the call numbers for the following titles.

a. 823.8   Brook, G. L. *The Language of Dickens*

b. 823.8   Churchill, R. C. *A Bibliography of Dickensian Criticism*

c. 823.8   Dickens, Charles. *Eine Geschichte von zwei Städten* [a German translation of *A Tale of Two Cities*]

d. 823.8   Dickens, Charles. *Hard Times*

e. 823.8   Dickens, Charles. *Historia de dos Ciudades* [a Spanish translation of *A Tale of Two Cities*]

f. 823.8   Dickens, Charles. *Paris et Londres en 1793* [a French translation of *A Tale of Two Cities*]

g. 823.8   Dickens, Charles. *Les temps difficiles* [a French translation of *Hard Times*]

h. 823.8   Dickens, Charles. *Schwere Zeiten* [a German translation of *Hard Times*]

i. 823.8   Dickens, Charles. *A Tale of Two Cities*. 1934

j. 823.8   Dickens, Charles. *A Tale of Two Cities*. 1970

k. 823.8   Dickens, Charles. *Zwei Städte, Roman aus der französischen Revolution von Charles Dickens* [a German translation of *A Tale of Two Cities* by B. Dedek, 1924]

l. 823.8   *Dickens Studies Newsletter*

m. 823.8   *The Dickensian: A Magazine for Dickens Lovers*

n. 823.8   Hayward, A. L. *The Dickens Encyclopedia*

o. 823.8   *Twentieth Century Interpretations of A Tale of Two Cities: A Collection of Critical Essays*

CHAPTER THIRTEEN
LIBRARY OF CONGRESS
CLASSIFICATION

During most of the nineteenth century, the Library of Congress collection was organized according to a system devised by Thomas Jefferson. When the library moved into its new building in 1897, however, the Jeffersonian system was found to be inadequate for a collection that had grown to over one and a half million pieces. Two other classification systems, the Dewey Decimal Classification (DDC) and Charles A. Cutter's Expansive Classification (EC), had emerged during the last few decades of the century and were in use in many other libraries in the nation, but neither was considered suitable for the Library of Congress. It was decided to construct a new system, to be called the *Library of Congress Classification* (LCC), and work began on its development.

From the beginning, individual classes were developed by different groups of specialists under the direction of J.C.M. Hanson and Charles Martel; the schedules, each of which contains an entire class, a subclass, or a group of subclasses, were published separately. Thus, unlike most other classification systems, LCC was not the product of one master mind. Indeed, it has been called "a coordinated series of special classes."[1]

Today, the Library of Congress Classification consists of twenty-one classes displayed in over forty separately published schedules. Its provisions are continually updated, and information on additions and changes is made widely available to the library community. Although LCC was originally designed expressly for the Library of Congress collection, it has been adopted by most large academic and research libraries, as well as by some large public libraries. During the 1960s in particular, there was a trend among academic libraries previously using DDC or other systems to switch to LCC. There were several reasons for the trend: (1) the basic orientation of LCC toward research libraries; (2) the economic advantage offered by LC cataloging services—libraries can simply adopt whole call numbers as they appear on LC cataloging records; and (3) the increasing ease with which many libraries can bring up full LC records online and add them to their own catalog databases.

---

[1]Arthur Maltby. *Sayers' Manual of Classification for Librarians*. 5th ed. London: Andre Deutsch, 1975. P. 175.

The fact that LCC is used in so many libraries has had some impact on its development: Library of Congress catalogers no longer focus solely on LC's own needs as they revise and expand the schedules.

HISTORY

From its earliest days, the two persons primarily responsible for the design and working out of the new Library of Congress Classification were J. C. M. Hanson and Charles Martel. They chose Cutter's Expansive Classification (EC) (see discussion on pages 379–382) as their chief guide, with considerable modification of the EC notation. Some of the early parallels, particularly for class Z (Book arts in Cutter; Bibliography and Library science in LCC), were very close. Table 13-1, a comparison of Cutter's outline and Hanson's first outline, shows how much the two schemes resemble each other in broad divisions.

For notation, it was decided at the outset to use a three-element pattern: first, single capital letters for main classes (H for Social sciences, P for Language and literature, Q for Science, and so on) with one or two capital letters for their subclasses (H for General works on social sciences, HA for Statistics, QD for Chemistry, and so on); second, arabic integers from 1 to 9999 for subdivisions; and third, Cutter numbers (letter/number strings read decimally) for individual books.[2] Gaps were left for future expansion. (Before many decades, parts of the schedules became crowded as knowledge developed. To accommodate new topics, decimal expansions of the original integers were allowed in some cases and so was the use of Cutter numbers for some topical subdivisions. More recently, three capital letters have been used for some subclasses.)

Class Z was chosen as the first schedule to be developed because its subject matter included the bibliographic works necessary for work on all the other schedules. The class Z draft was adopted by the Library of Congress in 1898, and the schedule was published in 1902. A full system outline appeared in 1904, by which time the classification of classes D, E–F, M, Q, R, S, T, U, and Z had been completed and work was under way on classes A, C, G, H, and V. By 1948, all but one schedule had been completed and published; the exception was class K (Law). The first schedule of this class, KF (United States law), was published in 1969, and schedules for other subclasses of law have appeared since. Schedules for some subclasses of law, however, are still under development and are published as they are completed.

[2]J. C. M. Hanson. "The Library of Congress and Its New Catalogue: Some Unwritten History." In *Essays Offered to Herbert Putnam by His Colleagues and Friends on His Thirtieth Anniversary as Librarian of Congress: 5 April 1929*. New Haven, Yale University Press, 1929. Pp. 186–187.

TABLE 13-1   Cutter's Outline and Hanson's First Outline

Cutter's Outline	Hanson's First Outline
General works	General works
Philosophy	Philosophy
Religion	Religion
Ecclesiastical history	
Biography	Biography and auxiliary studies of history
History and allied subjects	History
Geography and travels	Geography and allied subjects
Social sciences	Political science
	Law
Sociology	Sociology
Government; Politics	
Law; Women; Societies	Women, Societies, etc.
	Sports and amusements
	Music
	Fine arts
	Philology; Literature
Science in general; Physical sciences	Science; Mathematics; Physical sciences
Natural history in general; Microscopy; Geology; Biology	Natural history, general; Geology
Botany	Zoology; Botany
Zoology	
Medicine	Medicine
Useful arts	Useful arts; Agriculture
Engineering; Building	Manufactures
Manufactures; Handicrafts	Engineering
Defensive and Preservative arts	Military and Naval science; Lighthouses; Lifesaving; Fire extinction
Recreative arts: Sports; Theatre; Music	
Fine arts	Special collections
Language	
Literature	
Book arts	Bibliography (Book arts)

BASIC PRINCIPLES AND STRUCTURE
Overall Characteristics

Like the other classification systems originating in the nineteenth century, the Library of Congress Classification is basically a classification by discipline. LCC's main classes, established to accommodate all subject areas represented in LC's collection, correspond to major academic areas or disciplines. Main classes are divided into subclasses, which, in turn, reflect individual disciplines or their branches. Classes or subclasses are then further subdivided by topic and/or by form, place, or time. The system is thus hierarchical, progressing from the general to the specific. One striking difference between LCC and most other modern classification systems is that it is essentially an enumerative scheme in that most subject subdivisions are listed in highly specific detail, and compound or multifaceted subjects are specifically listed as such in the schedules. Even many common divisions, including those for form, are also individually listed under their applicable subjects. Such detailed enumeration means that relatively little notational synthesis, or number building, is required. There are many auxiliary tables, but these are included mainly as a device for saving space in the schedules; they are usually used for pinpointing specific numbers within a range of numbers given after a caption in a schedule. Thus auxiliary tables in LCC have quite a different purpose from those in the Dewey Decimal Classification and other systems, where numbers can be quite literally "built." LCC's degree of enumeration is only one way in which it differs dramatically from DDC. Another is that because of the use of letters as notation for representing main classes and subclasses, there is room for a substantially larger number of them.

It should be borne in mind that in its details LCC was not designed as a universal system (i.e., a system that details all existing subjects), but rather as one specifically tailored to Library of Congress needs. In other words, it was based on the "literary warrant" of the materials already in, and being added to, the Library of Congress itself. To a considerable extent, this is still true, a fact that partly explains the seemingly uneven distribution of LCC notation, especially its preponderance in history and other social sciences. Table 13-2 shows the current state of LCC classes and subclasses in terms of what the schedules are and how many volumes are devoted to each. The table should give a good picture of how LCC's coverage is distributed over areas of knowledge. A list of separately published schedules of LCC appears on the inside cover of each schedule.

Main Classes

The rationale for the arrangement of LCC's main classes was explained by Charles Martel,[3] one of the persons responsible for the original planning and supervision of the development of the system. The class of general works (A), not limited to any particular subject, leads the

[3]Leo E. LaMontagne. *American Library Classification with Special Reference to the Library of Congress.* Hamden, Conn.: Shoe String Press, Inc., 1961. P. 254.

TABLE 13-2   LCC Main Classes as Published

A　General works
　　1 volume
B　Philosophy, Psychology, Religion
　　4 volumes: B–BJ; BL, BM, BP, BQ; BR–BV; BX
C　Auxiliary sciences of history
　　1 volume
D　History: General and Old World
　　4 volumes: D–DJ; DJK–DK; DS; DT–DX
E–F　History: America
　　1 volume
G　Geography, Maps, Anthropology, Recreation
　　1 volume
H　Social sciences
　　2 volumes: H–HJ; HM–HX
J　Political science
　　1 volume
K　Law
　　8 volumes: K; KD; KDZ, KG–KH; KE; KF; KJ–KKZ; KJV–KJW;
　　　KK–KKC
L　Education
　　1 volume
M　Music and books on music
　　1 volume
N　Fine arts
　　1 volume
P　Language and Literature
　　13 volumes: P–PZ (Tables); P–PA; PA (Supplement); PB–PH; PG;
　　　PJ–PK; PL–PM; P–PM (Supplement); PN, PR, PS, PZ; PQ: pt 1; PQ: pt
　　　2; PT: pt 1; PT: pt 2
Q　Science
　　1 volume
R　Medicine
　　1 volume
S　Agriculture
　　1 volume
T　Technology
　　1 volume
U　Military science
　　1 volume
V　Naval science
　　1 volume
Z　Bibliography and Library science
　　1 volume

scheme. It is followed by the class containing philosophy and religion (B), which sets forth theories about human beings in relation to the universe. The next classes in the sequence, history and geography (C–G), cover such concepts as the human abode and the source of humanity's means of subsistence, human beings as affected by and affecting their physical milieu, and the mind and soul of humanity in transition from primitive to advanced culture. The next group, classes H to L, deals with the economic and social evolution of human beings. Classes M to P, for music, fine arts, and language and literature, concern human aesthetic and intellectual development and state. Classes B to P form the group of the philosophico-historical and philological sciences. The second large group, classes Q to V, embraces the mathematico-historical, natural, and applied sciences. Bibliography, which in many libraries may be distributed throughout different subject classes, shares the same class (Z) with librarianship.

Because different persons were responsible for the development of the individual classes, a given class may display unique features. The use of auxiliary tables and the degree and method for notational synthesis often vary from schedule to schedule. However, certain features are shared by all schedules: the overall organization, the notation, the method and arrangement of form and geographic divisions, and many auxiliary tables. (These will all be discussed in detail later in the chapter.) The organization of divisions within a class, subclass, or subject originally followed a general pattern, often called *Martel's seven points*. Briefly, these are (1) general form divisions, (2) theory/philosophy, (3) history, (4) treatises or general works, (5) law/regulation/state relations, (6) study and teaching, and (7) special subjects and subdivisions of subjects. Subsequent additions and changes have clouded this pattern to some extent, but it is generally still discernible.

Subclasses

Each of the main classes, with the exception of E, F and Z, is divided into subclasses that represent disciplines or major branches of the main class. Class Q, for example, is divided into the following subclasses:

Q   Science (general)
  QA   Mathematics
  QB   Astronomy
  QC   Physics
  QD   Chemistry
  QE   Geology
  QH   Natural history (general). Biology (general)
  QK   Botany

QL Zoology
QM Human anatomy
QP Physiology
QR Microbiology

Divisions

Each subclass is further divided into divisions that represent components of the subclass. For example, the subclass chemistry has the
following divisions:

QD *Chemistry*
23.3–26.5 Alchemy
71–142   Analytical chemistry
146–197   Inorganic chemistry
241–441   Organic chemistry
450–731   Physical and theoretical chemistry
901–999   Crystallography

Each of the divisions, in turn, has subdivisions specifying different
aspects of the subject, such as form, time, place, and more detailed
subject subdivisions. Table 13-3 shows a portion of the subdivisions
under Inorganic chemistry.

NOTATION

Symbols

As mentioned earlier, the Library of Congress Classification uses a
mixed notation of letters and arabic numerals to construct call numbers.
Main classes are represented by a single letter, e.g., K (Law), N (Fine arts),
and Q (Science). Most subclasses are represented by double or triple
letters, e.g., QD (Chemistry), DJK (History of Eastern Europe), and KFF
(Law of Florida). Classes E, F, and Z, the earliest classes to be developed,
have not been divided into subclasses.

An interesting feature of the LCC notation is that, in many schedules,
the single letter stands for the class as a whole as well as for its first
subclass (usually general works relating to the subject as a whole, but
sometimes its most prominent subclass), e.g.,

Class P: Language and literature
Subclass P: Philology and linguistics (General)

Class N: Fine arts
Subclass N: Visual arts (General)

TABLE 13-3   Portion of Subdivisions under Inorganic Chemistry

QD Chemistry
Inorganic Chemistry

	Cf. QD475, Physical inorganic chemistry
	QE351+, Mineralogy
146	Periodicals, societies, congresses, serial collections, yearbooks
147	Collected works (nonserial)
148	Dictionaries and encyclopedias
149	Nomenclature, terminology, notation, abbreviations
	History
.5	General works
.7	By region or country, A–Z
150	Early works through 1800
	General works, treatises, and advanced textbooks
151	1801–1969
.2	1970–
.5	Elementary textbooks
152	Addresses, essays, lectures
.3	Special aspects of the subject as a whole
153	Study and teaching. Research
154	Problems, exercises, examinations
155	Laboratory manuals
.5	Handbooks, tables, formulas, etc.
156	Inorganic synthesis
157	Electric furnace operations
	Cf. QD277, Electric furnace operations (Organic)
161	**Nonmetals**
162	Gases
163	Chemistry of the air
	Cf. TD881+, Air pollution
165	Halogens: bromine, chlorine, fluorine, iodine
167	Inorganic acids
	Cf. QD477, General theory of acids and bases
169	Other, A–Z
	.C5 Chalcogenides
	Heavy water, *see* .W3
	.W3 Water
	Cf. GB697, Natural water chemistry
	Metals
	Cf. TN600P+, Metallurgy
171	General works, treatises, and textbooks
172	By group, A–Z
	.A3 Actinide elements
	.A4 Alkali metals
	.A42 Alkaline earth metals
	.I7 Iron group

TABLE 13-3   (Continued)

QD Chemistry
Inorganic Chemistry

.M4	Magnesium group
.P8	Platinum group
.R2	Rare earth metals. Rare earths
.S6	Spinel group
.S935	Superheavy elements
.T52	Titanium group
.T6	Transition metals
.T65	Transplutonium elements
.T7	Transuranium elements

Divisions within subclasses are represented by arabic numbers from 1 to 9999 (as integers), with possible decimal extensions and/or, sometimes, with further subdivision indicated by Cutter numbers. A book number (also in the form of a Cutter number) and in most cases the year of publication complete the call number. Typical forms of LC call numbers are as follows:

		Class number
Z	LB	One, two, or three capital letters
8587	1715	Integer 1 to 9999
.8		Possible decimal extension
.A46	.G53	*Book number*
1991	1990	*Year of publication*

		Class number
DS	KFF	One, two, or three capital letters
63	300	Integer 1 to 9999
.2		Possible decimal extension
.S65	.T78	Cutter number for further subdivision of subject
G648	A25	*Book number*
1990	1989	*Year of publication*

No LC call number contains more than two Cutter numbers. Call numbers for certain types of maps and atlases, however, may contain three letter–number combinations that appear to have triple Cutter numbers.

An important characteristic of LCC notation is that it is not hierarchical beyond the class/subclass level. In other words, the notation does not necessarily reflect whatever general/specific relationships are inherent in the scheme itself. There has been some criticism of LCC's nonhierarchical notation.[4] On the other hand, the absence of notational hierarchy can be viewed as an advantage for LCC. For one thing, the majority of its class numbers are thereby relatively brief and are thus easily manageable for shelving purposes. For another, in part because relationships are largely ignored, LCC notation is remarkably hospitable.

Hospitality

A classification system with its attendant notation is said to be *hospitable* if it can readily accommodate expansion. Compared with the Dewey system especially, the LCC notation stands out for its hospitality. One reason is that, from the beginning, generous notational provision was made for future expansion. At the class level, the alphabet provides a broad base for division by major subject area or discipline, broad enough that not all letters are used; I, O, X, and Y have not been assigned to any subjects and so are available for later or specialized use. At the subclass level, generous gaps have been left between two-letter combinations, and these, too, are available for future expansion or specialized use. (An example of specialized use is found in the LCC-based National Library of Medicine Classification; it has adopted the vacant letter W for Medicine and the unused span QS–QZ for Preclinical sciences.) Finally, there is the option of interpolating three-letter combinations to denote new subclasses.

Within subclasses, expansion is usually achieved by using vacant numbers, but when this is not feasible, two other methods can be used: decimal extension and Cutter numbers. Regarding decimal extensions, the absence of hierarchy allows their use for coordinate subjects or even subjects broader than those represented by shorter numbers. For Cutter numbers, their alphabetical base and broad decimal extendability make them especially suitable for alphabetical arrangement of subtopics or for geographic subdivision.

Mnemonics

LCC lacks the mnemonic aids found in some other systems. There is some use of mnemonics in class A, where the second letter for the subclass is taken from the name of the subject covered, e.g., AC for Collections, AE for Encyclopedias, AS for Societies, etc.

[4]Maltby. Op. cit. P. 180.

EVALUATION OF THE LIBRARY OF CONGRESS CLASSIFICATION[5]

The Library of Congress Classification has both strong and weak points, both supporters and detractors. Ideally, someone making decisions on a classification system for a *new* collection would look for one with provisions most suitable for the nature and size of that collection. A medical library, for instance, is best organized by a classification system with deeply detailed provisions for medical topics. Other considerations include the availability of cataloging copy (i.e., of ready-to-use records) and frequency of update of provisions. For existing collections already classed by one system or another, one thing can be said with some force: There must be strong reasons for change, because accomplishing a change is very demanding in terms of personnel and other resources.

In this context, the following lists of LCC's merits and weaknesses may be helpful.

Merits

1. It is a practical system that has proved to be satisfactory. "It is a triumph for pragmatism."[6]
2. It is based on the literary warrant of the materials in the Library of Congress collection, the nature and content of which are a reasonable parallel to those in academic and research libraries.
3. It is largely an enumerative system that requires minimal notational synthesis.
4. Each schedule was developed by subject specialists rather than by a "generalist" who cannot be an expert in every field.
5. Its notation is compact and hospitable.
6. There are frequent additions and changes, stemming for the most part from what is needed in the day-to-day cataloging work at LC, and these are made readily available to the cataloging community.
7. The need for reclassification of large blocks of material is kept to a minimum because, to ensure stability of class numbers, few structural changes have been made over the years. (This advantage is also a disadvantage; see point 6 under "Weaknesses," below.)

[5]Cf. Maltby. Op. cit. Pp. 187, 174–189. See also J. Mills. *A Modern Outline of Library Classification.* London: Chapman & Hall, Ltd., 1967. Pp. 89–102. And A. C. Foskett. *The Subject Approach to Information.* 4th ed. Hamden, Conn.: Linnett Books; London: Clive Bingley, 1982. Pp. 409–417.

[6]Maltby. Op. cit. P. 187.

Weaknesses

1. Its scope notes are inferior to those of DDC.
2. There is much national bias in emphasis and terminology.
3. Too few subjects are seen as compounds. Multitopical or multielement works for which specific provisions have not yet been made cannot be classified with precision.
4. Alphabetical arrangements are often used in place of logical hierarchies.
5. There is no clear and predictable theoretical basis for subject analysis.
6. As a result of maintaining stability, parts of the classification are obsolete in the sense that structure and collocation do not reflect current conditions.
7. It is expensive to keep an up-to-date working collection of schedules, supplements, new announcements of changes, and cumulations of additions and changes.

THE SCHEDULES: REVISION AND PUBLICATION PATTERNS

Revision

Revision and expansion of LCC take place continuously. Changes are the responsibility of the Cataloging Policy and Support Office at the Library of Congress, with assistance from LC catalogers. Additions and changes often originate with subject catalogers who become aware of subjects not previously provided for or anomalies as they attempt to find classification placements for new materials. Proposals are reviewed at weekly meetings of an editorial committee made up of representatives of the office and other catalogers; if approved, a new or changed number is put into effect immediately. Additions and changes are first published in the quarterly, *LC Classification—Additions and Changes*, each issue of which lists all new and changed numbers in one alphabetical sequence by class. Two other publications are helpful in keeping LCC current.

    1. *Library of Congress Classification Schedules: A Cumulation of Additions and Changes*,[7] issued annually by the Gale Research Company of Detroit, contains cumulations of additions and changes that appear in LC's quarterly publication. The additions and changes to each schedule are cumulated and published in a separate volume, alleviating the need

---

[7]*Library of Congress Classification Schedules: A Cumulation of Additions and Changes through [previous year]*. Rita Runchock and Kathleen Droste, eds. Detroit: Gale Research, Inc., 1974–.

to consult over two hundred quarterly issues of *LC Classification—Additions and Changes* in search of new or changed numbers.

2. *Library of Congress Classification Schedules Combined with Additions and Changes through [previous year]*[8] offers the advantage of consulting in one place all currently valid numbers in one source.

Publication Patterns for Revised Schedules

There is no regular timetable for issuing revised editions for individual LCC schedules; new issues are prepared as needed, independently of one another. Class Q is in its seventh edition, while many of the P schedules are still in their first edition.

In using current LCC schedules, it is important to note that there are four different types of new editions.

New Schedules   Occasionally, a schedule appears for a class or subclass on which work has recently been completed and which has never been published before. Examples are the schedules for the subclasses of class K, Law.

Reissues with Supplementary Pages   When the stock of a particular schedule is exhausted and no revised edition is planned for the near future, a reprint edition is issued, with additions and changes up to the time of reprinting interfiled in one alphanumeric sequence separate from the main sequence and index. Many reissues of older schedules appear in this format, e.g., the schedules for classes E–F and parts of P.

Cumulative Editions   These are new editions that are essentially a cumulation of the provisions of the previous edition with additions and changes interfiled. Because relatively little revamping of the classification is involved, the preparation of such an edition is normally performed by an editorial staff, and the work is fairly mechanical and speedy. The third edition (1988) of schedule PN, PR, PS, PZ and the seventh edition of schedule Q (1989) were prepared in this manner. For reasons of size, some schedules originally published in one volume have been divided and then cumulated and published in parts, e.g., classes B and H. In other cases, when a part of a class needs substantial revision, it may be extracted from the main schedule and developed and published separately, e.g., the schedules for DS, History of Asia; and DT–DX, History of Africa, Australia, New Zealand; etc.

---

[8]*Library of Congress Classification Schedules Combined with Additions and Changes through [previous year]*. Rita Runchock and Kathleen Droste, eds. Detroit: Gale Research, Inc., 1988–.

Revised Editions   These are new editions that have undergone considerable revamping and revision, in a process that requires reviewing and rethinking much of the entire schedule. The preparation of such an edition involves not only individual catalogers but also the staff of the Cataloging Policy and Support Office; many numbers are changed, and terminology is updated. Since such thorough revision normally requires a great deal more time and effort than preparing a cumulative edition, revised editions appear relatively rarely. The fourth edition of schedule H–HJ (1981) is a revised edition.

Indexes

With very few exceptions, each schedule contains its own index, and the Library of Congress has yet to produce a general index to all the schedules. Two indexes compiled by groups not associated with the Library of Congress appeared some years ago and are of limited help to today's classifiers: *An Index to the Library of Congress Classification*[9] and *Combined Indexes to the Library of Congress Classification Schedules.*[10] *Library of Congress Subject Headings*, which lists LCC numbers after many of the headings, also has been used as a partial alphabetical key to the classification schedules.

APPLYING THE LIBRARY OF CONGRESS CLASSIFICATION: INSTRUCTIONS AND EXAMPLES

The Library of Congress Classification is highly enumerative with little need for synthesis. There are, however, many places in the schedules where the classifier needs to use tables, and the applicational rules for these must be learned. Furthermore, in some cases, LCC's use of Cutter numbers is quite complex.

The following instructions and examples are based on LCC schedules H, P, Q, and S. They cover such matters as characteristics of arrays of numbers within classes or subclasses, types of LCC tables, the special Cutter number table used with LCC, Cutter numbers as part of class numbers, double and successive Cutter numbers, and Cutter number variations such as "A" and "Z" Cutter numbers. The focus is on understanding how LCC works in order to use it according to Library of Congress policies and practices. In most collections classified by LCC, a

[9]*An Index to the Library of Congress Classification.* J. McRee Elrod, Judy Inouye, and Ann Craig Turner, eds. Ottawa: Canadian Library Association, 1974.

10*Combined Indexes to the Library of Congress Classification Schedules.* Compiled by Nancy B. Olson. 15 vols. Washington: U.S. Historical Documents Institute, Inc., 1974.

large number of new records originate from LC itself; it is generally considered important that records prepared locally should be consistent and compatible with Library of Congress practice.

Format of Schedules

To use the Library of Congress system efficiently, one must be familiar with the format and physical characteristics of the schedules. As noted earlier, the scheme comprises over forty separately published schedules with a full set running to over 10,000 pages. The schedules are similar in format, with the following elements found in most of them: (1) a preface, (2) a synopsis of the subclasses, (3) an outline of the major divisions within subclasses, (4) the main array of provisions giving all details except those which need to be extrapolated through the use of tables, (5) any applicable tables, (6) an index, and (7), for schedules that have not been revised for some time, supplementary pages of additions and changes.

Class Numbers [MARC Field 050, Subfield ‡a]

The primary task in classifying according to any system is the same as it is in subject cataloging: identifying the subject content of and the principal concepts in the work in hand. The next task is to express that content (even when multiple concepts are involved) as accurately as possible within the provisions of the classification system with which one is working. Given the structure and nature of LCC, most subjects can be found enumerated in the schedules, with whatever form, period, geographic, and topical subdivisions as provided; thus no notational synthesis is required. In other cases, there are tables to be used as directed, usually within a range of numbers listed in the main schedule. Finding the optimal classification placement often requires judicial use of whatever indexes are available, careful attention to any scope notes or other placement directions pertaining to the subject at issue, and persistent study of the list of captions preceding and following what one has selected as a starting point. It may involve using a table or constructing complicated Cutter numbers. And it also requires a patient search for applicable additions or changes.

Table 13-4, taken from the schedule for class Q, Science, shows typical divisions of a scientific subject and also illustrates the possible helpfulness of *compare* and *see* references.

As can be seen from Table 13-4, the numbers QC120–129.5 contain form, period, and geographic divisions of the subject, Descriptive and experimental mechanics. A journal on this subject is classed in QC120, and a current treatise on the subject is classed in QC125.2. Numbers

TABLE 13-4   Portion of Divisions of a Subject: Class Q, Science: QC, Physics

	QC Physics
	Descriptive and Experimental Mechanics

	Cf. QC73+, Force and energy (General)
	QC176+, Solid-state physics
	TA349+, Applied mechanics
	For theoretical and analytical mechanics, *see* QA801+
120	Periodicals, societies, congresses, serial collections, yearbooks
121	Collected works (nonserial)
.6	Dictionaries and encyclopedias
.8	Nomenclature, terminology, notation, abbreviations
	History
	For general history of mechanics, *see* QA802
122	General works
.2	By region or country, A–Z
123	Early works through 1800
	General works, treatises, and advanced textbooks
125	1801–1969
.2	1970–
127	Elementary textbooks
.3	Popular works
.4	Juvenile works
.6	Addresses, essays, lectures
128	Study and teaching. Research
129	Problems, exercises, examinations
.5	Laboratory manuals
131	Special aspects of the subject as a whole
	Dynamics
	Cf. QA845+, Analytic mechanics
133	General works, treatises, and textbooks
135	Kinematics
136	Vibrations
	Cf. QA865+; QA935+, Analytic mechanics
	QC231+, Sound
	TA355, Engineering
	Fluids. Fluid mechanics
	Including liquids
	Cf. QA901+, Analytic mechanics
	TA357+, Applied fluid mechanics
138	Periodicals, societies, congresses, serial collections, yearbooks
139	Dictionaries and encyclopedias
140	Nomenclature, terminology, notation, abbreviations
141	History
142	Early works through 1500

TABLE 13-4   (Continued)

<table>
<tr><td colspan="2" align="center">QC Physics
Descriptive and Experimental Mechanics</td></tr>
<tr><td></td><td>General works, treatises, and textbooks</td></tr>
<tr><td>143</td><td>1501–1700</td></tr>
<tr><td>144</td><td>1701–1800</td></tr>
<tr><td>145</td><td>1801–1969</td></tr>
<tr><td>.2</td><td>1970–</td></tr>
<tr><td>.24</td><td>Juvenile works</td></tr>
<tr><td>.26</td><td>Addresses, essays, lectures</td></tr>
<tr><td>.28</td><td>Study and teaching</td></tr>
<tr><td>.3</td><td>Handbooks, tables, formulas, etc.</td></tr>
<tr><td>.4</td><td>Special properties of liquids, A–Z</td></tr>
<tr><td></td><td>.A25 Acoustic properties</td></tr>
<tr><td></td><td>.C6   Compressibility</td></tr>
<tr><td></td><td>.D5   Diffusion</td></tr>
<tr><td></td><td>.E45 Electric properties</td></tr>
</table>

beginning with QC133 provide topical divisions of the subject, such as Dynamics, Fluids, etc. Each of the topical divisions may have its own subdivisions, depending on the amount of material on that subject in the Library of Congress collection. More elaborate subdivisions appear under Fluids and Fluid mechanics than under Dynamics; thus a handbook on Fluid mechanics is classed in QC145.3. When no form divisions are provided under a particular subject, the number designated for General works is used for all forms; a handbook on Dynamics is therefore classed in QC133.

Cutter Numbers[11] [MARC Field 050, Subfield ‡b]

As mentioned earlier, the Cutter number is used in LCC for two purposes: as a further extension of the class number[12] and as an item or book number. A Cutter number consists of a capital letter followed by an arabic number; the number is read decimally, and the decimal point precedes the letter, e.g., .T7, .T7324 .T745, and .T8. The decimal feature of Cutter numbers is important, because it allows for infinite interpolation on the decimal principle.

[11]"Call Number." In Library of Congress, Subject Cataloging Division. *Subject Cataloging Manual: Shelflisting.* Washington: Library of Congress, 1987. G060.
[12]In this case, it is included in subfield ‡a, e.g., ‡a UF555.G7 ‡b W47 1991 and ‡a DA125.N4 ‡b G55 1991.

TABLE 13-5   Cutter Table

1. After initial *vowels*,

for the second letter:	b	d	l–m	n	p	r	s–t	u–y
use number:	2	3	4	5	6	7	8	9

2. After the initial letter *S*,

for the second letter:	a	ch	e	h–i	m–p	t	u	w–z
use number:	2	3	4	5	6	7	8	9

3. After the initial letters *Qu*,

for the third letter:	a	e	i	o	r	t	y
use number:	3	4	5	6	7	8	9

for initial letters *Qa–Qt*, use: 2–29

4. After other initial *consonants*,

for the second letter:	a	e	i	o	r	u	y
use number:	3	4	5	6	7	8	9

5. For *expansion*,

for the letter:	a–d	e–h	i–l	m–o	p–s	t–v	w–z
use number:	3	4	5	6	7	8	9

Because in most cases LCC's subject provisions are developed in greater detail than those in the Dewey system, not as many books are likely to be given the same class number. Therefore, the elaborate Cutter tables used with that system are not needed for constructing LCC book numbers. Instead, a relatively simple Cutter table[13] (shown above as Table 13-5) is used.

Letters not included in the foregoing table are assigned the next higher or lower number as required by previous assignments in the particular class. The arrangements in the following examples illustrate possible applications of this table:

Vowels		S		Q		Consonants	
IBM	.I26	Sadron	.S23	*Qadduri	.Q23	Campbell	.C36
Idaho	.I33	*Scanlon	.S29	*Qiao	.Q27	Ceccaldi	.C43
*Ilardo	.I4	Schreiber	.S37	Quade	.Q33	*Chertok	.C48
*Import	.I48	*Shillingburg	.S53	Queiroz	.Q45	*Clark	.C58
Inman	.I56	*Singer	.S57	Quinn	.Q56	Cobblestone	.C63
Ipswich	.I67	Stinson	.S75	Quorum	.Q67	Cryer	.C79
*Ito	.I87	Suranyi	.S87	Qutub	.Q88	Cuellar	.C84
*Ivy	.I94	*Symposium	.S96	*Qvortrup	.Q97	Cymbal	.C96

*These Cutter numbers reflect the adjustments made to allow for a range of letters on the table, e.g., l–m, or for letters not explicitly stated, e.g., h after an initial consonant.

[13]"Call Number." P. 26.

Since the table provides only a general framework for the assignment of numbers, the symbol for a particular name or work is constant only under a particular class number. Each entry must be added to the existing entries in the shelflist in such a way as to preserve alphabetical order in accordance with filing rules.

Cutter number as part of class number

In Table 13-3, under QD149.7, the caption "By region or country, A–Z" indicates that Cutter numbers are to be used for geographic division of the subject. In Table 13-4, QC145.4 carries the caption "Special properties of liquids, A–Z." This means that individual properties are represented by Cutter numbers after the main class number. The class number for the subject of diffusion of fluids contains the following elements:

QC   The double letters for the subclass, Physics
145.4   The arabic number meaning special properties of liquids
.D5   The Cutter number for diffusion

Cutter number as book number

Each call number contains a book number generally based on the main entry of the work. Its main purpose is to distinguish different works on the same subject that have been given the same class number. A work about macroeconomics by Ball is assigned the number HB172.5.B35, and another work on the same subject by Beneassy is classed in HB172.5.B45. If the Cutter number taken from the table has already been assigned to another work, it is adjusted for the work being classified. For example, a work about macroeconomics by Barro received the call number HB172.5.B36. If the same author has written more than one work on a subject, the Cutter numbers are adjusted in a similar manner. For example:

Hamlet, Peter
QD31.2.H35   *Introductory chemistry: a new view*
QD31.2.H352   *Introductory, organic, and biochemistry: a new view*

In order to place a translation of a work with the original text, the call number of the original work with an extension of the book number is assigned to the translation. For example:

Remmert, Reinhold
QA331.R46   *Funktionentheorie* (original work in German)
QA331.R4613   *Theory of Complex Functions* (an English translation of the above title)

TABLE 13-6   Table for Translations

.x	Cutter number for original work
.x12	Polyglot
.x13	English translation
.x14	French translation
.x15	German translation
.x16	Italian translation
.x17	Russian translation
.x18	Spanish translation

The Table for Translations[14] (see Table 13-6) is used unless there are specific instructions for subarranging translations in the schedules.

The notations in Table 13-6 may be adjusted to accommodate translations in other languages. For instance, for a Bulgarian translation, one may use .x13 if the original work is in English or .x125 if the original is in a language other than English.

Double cutter numbers

When a class number includes a Cutter number as a subdivision, a second Cutter number is added as the book number, resulting in a double Cutter number.[15] For example, a work about distributed processing is assigned the following call number:

> *Fault-tolerant distributed computing.* 1990
> QA   The double letters meaning Mathematics
> 76.9   The arabic number meaning topics about Computers
> .D5   The first Cutter number for the topic Distributed processing
> F38   The book number for the main entry under the title, *Fault ...*
> 1990   The date of publication

Note that only one decimal point, preceding the first Cutter number, is required for double Cutter numbers. (The first decimal in the call number above results from numerical expansion of the schedule notation and thus is not part of the Cutter sequence.)

Call numbers for biography often contain double Cutter numbers, one for the biographee and one for the biographer, e.g., a biography of Earvin Johnson, a basketball player, by James Haskins:

[14]"Translations." In Library of Congress, *Subject Cataloging Manual: Shelflisting.* Op. cit. G150. P.1.

[15]In rare instances, both Cutter numbers may be extensions of the class number, and the call number will therefore not include a book number.

Sports great Magic Johnson / James Haskins. 1989
- GV   The double letters for Recreation and leisure
- 884   The arabic number meaning a biography associated with basketball
- .J63   The first Cutter number for Johnson
- H38   The second Cutter number for Haskins
- 1989   The date of publication

Successive cutter numbers

Successive Cutter numbers are a series of Cutter numbers (e.g., .F3, .F4, .F5) or decimal extensions of a Cutter number (e.g., .F32, .F33, .F34, .F35) in an established sequence. They are used when certain works are to be grouped on the shelves in an established order. An example is the additional digits for a translation (e.g., 14, French) attached to a book number. Frequently, in the schedules and in tables, there are instructions to use successive Cutter numbers. Further examples showing the use of successive Cutter numbers are found on pages 355, 363–365.

A and Z cutter numbers

In some cases, under a class number, a span of Cutter numbers at the beginning or at the end of the alphabetical sequence is assigned special meanings. These spans are called "A" Cutter numbers or "Z" Cutter numbers, respectively. The "A" Cutter numbers are used most frequently for form divisions such as periodicals or official publications.

QC **PHYSICS**
174.4   **Quantum statistics**
  .A1A–Z   Periodicals, societies, congresses, serial collections, yearbooks
  .A2A–Z   Collected works (nonserial)
  .A6–Z   General works, treatises, and textbooks

The Cutter numbers .A1 and .A2 are used for serial publications and nonserial collected works. .A3–.A5 are not used at present. A treatise on quantum statistics by an author named Adams, which is normally assigned the Cutter number .A3 according to the Cutter table, will receive a Cutter number greater than .A6.

The "Z" Cutter numbers are often assigned to special divisions of the subject such as biography and criticism of a literary author or corporate bodies associated with the subject.

UA	ARMIES: ORGANIZATION, DISTRIBUTION, ETC.
	By region or country
	Europe
	France
	Army
	Artillery
705.A1–5	Documents
.A6–Z4	General works
.Z5A–Z	Bataillons d'artilerie a pièd
.Z6	Regiments. By number

Dates in Call Numbers

Dates appear in LC call numbers in two functions. A date may be part of the class number; at various points in the schedules, dates are listed explicitly, or there are instructions about using them. A date also may be part of a book number; the date of imprint or copyright is now added to the Cutter numbers for all monographs and to later editions of serials.

Date as part of class number

The following example shows a case in which a date is called for as part of a class number.

HB	Economic theory
3717	History of crises
1929	Date of the crisis

In such cases, the book number and date of publication follow the first date to complete the call number, i.e., HB3717 1929 .G36 1987.

Date of publication in book numbers

The date of publication is added to a book number for all monographic publications (including most types of nonprint materials) and to later editions of serials. An example is shown below.

Statistical inference for branching processes / Peter Guttorp. 1991

QA	Mathematics
274.76	Branching processes
.G88	Book number based on the main entry, Guttorp
1991	Date of publication

Since different editions of the same work receive the same class and book numbers, they are distinguished by dates of publication.

	Reagan, Nancy
E878.R43A3 1989	*My turn : the memoirs of Nancy Reagan* (Random House, c1989)
E878.R43A3 1990	*My turn : the memoirs of Nancy Reagan* (Thorndike Press, large print edition, 1990)

	Heyne, Paul T.
HB171.5.H46 1987	*The economic way of thinking.* 5th ed. 1987
HB171.5.H46 1990	*The economic way of thinking.* 6th ed. 1990

If different dates are shown in the work, the date to be used in the call number is based on the imprint or copyright date given in the "publication, distribution, etc." area in the bibliographic record.

If there is more than one edition of the same work published in the same year, a lowercase letter (called a *work letter*) is added to the date. The work letters are assigned in the following manner:

[date]   Original work
[date]a A facsimile or photocopy edition, the date being that of the original
[date]b A variant edition published in the same year
[date]c Another variant edition
etc.

Works Entered under Corporate Headings[16]

In assigning book numbers and dates to call numbers for works with main entry under corporate bodies, the procedures outlined below are followed except when the schedules provide specific instructions to the contrary.

Monographs
Under the same class number, all works entered under the same corporate heading (disregarding any subheadings) are assigned the same Cutter (book) number. The date is added to distinguish between different titles.

RA997
.U48   United States. Congress. Senate. Special
1974   Committe on Aging. Subcommittee on
            Long-term Care.
            Nursing home care in the ... 1974.

---

[16]"Corporate Bodies." in Library of Congress, *Subject Cataloging Manual: Shelflisting.* Op. cit. G220.

RA997
.U48   United States. Congress. House. Select Committee
1980   on Aging.
Elder abuse, the hidden problem ... 1980.

If there is more than one work by the corporate body in the same year, successive work letters (i.e., [date]a̲, [date]b̲, etc.) are added to the imprint dates in the call numbers.

Serials
For serial publications entered under the same corporate heading, successive work letters (i.e., a̲, b̲, c̲, etc.) are added to the Cutter (book) number, since call numbers for serials do not contain dates of publication.

TC425
.M7U54a   United States. Missouri River Basin Commission.
Standing Committee for Development of
Priority Listing.
Annual report : basin priority listing ...

TC425
.M7U54b   United States. Missouri River Basin Commission.
Priorities report—Missouri River Basin ...

EXERCISE A

Assign LC call numbers to the following works.

1. *Railway Imperialism* / edited by Clarence B. Davis and Kenneth E. Wilburn, Jr., with Ronald E. Robinson. 1991

2. *Beyond Ambition : How Driven Managers Can Lead Better and Live Better* / Robert E. Kaplan with Wilfred H. Drath and Joan R. Kofodimos. 1991

3. *Norbert Wiener, 1894–1964* / by Pesi R. Masani. 1989 [Wiener was a mathematician.]

4. *Creating Period Gardens* / Elizabeth Banks. 1991

5. *Solomon's House Revisited : The Organization and Institutionalization of Science* / Tore Fransgsmyr, editor. 1990 [main entry under: Nobel Symposium (75th : 1989 : Stockholm, Sweden)]

6. *Creativity in the Arts and Science* / William R. Shea and Antonio Spadafora, eds. 1990 [Proceedings of the Third Locarno International Conference on Science and Society, held in October 1988; main entry under the title]

7. *Accumulation of Organic Carbon in Marine Sediments : Results from the Deep Sea Drilling Project* / Ruediger Stein. 1991

8. *Banach Lattices* / Peter Meyer-Nieberg. 1991

9. *America and the New Economy : How New Competitive Standards are Radically Changing American Workplaces* / Anthony Patrick Carnevale. 1991 [a book on labor productivity in the United States]

10. *Yen for Development : Japanese Foreign Aid & the Politics of Burden-Sharing* / edited by Shafiqul Islam. 1991 [main entry under the title]

11. *Leadership : The Inner Side of Greatness : A Philosophy for Leaders* / by Peter Koestenbaum. 1991 (The Jossey-Bass management series)

12. *Creating Effective Boards for Private Enterprises : Meeting the Challenges of Continuity and Competition* / John L. Ward. 1991

13. *Varieties of Social Explanation : An Introduction to the Philosophy of Social Science* / Daniel Little. 1991

14. *Taxation in the Global Economy* / edited by Assaf Razin and Joel Slemrod. c1990 [a book on tax on foreign income in the United States]

15. *New Directions in Telecommunications Policy* / edited by Paul R. Newberg. 1989 [main entry under the title]

16. *Self Employment : A Labor Market Perspective* [for women in the United States] / Robert L. Aronson. 1991

17. *Translating Poetry : The Double Labyrinth* / edited by Daniel Weissbort. 1989 [main entry under the title]

18. *Paleontology of Vertebrates* / Jean Chaline. 1990 [an English translation]

TABLES

Tables represent recurring patterns of subdivision. Although LCC relies to a lesser extent on the use of general auxiliary tables than do many other modern library classification schemes, it still requires considerable use of tables, most of which were designed to save space in the schedules. Those familiar with other classification systems will find a basic difference between LCC tables and those used in other systems. The tables in the Dewey system, for instance, provide additional segments to be *attached* to a main class number, extending it lengthwise to render it more specific. In LCC, with the exception of tables for subdivisions that are represented by Cutter numbers, the tables are a device for locating the desired number within a range of numbers given in the schedule. Usually, the number given in the table is *added* (in the arithmetic sense) instead of attached to the base number from the schedule. The base number is normally the one *preceding* the span of numbers (given in the schedule) for which the table is to be used. In many schedules, the base number is given in a footnote on the same page where the instruction for using a table appears.

There are two types of auxiliary tables in LCC: tables of general application and tables of limited application. Tables of general application include (1) the biography table, (2) the translation table mentioned earlier, and (3) certain geographic tables based on Cutter numbers. These tables were used initially with only a few schedules but are now applicable throughout the schedules whenever called for. In turn, there are two kinds of LCC tables that are limited in their application: one applies to a whole class or subclass, and the other (referred to as *tables for internal subarrangement*) applies only according to specific directions in the schedules.

Tables of General Application

Several tables for general application are discussed below, with illustrations: three tables for geographic division and the biography table.

Tables for geographic division by means of Cutter numbers

Regions and countries in one alphabet
The table "Regions and Countries in One Alphabet" provides alphabetical arrangement of countries by means of Cutter numbers. It is used whenever the schedule gives the instruction "By country, A–Z" or "By region or country, A–Z." This table (sometimes with the caption "Table of Countries in One Alphabet") is printed in the schedules of classes C, D, E–F, H, T, U, and V and *Subject Cataloging Manual: Shelflisting*.[17] Table 13-7 shows portions of the table. The complete table is given in Appendix D of this book.

---

[17]"Regions and Countries Table." In Library of Congress, *Subject Cataloging Manual: Shelflisting*. Op. cit. G300.

TABLE 13-7   Regions and Countries Table (Portions)

Abyssinia *see* Ethiopia.		Cuba	.C9
Afghanistan	.A3	Cyprus	.C93
Africa	.A35	Czechoslovakia	.C95
Africa, Central	.A352		
Africa, East	.A353	****	
Africa, Eastern	.A354		
Africa, French-	.A3545	Formosa *see* Taiwan.	
speaking West		France	.F8
Africa, North	.A355	French Guiana	.F9
Spain	.S7	United States	.U6
Sri Lanka	.S72	Upper Volta *see*	
Sudan	.S73	Burkina Faso.	
Surinam	.S75	Uruguay	.U8
Swaziland	.S78	Vatican City	.V3

The following examples illustrate its application.

Managing socialism : from old cadres to new professionals in revolutionary Cuba / Frank T. Fitzgerald. 1990

HD   Economic history and conditions

8038   Professions (General)

.C9   Cuba (according to the table of "Regions and Countries in One Alphabet")

F58   Cutter number for the main entry, Fitzgerald

1990   The date of publication

The politics of survival : artisans in twentieth-century France / Steven M. Zdatny. 1990

HD   Economic history and conditions

2346   Small and medium industry, artisans, handicrafts, trades: By region or country, A–Z

.F8   France (according to the table of "Regions and Countries in One Alphabet")

Z38   Cutter number for the main entry, Zdatny

1990   The date of publication

Although the table is applied universally, the Cutter number assigned to a particular country may sometimes vary under different class numbers, depending on what already *exists* in the LC shelflist. For example, although, in the table, .U6 is the Cutter number listed for the United States, in the following example, .U5 is assigned.

Caught in the crossfire : a year on abortion's front line / Sue Hertz. 1991
HQ   The family, marriage, woman
767   Abortion
.5   By region or country, A–Z
.U5   United States
H47   Cutter number for the main entry, Hertz
1991   The date of publication

United States
This table, containing a list of the states and regions of the United States in alphabetical order (sometimes with the caption "Table of States"), is used when the instruction "By state, A–W" or "By region or state, A–Z" is given in the schedule. The table is printed in schedules G, H, T, U, and V, in *Subject Cataloging Manual: Shelflisting,*[18] and in Appendix D of this book. The following examples illustrate its use.

California festivals : your guided tour to over 300 California festivals / Carl Landau and Katie Landau with Kathy Kincade. 1990
GT   Manners and customs (General)
4810   Festivals and holidays in the United States, by state, A–W
.C2   California (according to the table "United States")
L36   Book number based on the main entry, Landau
1990   Date of publication

Habits of industry : white culture and the transformation of the Carolina Piedmont / Allen Tullos. c1989
HC   Economic history and conditions
107   United States, by region or state
.N8   North Carolina (according to the table "United States")
T85   Book number based on the main entry, Tullos
1990   Date of publication

Canadian provinces
This table, printed in schedule T, *Subject Cataloging Manual,*[19] and in Appendix D of this book, is used when the instruction "By province, A–Z" or "By region or province, A–Z" is given under a class number for Canada. Its application is similar to that of the table for United States.

[18]"American States and Canadian Provinces." In Library of Congress, *Subject Cataloging Manual: Shelflisting.* Op. cit. G302. Pp. 1–2.
[19]Ibid. P. 2.

Sustaining the living land : the report of the British Columbia Task Force on Environment and Economy. c1989

HC   Economic history and conditions
117   Canada (the seventh number in the range HC111–120 assigned to Canada in the main schedule, chosen according to the internal table above the number HC94), by state, etc., A–Z
.B8   British Columbia (according to the table "Canadian Provinces")
B76   Book number based on the main entry: British Columbia Task Force on Environment and Economy
1989 Date of publication

Biography table

When works about a person, including autobiography, letters, speeches, and biography, are classed in a number designated for individual biography, they are subarranged according to the biography table. This table (reproduced in Table 13-8) contains extensions (in the form of successive Cutter numbers) of the Cutter number (represented by .x in the table) assigned to the individual or biographee.

TABLE 13-8   Biography Table

.x	Cutter number for the biographee
.xA2	Collected works. By date
.xA25	Selected works. Selections. By date Including quotations
.xA3	Autobiography, diaries, etc. By date
.xA4	Letters. By date
.xA5	Speeches, essays, and lectures. By date Including interviews
.xA6–Z	Individual biography, interviews and criticism. By main entry Including criticism of selected works, autobiography, quotations, letters, speeches, interviews, etc.

Application of the biography table results in double Cutter numbers; the first Cutter number is for the biographee and the second is taken from the table. The use of "A" Cutter numbers in this table results in works written by the biographee to be filed before works written by other people about him or her. The following example illustrates the use of the biography table.

The Letters of Sigmund Freud to Eduard Silberstein, 1871–1881 /
edited by Walter Boehlich ; translated by Arnold J. Pomerans.
1990
BF   Psychology
173   Psychoanalysis
.F85   The first Cutter number for Freud
A4   The second Cutter (for letters) from the Biography
        Table
1990   The date of publication

Tables of Limited Application

Tables applicable to an individual class or subclass

Many LCC schedules contain tables that apply to an entire class or
subclass. Examples are the author tables used throughout the schedules
for class P, Language and Literature; the form tables used in the schedules of class K, Law; and the geographic tables in class H, Social Sciences,
and in class S, Agriculture. These may be Cutter tables, numerical tables,
or a combination of both; they usually appear at the end of the schedule
to which they apply, immediately before the index.

In using a table that contains Cutter numbers, the appropriate Cutter
number, adjusted if necessary, is simply attached to the main number
from the schedule.

In applying a numerical table, the following steps should be followed:

1. Find the range of numbers in the schedule within which the
   subject being represented falls, and note its base number.
2. Determine the appropriate table to be applied to the specific
   range of numbers.
3. Select the number in the table that represents the specific subject
   or aspect appropriate to the item being classified, and fit the
   number (usually by simple substitution or addition) into the
   range of numbers from the schedule.

Geography tables in class S
An example of a set of numerical tables is the "Geographical Distribution
Tables" in class S, Agriculture, a portion of which is reproduced in Table
13-9.

The following example illustrates the application of Table II below.
(In a table of this kind, of which there are many in LCC, the captions
in the third column apply to both sets of numbers: those in the first

TABLE 13-9   Geographical Distribution Tables (Portions) from Class S

In countries to which two numbers are assigned:
(1) General
(2) Local, A–Z

I	II	
21		America
22		North America
23		United States
	****	
55	33	Europe
57–58	35–36	Great Britain. England
	****	
85–86	63–64	Soviet Union
87–88	65–66	Spain

column, which is Table I, and those in the second column, which is Table II.)

> *The disappearing Russian forest : a dilemma in Soviet resource management* / Brenton M. Barr & Kathleen E. Braden. c1988
>
> SD   Forestry
> 207   The number meaning a history of forestry in the Soviet Union
> .B37   The Cutter number for the main entry, Barr
> 1988   The date of publication

The number SD207 is determined by following the steps outlined above:

1. In schedule S, the numbers SD145–246 have been assigned to the history of forestry subdivided geographically.
2. These class numbers are to be used with Table II for specific countries.
3. The number 63 (meaning the Soviet Union in general) from Table II is added to the base number 144 as given in the schedule.

Geography tables in class H
The "Tables of Geographical Divisions" (in class H) are a group of ten tables providing detailed geographic divisions. They are used with spans of numbers given in the main schedules with specific instruction concerning which table is to be used in a particular case. For example, to classify a work about the standard of living in England by Christopher Dyer, the first step is to find the appropriate class number or numbers in the schedule.

TABLE 13-10 Tables of Geographical Divisions (Portions)

I	II	III	IV	V		VI	VII	VIII	IX	X
1	1-2	1-2	1-2	1	America, Western Hemisphere	1				
2	3-4	3-4	3-4	2	North America	2				
3	5-6	5-6	5-8	3-6	United States					
4	7-8	8-10	9-12		Northeastern States. New England					
5	9-10	11-13	13-16		Middle Atlantic States. Middle States					
6	11-12	14-16	17-20		Southern States					
7	13-14	17-19	21-24		Central States. Plains States					
8	15-16	21-22	25-28		Great Lakes region					
9	17-18	23-25	29-32		Mississippi Valley					
10	19-20	26-28	33-36		Southwestern States					
11	21-22	29-31	37-40		Northwestern States. Rocky Mountain region					
12	23-24	32-34	41-44	7-10	Pacific States					121-130
13	25	35	45		States, A-W Including regions and counties Cities, A-Z					
14	27	38	49		Canada	10	11-20	1-10	1-10	151-160
15	29-30	41-43	53-56	10.25	Saint Pierre and Miquelon Islands	10.25	20.25	10.25	10.25	160.25
15.25	30.25	43.25	56.25		Greenland, see 99.5					
15.5	30.5	43.5	56.5	10.5	Latin America	11.5	20.5	10.5	10.5	160.5
16	31-32	44-46	57-60	11	Mexico	12	21-30	11-20	11-15	161-170
17	33-34	47	61-64	13	Central America	13	31-35	21-25	16-20	171-175
17.5	35-36	48	65-68	13.5	Belize. British Honduras	13.25	36-40	26-30	20.5	181-185
18	37-38	49-51	69-72	14	Costa Rica	13.5	41-50	31-40	21-25	191-195
19	39	52-54	73-74	15	Guatemala	13.75	51-60	41-50	26-30	201-205
20	40	55-56	75-76	16	Honduras	14	61-70	51-60	31-35	206-210
21	41	57-58	77-78	17	Nicaragua	14.25	71-80	61-70	36-40	216-220
22	42-43	59-60	79	18	Panama	14.5	81-85	71-75	41-45	221-225
22.5	43.5	61	80	18.5	Panama Canal Zone	14.75	86-90	76-80	45.5	226-230
23	44	62-64	81-84	19	Salvador	15	91-100	81-90	46-50	231-235

TABLE 13-10 (Continued)

I	II	III	IV	V		VI	VII	VIII	IX	X
					South America					
38	73–74	110–112	145–148	40	Paraguay	44–45	241–250	231–240	116–120	381–390
39	75–76	113–115	149–152	41	Peru	46–47	251–260	241–250	121–125	391–400
40	77–78	116–118	153–156	42	Uruguay	48–49	261–270	251–260	126–130	401–410
41	79–80	119–121	157–160	43	Venezuela	50–51	271–280	261–270	131–135	411–420
42	81–82	122–124	161–164	44	Europe	52–53	281–290	271–280	136–140	421–430
42.8	82.5	124.5	164.5	44.5	European Economic Community countries	53.5	289.5	280.5	140.5	430.5
43	83–84	125–127	165–168	45	Great Britain	54–58	291–300	281–300*	141–150*	431–440
44	85–86	128–130	169–172	46	England and Wales	60–61	301–310			441–450
45	87–88	131–132	173–176	47	Scotland	62–63	311–320			451–460
45.5	88.5	132.5	176.5	47.5	Northern Ireland	63.5	320.5			460.5
46	89–90	133–135	177–180	48	Ireland, Irish Republic	64–65	321–330	300.3	150.3	461–470
47	91–92	136–138	181–184	49–52	Austria	66–67	331–340	301–320	151–160	471–480
47.3	92.3	138.3	184.3	52.3	Czechoslovakia	69.3	340.3	320.3	160.3	480.3
47.5	92.5	138.5	184.5	52.5	Hungary	69.5	340.5	320.5	160.5	480.5
47.9	92.9	138.9	184.9	52.9	Liechtenstein	69.9	340.9	320.9	160.9	480.9
48	93–94	139–141	185–188	53–56	France	70–74	341–350	321–340	161–170	481–490
48.5	94.5	141.5	188.5	56.5	Monaco	74.5	350.5	340.5	170.5	490.5
49	95–96	142–144	189–192	57–60	Germany Including West Germany	75–79	351–360	341–360	171–180	491–500
49.5	96.5	144.5	192.5	60.5	East Germany	79.5	360.5	360.5	180.5	500.5
51	99–100	148–150	197–200	62–65	Italy	85–89	371–380	371–390	186–195	511–520
51.3	100.3	150.3	200.3	65.3	San Marino	89.3	380.3	390.3	195.3	520.3
51.5	100.5	150.5	200.5	65.4	Malta	89.5	380.5	390.5	195.5	520.5
52	101–102	151–153	201–204	65.5	Benelux countries. Low countries	90–94	381–390	391–400	196–200	521–530
53	103–104	154–156	205–208	66–69	Belgium	95–99	391–400	401–410	201–205	531–540
54	105–106	157–159	209–212	70–73	Netherlands	100–104	401–410	411–420	206–210	541–550
54.5	106.5	159.5	212.5	73.5	Luxemburg	104.5	410.5	420.5	210.5	550.5

*Class the constituent countries of Great Britain as particular localities of Great Britain in the Local, A–Z number provided.

HD   ECONOMIC HISTORY AND CONDITIONS
                  Labor
                  Wages and cost of living. Standard of living
6981–7080   By region or country. Table I

The instruction calls for the use of Table I. A portion of an updated version of the "Tables of Geographical Divisions" is reproduced as Table 13-10. The number designated for England in Table I is 44. This number is added to the base number HD6980 (*not* to 6981, which is the first number in the range, not the base number) to obtain the desired number, HQ7024. Attaching the book number for the main entry and the date of publication yields the desired call number, HD7024.D94 1989. This number is analyzed below.

> *Standards of living in the later Middle Ages : social change in England, 1200–1520* / Christopher Dyer. 1989
> HD   Economic history and conditions
> 7024   Standard of living in England
> .D94   Cutter number for the main entry, Dyer
> 1989   The date of publication

Since the schedule does not provide for period subdivision, the chronologic aspect of the book is not represented in the class number.

Author tables in class P
The author tables in class P, which are similar to those for philosophers in class B, present special features because provision has to be made for a large number of related works. Their use is illustrated below. Works written by and those about an individual literary author are classed together in LCC. Each author is assigned a range of numbers, a number, or a Cutter number. The literature tables used with authors, originally published in the appropriate schedules of class P, have been revised, renumbered, and published in a separate volume entitled *Classification—Class P–PZ: Language and Literature Tables* (1982). These tables provide patterns for subarrangement of works by and about literary authors. The following examples illustrate the use of author tables in class P.

> *The works of Mark Twain.* 1972–
> PS   American literature
> 1300   First number (according to Table XXXI) in the range of 1300–1348 assigned to Clemens, Samuel Langhorne (Mark Twain) for collected works
> .F72   Book number (also according to Table XXXI) for a work published in 1972

The adventures of Tom Sawyer / by Mark Twain. 1991
PS   American literature
1306   The number (within the range of 5–22 designated for
        separate works by an author with 49 numbers in
        Table XXXI) assigned specifically to *The adventures
        of Tom Sawyer*
.A1   The Cutter number meaning (according to Table
        XLI, "Separate works with one number) the text of
        the work arranged by date (if no editor is given)
1991   The date of publication

Works of Edgar Allan Poe. 1990
PS   American literature
2603   The fourth number (3) in the range 0–49 in Table
        XXXI for selections fitted into the range of numbers
        PS2600–2648 assigned to Poe in the schedule
1990   The date of publication

No Cutter number is assigned to this work because the author's name,
Poe, is already implied in the class number and no editor is given.

The following examples illustrate the application of Table XXXII for
an author assigned nineteen numbers.

Pope's Dunciad of 1728 : a history and facsimile / David L.
Vander Meulen. 1990
PR   English literature
3625   Number assigned to *Dunciad* in the schedule (among
        the range of numbers (25–30) for separate works
        according to Table XXXII, i.e., PR3625–3630 for
        Pope)
.A1   Texts (according to Table XLI for separate works
        with one number)
1990   The date of publication

Women's place in Pope's world / Valerie Rumbold. 1989
PR   English literature
3633   Number for a general criticism (13.A5–Z in Table
        XXXII) of Pope
.R84   The Cutter number for the main entry, Rumbold
1989   The date of publication

Tables for internal subarrangement

Tables designed for use with specific spans of numbers are scattered
throughout the schedules. Such tables are used for subarrangement
within a span of numbers and may contain form, period, geographic,

and/or subject elements. They range from a few lines of instructions to several pages and are usually found at the beginning of or immediately following the spans of numbers involved.

Table 13-11 contains an example of a table for internal subarrangement from schedule H–HJ, following HC92.

TABLE 13-11   Internal Table

HC		ECONOMIC HISTORY AND CONDITIONS	HC
		By region or country	
		Class here general works only; for particular industries, *see* HD	
		Under each country (local numbers used under countries only):	
10 nos.	*5 nos.*		
		Collected works	
		Documents	
(1.A1–3)	(1.A1–3)	Serial documents	
		Separate documents	
(1.A4)	(1.A4)	Administrative documents. By date	
		Other documents, *see* General works	
(1.A5–Z)	(1.A5–Z)	Periodicals. Societies. Serials	
(2)		Dictionaries. Encyclopedias	
(2.2)		Directories	
		For trade directories, *see* HF54+	
(2.5)	(1.5)	Biography	
		For particular industries, *see* HD	
		.A2 Collective	
		.A3–Z Individual	
(3)	(2)	General works	
(3.5)	(2.5)	Natural resources	
		By period.	
		Period divisions vary for different countries	
(4)		Early	
		Including Medieval	
(5)		Later	
	(3)	Local (used under countries only)	
(7)		By state, etc., A–Z	
(8)		By city, A–Z.	
		For local annual reviews of "Commerce," "Finance," "Trade," etc., *see* HF3163 and HF3221+, subdivision (10) under each country; general, HC14	
(9)	(4)	Colonies	
		Including exploitation and economic conditions	
		For colonial administration and policy, *see* JV	
(10)	(5)	Special topics (not otherwise provided for), A–Z	
		For list of topics, *see* HC79	

In the schedule, Mexico is assigned the range of numbers HC131–140. Therefore, the call number assigned to a work on the economic conditions of Mexico by Cypher is HC135.C97 1990, which is analyzed below.

> *State and capital in Mexico : development policy since 1940 /*
> James M. Cypher. 1990
> HC   Economic history and conditions
> 135   The fifth number (under the 10 nos. column in Table
>   13-11, meaning a work about the later period)
>   in the span of numbers 131–140 assigned to
>   Mexico
> .C97 The book number based on the main entry, Cypher
> 1990 The date of publication

A work about the economic conditions of Chiapas, Mexico, by Benjamin is assigned the number HC137.C47B46 1989, as shown below.

> *A rich land, a poor people : politics and society in modern Chiapas /*
> Thomas Benjamin. 1989
> HC   Economic history and conditions
> 137   The seventh number (under the 10 nos. column in
>   Table 13-11, meaning a local subdivision by state)
>   in the span of 131–140
> .C47 The first Cutter number for the state, Chiapas
> B46   The book number based on the main entry,
>   Benjamin
> 1989 The date of publication

In numerical tables, some numbers appear in parentheses, e.g., (1), (2), (3), etc. These are treated as variable rather than constant numbers, successively designating the first number, the second number, and so on. In other words, the parenthesized numbers are ordinal numbers. For example, the numbers HC186–190 assigned to Brazil would be matched to those in the table in the following manner:

HC186   (1)
HC186.5 (1.5)
HC187   (2)
HC187.5 (2.5)
HC188   (3)
HC189   (4)
HC190   (5)

TABLE 13-12   Portion of Internal Table, Containing Another Small Table

HD		ECONOMIC HISTORY AND CONDITIONS

Special industries and trades
TABLES OF SUBDIVISIONS UNDER INDUSTRIES AND TRADES
(HD9000–9999)

Under each:

A	B	
(20 nos.)	(11 nos.)	
0.1	0.1	Periodicals. Societies. Serials
		For manufacturers' associations formed with particular reference to labor questions, *see* HD6941+
.2	.2	Yearbooks
.3	.3	Directories
		****
		By region or country
	1	United States.
1	.1	Periodicals. Societies. Serials
		****
7	.7	By region or state, A–Z
8	.8	By city, A–Z
9	.9	By firm, etc., A–Z
		****
		Other regions or countries
		Under each country:
		.x Periodicals. Societies. Serials
		.x2 General works. History
		Including biography
		.x3 Local, A–Z
		.x4 By firm, etc., A–Z
14	5	America. By region or country, A–Z
15	6	Europe
		Subarranged like America
		****

Table 13-12 shows a portion of an internal table also found in class H, following HD9999. For example, chemical industries are given the span of numbers HD9650–9660. Therefore, Table B is used with this topic. A work about the Union Carbide Corporation, a chemical company in the United States entered under the first author Dembo, is classed in HD9651.9.U55D45 1990.

Abuse of power : social performance of multinational corporations :
the case of Union Carbide / by David Dembo, Ward Morehouse,
and Lucinda Wykle. 1990
HD   Economic history and conditions
9651 United States
.9   By firm, etc., A–Z
.U55 The Cutter number for Union Carbide
D4   The Cutter number for the main entry, Dembo
1990 The date of publication

Table 13-12 contains a small table (using successive Cutter numbers,
.x, .x2, .x3, .x4) under "America: By region or country, A–Z." Note that
the first Cutter number in the small table is .x (e.g., .V4 for a periodical
on the economic conditions of Venezuela) instead of .x1 (.V41) because
the use of a Cutter number ending in the digit "1" limits the possibility
of interpolation and is therefore generally avoided. Furthermore, the
digit 1 is used to introduce a successive Cutter number for a translation,
e.g., .V414 for a French translation and .V415 for a German translation
of a work assigned the Cutter number .V4.

An example of applying the small internal table is shown below.

Revolution in the factory : the birth of the Soviet textile industry,
1917–1920 / William B. Husband. 1990
HD   Economic history and conditions
9865 The number (within the span 9850–9869) matching
      notation 15 in Table A, meaning textile industries
      in a European country
.S652 The Cutter number (.S65) for the Soviet Union with
      the successive element 2 (.x2 in the small table) for
      a general work
H87   The book number based on the main entry, Husband
1990 The date of publication

In many cases, call numbers are constructed by using a combination
of different types of tables. An example is given below.

Privatisation and competition : a market prospectus / edited by
Cento Veljanovski. 1989
HD   Economic history and conditions
4145 A general work on industry in Great Britain
.P68 The Cutter number for the main entry under the
      title, *Privatisation ...*
1989 The date of publication

In this example, the number 4145 is constructed as follows:

1. Locate the appropriate range of numbers in the schedule:

HD4001–4420.7   Industry
> The state and industrial organization State industries. Public works. Government ownership
> By region or country
> > Other regions or countries. Table IX

(Footnote in schedule: Add country number in table to 4000.)

2. Consult Table IX for the numbers assigned to Great Britain:

141–150

3. Consult the 10 nos. column in the internal table under HD4001–4420.7:

(5) General works

4. Choose the fifth number in the range 141–150: 145
5. Add 145 to 4000: 4145

EXERCISE B

Assign LC call numbers to the following works.

1. *Financial Liberalization, Money Demand, and Monetary Policy in Asian Countries* / Wanda Tseng and Robert Corker. 1991

2. *Antonio Gramsci : Architect of a New Politics* / Dante Germino. 1990 [Gramsci (1891–1937) was an Italian communist.]

3. *Charlotte Brontë* / Penny Boumelha. 1990

4. *Ben Jonson's 1616 Folio* [a textual criticism] / edited by Jennifer Brady and W.H. Herendeen. 1991

5. *The Masque of Stuart Culture* / Jerzy Limon. c1990

6. *The Book of the Laurel* / John Skelton ; edited by F.W. Brownlow. c1990

7. *Last Lines : An Index to the Last Lines of Poetry* / Victoria Kline. c1992

8. *Medieval Literature : Texts and Interpretation* / edited and with an introduction by Tim William Machan. 1991

9. *The Makings of Happiness* / Ronald Wallace. 1991

10. *Close Connections : Caroline Gordon and the Southern Renaissance* / Ann Waldron. 1987

11. *The Second Part of King Henry VI* / William Shakespeare ; edited by Michael Hattaway. 1990

12. *The Victorian Serial* / Linda K. Hughes and Michael Lund. 1991 [a book about 19th century English literary journals]

13. *Jane Austen and the Fiction of Culture : An Essay on the Narration of Social Realities* / Richard Handler & Daniel Segal. c1990

14. *Mark Twain's Own Autobiography : The Chapters from the North American Review* / with an introduction and notes by Michael J. Kiskis. c1990

CHAPTER FOURTEEN
NATIONAL LIBRARY OF
MEDICINE CLASSIFICATION
AND OTHER MODERN
CLASSIFICATION SYSTEMS

The preceding two chapters present two classification systems used by most of the general libraries in the United States as well as around the world. This chapter discusses in some detail one of the systems designed for special libraries and briefly some of the other library classification systems developed over the past century.

NATIONAL LIBRARY OF MEDICINE CLASSIFICATION

The National Library of Medicine (NLM) has developed its own classi-fication system as well as its own indexing thesaurus—*Medical Subject Headings* (MeSH), described in Chapter 10. The NLM Classification is an example of a special-subject classification system that was expressly designed to be fully compatible with an extensive, existing general classification system. In this case, the general system is the Library of Congress Classification (LCC), which, as noted in Chapter 13, was in turn designed with many "empty spaces" in its notational array of main classes and major subclasses. What the original designers of the NLM Classification proposed was a classification scheme that would (1) fol-low LCC in both style of classification and general pattern of notation, (2) develop its own classification scheme for medicine and related sub-jects, fitting it into LCC's vacant class W, and (3) develop its own scheme for the preclinical sciences, using LCC's vacant subclasses QS through QZ (in LCC main class Q for science). In response, the Library of Congress agreed with NLM that the main class W and subclasses QS to QZ would be permanently excluded from LCC.

For any material in its collection that would not be classed appro-priately under either medicine or the preclinical sciences, NLM uses LCC as it stands except for class R (Medicine), subclasses QM, QP, and QR (Anatomy, Physiology, and Microbiology, respectively), and the class Z provisions for medicine-related bibliographies.

The resulting system has many advantages for a specialized medical library such as NLM. The classificational development of the subject matter that is its primary concern is fully under its control, while provisions for peripheral subjects are developed and kept up to date by outside specialists, in this case the Library of Congress staff. Yet the two parts of the system are fully compatible. More specifically, its advantages are (1) currency in arrangement of medical material and in terminology, (2) compatibility in terminology with *Medical Subject Headings*,[1] (3) compatibility in notation with LCC, (4) the presence of NLM call numbers in both the NLM catalog and its online database, CATLINE, and (5) the presence, on most, if not all, LC records for materials in health sciences, of both NLM class numbers and LCC class numbers. The last, which results from NLM's involvement in the Library of Congress cooperative cataloging program, is especially helpful to libraries with collections classified by both LC and NLM systems.

Brief History and Current Status

In the early 1940s, a survey at the U.S. Army Medical Library (now the National Library of Medicine) indicated the need for a specialized classification scheme for the books in the library. In 1948, a preliminary edition of such a scheme was prepared by Mary Louise Marshall. This edition was modified and revised by Dr. Frank B. Rogers in 1950 and published in 1951 as the first edition of the *Army Medical Library Classification*.[2] The second edition was published in 1958 under the title *National Library of Medicine Classification*. The third edition appeared in 1964, the fourth in 1978, and a revision of the fourth in 1981.[3]

Although originally designed for the Army Medical Library, now the National Library of Medicine (NLM), the NLM scheme is also used by most of the other major medical libraries in this country.

Basic Principles and Structure

The NLM Classification comprises two major subject groups, the preclinical sciences and medicine. The first group is divided into eight subclasses, QS through QZ. The second group, class W, contains thirty-three major divisions within medicine and related subjects; the first is

---

[1]National Library of Medicine (U.S.). *Medical Subject Headings*. Bethesda, Md.: National Library of Medicine, Library Operations, Medical Subject Headings Section, 1975–.

[2]United States Army Medical Library. *Army Medical Library Classification: Medicine. Preclinical Sciences: QS–QZ, Medicine and Related Subjects: W.* 1st ed. Washington: Government Printing Office, 1951.

[3]National Library of Medicine (U.S.). *National Library of Medicine Classification: A Scheme for the Shelf Arrangement of Books in the Field of Medicine and Its Related Sciences.* 4th ed. revised. NIH Publication no. 81-1535. Bethesda, Md.: U.S. Department of Health and Human Services, Public Health Service, National Institutes of Health, National Library of Medicine, 1981.

the medical profession as a whole, followed by diseases, physiologic systems, medical specialties, hospitals, nursing, and the history of medicine. An outline of the first-order divisions of the NLM Classification is shown in Table 14-1.

TABLE 14-1   Outline of National Library of Medicine Classification

PRECLINICAL SCIENCES

QS	Human anatomy	QW	Microbiology and immunology
QT	Physiology	QX	Parasitology
QU	Biochemistry	QY	Clinical pathology
QV	Pharmacology	QZ	Pathology

MEDICINE AND RELATED SUBJECTS

W	Medical profession	WK	Endocrine system
WA	Public health	WL	Nervous system
WB	Practice of medicine	WM	Psychiatry
WC	Infectious diseases	WN	Radiology
WD 100	Deficiency diseases	WO	Surgery
WD 200	Metabolic diseases	WP	Gynecology
WD 300	Diseases of allergy	WQ	Obstetrics
WD 400	Animal poisoning	WR	Dermatology
WD 500	Plant poisoning	WS	Pediatrics
WD 600	Diseases by physical agents	WT	Geriatrics. Chronic disease
WD 700	Aviation and space medicine	WU	Dentistry. Oral surgery
WE	Musculoskeletal system	WV	Otorhinolaryngology
WF	Respiratory system	WW	Ophthalmology
WG	Cardiovascular system	WX	Hospitals
WH	Hemic and lymphatic systems	WY	Nursing
WI	Gastrointestinal system	WZ	History of medicine
WJ	Urogenital system		

Within a particular schedule for a subclass and, in some cases, under a main subject, the numbers 1 to 33 (e.g., WI 1–33.1 and WO 201–233.1) are used for form divisions such as collections, history, dictionaries and encyclopedias, tables and statistics, and atlases. In the schedules for physiologic systems, form divisions are followed by general divisions and then divisions by organ. At the beginning of each class, a brief outline of the class is given. For example:

GASTROINTESTINAL SYSTEM

WI 1–250   General
WI 300–387   Stomach
WI 400–575   Intestines
WI 600–650   Anus and Rectum
WI 700–770   Liver and Biliary Tract

WI 800–820   Pancreas
WI 900–970   Abdomen and abdominal surgery

Divisions by organ have priority over diseases, which are subsumed under the organ or region chiefly affected, regardless of special emphasis on diet, drug, or other special form of therapy.

Books treating several subjects that fall into different areas of the classification are classed by emphasis. If no emphasis is apparent, they are classed with the first subject treated.

Notation

As mentioned earlier, it was planned from the beginning that the notation for the NLM Classification would be compatible with that for LCC and that, for material that did not fall within the areas covered by its own system, NLM would use provisions from LCC proper. One necessary condition for the implementation of these plans was that NLM would not use the LC schedules for class R (Medicine) and subclasses QM through QR (Anatomy, Physiology, and Microbiology); another was that LC would not seek to develop class W or subclasses QR through QZ, which were, in a sense, "ceded" to NLM. Within these limitations, the NLM notational system is compatible with that for LCC.

Class numbers [MARC field 060, subfield ‡a]

A typical class number consists of one or two capital letters followed by an arabic number of up to three digits with possible decimal extensions, e.g., **W 1**, **QS 22.1**, **QY 350**, **W 40.1**, and **WK 700**. Triple capital letter combinations are used in classifying some nineteenth-century publications. Also, in some cases, Cutter numbers are used for subject subdivision. With respect to notational capacity, the NLM Classification allows a range of 1 to 999 integers under each main class or subclass, in contrast to the range of 1 to 9999 in LCC. The NLM Classification is a relatively broad classification system, leaving specificity in subject analysis to the MeSH system and its tree structures.

Cutter numbers [MARC field 060, subfield ‡b]

NLM Cutter numbers, used primarily for book numbers and occasionally for subject subdivisions, differ from those used in LCC. The difference springs from the fact that there may be a large number of works written on any one of the topics enumerated in the NLM scheme for which the relatively simple Cutter number table used for book numbers in LCC does not suffice. Instead, NLM uses the more detailed

Cutter-Sanborn Three-Figure Author Table[4] for book numbers. Even then, numbers from this table may need to be adjusted to accommodate large numbers of books under crowded class numbers. Work letters, taken from the first word in the title, disregarding initial articles, are added to distinguish works on the same subject by the same author, and publication dates are routinely added to records for monographs, as they are in LC cataloging. Illustrations of NLM book numbers appear in the cataloging examples on pages 377–379. Note that NLM does not use a period before the book number, even though the numbers are read decimally.

Examples of Cutter numbers used for subject subdivisions, where a simpler Cutter number scheme suffices, are given below.

QW	MICROBIOLOGY AND IMMUNOLOGY
138	Enterbacteriaceae
138.5	Specific organisms, A–Z
.E8	Escherichia
.K5	Klebsiella
.P7	Proteus
.S2	Salmonella
.S3	Serratia
.S4	Shigella
.Y3	Yersinia

Cutter numbers are not used as item numbers for nonprint materials. Instead, a medium code consisting of a serial number following a brief alphabetical notation representing type of materials (e.g., AC for sound recordings, SL for slides, VC for videorecordings, etc.), is used. For examples, see page 379.

Geographic table

There is only one auxiliary table in the NLM Classification system, Table G for geographic subdivisions, which is based on a modified Cutter pattern. The world is divided into ten regions, each of which is assigned a capital letter as follows:

A	United States	J	Asia
D	America	K	Australia
F	Great Britain	L	Pacific islands
G	Europe	M	International
H	Africa	P	Polar Regions

[4]Charles Ammi Cutter. *Cutter-Sanborn Three-Figure Author Table.* Swanson-Swift revision. Chicopee, Mass.: H. R. Huntting Company, 1969.

Within each region, subdivisions are provided for subordinate units. For example,

AA1   United States
AA4   Alabama
AA5   Alaska
AA6   Appalachian

****

FA1   Great Britain
FE5   England
FI7   Northern Ireland
FM2   Isle of Man
FS2   Scotland
FW3   Wales

****

M   International agencies (General or not listed below)
MA4   Allied Forces
MF6   Food and Agricultural Organization of the United Nations
MI3   International Labor Office
MI8   Islamic Countries

Table G is used mainly with serial government publications and with hospital publications. However, there are some numbers in the schedules that expressly call for the use of Table G. For example:

QV   **PHARMACOLOGY**
11   History (Table G)
11.1   General coverage (Not Table G)
          ****
32   Laws (Table G)
32.1   General coverage (Not Table G)

In these cases, the decimal extension .1 is used for material covering areas broader than any of the areas represented in Table G. A history of pharmacology in a particular geographic area is classed in QV 11 plus a number from Table G, while a general history of pharmacology is classed in QV 11.1.

Index

There is a detailed index to the NLM schedules, with major terms chosen to conform with those in MeSH. At any one time, of course, the degree of conformity depends in large part on whether revisions in the two tools have kept pace with each other. At present, because the latest edition of the classification was published in 1981, there are noticeable discrepancies between the index terms and current MeSH headings.

In the index, major terms are arranged alphabetically with subterms indented under them. Each major term or subterm is followed by a class number or range of numbers, including numbers from LCC. Indented terms represent aspects of the subject that are more specific or have their own numbers different from the general number. *See also* references and general references follow the subterms. The examples below show these features.

> Lasers   TK 1660–1750
> Biomedical application   WB 117
> In dentistry (General)   WU 26
> In surgery (General)   WO 500
> Physics   QC 454.L3
> Used for other purposes, by subject
> *See also* special topics under Radiation, Nonionizing

Classification of Special Types of Materials

Certain types of materials receive special treatment in the NLM Classification. These include bibliographies, serial publications, and early publications.

Bibliography

The call number for a bibliography in a topic listed in the NLM schedules begins with the letter Z, followed by the class number for the particular subject of the bibliography. A bibliography outside the scope of the NLM Classification is assigned a number from class Z of the Library of Congress Classification. Examples of class numbers for bibliographies are shown below.

> **Z 675.D3**   A list of general holdings of a dental library
> **Z 7144.I8**   A bibliography of isotopes
> **ZQT 35**   A bibliography of biomedical mathematics
> **ZW 1**   A bibliography of general medical serials
> **ZWB 100**   A bibliography of monographic works on general medicine
> **ZWD 700**   A bibliography of aviation and space medicine

Serial publications

Serial publications are given different treatment according to the type of publication they represent. There are seven categories:

1. *Biomedicine.* Serials that are not restricted to medical topics but are important to medicine and related fields are classed in W1.
2. *Information science and general reference materials.* These serials are classed in the appropriate LCC numbers.
3. *Congresses.* Serial publications of numbered congresses are classed in W3, unless they fall in category 2 or originate from the meetings of one society, in which case they are classed in W1.
4. *Hospitals.* Serial publications of hospitals that do not contain clinical material are classed in WX2. Reports of the government administration of hospitals are classed in W2.
5. *Statistics and administrative reports.* Serial government publications of an administrative or statistical nature are classed in W2.
6. *Schedule numbers for special forms.* Some publication forms are individually listed in the schedules with the numbers marked with an asterisk (*). They are used for both monographs and serial publications, e.g.,

WB	**PRACTICE OF MEDICINE**
*22	Directories (of health resorts and/or special systems of therapeutics) (Table G)
*22.1	General coverage (Not Table G)

7. *Indexes and bibliographies.* Indexes or bibliographies issued serially are classed according to the instructions for classing bibliographies given above.

Early publications

1. *Nineteenth century titles.* A "Special Schedule for 19th Century Publications," which is a simplified version of the NLM Classification, is provided for the classification of such publications, except nineteenth-century bibliographies. This special schedule appears at the end of the NLM schedules. An excerpt from this special schedule is shown below:

QS	Anatomy
QS 22	Directories (Table G)
QSA	Histology
QSB	Embryology

****

WB	Practice of medicine
WB 22	Directories (Table G)

WBA	Popular medicine
WBB	Diagnosis

2. *Early printed books.* Books published before 1801 and Americana are classed in WZ 220–294, a section of the classification specially designed for such works.

Cataloging Examples

Application of the NLM Classification system is illustrated in the following examples for books as well as nonprint materials. All MARC records of medical literature prepared by the National Library of Medicine for the Library of Congress in shared cataloging contain both class R (LCC) and class W (NLM) numbers, as shown in some of the following examples.

Medical use of snake venom proteins / editor, Kurt F. Stocker. c1990

WD	Animal poisoning
410	Reptiles
M489	Cutter number for the main entry, *Medical use ...*
1990	Date of publication

[LC call number: RM666.S52M43 1990]

Medical microbiology / Patrick R. Murray ... [et al.]. 1990

QW	Microbiology and immunology
4	General works
M4862	Cutter number for the main entry, Murray
1990	Date of publication

[LC call number: QR46.M4683 1990]

Encyclopedia of health information sources : a bibliographic guide to approximately 13,000 citations for publications, organizations, and other sources of information on more than 450 health-related subjects / Paul Wasserman, editor, Suzanne Grefsheim, associate editor. c1987

W	Medical profession
22	Directories (Table G)
AA1	United States *(from Table G)*
E54	Cutter number for the main entry under the title, *Encyclopedia ...*
1987	Date of publication

[LC call number: Z6658.E54 1987]

Medical publishing in 19th century America ... / Francesco Cordasco. 1990
WZ   History of medicine
345   Medical writing and publishing
C794m   Cutter number for the main entry, Cordasco, and
        work letter (m) for the title
1990   Date of publication
[LC call number: Z473.C764 1990]

Essentials of human anatomy & physiology / Elaine N. Marieb. c1991
QS   Human anatomy
4   General works
M334e   Cutter number for the main entry, Marieb, and
        work letter (e) for the title
1991   Date of publication
[LC call number: QP34.5.M455 1991]

Ethical dilemmas in pediatrics : a case study approach / Edwin N. Forman, Rosalind Ekman Ladd. c1991
WS   Pediatrics
21   Pediatrics as a profession. Ethics. Peer review
F724e   Cutter number for the main entry, Forman, and
        work letter (e) for the title
1991   Date of publication
[LC call number: RJ47.F67 1991]

Medicaid spending in the 1980s : the access-cost containment trade-off revisited / Deborah Chang and John Holahan. c1990
W   Medical profession
275   Medical, dental, pharmaceutical and/or
        psychiatric service plans, by country (Table G)
AA1   United States *(from Table G)*
C423m   Cutter number for the main entry, Chang, and
        work letter (m) for the title
1990   Date of publication
[LC call number: RA395.A3C472 1990]

Medicine women, curanderas, and women doctors / by Bobette Perrone, H. Henrietta Stockel, and Victoria Krueger. c1989
WB   Practice of medicine
50   Medical practice (Table G)
AA1   United States *(from Table G)*
P45m   Cutter number for the main entry, Perrone, and
        work letter (m) for the title
1989   Date of publication
[LC call number: R692.P47 1989]

Evaluation and management of acid related disorders
[videorecording] : current trends and future directions /
Gardiner-Caldwell SynerMed. 1990

WI	Gastrointestinal system
350	Peptic ulcer
VC	Medium code for videorecordings
no. 18	Serial number
1990	Date of manufacture

C-section rates [sound recording] : is your hospital vulnerable? 1989

WQ	Obstetrics
16	Tables. Statistics
AC	Medium code for sound recordings
no. 1	Serial number
1989	Date of manufacture

OTHER MODERN LIBRARY CLASSIFICATION SYSTEMS

In addition to the library classification systems discussed previously, a number of other systems have been developed in modern times. The following brief account presents the salient characteristics of the most notable, along with information on their conception and development. They are listed in chronologic order by date of publication of their first editions.

Although some of the systems are no longer in use, they are included here not only because they are part of the history of librarianship but also because they illustrate different ways of classifying bibliographic materials. Often, those who are involved in designing new retrieval schemes conclude that appropriate classification is one of the keys to effective design. A comparison of the different principles and structures that characterize the many classification systems can be a fruitful exercise.

Expansive Classification (Charles Ammi Cutter, 1837–1903)

Brief history

Cutter first designed the Expansive Classification (EC) for the Boston Athenaeum, where he was librarian. He later recognized its value as a general library classification system and, with certain modifications and refinements, made it available to other libraries by publishing it over the years 1891–1893.[5]

---

[5]C. A. Cutter. *Expansive Classification: Part 1: The First Six Classifications.* Boston: C. A. Cutter, 1891–1893.

Cutter continued work on his seven-stage scheme, the first of which was intended for small libraries and the seventh for a collection of 10 million volumes. Unfortunately, he died before its completion. EC was adopted by a number of American libraries. However, perhaps particularly because there has never been a mechanism or organizational support for updating the scheme, libraries have long ceased to adopt it. The latest survey, conducted in the 1970s, revealed that it was used then by only a dozen American and Canadian libraries, most of which were special or small public libraries.[6]

Basic principles and characteristics

The Expansive Classification is perhaps best known today because it served as a model for the early development of the Library of Congress Classification (LCC). However, it presents several interesting features in its own right. The most striking is that the same basic organizational approach to recorded knowledge was developed at several levels of fullness. Cutter was very much aware of the fact that a village library and a national library have vastly different needs, so he decided to work out a system that could meet the needs of all sizes of libraries. EC was therefore prepared in seven versions, called *classifications*, in increasing fullness of detail. The first has eight main classes with rather broad subdivisions. The second has fifteen main classes, and the third through sixth have twenty-seven; these are shown in Table 14-2. The idea of providing varying degrees of fullness to suit the needs of individual libraries is in keeping with Cutter's proposal of the full, medium, and short catalogs for libraries of different sizes.[7] A similar principle, followed to a lesser degree, was adopted by both DDC (two versions, full and abridged) and the Universal Decimal Classification (three versions, full, medium, and abridged).

In arranging the subdivisions of each main class, Cutter claims to have followed an evolutionary order, i.e., placing the subdivisions of each subject in the order that evolutionary theory assigns to their appearance in creation. For example, Science in general proceeds from the molecular to the molar (in physics, the whole as distinguished from its constituent elements), from number and space, through matter and force, to matter and life. In Book arts, the subdivisions follow the history of the book from its production through its distribution, to its storage and use in libraries, and ends with its description, i.e., bibliography.

---

[6]Robert L. Mowery. "The Cutter Classification: Still at Work." *Library Resources & Technical Services,* **20:**154–156, Spring 1976.

[7]Charles A. Cutter. *Rules for a Dictionary Catalog.* 4th ed., rewritten. Washington: Government Printing Office, 1904. P. 13.

TABLE 14-2   Outline of the Expansive Classification

A	General works
B	Philosophy
BR	Religion (except the Christian and Jewish)
C	Christian and Jewish religions
D	Ecclesiastical history
E	Biography
F	History
G	Geography and travels
H	Social Sciences
I	Sociology
J	Government; Politics
K	Legislation; Law; Woman; Societies
L	Science in general; Physical sciences
M	Natural history
N	Botany
O	Zoology
Q	Medicine
R	Useful arts (technology)
S	Engineering; Building
T	Manufactures; Handicrafts
U	Defensive and preservative arts
V	Recreative arts: Sports; Theatre
VV	Music
W	Fine arts
X	Language
Y	Literature
Z	Book arts

For notation, Cutter used capital letters for main classes and subdivisions. For example:

X	Language
XDG	Grammar
XDHZ	Parts of speech
XDI	Noun
XDIW	Adjective

The notation is thus kept shorter than that in a system using only arabic numerals. However, it is not expressive.

For forms and geographic areas, Cutter devised two tables of common subdivisions, designated by arabic numerals, that were applicable throughout the system. The following lists, the first in its entirety, the second an excerpt, illustrate these tables.

Forms
.1   Theory; Philosophy
.2   Bibliography
.3   Biography
.4   History
.5   Dictionaries; Encyclopedias
.6   Yearbooks; Directories
.7   Periodicals
.8   Societies
.9   Collections

For example, XDG.4 designates History of grammar.

Areas
30   Europe
32   Greece
35   Italy
45   England, Great Britain
47   Germany
80   America
83   United States

For example, with IU denoting Schools, IU45 is for English schools and IU83 is for schools in the United States.

For subarrangement of books on the same subject, Cutter devised an extensive system of author or book numbers to be used with his classification. Ironically, this part of Cutter's achievement, which has become known as the *Cutter number system,* has survived the classification itself; it is now widely used with the Dewey and the NLM systems, and a simplified version is used with the Library of Congress Classification.

Universal Decimal Classification

Brief history

The Universal Decimal Classification (UDC) was an adaptation of the Dewey Decimal Classification. It was originally developed for the purpose of compiling a classified index to a universal bibliography which would list all publications, including books and articles in periodicals. This project was initiated in 1895 by the Institut International de Bibliographie (IIB) located in Brussels, which later became the Fédération Internationale de Documentation (FID). Paul Otlet and Henri La Fontaine of Belgium, who were responsible for the initial development of UDC, decided to base the new system on DDC, which had become the most successful and best-known library classification system by the end of the nineteenth century. Because much more detail and minute speci-fications were needed for an indexing tool than were available in DDC, the institute obtained Melvil Dewey's permission to expand and modify DDC to suit the purpose of a universal bibliography.

The first complete (international) edition in the French language was published between 1904 and 1907[8] under the title *Manual du répertoire bibliographique universel.*

Over the years, the project of the universal bibliography was aban-doned, but the development of UDC as a general scheme for classifica-tion and indexing continued. It has been adopted widely in Europe. It now appears in three versions with varying details—full, medium, and abridged—and has been translated into over twenty languages. How-ever, not all these are complete editions that encompass all classes. Only parts of the full edition are available in English.

Until 1985, UDC in its entirety (i.e., covering all subjects) was avail-able in the English language only in the abridged version.[9] In 1985, part 1 (containing the Systematic Tables) of *Universal Decimal Classification: International Medium Edition English Text,*[10] covering all subjects, was published, to be followed by part 2, Index.

The system is now maintained by the FID. A major difficulty has been the slow process in updating because of the very involved and complicated mechanism for revision, sometimes called a hyperde-mocratic procedure. This mechanism ensures universal input but is extremely time-consuming.

UDC also has been known under various other names: Classification Internationale Décimale, the International Decimal Classification, the Expanded Dewey, and the Brussels Expansion of Dewey.

Developments in modern knowledge have placed a certain strain on a classification system such as DDC, which originated in the nineteenth century. The same strain is apparent in UDC. New knowledge con-stantly comes into being, and existing knowledge is continuously rede-fined and realigned. As in the case of DDC, editors of UDC also have been making constant efforts to keep pace with knowledge while at-tempting to maintain a certain degree of stability.

In adopting the basic structure of DDC, UDC also has inherited its intrinsic weaknesses. Over the years, attempts have been made to rectify or mitigate some of the basic problems without uprooting the system. In addition to continuous expansion of details in order to keep pace with

[8]Amitabha Chatterjee and Gobinda Gopal Choudhury. "UDC: International Medium Edition—English Text: A Critical Appraisal." *International Classification,* **13** (3): 137, 1986.
[9]*Universal Decimal Classification.* 3rd abridged English ed. B.S. 1.000A. London: British Standards Institution, 1961.
[10]*Universal Decimal Classification.* International medium ed., English text. B.S. 1.000M. London: British Standards Institution, 1985–1988.

TABLE 14-3   Outline of Universal Decimal Classification

0   Generalities of knowledge
1   Philosophy. Metaphysics. Psychology. Logic. Ethics
2   Religions. Theology
3   Social sciences. Statistics. Politics. Economics. Trade. Law. Government.
    Military Affairs. Welfare. Insurance. Education. Folklore
4   (Currently vacant. Formerly Linguistics; Philology)
5   Mathematics and Natural sciences
6   Applied sciences. Medicine. Technology
7   The arts. Recreation. Entertainment. Sport
8   Language. Linguistics. Literature.
9   Geography. Biography. History

knowledge and proliferation of literature, many relocations have been made over the years. A major relocation has been made by moving the language class to the literature class, a move resulting in a better collocation of related subjects and an entire vacant class for future use.

Basic principles and characteristics

UDC follows the basic outline of the Dewey system in its main classes and major subdivisions; these are delineated in Table 14-3. It is thus a general classification scheme covering all fields of knowledge. The DDC provisions, however, required extensive expansion in order to meet the needs of a system intended to serve as an indexing tool for a universal bibliography. In the subsequent proliferation of subject subdivisions, the progression is from the general to the specific, and division is based as far as possible on mutually exclusive classes. Efforts are also made to collocate related topics.

The latest official statement of UDC's guiding characteristics appears in the International Medium Edition—English Text:[11]

1. It is a general classification covering the universe of information.
2. It is a documentary classification.
3. It has been developed into a faceted classification from an enumerative one.
4. It was designed for bibliographic use but has proved eminently suitable for library use.
5. It is an aspect classification in which a phenomenon is classed according to the concept or discipline in which it is considered.

[11]Chatterjee and Choudhury. Op. cit. P. 137.

Because of its initial purpose and later development, UDC has moved a long way from DDC in several aspects. An attempt has been made to remove all national biases; however, a western, or occidental, viewpoint is still detectable.

For notation, UDC followed DDC in adopting a base notation of arabic numerals, including a decimal after the third digit; such notation is particularly advantageous for an international bibliographic system because it is universally recognizable with virtually infinite possibilities for expansion. UDC notation departs from DDC notation in not requiring three-digit integers as base numbers; in other words, UDC does not use zeros as fillers. For example, Religion is represented by 2 instead of 200, as it is in DDC. Divisions and subdivisions of main classes are represented by additional digits, e.g., 63, Agriculture; 633, Field crops; 633.1, Cereal, corn, grain.

As noted above, because it serves as an indexing tool, UDC is required to have many more detailed subdivisions than a scheme designed mainly for shelving purposes. Perhaps for this reason, over the years, UDC has adopted modern classification theory more readily than DDC and has incorporated many of the features of a faceted scheme. It provides for a considerable degree of synthesis through combining subjects and concepts by means of auxiliary devices. There are common auxiliaries—such as form, period, and place—that apply to all classes, and special auxiliaries apply to certain parts of the schedules. The distinguishing aspect of UDC's provisions for synthesis, however, is that topics and subtopics in disparate parts of the schedules can be combined as required by means of connecting symbols (called *facet indicators*) that not only provide links but show the nature of the relationship. Table 14-4 lists facet indicators and their meanings. The following examples show that UDC notation is both hierarchical (i.e., capable of representing hierarchical relationships) and expressive (i.e., capable of representing associative relationships).

Following are examples of UDC numbers:

975.5 + 976.9	History of Virginia and Kentucky
975.5	History of Virginia
976.9	History of Kentucky

026:61 (058.7)	Directory of medical libraries
026	Libraries
61	Medicine
058.7	Directory

TABLE 14-4   Facet Indicators in UDC

Symbol	Meaning
+	Combining two separate numbers
/	Combining two or more consecutive numbers
:	Simple relationships between two subjects
::	Connecting symbol indicating the order of the component numbers in a compound number
=	Language
(0 ...)	Form
(1/9)	Place
(=0/9)	Race and nationality
"..."	Time
A/Z	Alphabetical subarrangement
.00 . . .	Point of view
=05	Persons
[...]	Denoting subordinate concepts
*	Connecting non-UDC numbers to a UDC number

61 (038) =20=50	Italian-English dictionary of medicine
61	Medicine
038	Dictionary
20	English
50	Italian

850"19"	Twentieth-century Italian literature
850	Italian literature
19	Twentieth century

UDC is a powerful system, one that is particularly suited to the machine environment; retrieval algorithms can be written that can either refine or expand subject searches just through operations on the class numbers. However, UDC takes its basic intellectual structure from a scheme (Dewey) that originated fairly late in the nineteenth century when the general intellectual consensus was that revolutionary changes in scholarly disciplines were no longer likely. In reality, new knowledge constantly comes into being, and existing knowledge is continuously redefined and realigned. Both DDC and UDC, therefore, are under considerable strain. For retrieval effectiveness, both need to keep pace with the current states of and relationships among the many fields of knowledge. However, to avoid the need of massive reclassification, each system also attempts to maintain a certain degree of stability. The editors of both systems do their best to rectify or mitigate anomalies without uprooting their systems. Still, in addition to continuous expansion of details in order to keep pace with knowledge and proliferation of literature, there have been many relocations in each system over the years.

Subject Classification (James Duff Brown, 1862–1914)

Brief history

The Subject Classification has now faded into obscurity, but nonetheless it has interesting features. The classification originated as a protest. Toward the end of the nineteenth century, the Dewey system, already widely used in the United States, was gradually gaining ground in Britain also; Brown, dissatisfied with the system because of its obvious American bias and other weaknesses, set out to devise a British system. The Subject Classification (SC) first appeared in 1906, with a second edition in 1917, three years after Brown's death. The third (1939) edition was edited by J. D. Stewart.

Prior to his work on SC, Brown was responsible for two other schemes. The Quinn-Brown Classification (in collaboration with John Henry Quinn) was developed in 1849. It was modified by Brown and published in 1898 as Adjustable Classification.[12]

Although SC had enough viability in its early years to merit the 1939 edition, in the end it failed to win over British libraries, and only a small number adopted it. Failure to keep the system up to date may have been the crucial factor in its obsolescence.

Basic principles and characteristics

In its arrangement of the main classes, SC follows an order of "scientific progression." Brown's theory was that in the order of things, matter and force came first; they gave rise to life and then to mind. Finally, mind was followed by the making of its record. Table 14-5 shows the SC outline.

Brown is most famous for his "one-place theory," which assumes that materials on a concrete subject are more useful grouped together in one place than scattered according to the author's standpoint or discipline. This is the major difference between his system and other schemes such as DDC and LCC. Although the subject Iron may be treated from such standpoints as Metallurgy, Mineralogy, Inorganic chemistry, Geology, Economics, and Industry, in SC all materials on the subject Iron are grouped together with locations determined on the principle of placing each subject as near as possible to the science on which it is based. Hence Iron is classed under Mineralogy, Apple under Botany, and Music under

---

[12]James Duff Brown. *Adjustable Classification for Libraries, with Index*. London: Library Supply Company, 1898.

TABLE 14-5   Outline of Subject Classification

A	Generalia
	Matter and force
B–D	Physical science
	Life
E–F	Biological science
G–H	Ethnology. Medicine
I	Economic biology. Domestic arts
	Mind
J–K	Philosophy and religion
L	Social and political science
	Record
M	Language and literature
N	Literary forms. Fiction. Poetry
O–W	History and geography
X	Biography

Acoustics, which is, in turn, a subdivision of Physics. Applications follow their theoretical base, e.g., Chemical technology under Chemistry and Mining under Geology.

Brown adopted a simple mixed notation; main classes are represented by single capital letters and subdivisions by arabic numerals. For example:

N	Literary forms and texts
N000	Fiction
N100	Poetry
N110	Forms of poetry
N114	Lyric poetry—English

Brown also provided a Categorical Table for commonly used subdivisions; its provisions can be used throughout the scheme. Thus limited notational synthesis is provided by combining the main number with a number from the Categorical Table (for the subdivision of subjects) representing form or other divisions, as shown below:

.0	Generalia
.00	Catalogues. Lists
.01	Monarchs. Rulers
.02	Subdivisions for rearrangement
.1	Bibliography
.2	Encyclopedias. Dictionaries
.10	History (for general use in all classes)

For example,

I229.10   History of gardening in England.

Colon Classification (Shiyali Ramamrita Ranganathan, 1892–1972)

Brief history

The Colon Classification (CC) was developed by S. R. Ranganathan, a prominent librarian from India who is considered by many to be the foremost theorist in the field of classification because of his contributions to the theory of facet analysis and synthesis. His writings on classification, the best known of which is *Prolegomena to Library Classification* (3rd ed., 1967), form the basis of modern classification theory. The Colon Classification is a manifestation of Ranganathan's theory, which has had a major influence on all currently used classification and indexing systems. CC itself, however, has not been widely used even in India.

The first edition of *Colon Classification* was published in 1933. The sixth edition[13] appeared in 1963. Over the years, as Ranganathan refined and redefined his thinking about classification, each edition reflected the progress of his theory. Drastic changes took place between editions, and stability was sacrificed for the sake of keeping up with knowledge as well as with classification theory.

Ranganathan died before completing the seventh edition, which had been in preparation for many years. M. A. Gopinath continued what was begun by Ranganathan. In 1987, the first (containing the schedules) of three projected volumes of the seventh edition was published.[14]

Basic principles and characteristics

In the colon classification, knowledge is divided into more or less traditional main classes; these are shown in Table 14-6. However, the similarity between CC and other classification systems ends here.

CC is a faceted scheme. Each class is broken down into its basic concepts or elements according to certain characteristics, called *facets*. In isolating these component elements, Ranganathan has identified five fundamental categories, often referred to as *PMEST: Personality* (entity in question), *Matter* (materials, substances, properties, etc.), *Energy* (operations, processes, activities, etc.), *Space* (geographic areas and features), and *Time* (periods, dates, seasons, etc.). When classifying a document, the classifier identifies component parts that reflect every aspect and element of the subject content and puts them together according to a structural procedure, called a *facet formula*, which has been individually designed for each main class. Thus, unlike enumerative classification

---

[13]S. R. Ranganathan. *Colon Classification*. 6th ed., reprinted with amendments. Bombay: Asia Publishing House, 1963.

[14]S. R. Ranganathan. *Colon Classification*. Ed. 7, revised and edited by M. A. Gopinath. Bangalore: Sarada Ranganathan Endowment for Library Science, 1987. Cf. P. Dhyani. "Colon Classification Edition 7—An Appraisal." *International Classification*, 15(1):13, 1988.

TABLE 14-6   Outline of Colon Classification, Main Classes

Main Classes

01	Generalia	L	Medicine
1	Universe of subjects	M	Useful arts
2	Library science	Δ	Mysticism
3	Book science	N	Fine arts
4	Mass communication	O	Literature
8	Management	P	Linguistics
B	Mathematics	Q	Religion
C	Physics	R	Philosophy
D	Engineering	S	Psychology
E	Chemistry	T	Education
F	Technology	U	Geography
G	Biology	V	History
H	Geology	W	Political science
I	Botany	X	Economics
J	Agriculture	Y	Sociology
K	Zoology	Z	Law

schemes, CC does not list complete ready-made numbers in its schedules. A combination, or *synthesis,* of notation is tailored for each work in hand.

In addition to subject subdivisions in each main class, there are certain common subdivisions (called *isolates* in the CC system) which can be applied throughout the entire scheme. These include form and language isolates.

The basic ideas of facet analysis and synthesis had been present in the earlier classification schemes, notably in the form divisions in Dewey's system, the common subdivisions and the local list in Cutter's classification, and the Categorical Table in Brown's classification. But it was left to Ranganathan to systematize and formalize the theory. Its influence is particularly apparent in the revision of UDC and Bibliographic Classification. In addition, revision of DDC, particularly in recent editions, shows increasing use of facet analysis and synthesis, most noticeably in the five auxiliary tables added in the eighteenth edition.

Notation for the Colon Classification is extremely mixed and complex. It combines arabic numerals, capital and lowercase letters, some Greek letters, brackets, and certain punctuation marks. The Generalia classes are represented by arabic numerals. Main classes are shown by capital letters of the Roman alphabet and certain Greek letters. Basic concepts and elements under each main class are represented mainly by arabic numerals.

L	Medicine
2	Digestive system
27	Large intestine
2721	Caecum

Common subdivisions, called *common isolates*, are shown in lower-case letters, capital letters, or arabic numerals.

4	Asia
5	Europe
52	Italy
5215	Sicily

r	Dry
u	Rainy
v	Monsoonish

L	1700–1799 A.D.
N	1900–1999 A.D.
Z	Future

In formulating a class number, certain punctuation marks are used as facet indicators to show the nature of the element being presented. The following meanings have been assigned to them:

(,) connecting symbol for Personality
(;) connecting symbol for Matter
(:) connecting symbol for Energy
(.) connecting symbol for Space
(') connecting symbol for Time

In the seventh edition, additional connecting symbols were introduced, e.g., = (equal to) as in the space isolate 1=(Q,7) for Muslim area of the world, where 1 means the world and Q,7 means Islam.

Following are examples of CC class numbers:

Research in the cure of the tuberculosis of lungs by x-ray, conducted in India in 1950s
L,45;421:6;253:f.44'N5

L	Medicine
45	Lungs
421	Tuberculosis
6	Treatment
253	X-ray
f	Research
44	India
N5	1950

Discharge of partnership in Indian law
Z,44,315,7
Z   Law
44   India
315   Partnership
7   Discharge

Eradication of virus in rice plants in Japan (1971)
J,381;421:5.42'N7
J   Agriculture
381   Rice
421   Virus disease
5   Prevention
42   Japan
N7   1970s

Bibliographic Classification (Henry Evelyn Bliss, 1870–1955)

Brief history

Henry Evelyn Bliss, for nearly half a century a librarian at the College of the City of New York, devoted more than thirty years of his life to the study of classification and the development of Bibliographic Classification (BC). The publication of the scheme took thirteen years, from 1940 to 1953. In the course of its development, Bliss also produced numerous articles and books on classification. Among his best known works are *Organization of Knowledge and the System of the Sciences* (1929) and *Organization of Knowledge in Libraries and the Subject Approach to Books* (1933; 2nd ed., 1939). The latter embodies the theory on which his classification scheme was based and includes an outline of the scheme.

Before the full schedules were published, an expansion of the outline appeared in a one-volume work entitled *A System of Bibliographic Classification* (1935).

Although BC was not widely adopted in the United States, it received much attention in Britain. In 1967, an abridged *Bliss Classification* was published there by the School Library Association. A Bliss Classification Association was formed in Britain, which has assumed responsibility for maintaining and updating the scheme. A second edition, entitled *Bliss Bibliographic Classification*,[15] under the editorship of J. Mills and V. Broughton, began publication in 1977 in separate volumes. Currently, not all schedules have been published.

[15]Henry Evelyn Bliss. *Bliss Bibliographic Classification*. 2nd ed. J. Mills and Vanda Broughton, eds., with the assistance of Valerie Lang. London; Boston: Butterworths, 1977–

Basic principles and characteristics

From the beginning, several principles guided Bliss's work. These are consensus, collocation of related subjects, subordination of special to general, gradation in speciality, and the opportunity for alternative locations and treatments.

Respecting *consensus*, Bliss asserted that "knowledge should be *organized in consistency* with *the scientific and educational consensus*, which is *relatively stable* and tends to become more so as theory and system become more definitely and permanently established in general and increasingly in detail."[16] He believed that such an order would be the most helpful to library users, and he tried to reflect scientific and educational consensus in arranging his main and subordinate classes.

The original Bliss Classification was essentially an "aspect" classification, or classification by discipline, in which information on individual "phenomena" is scattered over many disciplines and subdisciplines; e.g., Iron is subordinated variously to Chemistry, Chemical technology, Mineralogy, Mining, Industrial economics, and so on.

Bliss acted on his ideas of *collocation of related subjects* by bringing them into close proximity in his schedules. For example, certain pure sciences are collocated with the appropriate technology. This idea is similar to Brown's. However, Bliss did not carry it to the extremes Brown used in Subject Classification. Bliss brought together only those pure sciences and technology which are most likely to be used together by readers.

In developing subclasses and subdivisions, Bliss followed the principle of *subordination of special to general* in bringing special subjects under comprehensive general subjects. In arranging coordinate topics under them, the principle of *gradation in speciality* was followed. The premise of this principle is that certain derivative subjects draw on the findings of other subjects. In a classification scheme, the subject that borrows from another is considered to be more specialized than the latter and should follow it. For example, mathematics is a science that many other sciences draw on, and therefore, it is placed at the very beginning of the classification.

Bliss recognized that frequently a subject may be placed with equal usefulness in two or more possible locations in the scheme. In order to render the system useful to the largest number of users, *alternative locations* are provided in the scheme for these subjects. For example, Economic history can be subordinated to General history or classed in Economics. There are a large number of alternative provisions in BC, and this feature is enhanced even further in the new edition. Alternative locations might be to place Religion between History and the Occult or to put it at the end of the scheme, or to concentrate all Technology together

[16]Henry Evelyn Bliss. *The Organization of Knowledge in Libraries*. 2nd ed. New York: H. W. Wilson Company, 1939. Pp. 42–43.

in class U instead of subordinating the more science-oriented ones with the appropriate science (e.g., Chemical technology with Chemistry).

Bliss also realized that in some cases a body of material may be organized in different but equally useful ways. He made many provisions for *alternative treatment* in the schedules. A notable example is his four modes of classifying literature:

1. Separating literary history from texts
2. Literary history and texts together
3. Combination of (1) for modern literature and (2) for earlier literature
4. Same as (3) except the modern texts are classed by form rather than by author

In the new edition,[17] the editors have taken into consideration the advances in classification theory that have developed since Bliss died, particularly the principles (based on Ranganathan's work) of facet analysis, explicit citation orders, and explicit filing order. While the main outline of the first edition was largely retained, many of the internal details have undergone radical revision. Each class has been given a fully faceted structure. Furthermore, the vocabulary has been thoroughly revised and greatly enlarged, as well as organized into explicitly named facets and arrays.

At the beginning of the scheme, the new edition provides classes for comprehensive works (called *Generalia attributes, Generalia processes,* and *Generalia entities*) but with the option of placing these works with the most suitable "aspect" or discipline. Many new subjects have been added, such as Media science, Recording and reproduction techniques, Data processing, etc.

Bliss's notation was simple, with Generalia classes represented by arabic numerals, subject classes by single capital letters, and subclasses and subdivisions by a combination of capital letters.

U	Technology, useful arts
UE	Engineering
UHC	Construction techniques
UHV	Architecture, planning and building
UJ	Architectural practice and design

Bliss constantly emphasized the desirability of brief notation. The wide base provided by the use of the letters in the alphabet makes brevity more easily achievable but, inevitably, entails a sacrifice of expressivity. Many classificationists have chosen brevity over expressivity. The new BC edition has retained most of the notational features of the original. In the earlier edition, lowercase letters and arbitrary symbols also were

[17]J. Mills. "The New Bliss Classification." *Catalogue and Index,* 40:1, 3–6 Spring 1976.

used, but these have been abandoned in the new edition. Table 14-7 shows an outline of the current schedules.

TABLE 14-7   Outline of Bliss Bibliographic Classification (Second Edition)

2	Generalia: physical forms and documents
3	Generalia: forms of arrangement and presentation
	Phenomena
4	Attributes (e.g., structure, order, symmetry, colour)
5	Activities and processes (e.g., organising, planning, change, adaptation)
6	Entities (e.g., particles, atoms, molecules, minerals, organisms, communities, institutions, artefacts)
7	Universe of knowledge
	Communication and information
8	Data processing, Computer science
	Records, Documentation
9	Individual and mass communication
	Disciplines
A	Philosophy
AL	Logic
AM	Mathematics
AW	Statistics and probability
AX	Systemology, Organisation theory, Management
AY	Science and technology
AZ	Science
B	Physics
BR	Technologies based primarily on physics (*Alternative* is UG)
C	Chemistry

(continued on page 396)

There are six auxiliary schedules containing concepts that occur in some way or another in all or most subjects. Their provisions may be applied to any class in the system. Notation for the auxiliaries is similar to that used in the main schedules: arabic numerals, capital letters, or a combination thereof. Table 14-8 contains excerpts from the auxiliary schedules.

The faceted structure of both the main schedules and the auxiliary schedules allows a great degree of synthesis. The following examples show Bliss class numbers:

C	Chemistry
C5V	Bibliography
C6C	Chemical Research
P	Religion
POZ	Religion in individual countries
POZ RB	Religion in China
POZ Y	Religion in the U.S.
POZ YG	Religion in the south

TABLE 14-7   (Continued)

CT	Materials science and technology (*Alternative* is UEV)
D	Astronomy
DG	Space science
DH	Earth sciences
E	Biology
EV	Microbiology
F	Botany
G	Zoology
H	Man, Anthropology
HA	Human biology
HH	Health sciences, Medicine
I	Psychology
J	Education
K	Social sciences
KA	Sociology
KY	Travel and description
L	History
L9	Biography
M	Europe
N	America
OA	Australia
OH	Asia
OS	Africa
P	Religion (*Alternative* is Z)
PX	The occult
PY	Morals, ethics
Q	Social welfare and administration
R	Political science
RO	Public administration
S	Law
T	Economics
TX	Management of enterprises
U	Technology, Useful arts
UA	Agricultural industry (*Alternative* is GZ)
UD	Mining technology
UE	Engineering
UO	Transport technology
US	Military science and technology
UY	Recreative arts
V	Arts, Fine arts
VV	Music
VY	Performing arts
W	Philology: Language and literature
WA	Linguistics
WI	Individual languages and their literatures
YU	Literature: General and comparative
Z	Religion, Occult, Morals (*Alternative* is P)

Table 14-8   Excerpts from Auxiliary Schedules in BC

Schedule		Divisions
1 Common subdivisions	2EN	Nonbook materials
	2WH U	Government publications
	5V	Bibliographies
	6C	Research in the subject
	7	History (*see* Schedule 4)
	8	Places, localities in the subject (*see* Schedule 2)
	9	Biography
1A Persons	A	Persons in the subject
	CP	Relations to community, society
	JD	Minority groups
	NS	Families
	RC	Refugees
2 Place	AS	Regions by climate
	BAJ	Regions by land and resource use
	BC	Urban
	D	Europe
	O	Asia
	RB	China
	X	America
	Y	U.S.A.
3 Language	G	American aboriginal languages
	PB	Indo-European languages
	WB	Germanic
	X	German, Dutch, English
3A Ethnic groups	BS	Europiforms
	G	American aborigines
	KY	Northeast Asian groups
	L	Japanese
4 Periods of time	DF	4000 B.C.
	EV	000 A.D.
	FX	1300
	GZ	1500
	Q	1900
	S	2000

TOPICS FOR DISCUSSION

1. In the second edition of DDC, in which Dewey declared the policy of the "integrity of numbers," he assigned topics to all one-hundred divisions and to all but twenty-one of the 1000 numbers in the

000–999 sequence. Nineteen of the twenty-one vacant numbers occurred in the 000 class, General works. Like his contemporaries, Dewey assumed that technology had reached its summit and there was nothing left to be invented. In establishing the scheme, he saw fit to use up the available numbers even in places where he did not need to; for instance, he assigned 570, 580, and 590 to Biology, Botany, and Zoology, respectively, making them coordinate topics, when the latter two should have been subsumed under 570 according to the hierarchical principle; 580 and 590 could have been left vacant and saved for future use. Find other similar examples of distorted hierarchy in the system, and discuss the reasons and consequences of this irregular practice, particularly in terms of difficulties in maintaining logical collocation and inserting new subjects in later editions.

2. Most online catalogs have the capability of searching by class or call numbers. What are the advantages of searching by class numbers? How does class-number searching complement searching by verbal subject access points?

3. Discuss the effect of hierarchical notation in online searching by class numbers.

4. In the 800 (Literature) class of DDC, literary works by individual authors are scattered according to their literary form, e.g., T. S. Eliot's drama in 822.912, his poetry in 821.912, and his essays in 824.912. Discuss the advantages and disadvantages of such an arrangement. Also, consider the problems in classifying Eliot's collected works and criticism of his works in general.

5. In a hierarchical notational system such as DDC, specificity entails long numbers. Yet in practice, particularly as a shelving device, long numbers create problems. Discuss some of these problems and possible solutions. Compare this aspect of DDC with the nonhierarchical notation of LCC.

6. During the 1960s, many libraries, particularly academic libraries, reclassified from DDC to LCC. Identify some of the reasons for the switch. One frequently cited rationale is that LCC is more specific than DDC. Another claims that LCC is more stable than DDC. Evaluate some of these justifications.

7. Discuss the purpose and functions of unique call numbers both in shelf arrangement and in online retrieval.

8. Compare the Dewey Decimal Classification and the Library of Congress Classification in terms of the following topics: form subdivisions, geographic subdivisions, notation, Cutter numbers, and treat-

ment of a specific subject (e.g., library science, chemistry, literature, etc.).

9. Using LCC as an example of an enumerative classification scheme and DDC as an example of a partially faceted scheme, compare the two kinds of classification systems in terms of application in libraries and in terms of online searching.

10. The National Library of Medicine is a broad classification, i.e., one that does not provide minute and narrow subjects. Discuss the advantages and disadvantages of such a system in terms of its function as a shelving device and in terms of online searching.

PART V
USMARC FORMATS
AND PRODUCTION
OF CATALOGING
RECORDS

BASIC TOOLS

USMARC Concise Formats. Prepared by Network Development and MARC Standards Office. Washington: Cataloging Distribution Service, Library of Congress, 1991.

USMARC Format for Authority Data, Including Guidelines for Content Designation. Prepared by Network Development and MARC Standards Office. Washington: Cataloging Distribution Service, Library of Congress, 1987.

USMARC Format for Bibliographic Data, Including Guidelines for Content Designation. Prepared by Network Development and MARC Standards Office. Washington: Cataloging Distribution Service, Library of Congress, 1988.

USMARC Format for Classification Data, Including Guidelines for Content Designation. Prepared by Network Development and MARC Standards Office. Washington: Cataloging Distribution Service, Library of Congress, 1990.

USMARC Format for Holdings Data, Including Guidelines for Content Designation. Prepared by Network Development and MARC Standards Office. Washington: Cataloging Distribution Service, Library of Congress, 1989.

BACKGROUND READING

Attig, John. "The USMARC Formats—Underlying Principles." *Information Technology and Libraries*, 1(2):169–74, June 1982.

Avram, Henriette D. *MARC: Its History and Implications.* Washington: Library of Congress, 1975.

Byrne, Deborah J. *MARC Manual: Understanding and Using MARC Records*. Englewood, Colo.: Libraries Unlimited, 1991.

Crawford, Walt. *MARC for Library Use: Understanding Integrated US-MARC*. Boston: G. K. Hall & Company, 1989.

Hyman, Richard Joseph, "Automated Catalog Access." In *Information Access: Capabilities and Limitations of Printed and Computerized Sources.* Chicago: American Library Association, 1989.

Library of Congress, MARC Development Office. *Information on the MARC System.* 4th ed. Washington: Library of Congress, 1974.

Library of Congress. Network Development and MARC Standards Office. *Format Integration and Its Effect on the USMARC Bibliographic Format.* Washington: Library of Congress, Cataloging Distribution Service, 1988.

McCallum, Sally H. "Format Integration Implementation Plans." *Information Technology and Libraries,* **9**:155–161, June 1990.

The USMARC Formats: Background and Principles. Prepared by MARBI, American Library Association's ALCTS/LITA/RASD Machine-Readable Bibliographic Information Committee in conjunction with Network Development and MARC Standards Office. Washington: Library of Congress, 1989.

CHAPTER FIFTEEN
USMARC FORMATS

In the Anglo-American library environment, what it takes to make a cataloging record machine readable was outlined briefly in Chapter 1. This chapter elaborates the discussion of USMARC formats in terms of both historical background and their basic structure.

USMARC: HISTORY[1]

In the late 1950s, the Library of Congress began investigating the possibility of automating its internal operations. In the early 1960s, a study was made with financial support from the Council on Library Resources to determine the feasibility of applying automated techniques to the operations of LC. Another study was made of the possible methods of converting the data on LC cards to machine-readable form for the purpose of printing bibliographic products by computer. These studies generated a great deal of interest and enthusiasm. As a result, a pilot project, called *MARC*, was initiated in January 1966 to test the feasibility and utility of having LC distribute machine-readable cataloging data to user libraries. For the pilot project, sixteen libraries of different types and geographic locations were chosen to receive MARC tapes. Trial distribution began in October 1966; by June 1968, approximately 50,000 cataloging records for English-language book materials had been converted to machine-readable form and distributed to the participating libraries. The results of the MARC pilot project were sufficiently encouraging for LC to proceed on a full-scale basis. The original MARC book format was refined and became the MARC II format for monographs.

The MARC Distribution Service was established in March 1969 to disseminate MARC records to subscribing libraries and institutions. It has been doing so, in increasing volume, ever since. Initially, the tapes included records for currently cataloged English-language mono-

[1]Henriette D. Avram. *MARC: Its History and Implications.* Washington: Library of Congress, 1975. Walt Crawford. *MARC for Library Use: Understanding Integrated USMARC.* Boston: G. K. Hall & Co., 1989. Pp. 203–241.

graphic material only,[2] but over the years, the coverage has been broadened to include material of other types and in other languages.

The MARC structure was adopted as a national standard (ANSI Standard Z39.2)[3] in 1971 and as an international standard (ISO Standard 2709)[4] in 1973.

In 1973, an American Library Association committee that had been working on machine-readable form of bibliographic information became a MARC advisory committee working with LC on changes and refinements of the MARC formats. (The committee is known by its acronym, *MARBI*.) Other representatives from the American library and bibliographic community also participate in the continuing development of MARC.

Initially, the MARC formats were intended to be communications formats for the purpose of transmitting machine-readable data from the Library of Congress to users in the library community. With their wide adoption and use, the LC MARC formats later became known as *US-MARC*. In 1982, a set of principles was prepared and published.[5] The Library of Congress continues to have ultimate responsibility for the maintenance and publication of the USMARC formats, but all proposed changes are discussed at MARBI meetings and published after MARBI approval.

TYPES OF MARC FORMATS[6]

There are currently four types of MARC formats: (1) for bibliographic data, (2) for authorities data, (3) for classification data, and (4) for holdings data. These formats have been published in separate volumes. For those who do not need the details in the individual formats, a concise version including all formats, entitled *USMARC Concise Formats*, also has been published.[7]

---

[2]Library of Congress, MARC Development Office. *Information on the MARC System.* 4th ed. Washington: Library of Congress, 1974. P. 1.

[3]American National Standards Institute. *American National Standard Format for Bibliographic Information Interchange on Magnetic Tape.* ANSI Z39.2-1971. New York: ANSI, 1971.

[4]International Organization for Standardization. *Documentation—Format for Bibliographic Information Interchange on Magnetic Tape.* ISO 2709-1973(E). Geneva: The Organization, 1973.

[5]John Attig. "The USMARC Formats—Underlying Principles." *Information Technology and Libraries,* 1(2):169–174, June 1982.

[6]*The USMARC Formats: Background and Principles.* Prepared by MARBI, American Library Association's ALCTS/LITA/RASD Machine-Readable Bibliographic Information Committee in conjunction with Network Development and MARC Standards Office. Washington: Library of Congress, 1989.

[7]*USMARC Concise Formats.* Prepared by Network Development and MARC Standards Office. Washington: Cataloging Distribution Service, Library of Congress, 1991.

1. *USMARC Format for Bibliographic Data*[8] is designed to cover bibliographic information for various types of materials, including books, archival and manuscript materials, computer files, maps, music, visual materials, and serials. Initially, separate formats for different media of data—books, serials, etc.—were prepared, and there have been differences in the provisions for each medium of material, differences that cause problems in application.[9] For example, bibliographic items that manifest more than one set of characteristics, such as nonprint materials in serial form, cannot fit adequately into one format. Although bibliographic items in many media may be issued in serial form, provisions for the serial nature are inconsistent among the various formats. Comparable elements in different formats are not always handled consistently. Furthermore, the multiplicity of formats makes maintenance and systems support difficult and cumbersome. As a result, many considered an integrated format, i.e., a single format for all bibliographic data, would be desirable. In the early 1980s, work toward integrating various MARC formats began. The first step toward format integration was the inclusion of six individual MARC bibliographic formats in one publication, *MARC Formats for Bibliographic Data* (1980). Beginning in 1980, MARBI and LC have worked toward making the formats for different types of materials more consistent and compatible. Proposed changes to specific formats are examined across all the formats. The ultimate aim is to produce a single format for all bibliographic types. This intent was evident when in 1988 the first edition of *USMARC Format for Bibliographic Data, Including Guidelines for Content Designation* replaced *MARC Formats for Bibliographic Data*. In order to achieve the single format, many fields, subfields, and indicators had to be revised and others deleted or added. Because of the enormous amount of details and implications in terms of cost of implementation, particularly its impact on existing records and databases, work proceeded slowly but steadily.

In 1988, the Library of Congress submitted *Proposal 88-1: Format Integration*[10] for consideration at the MARBI meetings. The proposal was accepted as a whole, with some details to be refined later. In order to make the integrated bibliographic format suitable for all types of materials, the proposed format contains data elements that can be used to describe many forms of material and provides the means for describing their serial-related aspects. Subfields and indicator values are made uniform across fields. Because implementing format integration entails great cost in terms of systems design and will have great impact on

[8]*USMARC Format for Bibliographic Data, Including Guidelines for Content Designation.* Prepared by Network Development and MARC Standards Office. Washington: Cataloging Distribution Service, Library of Congress, 1988.

[9]Walt Crawford. *MARC for Library Use: Understanding Integrated USMARC.* Boston: G. K. Hall & Co., 1989. Pp. 221–222.

[10]*Proposal 88-1: Format Integration.* Washington: Library of Congress, 1987.

existing records, implementation is set for 1993, to allow time for adjustment and transition.

2. *USMARC Format for Authority Data*[11] is intended for use by personnel involved in the creation and maintenance of authority records. It contains specifications for encoding and identifying data elements in authority records, including those for name headings, name/title headings, uniform title headings, topical term headings, extended headings (i.e., headings with subdivisions), and references to headings.

3. *USMARC Format for Classification Data*[12] is designed for identifying data elements in classification records. In effect, a classification record is an "authority record" for a class number. It is intended for use by personnel involved in (a) the creation and maintenance of classification records, (b) the publication of classification schemes from machine-readable data, and (c) the design and maintenance of systems for the communication and processing of classification records. The format contains features particularly amenable to the two major classification schemes in use in the United States: Dewey Decimal Classification (DDC) and Library of Congress Classification (LCC).[13]

4. *USMARC Format for Holdings Data*[14] is designed for identifying the data elements in MARC holdings reports (i.e., reports indicating the holdings of individual libraries) for both serial and nonserial items. As such, it contains provisions for recording copy-specific information of any particular item, plus information that is peculiar to the holding library. It is designed to allow the potential use of the format to interface with automated control systems such as union catalogs, serials check-in, and interlibrary loan systems. It is intended for use by personnel involved in the creation and maintenance of USMARC holdings information.

ARCHITECTURE OF USMARC FORMATS

The general architecture of the various formats is similar. The separately published formats, which include instructions on application as well as the format definitions and provisions themselves, are enormously com-

---

[11]*USMARC Format for Authority Data, Including Guidelines for Content Designation.* Prepared by Network Development and MARC Standards Office. Washington: Cataloging Distribution Service, Library of Congress, 1987.

[12]*USMARC Format for Classification Data, Including Guidelines for Content Designation.* Prepared by Network Development and MARC Standards Office. Washington: Cataloging Distribution Service, Library of Congress, 1990.

[13]The format was developed to facilitate the conversion of classification schemes into machine-readable form. DDC, already in a machine-readable form designed for editing the schedules, will be converted to the MARC format. Plans are also underway to convert LCC into MARC format.

[14]*USMARC Format for Holdings Data, Including Guidelines for Content Designation.* Prepared by Network Development and MARC Standards Office. Washington: Cataloging Distribution Service, Library of Congress, 1989.

plex and detailed. For beginners and those interested in an overview of the formats, the concise version offers essential details sufficient for an understanding of the architecture of MARC formats.

It is helpful to consider the basic structure of the USMARC formats in three perspectives: the various elements, the units that appear in a record, and the three main parts of a record. It should be borne in mind that a MARC record in the communications format is a sequential string of characters—a blank space is also a character—with each character having a number or "address" within the string. The OCLC MARC records shown throughout this book represent re-formatted records for easy reading.

Figure 15-1 shows a cataloging record in the MARC communications format (along with a field-by-field analysis) before individual elements are formatted for display. For re-formated records for the same book, see pages 16, 18, and 20-22.

Elements of a MARC Format

Three elements form the basis of the USMARC format: (1) the record structure, (2) the content designation, and (3) the data content.

1. The *record structure* is the overall framework for the MARC record.

2. The *content designation* refers to the set of symbols by which data in the record are identified and manipulated; these include field tags, indicators, and subfield codes (see explanation below).

3. The *data content* consists of record-specific information (bibliographic data, authority data, classification data, etc.), field by field. Data content is what is usually thought of as "catalog information."

Units in a MARC Record

Another way to look at what constitutes a MARC record is in terms of units. The term *unit* here refers to an item of MARC-tagged information. Any MARC record consists of the following units:

1. *Data element.* This is the lowest unit of information, e.g., an entry such as record status, an International Standard Book Number, or a copyright date. An element may be of fixed or variable length.

   a. *Fixed-length element.* This is an element that is always expressed by the same number of characters; e.g., the coded form of a language is always three characters long.

   b. *Variable-length element.* This is an element (such as an author's last name, a series title, an edition statement, etc.) the length of which cannot be predetermined.

```
                                            00889cam  2200
265 a 45e0001001300000005001700013008004100030010002200071040001300093020003200032001
060200032001380500020001700820016001900490009002061000029002152450055002442250001
200299260003700311300001900348440003675040053004115050089004646500003500555365
0003500588ocm13559686 19920401113815.0860421s1987    nyu    b   001 0 eng
a  86010247 //r91 aDLCcDLC a0070335370 (v. 1) :c$28.95 a0070335389 (v. 2) :c
$27.9500aZ711b.K32 198700a025.5/2219 akUKK1 akatz, William A.,d1924-10aIntroduc
tion to reference work /cWilliam A. katz. a5th ed. aNew York :bMcGraw-Hill,cc1
987. a2 v. ;c24 cm. 0aMcGraw-Hill series in library education aIncludes biblio
graphical references and indexes.0 av. 1. Basic information sources -- v. 2. Ref
erence services and reference processes. 0aReference services (Libraries) 0aRefe
rence booksxBibliography.
```

(a)

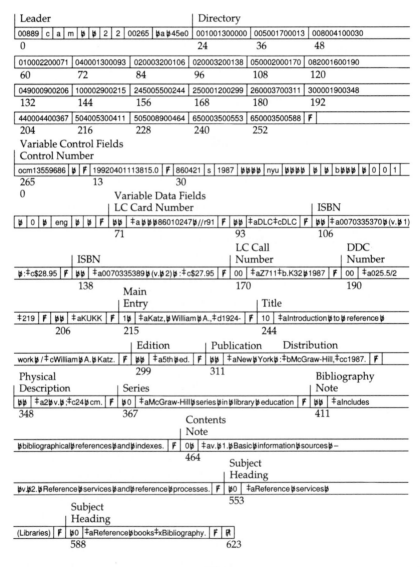

(b)

FIGURE 15-1   (a) A bibliographic record in MARC communications format. (b) A field-by-field analysis. ($\ddagger$ = delimiter; F = field terminator; R = record terminator)

2. *Field.* This is a collection of data elements, e.g., a main entry consisting of the data elements for the person's name and possibly a title of nobility or the dates of his or her birth and death; a field sometimes consists of only one data element, e.g., the LC Control Number.

All of the fields in a MARC record end with a field terminator, ¶ or Ꞙ (an F with a slash through it); these, however, are often not displayed on a catalog screen. Each field terminator indicates that the next character in the MARC string begins a new field.

3. *The record itself.* This is a collection of fields treated as a unit, e.g., a bibliographic record, an authority record, and a classification record; in a string of records, each one ends with a record terminator, Ʀ (an R with a slash through it).

Component Parts of a MARC Record

A final way to look at what makes up a MARC record is to consider its distinct parts. There are three main components: (1) the leader, (2) the directory, and (3) the variable fields. Figure 15-2 shows the three-part structure.

| Leader | Record directory | Variable fields |

FIGURE 15-2   USMARC record structure.

1. The *leader,* fixed at twenty-four characters (positions 0–23), is the first field in a MARC record. It provides particular information for processing the ensuing record, data such as total length, status (e.g., new, deleted, or corrected), type (books, maps, sound recordings, or name authority or subject authority), base address of data, and encoding level (full, minimal, complete, incomplete, etc.).

2. The *directory* is a computer-generated index to the locations of the variable control and data fields within a record. It is similar to the table of contents in a book. It lists the variable fields in the record and gives their respective locations by starting character position. The directory consists of a series of fixed-length (twelve characters each) entries, one for each of the variable fields that contain data presented later in the record. The elements in each directory entry are the field tag (such as 100 for a personal name main entry), the field length (how many characters—letters, numbers, punctuation marks, subfield codes, and blanks—are in that field), and its starting character position in the record. The directory ends with a field terminator.

A record's directory will have as many of these twelve-character entries as there are fields in the record. In modern systems, directory data are system-computed after a record is entered—the cataloger does not have to supply it. Figure 15-3 shows the outline of a directory entry.

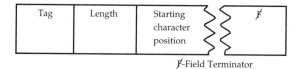

ℱ-Field Terminator

FIGURE 15-3   Outline of directory entries.

3. The *variable fields* contain the essence of the record, i.e., cataloging, authority, classification, or holdings data. Each variable field is identified by a three-character numeric tag stored in the directory. The field tag identifies the nature of each field in the record. At the end of each variable field is a field terminator, shown as a ¶ or an ℱ.

There are two types of variable fields: (1) variable control fields and (2) variable data fields. The *variable control fields* are numbered 00X (e.g., 001, 005, or 008); they may contain either a single data element or a series of fixed-length data elements identified by relative character position. The *variable data fields* are numbered 01X to 8XX; most of the fields in the range of 010 to 09X are for various numbers or codes (e.g., 020 for ISBN, 050 for LC call number, and 082 for DDC number), while the ones in the range of 100 to 8XX are for bibliographic and subject information, i.e., the main entry through the tracings. Two kinds of content designation are used within variable data fields: indicators and subfield codes. The indicators are two one-character positions that contain values that interpret or supplement the data found in the field. Not every field has indicators; those which have not been defined are shown as blanks in the string. The subfield codes, each preceded by a character [a dagger (‡) or a dollar sign ($)] called a *delimiter* and followed by an alphabetic or numeric character, identify the data elements within the field that require separate manipulation; examples are ‡d and ‡2. Each subfield code is followed by the appropriate data. Figure 15-4 shows an example of a variable data field and its corresponding directory entry in a bibliographic record.

Some fields, such as the 100 (main entry) or 250 (edition) field, occur only once in each record. Others, such as those for subject headings or index terms, may be repeated. Similarly, some subfields are also repeatable. The repeatability (R) or nonrepeatability (NR) of each field and subfield is indicated in the formats.

What a given content designator means varies considerably from one MARC format to another. This is shown in the contrast between the

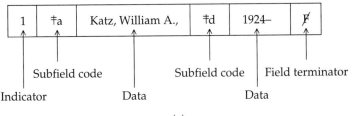

(a)

Field tag Field Length Starting character position

(b)

FIGURE 15-4   (a) A variable data field in a bibliographic record. (b) Corresponding directory entry.

two tables included in the first chapter (pages 17 and 24) for bibliographic and authority data, respectively. Nevertheless, there are similar patterns. The schemas below, for bibliographic data, illustrate the sort of thing that may be found in other formats.

Variable data fields in the bibliographic record are grouped into blocks identified by the first character of the tag, which normally indicates the function of the data within the record.

0XX Control information, identification and classification numbers, etc.
1XX Main entries
2XX Titles and title paragraph (title, edition, imprint)
3XX Physical description, etc.
4XX Series statements
5XX Notes
6XX Subject access fields
7XX Added entries other than subject or series; linking fields
8XX Series added entries, etc.
9XX Reserved for local implementation

Within each block, the type of information (e.g., personal name, corporate name, uniform title, and geographic name) is often identified by the second and third characters of the tag.

X00 Personal names
X10 Corporate names
X11 Meeting names
X30 Uniform titles
X40 Bibliographic titles
X50 Topical terms
X51 Geographic names

Indicators and subfield codes are defined for each field. For example, the main entry personal name field (tag 100) in a bibliographic record uses the first indicator position to specify the type of personal name according to the following codes:

0 Forename
1 Single surname
2 Multiple surname
3 Family name

The second indicator, left as a blank, is undefined.

If the main entry is in the form of a personal name, the most commonly used subfield codes are the following:

Code	Subfield
‡a	Personal name
‡b	Numeration
‡c	Titles and other words associated with a name
‡d	Dates associated with a name

For example, see Figure 15-4.

Wherever feasible, parallel content designation is used in the various formats. For example, the same subfield codes shown above are used in fields containing personal names in both the bibliographic and authority formats.

As shown in Chapter 1 of this book, the MARC record may be manipulated for various types of display: record with MARC coding, catalog card, and various formats of display in online catalogs. Thus the same cataloging information, once coded, may be manipulated for use in different environments and for different purposes—catalog entries, acquisitions lists, circulation records, etc. The flexibility is great, and the display depends on the design of each local system.

CHAPTER SIXTEEN
PRODUCING CATALOGING
RECORDS

The preceding chapters have focused primarily on the intellectual operations of preparing a bibliographic record: drafting a description, determining access points (both those based on names and titles and those based on subject content), ensuring uniform and unique headings, and coding cataloging information for computer manipulation. This chapter treats more practical questions: how and by whom cataloging is done, and how a record is physically added to a catalog or other bibliographic list.

The operations involved in getting an item into a library collection and providing and maintaining physical and intellectual access to it are usually referred to as *technical services*. Book selection, acquisition, cataloging, binding, and preservation are all part of technical services. Today, in most large libraries, the first three of these make heavy use of computers. In terms of how library operations are organized, automation departments may or may not be considered one of the technical services, but they are heavily involved in the major technical services operations in any case. Cataloging is usually the largest technical services department.

In cataloging any given item, there are two ways to proceed. The first is to make the fullest possible use of records prepared elsewhere— records that are called *cataloging copy*. The second is to do the cataloging in-house, from scratch. The first is called *copy cataloging*, and the second is called *original cataloging*. In any given library with a general collection, it is usual to find a mix of both, with fully original cataloging restricted to items for which no outside record is available. The more specialized the library or indexing agency, of course, the fewer outside records are likely to be suitable if they can be found at all.

In strict copy cataloging, a local cataloging record is based on an outside record with minimum modification to fit the item being cataloged. Nonetheless, in many cases of copy cataloging, there may be a high level of professional judgment needed once a candidate outside record is found: first, to be sure that the record in question matches the item in hand; second (if it does match), to determine whether the item was adequately cataloged by the originating agency; and third, to alter, add, or delete cataloging elements to suit local needs. Thus there are elements of original cataloging even in what is usually considered copy cataloging. In general libraries, nevertheless, most local cataloging departments stay as close as possible to strict copy cataloging because doing so has been found to bring about a large increase in the productivity of cataloging staff.

Where do outside records come from? Where can they be found? Two facets of cataloging come into play here: centralized cataloging and shared cataloging. *Centralized cataloging* describes the situation in which cataloging records are prepared by one agency and made available to subscribers; *shared cataloging* describes the situation in which cataloging records are contributed by two or more libraries or agencies and made available to one another. The Library of Congress (LC) has been the prime figure in centralized cataloging in this country, beginning with its printed card service initiated in 1901 and which, for many years, amounted to duplicates of records prepared by its own staff for its own use.

By 1950, even LC could not keep up with its current cataloging, so it began welcoming cataloging records prepared by other major libraries. It used these records to supplement its own cataloging and also made them available to other libraries. Shared cataloging has been a major force in American cataloging ever since.

Besides shared bibliographic records, there is another kind of cataloging information that the library community benefits from sharing. This is name and subject authority data. As discussed in Chapter 8, the Library of Congress has been making its subject authority list available since early on in its history, through publishing what is now entitled *Library of Congress Subject Headings* (LCSH), also issued in microform. In 1986, LCSH became available in machine-readable form, first on magnetic tape as the *Subject Authorities* and later also on CD-ROM as *CDMARC Subjects.*

In 1974, the Library of Congress began issuing its name authority records, first serially in book form,[1] then on microfiche, and finally on magnetic tape as the *Name Authorities* and on CD-ROM as *CDMARC Names.*

At first, LC was almost the only agency involved in the large-scale collection and distribution of cataloging records. Now, spurred by the potential of using computer technology to facilitate library operations, there are many others, particularly the cooperatives called *bibliographic networks* or *bibliographic utilities.*

Bibliographic utilities are agencies with large cataloging databases that provide a wide range of bibliographic services to members or

---

[1]Library of Congress. *Library of Congress Name Headings with References.* Washington: Library of Congress, 1974–1983.

subscribers. Some are networks in which members contribute their original cataloging records to be shared with other members. There are also many commercial and government-supported processing centers that provide precataloged books to libraries. Some of them create their own cataloging records; others adapt cataloging copy and either make it directly available to libraries or use it in their own products. Such processing centers offer a variety of services often tailored to an individual library's needs. Most provide catalog cards with books, and some process books and other materials (complete with spine markings, book pockets, and cards) which are then ready to be shelved upon receipt. Other centers cater to specific types of libraries.

MAJOR SOURCES OF CATALOGING COPY

Library of Congress

The Library of Congress makes catalog copy available through several different vehicles, most of which are under the direction of the Cataloging Distribution Service (formerly the Card Distribution Service). These include printed card sets, printed catalogs, microfiche catalogs, Cataloging-in-Publication (CIP) data, and MARC tapes.

Printed sources

In 1942, LC began publishing *The Library of Congress Catalog: A Cumulative Catalog of Books Represented by Library of Congress Printed Cards,* which made available, en masse, the author (main entry) cataloging records of the vast holdings of the Library. In 1953, the title was changed to *National Union Catalog* (NUC), and the scope was enlarged to include cataloging records of contributing North American libraries with holdings information for many items. It was published by the Library of Congress regularly in nine monthly issues and cumulated quarterly, annually, and every five years. A subject catalog was published quarterly and also cumulated annually and quinquennially. In addition, there were separate catalogs for other formats and media, such as motion pictures, filmstrips and other materials for projection, manuscripts, microform masters, music, and newspapers. Catalogers used these catalogs to verify authors and titles and as sources for cataloging copy.

In 1983 the Library of Congress discontinued the print version of NUC and began issuing it on microfiche. The current NUC is issued in five sections: register (containing the bibliographic records), name index, title index, series index, and subject index. Records in the register are arranged in sequential order as they are entered, with entries in the indexes carrying the register numbers for reference. In this way, each record is entered only once, and the indexes are issued monthly, then quarterly, and then annually.

As was noted in Chapter 8, LC has published its subject authority information almost from the beginning, in print and later also in micro-form. Name authority data were issued serially in book form from 1974 to 1983 and in microform after that.

Cataloging-in-Publication (CIP)

The Library of Congress established the Cataloging-in-Publication (CIP) Program in 1971, with the objective of putting cataloging data for a publication inside the publication itself. The program represents a coop-erative effort between the Library of Congress and publishers, with the majority of American trade publishers participating. Selected federal government documents are also included. Publishers submit galleys of their books to the CIP Office at LC, where the material is processed through regular cataloging channels. LC cataloging staff supply the catalog data that require professional decisions: main entry, title proper, series statement, descriptive notes, subject headings, added entries, and Library of Congress and Dewey Decimal Classification numbers. For children's materials, a summary and alternative subject headings are also provided, as are National Library of Medicine subject headings and class numbers for medical books. The CIP information is then returned to the publisher for printing in the book, where it is displayed on the verso of the title page. Librarians or library assistants working with the book in hand can then prepare a complete cataloging record by filling in other title information, edition, imprint, physical description, and local call number. Another use of CIP data is for preliminary processing of a book while waiting for LC cards or for more complete cataloging data.

MARC records on magnetic tape

Since March 1969, LC has been distributing cataloging data in machine-readable form, coded according to the MARC format, for most of cur-rently cataloged monographs. Magnetic tapes containing these records are distributed to subscribers weekly. Libraries that have the necessary computer facilities can load data to local catalog databases or can use the tapes for various technical services functions.

The Library of Congress's own collection of MARC-coded records is referred to as the *LC MARC database*. It contains both records created by the LC staff and records submitted by cooperating libraries and verified by the Library of Congress. Although most of the records are for post-1966 English-language publications, there have been two special projects to convert earlier records into machine-readable form: the ear-lier RECON Project (retrospective conversion) and the ongoing CO-

MARC Project (cooperative machine-readable cataloging). The coverage of LC MARC is also being continuously enlarged in other ways. In 1988, for instance, the National Coordinated Cataloging Program (NCCP) was initiated, sponsored by the Council on Library Resources. Eight research libraries were chosen to contribute original cataloging records for certain categories of materials, particularly in non-English languages.

MARC records, both bibliographic records and authority records, are available through direct access to the LC MARC database, through subscriptions to magnetic tapes, and through bibliographic utilities. The latter have been playing an increasingly larger role over the last two decades.

Bibliographic Utilities

Large-scale networks

A *bibliographic utility*, as noted above, is an organization that offers bibliographic resources and services to subscribing libraries that the latter find uneconomical or infeasible to perform in-house. In recent years, a number of large bibliographic utilities have come into being, most of them starting from cooperative arrangements among small groups of participating libraries. Examples of bibliographic utilities include OCLC Online Computer Library Center begun as the Ohio College Library Center and later expanded to serve libraries in the United States and abroad, RLIN (Research Libraries Information Network, pronounced Arlin) begun in 1967 at Stanford University, UTLAS (University of Toronto Library Automation System) begun as the university's automation system and later expanded to serve other libraries, and WLN (Western Library Network) begun as the Washington Library Network serving libraries in the state of Washington and later expanded to serve many libraries outside the state. All have much in common, and in the beginning, each had special features that made it stand out.

OCLC Online Computer Library Center

Among the utilities, OCLC is the largest in scale and service—by 1991 its database totalled over 23 million records. It affords an apt example of what a bibliographic utility can do for a library.

OCLC was founded by Frederick G. Kilgour in 1967 as a consortium of forty-nine academic libraries in the state of Ohio. Its principal objectives were resource sharing and reduction of per-unit library costs.[2] It began operation in 1971 with its first subsystem, cataloging. Other subsystems, including serials control, online acquisitions, and online interlibrary loan requests, were implemented as time went on. Since 1973,

---

[2]Frederick G. Kilgour. "Ohio College Library Center." In *Encyclopedia of Library and Information Science*. New York: Marcel Dekker, 1977. Vol. 20, pp. 346–347.

access to its union catalog and services has been extended to libraries in states outside of Ohio and eventually abroad, an important step toward making OCLC the largest online bibliographic network in the country. To reflect its expanded scope, the name Ohio College Library Center was changed to OCLC Online Computer Library Center in 1977.

OCLC's cataloging subsystem consists of an online union catalog set up as a shared cataloging operation. Early use of the network leaned heavily toward off-line catalog card production using MARC tapes from the Library of Congress. Now libraries with proper equipment can download OCLC records to their own databases directly.

OCLC's Online Union Catalog contains all LC MARC records as well as cataloging records contributed by member libraries. Since 1985, UK (United Kingdom) MARC records also have been incorporated. The LC Name Authority File was loaded as a separate file in 1984, and in 1987, the LC Subject Authority File also was added. These authority files are kept current as new and corrected data are received. With millions of bibliographic records and a large number of authority records available online, member libraries have been able to reduce cataloging costs considerably. Furthermore, the records in OCLC's Online Union Catalog give each library's holdings information. When many libraries later converted to online catalogs, this information played an indispensable role.

The early OCLC computerized system allowed retrieval of records by only a limited number of search keys, none of which afforded subject access. In 1991, OCLC launched a new system, PRISM, which not only contains enhanced features and capabilities for facilitating online cataloging operations but also offers very sophisticated searching options. Furthermore, through OCLC's new EPIC service, users have subject access not only to records in the union catalog but also to those in other databases such as ERIC and MEDLINE.

Other networks and services

There are a number of other networks or agencies for providing bibliographic services to libraries. Some networks are nationwide or regional; some are centers that serve the individual units of multicampus universities. Also, as was noted at the beginning of this chapter, many commercial companies operate in this sector as well.

COMPUTER-ASSISTED CATALOGING

Depending on the type of catalog—card catalog, book catalog, microform catalog, online catalog (see the discussion in Chap. 1)—used in the library, cataloging records are displayed in appropriate formats. Libraries still using the card catalog produce cards by traditional methods, such as typing and printing, or order cards from the Library of Congress or commercial companies.

The focus of this section is the online cataloging environment, a situation in which, first, cataloging records are produced through the medium of large-scale computer-processing equipment and, second, local librarians work directly or indirectly with such equipment. Naturally, catalogers in a library with a COM or an online catalog work in an online cataloging environment. The situation is less clear in libraries with card catalogs, since catalog cards can be produced manually or from MARC databases. The strict sense of the term *computer-produced,* of course, covers the use of word-processing programs, and most suppliers of card sets use large-scale computer-processing equipment to generate their products. With respect to the latter, local catalogers do not deal directly with the process. For their daily work, they do not need to know how records are coded for machine manipulation. The catalogers in other libraries with card catalogs may have their cards produced by large computer systems with which they interact directly; they prepare (or at the least edit) the catalog data from which the system produces cards, and they are responsible for inputting new records in the proper format, that is, with all record elements tagged with appropriate codes and with all other needed processing information properly coded as well. The same is true in most cases when the end product is a microform catalog. Catalogers in these situations are working in an online cataloging environment even if their end product is not an online catalog.

In libraries with online catalogs, furthermore, it is not only catalogers and book selection and acquisitions personnel who need to know about how bibliographic records are coded but also reference librarians. For the latter, such knowledge is an important factor in retrieval effectiveness.

No matter how cataloging records are produced and displayed for consultation, the intellectual part of the cataloging process is still performed by human catalogers and is completed before the computer plays its part. This is true no matter how little fully original cataloging is done, because cataloging copy has to be screened and often altered before it can be used.

Online Cataloging Activities

The availability of facilities for the online processing of cataloging records has proved to be extremely helpful to libraries not only in terms of catalog cost savings but also in terms of reducing the time between an order request and appearance of the purchased item on the shelves. The following discussion describes some of the processes involved in online cataloging.

Searching

The main purpose of searching is to ascertain whether there is a record in the database that can serve as cataloging copy. Searching may be performed by means of search keys, which may consist of alphabetic characters, numeric characters, or both. Depending on the capabilities of the system in use, records also may be retrieved from a database by means of one or more of many access points. The most commonly used search keys derive from the following elements in a record: name, title, name-title, subject heading, LC control number, ISBN, ISSN, and a special control number in the database. The last one, barring keying mistakes, is unique to a given record. The others will frequently call up more than one record, because the computer will respond with all the records containing the same search key. In such a case, a list of the items containing only brief information will be displayed, and the searcher then decides which particular record in the list is to be displayed in full.

Once it is ascertained that a record is in the database, it can then be used for whatever purpose is desired. For cataloging, the next step is to compare the record with the item being cataloged. If they match without variations, the record then can be processed for local use. Cards can be printed from the record, the record can be added to the library's own catalog database or other technical services file, and so on.

However, if the record varies in certain details from the item being cataloged, or if it differs from local cataloging norms, it can be modified or edited to suit individual purposes. The modifying process is called *editing*.

Editing

Editing can be performed online. One great advantage of online cataloging is the instant feedback. In editing, changes are made in the information displayed on the screen, and the modified or edited record will be shown instantly, allowing the cataloger to ensure that all necessary modifications have been processed correctly.

Three basic methods are used in editing: substitution, insertion, and deletion. In *substitution*, one simply replaces existing data with other data. In more sophisticated online cataloging systems such as OCLC's new PRISM system, substitution can be made by copying data, such as a valid name heading, from the authority file to the bibliographic record; this process is referred to as *pasting*. When additional characters are required, they are inserted; conversely, unwanted characters are deleted.

Inputting cataloging records

To store original cataloging data in machine-readable form in a database, records must be input in coded form. When there is no record in the database that can be used as a cataloging copy for the item in hand, the cataloger creates an original cataloging record, adding all additional data and tags called for in the MARC format. In some cataloging agencies, the cataloger's role stops at preparing a paper worksheet showing the record as it is to be keyed; in others, the cataloger is also the one who inputs the record. The inputting process is made relatively easy in almost all modern systems because a MARC worksheet or workform with the most common field tags is displayed on the screen. Cataloging data are then entered in the appropriate fields.

Conversion and Maintenance of Cataloging Records

Conversion, sometimes called *retrospective conversion,* refers to the process of converting manually produced records to MARC records. It is an important step in a library's transition from the manual to the automated cataloging environment and in implementing an online catalog. Conversion involves coding data in cataloging or authority records according to the USMARC formats. It is a time-consuming task. During conversion, it is desirable to update manual records, particularly their access points, to reflect current practice. Many bibliographic utilities and commercial companies offer retrospective conversion services to libraries. Use of such services is often the most cost-effective means to effect the transition.

Maintenance refers to the process of correcting errors and keeping cataloging records compatible with current standards. It is an ongoing process. For example, when a heading is revised, the authority record and all bibliographic records bearing the heading should be revised to conform to the current heading; almost always, a changed heading requires changes in cross-references as well. In parallel, when new headings are established, cross-references are often required to link them to existing headings. In systems where authority files are integrated or linked with the bibliographic file, many heading changes can be accomplished automatically through making the change in the appropriate authority file. In systems with separate authority files, all changes must be made record by record. Record-by-record changes are sometimes necessary even with linked authority files; for instance, when the subject heading **Ophthalmoscope and ophthalmoscopy** is changed to two separate headings, it takes at least looking at the record and often at the item itself to know whether **Ophthalmoscopes** or **Ophthalmoscopy** (or both) should be assigned.

Maintenance is an ongoing process, because the catalog is dynamic; it grows and changes as cataloging standards are refined and the technology of cataloging is improved. Two important objectives in catalog maintenance are containing catalog costs and ensuring catalog quality. The ultimate goal, however, is to provide a catalog that serves the needs of its users.

CONCLUSION

Over the past century, library catalogs in the Anglo-American environment have come a long way from inventory lists to the sophisticated online catalogs of today. Physical changes are the most obvious, from book catalogs to card catalogs and microform catalogs to online catalogs. Standards for preparing catalog entries also have changed, more through evolutionary processes than through large-scale, drastic changes. While the vehicles of conveying cataloging information have experienced fundamental transformations, the content, or essence, of bibliographic information remains basically the same. Some may feel that the basic structure or approach of the catalog has not kept up with or has not taken full advantage of the technology now available. Much of the bibliographic and subject analysis apparatus in the online catalog was originally designed in a different age for a different form of catalog. It would seem short-sighted to simply mount the same tools online and make them perform basically the same functions as in the manual catalog. On the other hand, in view of the millions of existing bibliographic records and the enormous financial implications of drastic changes, it would be irresponsible to suggest that the traditional approach to bibliographic control be abandoned completely and that totally new approaches be developed for online systems. Many libraries are still in the transitional stage from the card catalog to the online catalog. Even among the existing online systems, there are various degrees of sophistication. The question is then: How do we maintain the catalog in such a way that it can continue to serve the diversified needs of a wide range of systems presently operating while at the same time remain viable and adaptable to systems in the future, some of which have yet to be developed? Herein lies the challenge ahead, for those engaged in the field of cataloging and classification.

APPENDIX A
BIBLIOGRAPHIC RECORDS IN
CARD AND MARC FORMATS

Main entry card

```
Z        Katz, William A., 1924-
711         Introduction to reference work / William A.
.K32      Katz. -- 5th ed. -- New York : McGraw-Hill,
1987      c1987.

             2 v. ; 24 cm. -- (McGraw-Hill series in library
          education)

             Includes bibliographical references and indexes.
          CONTENTS: v. 1. Basic information sources -- v. 2.
          Reference services and reference processes.
             ISBN 0-07-033537-0 (v. 1) : $28.95
             ISBN 0-07-033538-9 (v. 2) : $27.95


             1. Reference services (Libraries) 2. Reference books--
          Bibliography.   I. Title.  II. Series.

          Z711.K32 1987                         025.5'2
                                                86-10247 //r91
                                                         MARC
```

Shelflist card

```
Z        Katz, William A., 1924-
711         Introduction to reference work / William A.
.K32      Katz. -- 5th ed. -- New York : McGraw-Hill,
1987      c1987.

             2 v. ; 24 cm. -- (McGraw-Hill series in library
          education)

             ISBN 0-07-033537-0 (v. 1) : $28.95
             ISBN 0-07-033538-9 (v. 2) : $27.95




             1. Reference services (Libraries) 2. Reference books--
          Bibliography.   I. Title.  II. Series.

          Z711.K32 1987                         025.5'2
                                                86-10247 //r91
                                                         MARC
```

Subject entry cards

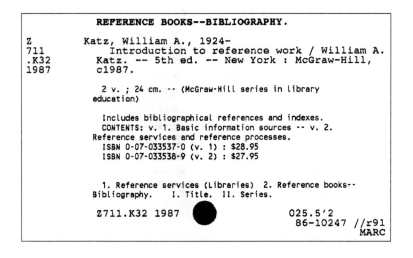

REFERENCE SERVICES (LIBRARIES)

```
Z          Katz, William A., 1924-
711            Introduction to reference work / William A.
.K32           Katz. -- 5th ed. -- New York : McGraw-Hill,
1987           c1987.

               2 v. ; 24 cm. -- (McGraw-Hill series in library
           education)

               Includes bibliographical references and indexes.
               CONTENTS: v. 1. Basic information sources -- v. 2.
           Reference services and reference processes.
               ISBN 0-07-033537-0 (v. 1) : $28.95
               ISBN 0-07-033538-9 (v. 2) : $27.95


               1. Reference services (Libraries)  2. Reference books--
           Bibliography.    I. Title.  II. Series.

           Z711.K32 1987                          025.5'2
                                                  86-10247  //r91
                                                            MARC
```

REFERENCE BOOKS--BIBLIOGRAPHY.

```
Z          Katz, William A., 1924-
711            Introduction to reference work / William A.
.K32           Katz. -- 5th ed. -- New York : McGraw-Hill,
1987           c1987.

               2 v. ; 24 cm. -- (McGraw-Hill series in library
           education)

               Includes bibliographical references and indexes.
               CONTENTS: v. 1. Basic information sources -- v. 2.
           Reference services and reference processes.
               ISBN 0-07-033537-0 (v. 1) : $28.95
               ISBN 0-07-033538-9 (v. 2) : $27.95


               1. Reference services (Libraries)  2. Reference books--
           Bibliography.    I. Title.  II. Series.

           Z711.K32 1987                          025.5'2
                                                  86-10247  //r91
                                                            MARC
```

Title added entry card

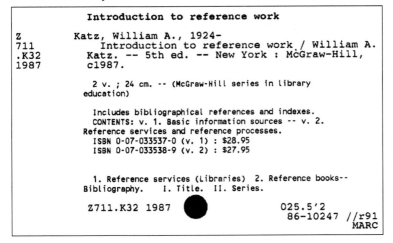

```
                    Introduction to reference work

Z           Katz, William A., 1924-
711             Introduction to reference work / William A.
.K32            Katz. -- 5th ed. -- New York : McGraw-Hill,
1987            c1987.

                2 v. ; 24 cm. -- (McGraw-Hill series in library
            education)

            Includes bibliographical references and indexes.
            CONTENTS: v. 1. Basic information sources -- v. 2.
            Reference services and reference processes.
            ISBN 0-07-033537-0 (v. 1) : $28.95
            ISBN 0-07-033538-9 (v. 2) : $27.95


            1. Reference services (Libraries)  2. Reference books--
            Bibliography.   I. Title.   II. Series.

            Z711.K32 1987          ●              025.5'2
                                                  86-10247  //r91
                                                          MARC
```

Series added entry card

```
                    McGraw-Hill series in library education

Z           Katz, William A., 1924-
711             Introduction to reference work / William A.
.K32            Katz. -- 5th ed. -- New York : McGraw-Hill,
1987            c1987.

                2 v. ; 24 cm. -- (McGraw-Hill series in library
            education)

            Includes bibliographical references and indexes.
            CONTENTS: v. 1. Basic information sources -- v. 2.
            Reference services and reference processes.
            ISBN 0-07-033537-0 (v. 1) : $28.95
            ISBN 0-07-033538-9 (v. 2) : $27.95


            1. Reference services (Libraries)  2. Reference books--
            Bibliography.   I. Title.   II. Series.

            Z711.K32 1987          ●              025.5'2
                                                  86-10247  //r91
                                                          MARC
```

Bibliographic records in USMARC format

```
▶ OCLC:      10375464           Rec stat:    c
  Entered:    19840120          Replaced:    19901229       Used:    19911221
  Type: a                Bib lvl: m         Source:         Lang:  eng
  Repr:                  Enc lvl:           Conf pub: 0     Ctry:  cau
  Indx: 0                Mod rec:           Govt pub:       Cont:
  Desc: a                Int lvl:           Festschr: 0     Illus:
                         F/B:       0       Dat tp:    r    Dates: 1984,1947 ¶
▶   1  010      84-55//r90 ¶
▶   2  040      DLC ‡c DLC ‡d OCL ¶
▶   3  020      0874773164 (pbk.) : ‡c $6.95 ¶
▶   4  050 00   PN1042 ‡b .D39 1984 ¶
▶   5  082 00   808.1 ‡2 19 ¶
▶   6  090      ‡b  ¶
▶   7  049      KUKK ¶
▶   8  100 2    Day Lewis, C. ‡q (Cecil), ‡d 1904-1972. ¶
▶   9  245 14   The poetic image / ‡c C. Day Lewis. ¶
▶  10  260      Los Angeles : ‡b J.P. Tarcher ; ‡a Boston : ‡b Distributed by
  Houghton Mifflin, ‡c 1984. ¶
▶  11  300      157 p. ; ‡c 21 cm. ¶
```

```
▶ OCLC:      20992991           Rec stat:    p
  Entered:    19900108          Replaced:    19900825       Used:    19920311
  Type: a                Bib lvl: m         Source:         Lang:  eng
  Repr: d                Enc lvl:           Conf pub: 0     Ctry:  enk
  Indx: 0                Mod rec:           Govt pub:       Cont:
  Desc: a                Int lvl:           Festschr: 0     Illus:
                         F/B:       1       Dat tp:    r    Dates: 1990,1978 ¶
▶   1  010      90-30465 ¶
▶   2  040      DLC ‡c DLC ¶
▶   3  020      0792702530 (lg. print) ¶
▶   4  050 10   PR6007.A95 ‡b B38 1990 ¶
▶   5  082 00   823/.912 ‡2 20 ¶
▶   6  090      ‡b  ¶
▶   7  049      KUKK ¶
▶   8  100 2    Blake, Nicholas, ‡d 1904-1972. ¶
▶   9  245 14   The beast must die / ‡c Nicholas Blake. ¶
▶  10  260      Bath, England : ‡b Chivers Press ; ‡a South Yarmouth, Mass., USA
  : ‡b Curley, ‡c 1990. ¶
▶  11  300      347 p. (large print) ; ‡c 22 cm. ¶
▶  12  490 0    Atlantic large print ¶
▶  13  500      Originally published: New York : Harper & Row, 1978. ¶
▶  14  500      "Atlantic mystery." ¶
▶  15  650  0   Large type books. ¶
```

SOURCE: The MARC records herein are taken and reproduced with permission from the OCLC database.

```
▶ OCLC:    21949176        Rec stat:    p
  Entered:  19900611        Replaced:    19910202      Used:    19920428
  Type: a          Bib lvl: m      Source:              Lang:  eng
  Repr: d          Enc lvl:         Conf pub: 0          Ctry:  meu
  Indx: 0          Mod rec:         Govt pub:            Cont:
  Desc: a          Int lvl:         Festschr: 0          Illus:
                   F/B:     0b      Dat tp:   r          Dates: 1990,1989 ¶
▶   1  010       90-41187 ¶
▶   2  040       DLC ‡c DLC ¶
▶   3  020       1560540567 (lg. print : alk. paper) ¶
▶   4  043       n-us--- ¶
▶   5  050 10    E878.R43 ‡b A3 1990 ¶
▶   6  082 00    973.927/092 ‡a B ‡2 20 ¶
▶   7  090       ‡b  ¶
▶   8  049       KUKK ¶
▶   9  100 1     Reagan, Nancy, ‡d 1923- ¶
▶  10  245 10    My turn : ‡b the memoirs of Nancy Reagan / ‡c Nancy Reagan with
William Novak. ¶
▶  11  260       Thorndike, Me. : ‡b Thorndike Press, ‡c 1990, c1989. ¶
▶  12  300       648 p. (large print) ; ‡c 23 cm. ¶
▶  13  500       "Thorndike Press large print edition published in 1990 by
arrangement with Random House, Inc."--T.p. verso. ¶
▶  14  500       "Thorndike large print"--P. [4] of cover. ¶
▶  15  600 10    Reagan, Nancy, ‡d 1923- ¶
▶  16  600 10    Reagan, Ronald. ¶
▶  17  650 0     Presidents ‡z United States ‡x Wives ‡x Biography. ¶
▶  18  650 0     Large type books. ¶
▶  19  700 10    Novak, William. ¶
```

```
▶ OCLC:    23836624        Rec stat:    n
  Entered:  19910416        Replaced:    19910525      Used:    19920326
  Type:   e        Bib lvl: m      Source:              Lang:  eng
  RecG:   a        Enc lvl:         Govt pub: f          Ctry:  dcu
  Relief:          Mod rec:         Base:     ^^^        Form:
  Desc:   a        Indx:    0       Dat tp:   s          Dates: 1991,    ¶
▶   1  010       91-682277/MAPS ¶
▶   2  040       DLC ‡c DLC ¶
▶   3  007       a ‡b j ‡d a ‡e a ‡f n ‡g z ‡h n ¶
▶   4  034 0     a ¶
▶   5  045 0     ‡b d1990 ¶
▶   6  050 00    G7611.H8 1990 ‡b .U5 ¶
▶   7  052       7611 ¶
▶   8  090       ‡b  ¶
▶   9  049       KUKK ¶
▶  10  110 1     United States. ‡b Dept. of State. ‡b Office of the Geographer. ¶
▶  11  245 10    Iraq, outlets for oil. ¶
▶  12  255       Scale not given. ¶
▶  13  260       [Washington, D.C. : ‡b Dept. of State, Office of the Geographer,
‡c 1991] ¶
▶  14  300       1 map ; ‡c 26 x 38 cm. ¶
▶  15  500       "1099 9-90 State (INR/GE)." ¶
▶  16  500       Shows pipelines, oilfields, selected oil refineries, and tanker
terminals. ¶
▶  17  500       From Geographic notes, no. 13, March 1, 1991. ¶
▶  18  650 0     Petroleum ‡z Iraq ‡x Transportation ‡x Maps. ¶
▶  19  650 0     Oil fields ‡z Iraq ‡x Maps. ¶
```

```
▶ OCLC:      22131444          Rec stat:     n
  Entered:   19900214          Replaced:     19900723     Used:      19920115
  Type: a              Bib lvl: m     Source:             Lang:  eng
  Repr: b              Enc lvl: L     Conf pub: 0         Ctry:  ilu
  Indx: 1              Mod rec:       Govt pub:           Cont:  b
  Desc: a              Int lvl:       Festschr: 0         Illus: b
             F/B:      0             Dat tp:    r         Dates: 1990,1913 ¶
▶   1  040     DLC ǂc ATL ¶
▶   2  007     h ǂb e ǂd a ǂe m ǂf c048 ǂg b ǂh a ǂi c ǂj a ¶
▶   3  007     h ǂb e ǂd b ǂe m ǂf c048 ǂg b ǂh a ǂi a ǂj a ¶
▶   4  020     0790533650 (microfiche) ¶
▶   5  050   4 BS1555 ¶
▶   6  090     ǂb  ¶
▶   7  049     KUKK ¶
▶   8  130 0   Bible. ǂp O.T. ǂp Daniel. ǂl English. ǂf 1913? ¶
▶   9  245 14  The book of Daniel ǂh microform : ǂb introduction, revised
version with notes, index and map / ǂc edited by R.H. Charles. ¶
▶  10  260     New York : ǂb H. Frowde ; ǂa Edinburgh : ǂb T.C. & E.C. Jack, ǂc
[1913?] ¶
▶  11  300     xlv, 152 p., [1] folded leaf of plates : ǂb col. map ; ǂc 17
cm. ¶
▶  12  440   4 The New-Century Bible ¶
▶  13  504     Includes bibliographical references. ¶
▶  14  533     Microfiche. ǂb Evanston : ǂc American Theological Library
Association, ǂd 1990. ǂe 1 microfiche. High reduction. Silver based film. ǂf
(ATLA monograph preservation program ; ATLA fiche 1987-3365) ¶
▶  15  630 00  Bible. ǂp O.T. ǂp Daniel ǂx Commentaries. ¶
▶  16  700 10  Charles, R. H. ǂq (Robert Henry), ǂd 1855-1931. ¶
▶  17  830 0   ATLA monograph preservation program ; ǂv ATLA fiche 1987-3365. ¶
```

```
▶ OCLC:      23838609          Rec stat:     n
  Entered:   19910423          Replaced:     19910525     Used:      19920325
  Type:  c             Bib lvl: m     Source:             Lang:  N/A
  Repr:                Enc lvl:       Format: c           Ctry:  nyu
  Accomp:              Mod rec:       Comp:   co          LTxt:  n
  Desc:  a             Int lvl:       Dat tp: s           Dates: 1990,      ¶
▶   1  010     91-752089/M ¶
▶   2  040     DLC ǂc DLC ¶
▶   3  028 32  M & M no. 5805 ǂb McGinnis & Marx Music Pub. ¶
▶   4  045 0   ǂb d1777 ¶
▶   5  048     ǂb wb01 ǂa ka01 ¶
▶   6  050 00  M1023 ǂb .M7 K. 314 1990b ¶
▶   7  090     ǂb  ¶
▶   8  049     KUKK ¶
▶   9  100 1   Mozart, Wolfgang Amadeus, ǂd 1756-1791. ¶
▶  10  240 10  Concertos, ǂm oboe, orchestra, ǂn K. 314, ǂr C major; ǂo arr. ¶
▶  11  245 00  Concerto in C major, K. 314, for oboe and piano (1777) / ǂc
Wolfgang Amadeus Mozart ; edited by Trevor Wye ; piano reduction by Robert
Scott. ¶
▶  12  260     New York, N.Y. : ǂb McGinnis & Marx Music Pub., ǂc c1990. ¶
▶  13  300     1 score (29 p.) + 1 part (11 p.) ; ǂc 31 cm. ¶
▶  14  500     Originally for oboe and orchestra. ¶
▶  15  650 0   Concertos (Oboe) ǂx Solo with piano. ¶
▶  16  700 10  Wye, Trevor. ¶
▶  17  700 10  Scott, Robert. ¶
```

```
▶ OCLC:       19173060         Rec stat:      c
  Entered:    19891109         Replaced:      19900414        Used:       19910911
  Type: a            Bib lvl: m         Source:              Lang:  dut
  Repr:              Enc lvl:           Conf pub: 0          Ctry:  ne
  Indx: 0            Mod rec:           Govt pub:            Cont:
  Desc: a            Int lvl:           Festschr: 0          Illus: a
                     F/B:      0        Dat tp:   s          Dates: 1988,        ¶
▶   1  010      89-155743/MN ¶
▶   2  040      DLC ‡c DLC ¶
▶   3  020      9012057523 ¶
▶   4  041 0    duteng ¶
▶   5  050 00   ML50.A199 ‡b N612 1988 ¶
▶   6  082 00   782.1/026/8 ‡2 20 ¶
▶   7  090      ‡b ¶
▶   8  049      KUKK ¶
▶   9  100 1    Adams, John, ‡d 1947- ¶
▶  10  240 10   Nixon in China. ‡s Libretto. ‡l Dutch & English ¶
▶  11  245 10   Nixon in China : ‡b opera in three acts / ‡c John Adams ;
  libretto, Alice Goodman. ¶
▶  12  260      Amsterdam : ‡b De Nederlandse Opera, ‡c c1988. ¶
▶  13  300      72 p. : ‡b ill. ; ‡c 20 x 22 cm. ¶
▶  14  500      Libretto. ¶
▶  15  500      Includes a synopsis in Dutch, English, French, and German, and
  the libretto in English with a Dutch translation by Rene Kurpershoek. ¶
▶  16  650 0    Operas ‡x Librettos. ¶
▶  17  600 10   Nixon, Richard M. ‡q (Richard Milhous), ‡d 1913- ‡x Drama. ¶
▶  18  700 10   Goodman, Alice. ¶
```

```
▶ OCLC:       22879352         Rec stat:      c
  Entered:    19901220         Replaced:      19920428        Used:       19920303
  Type:        a      Bib lvl: s         Source:      d       Lang:       eng
  Repr:               Enc lvl: 5         Govt pub:            Ctry:       ilu
  Phys med:           Mod rec:           Conf pub: 0          Cont:       r^^^
  S/L ent:  0         Ser tp:            Frequn:   g          Alphabt:    a
  Desc:        a                         Regulr:   r          ISDS:       1
                                         Pub st:   c          Dates:      1990-9999 ¶
▶   1  010      91-642205 ¶
▶   2  040      JED ‡c JED ‡d DLC ‡d NSD ‡d NST ¶
▶   3  012      2 ‡i 9103 ¶
▶   4  022 0    1058-2592 ¶
▶   5  042      lc ‡a nsdp ¶
▶   6  050 00   IN PROCESS ¶
▶   7  082 10   659 ‡2 12 ¶
▶   8  090      ‡b ¶
▶   9  049      KUKK ¶
▶  10  210 0    Advert. options plus ¶
▶  11  222 0    Advertising options plus ¶
▶  12  245 00   Advertising options plus : ‡b SRDS directory of out-of-home
  media. ¶
▶  13  246 13   SRDS advertising options plus ¶
▶  14  260      Wilmette, IL : ‡b Standard Rate & Data Service, ‡c c1990- ¶
▶  15  265      Standard Rate & Data Service, 3004 Glenview Rd., Wilmette, IL
  60091 ¶
▶  16  300      v. : ‡b ill. ; ‡c 28 cm. ¶
▶  17  310      Biennial ¶
▶  18  350      $127.00 ¶
▶  19  362 0    Vol. 1, no. 1 (1990-91)- ¶
▶  20  500      Title from cover. ¶
▶  21  650 0    Advertising ‡z United States ‡x Directories. ¶
▶  22  650 0    Marketing ‡z United States. ¶
▶  23  710 20   Standard Rate & Data Service. ¶
▶  24  850      DLC ‡a NN ‡a OC1 ¶
▶  25  890      Advertising options plus. ¶
```

```
▶ OCLC:     22773826        Rec stat:    c
  Entered:   19901204        Replaced:    19911204      Used:     19920305
  Type:     a      Bib lvl: s        Source:   d      Lang:    eng
  Repr:            Enc lvl:           Govt pub:        Ctry:    nju
  Phys med:        Mod rec:           Conf pub: 0      Cont:    ^^^^
  S/L ent:  0      Ser tp:  p         Frequn:   q      Alphabt: a
  Desc:     a                         Regulr:   r      ISDS:    1
                                      Pub st:   c      Dates:   1991-9999 ¶
▶  1   010      91-640899 ‡z sn90-3906 ¶
▶  2   040      NSD ‡c NSD ‡d DLC ‡d NST ‡d DLC ‡d CAS ¶
▶  3   012      2 ‡i 9111 ‡k 1 ‡l 1 ¶
▶  4   022 0    1054-1721 ¶
▶  5   030      JORCEM ¶
▶  6   042      nsdp ‡a lc ¶
▶  7   050 00   HD30.2 ‡b .J69 ¶
▶  8   082 00   658/.00285 ‡2 20 ¶
▶  9   090      ‡b ¶
▶ 10   049      KUKK ¶
▶ 11   210 0    J. organ. comput. ¶
▶ 12   222  0   Journal of organizational computing ¶
▶ 13   245 00   Journal of organizational computing. ¶
▶ 14   246 10   Organizational computing ¶
▶ 15   260      Norwood, N.J. : ‡b Ablex Pub. Corp., ‡c c1991- ¶
▶ 16   265      Ablex Pub. Corp., 355 Chestnut St., Norwood, NJ 07648 ¶
▶ 17   300      v. : ‡b ill. ; ‡c 26 cm. ¶
▶ 18   310      Quarterly ¶
▶ 19   350      $95.00 (institutions) ¶
▶ 20   362 0    Vol. 1, no. 1 (Jan.-Mar. 1991)- ¶
▶ 21   515      Vol. 1, no. 1 also numbered v. 2. ¶
▶ 22   650  0   Management ‡x Data processing ‡x Periodicals. ¶
▶ 23   650  0   Communication in organizations ‡x Automation ‡x Periodicals. ¶
▶ 24   850      DLC ¶
▶ 25   890      Journal of organizational computing. ¶
▶ 26   901      ‡c Ser ¶
▶ 27   936      Vol. 1, no. 2 (Apr.-June 1991) LIC ¶
```

```
▶ OCLC:     24761342        Rec stat:    c
  Entered:   19911111        Replaced:    19911202      Used:     19920409
  Type:     m      Bib lvl: m        Source:          Lang:    N/A
  File:     b      Enc lvl: I        Govt pub:        Ctry:    mnu
  Audience: d      Mod rec:          Frequn:   n      Regulr:
  Desc:     a                        Dat tp:   s      Dates:   1991,       ¶
▶  1   010      91-14847 ¶
▶  2   040      DLC ‡c CSS ¶
▶  3   020      0792901819 ¶
▶  4   041 0    ‡g eng ¶
▶  5   050 10   QA246.5 ‡b  1991 ¶
▶  6   082  0   515 ¶
▶  7   090      ‡b ¶
▶  8   049      KUKK ¶
▶  9   245 00   Exploring sequences and series ‡h computer file ¶
▶ 10   250      Version 1.0. ¶
▶ 11   260      St. Paul, MN : ‡b Minnesota Educational Computing Corp., ‡c
c1991. ¶
▶ 12   300      1 computer disk : ‡b sd., col. ; ‡c 3 1/2 in. + ‡e 1 manual. ¶
▶ 13   538      System requirements: Apple II series computers; 128K RAM;
ProDOS; BASIC and Assembler; 1 disk drive; monochrome or color monitor. ¶
▶ 14   500      Title from title screen. ¶
▶ 15   500      Edition statement from disk label. ¶
▶ 16   500      Copy-protected. ¶
▶ 17   521      Grades 7-12. ¶
▶ 18   500      Issued also on 5 1/4 in. computer disk. ¶
▶ 19   520      Provides students with a quick and convenient method for
generating sequences.  To generate a sequence, students supply the starting
number(s) and/or the algorithm.  Once a sequence is generated by the computer,
students can view the terms, find partial sums, or mathematically transform the
sequence to make a new one. ¶
▶ 20   500      "A-263"-- Disk label. ¶
▶ 21   650  0   Sequences (Mathematics) ‡x Software. ¶
▶ 22   650  0   Series ‡x Software. ¶
▶ 23   710 20   Minnesota Educational Computing Corporation. ¶
```

▶ OCLC: 24503853   Rec stat: n
  Entered: 19910717   Replaced: 19911005   Used: 19920415
  Type: j   Bib lvl: m   Source: Lang: ita
  Repr: Enc lvl: Format: n   Ctry: fr
  Accomp: di   Mod rec: Comp: or   LTxt:
  Desc: a   Int lvl: Dat tp: p   Dates: 1991,1990 ¶
▶   1 010   91-755165/R ¶
▶   2 040   DLC ‡c DLC ¶
▶   3 007   s ‡b d ‡c u ‡d z ‡e s ‡f n ‡g z ‡h n ‡i n ‡j m ‡k l ‡l n ‡m e ¶
▶   4 028 02 2292-45617-2 ‡b Erato ¶
▶   5 033 0   199009-- ‡b 6004 ‡c U8 ¶
▶   6 041 0   ‡d ita ‡e itaengfreger ‡h ita ‡g engfreger ¶
▶   7 045 0   ‡b d1708 ¶
▶   8 050 00 Erato 2292-45617-2 ¶
▶   9 090   ‡b ¶
▶ 10 049   KUKK ¶
▶ 11 100 1   Handel, George Frideric, ‡d 1685-1759. ¶
▶ 12 245 13 La Resurrezione ‡h [sound recording] / ‡c H¨andel. ¶
▶ 13 260   [France] : ‡b Erato, ‡c p1991. ¶
▶ 14 300   2 sound discs (1 hr., 56 min.) : ‡b digital ; ‡c 4 3/4 in. ¶
▶ 15 306   015600 ¶
▶ 16 500   Oratorio in 2 parts. ¶
▶ 17 500   Text by Carlo Sigismondo Capece. ¶
▶ 18 511 0   Nancy Argenta, Barbara Schlick, sopranos ; Guillemette Laurens,
  alto ; Guy de Mey, tenor ; Klaus Mertens, bass ; Amsterdam Baroque Orchestra ;
  Ton Koopman, conductor. ¶
▶ 19 518   Recorded Sept. 1990, Katholieke Kerk Maria Minor, Utrecht,
  Netherlands. ¶
▶ 20 500   Compact discs. ¶
▶ 21 500   Notes by Ton Koopman and Anthony Hicks in English, French, and
  German; libretto in Italian with English, French, and German translations (83
  p. : facsim.). ¶
▶ 22 650 0   Oratorios. ¶
▶ 23 650 0   Easter music. ¶
▶ 24 700 10 Capece, Carlo Sigismondo, ‡d 1652-1728. ‡4 lbt ¶
▶ 25 700 10 Argenta, Nancy. ‡4 prf ¶
▶ 26 700 10 Schlick, Barbara. ‡4 prf ¶
▶ 27 700 10 Laurens, Guillemette, ‡d 1957- ‡4 prf ¶

▶ OCLC: 25368531   Rec stat: n
  Entered: 19920122   Replaced: 19920229   Used: 19920509
  Type: i   Bib lvl: m   Source: Lang: eng
  Repr: Enc lvl: Format: n   Ctry: mau
  Accomp: ei   Mod rec: Comp: nn   LTxt: p
  Desc: a   Int lvl: Dat tp: p   Dates: 1978,1933 ¶
▶   1 010   92-788295/R ¶
▶   2 040   DLC ‡c DLC ¶
▶   3 007   s ‡b s ‡c u ‡d l ‡e u ‡f n ‡g j ‡h l ‡i c ‡j n ‡k n ‡l n ‡m u ¶
▶   4 033 2   1933---- ‡a 1970---- ‡b 3764 ‡c C2 ¶
▶   5 050 00 RZA 0937 ¶
▶   6 090   ‡b ¶
▶   7 049   KUKK ¶
▶   8 245 04 The Poet's voice ‡h [sound recording] / ‡c [selected and edited
  by Stratis Haviaras]. ¶
▶   9 260   Cambridge, Mass. : ‡b Harvard University Press, ‡c p1978. ¶
▶ 10 300   6 sound cassettes (ca. 1 hr. each) : ‡b analog + ‡e 1 booklet
  (11 p. ; 27 cm.) ¶
▶ 11 306   060000 ¶
▶ 12 518   Readings, recorded at Harvard University between 1933 and 1970.
▶ 13 500   In container (30 cm.). ¶
▶ 14 500   Accompanying booklet contains unattached contents page. ¶
▶ 15 520   Features a selection of modern American poets reading and
  commenting upon their works. ¶
▶ 16 505 0   Cassette 1. Ezra Pound (28:50) ; T.S. Eliot (32:40) -- Cassette
  2. Marianne Moore (28:10) ; William Carlos Williams (29:15) -- Cassette 3.
  Wallace Stevens (28:30) ; Robert Frost (29:30) -- Cassette 4. W.H. Auden
  (28:45) ; Robinson Jeffers (16:25) ; Theodore Roethke (10:05) -- Cassette 5.
  Randall Jarrell (32:50) ; John Berryman (35:20) -- Cassette 6. Robert Lowell
  (29:55) ; Sylvia Plath (24:35). ¶
▶ 17 650 0   American poetry ‡y 20th century. ¶
▶ 18 700 10 Haviaras, Stratis, ‡d 1935- ¶
▶ 19 700 10 Pound, Ezra, ‡d 1885-1972. ¶
▶ 20 700 10 Eliot, T. S. ‡q (Thomas Stearns), ‡d 1888-1965. ¶
▶ 21 700 10 Moore, Marianne, ‡d 1887-1972. ¶
▶ 22 700 10 Williams, William Carlos, ‡d 1883-1963. ¶
▶ 23 700 10 Stevens, Wallace, ‡d 1879-1955. ¶
▶ 24 700 10 Frost, Robert, ‡d 1874-1963. ¶

```
▶ OCLC:     22489442          Rec stat:    n
  Entered:   19900807    Replaced:   19901011    Used:      19920509
  Type:      g       Bib lvl: m       Source:    c    Lang:  eng
  Type mat:  v       Enc lvl: 1       Govt pub:       Ctry:  xxu
  Int lvl:   e       Mod rec:         Tech:      l    Leng:  060
  Desc:      a       Accomp:          Dat tp:    s    Dates: 1989,      ¶
▶   1   010        90-700072/F ¶
▶   2   040        Intellimation ‡c DLC ¶
▶   3   007        v ‡b f ‡c u ‡d c ‡e c ‡f a ‡g h ‡h r ¶
▶   4   007        v ‡b f ‡c u ‡d c ‡e a ‡f a ‡g h ‡h o ¶
▶   5   007        v ‡b f ‡c u ‡d c ‡e b ‡f a ‡g h ‡h o ¶
▶   6   050 10     HQ774 ¶
▶   7   082 10     155.4 ‡2 11 ¶
▶   8   090        ‡b  ¶
▶   9   049        KUKK ¶
▶  10   245 00     Seasons of life. ‡p Infancy and early childhood ‡h
[videorecording] / ‡c University of Michigan and WQED/Pittsburgh. ¶
▶  11   260        Santa Barbara, CA : ‡b Intellimation, ‡c 1989. ¶
▶  12   300        1 videocassette (60 min.) : ‡b sd., col. ¶
▶  13   500        Cataloged from contributor's data. ¶
▶  14   511 0      Host, David Hartman. ¶
▶  15   500        An Annenberg/CPB project. ¶
▶  16   500        Originally shown on PBS. ¶
▶  17   500        Closed-captioned for the hearing impaired. ¶
▶  18   521        College students and adults. ¶
▶  19   530        Issued as U-matic 3/4 in. or Beta 1/2 in. or VHS 1/2 in. ¶
▶  20   520        Looks at the developmental "clocks" of infancy and early
childhood, including the biological, social, and psychological ones which mark
definite stages of development at this time of life. ¶
▶  21   650 0      Infants. ¶
▶  22   650 0      Children. ¶
▶  23   650 0      Life cycle, Human. ¶
▶  24   700 11     Hartman, David, ‡d 1935- ¶
▶  25   710 21     University of Michigan. ¶
▶  26   710 21     WQED (Television program : Pittsburgh, Pa.) ¶
▶  27   710 21     Intellimation, Inc. ¶
▶  28   740 01     Infancy and early childhood. ¶
```

APPENDIX B
AUTHORITY RECORDS IN MARC FORMAT

Authority records for personal names

```
► ARN:       353039           Rec stat:     n
  Entered:   19840819         Replaced:     19840819
  Type:      z      Enc lvl:   n    Source:        Lang:
  Roman:     ▮      Upd status: a   Mod rec:       Name use: a
  Govt agn:  ▮      Ref status: a   Subj:     a    Subj use: a
  Series:    n      Auth status: a  Geo subd: n    Ser use:  b
  Ser num:   n      Auth/ref:  a    Name:     a    Rules:    c ¶
► 1    010     n  79121421  ¶
► 2    040     DLC ‡c DLC ¶
► 3    100 10  Reagan, Nancy, ‡d 1923-  ¶
► 4    400 10  Robbins, Anne Francis, ‡d 1923-  ¶
► 5    400 10  Reagan, Nancy Davis, ‡d 1923-  ¶
► 6    400 10  Davis, Nancy, ‡d 1923-  ¶
► 7    670     Her Nancy, 1980:  ‡b t.p. (Nancy Reagan) Acknowledgments (Nancy
  Davis Reagan) galley p. 4 (b. Anne Francis Robbins, 7/6/23) galley p. 9 (after
  her mother remarried she became officially Nancy Davis) ¶
► 8    670     Filmgoer's companion, 1974 ‡b (Davis, Nancy, b. 1924, m. Ronald
  Reagan) ¶
```

```
► ARN:       287741           Rec stat:     n
  Entered:   19840819         Replaced:     19840819
  Type:      z      Enc lvl:   n    Source:        Lang:
  Roman:     ▮      Upd status: a   Mod rec:       Name use: a
  Govt agn:  ▮      Ref status: a   Subj:     a    Subj use: a
  Series:    n      Auth status: a  Geo subd: n    Ser use:  b
  Ser num:   n      Auth/ref:  a    Name:     a    Rules:    c ¶
► 1    010     n  79054611  ¶
► 2    040     DLC ‡c DLC ¶
► 3    100 10  Ali, Muhammad, ‡d 1942-  ¶
► 4    400 10  Clay, Cassius, ‡d 1942-  ¶
► 5    400 00  Cassius X, ‡d 1942-  ¶
► 6    400 10  X, Cassius, ‡d 1942-  ¶
► 7    400 10  Ali, Muhammad, ‡d 1942-  ¶
► 8    400 00  Muhammad Ali, ‡d 1942-  ¶
► 9    670     His I am the greatest! [Phonodisc] 1963. ¶
► 10   670     Kaletsky, R. Ali and me, c1982 (a.e.) ‡b p. 11 (Cassius
  Marcellus Clay) ¶
```

SOURCE: The MARC records herein are taken and reproduced with permission from the OCLC database.

```
▶ ARN:       398314          Rec stat:      c
  Entered:   19840819        Replaced:      19910914
  Type:      z      Enc lvl:     n      Source:            Lang:
  Roman:     ∎      Upd status:  a      Mod rec:           Name use: a
  Govt agn:  ∎      Ref status:  a      Subj:        a     Subj use: a
  Series:    n      Auth status: a      Geo subd: a        Ser use:  b
  Ser num:   n      Auth/ref:    a      Name:        a     Rules:    c ¶
▶   1  010        n  80015879  ¶
▶   2  040        DLC ‡c DLC ‡d DLC ‡d DGPO ‡d DLC ¶
▶   3  100 10     Bush, George, ‡d 1924- ¶
▶   4  400 10     Bush, Dzhordzh Gerbert, ‡d 1924- ¶
▶   5  400 10     Bush, Dzh. ‡q (Dzhordzh), ‡d 1924- ¶
▶   6  400 10     Bush, George Herbert Walker, ‡d 1924- ¶
▶   7  510 10     United States. ‡b President (1989- : Bush) ¶
▶   8  670        His U.N. China debate. [Phonotape] 1971. ¶
▶   9  670        NUCMC data from Univ. of Virginia Lib. for Scott, H. Papers,
  1941-1983 ‡b (Bush, George Herbert Walker, 1924-) ¶
▶  10  670        WW Am. Pol., 1985/86: ‡b p. 1373 (Bush, George Herbert Walker,
  1924-; U.S. v.p.) ¶
▶  11  670        Bol'sh. sov. ˉenˉtˉsikl., 3rd ed. Ezhegodnik 1982: ‡b p. 574
  (Bush, Dzhordzh Gerbert, b. 1924; vice president of USA since 1981); Ezhegodnik
  1989: p. 354 (Bush. Dzh.; president of US since 1989) ¶
▶  12  670        His U.S. agricultural trade goals and strategy report, 1991,
  1990: ‡b t.p. (Message from the President of the United States transmitting the
  second annual U.S. long-term agricultural trade goals and strategy report for
  fiscal year 1991) ¶


▶ ARN:       2484292         Rec stat:      c
  Entered:   19890322        Replaced:      19890429
  Type:      z      Enc lvl:     n      Source:      c     Lang:
  Roman:     ∎      Upd status:  a      Mod rec:           Name use: a
  Govt agn:  ∎      Ref status:  a      Subj:        a     Subj use: a
  Series:    n      Auth status: a      Geo subd: n        Ser use:  b
  Ser num:   n      Auth/ref:    a      Name:        n     Rules:    c ¶
▶   1  010        n  88112497  ¶
▶   2  040        DGPO ‡c DLC ¶
▶   3  110 10     United States. ‡b President (1989- : Bush) ¶
▶   4  670        His Building a better America ... 1989: ‡b t.p. (Message from
  the President of the United States transmitting a supplement to his message
  delivered to the joint session of Congress, February 9, 1989) ¶


▶ ARN:       618798          Rec stat:      c
  Entered:   19840821        Replaced:      19900811
  Type:      z      Enc lvl:     n      Source:            Lang:
  Roman:     ∎      Upd status:  a      Mod rec:           Name use: a
  Govt agn:  ∎      Ref status:  a      Subj:        a     Subj use: a
  Series:    n      Auth status: a      Geo subd: n        Ser use:  b
  Ser num:   n      Auth/ref:    a      Name:        a     Rules:    c ¶
▶   1  010        n  81073496 ‡z n  82138607  ¶
▶   2  040        DLC ‡c DLC ‡d DLC ¶
▶   3  100 00     Diana, ‡c Princess of Wales, ‡d 1961- ¶
▶   4  400 10     Spencer, Diana Frances, ‡c Lady, ‡d 1961- ¶
▶   5  400 00     Di, ‡c Lady, ‡d 1961- ¶
▶   6  670        Dunlop, J. Diana and Diana, a royal romance, c1981 (subj.) ‡b
  p. 6, etc. (Lady Diana Frances Spencer; b. 1961) ¶
▶   7  670        Leete-Hodge, L. The Country Life book of the royal wedding,
  1981: ‡b table of contents (Diana, Princess of Wales) ¶
▶   8  670        Carretier, M.-P. Lady Di chez elle, c1987. ¶


▶ ARN:       230886          Rec stat:      c
  Entered:   19840818        Replaced:      19871001
  Type:      z      Enc lvl:     n      Source:            Lang:
  Roman:     ∎      Upd status:  a      Mod rec:           Name use: a
  Govt agn:  ∎      Ref status:  a      Subj:        a     Subj use: a
  Series:    n      Auth status: a      Geo subd: n        Ser use:  b
  Ser num:   n      Auth/ref:    a      Name:        a     Rules:    c ¶
▶   1  010        n  78095822  ¶
▶   2  040        DLC ‡c DLC ‡d DLC ¶
▶   3  053        PS3507.O726 ¶
▶   4  100 00     H. D. ‡q (Hilda Doolittle), ‡d 1886-1961. ¶
▶   5  400 10     Aldington, Hilda Doolittle, ‡d 1886-1961 ¶
▶   6  400 10     Helforth, John, ‡d 1886-1961 ¶
▶   7  400 10     Doolittle, Hilda, ‡d 1886-1961 ‡w nna ¶
▶   8  400 10     D., H. ‡q (Hilda Doolittle), ‡d 1886-1961 ¶
▶   9  670        Her Sea garden, 1916. ¶
```

Authority records for corporate names

```
▶ ARN:      2444280          Rec stat:      n
  Entered:   19890126        Replaced:   19890126
  Type:      z      Enc lvl:       n      Source:    c      Lang:
  Roman:     ▮      Upd status:  a      Mod rec:          Name use: a
  Govt agn: ▮      Ref status:  a      Subj:       a      Subj use: a
  Series:    n      Auth status: a      Geo subd: n      Ser use:  b
  Ser num:  n      Auth/ref:    a      Name:       n      Rules:    c ¶
▶   1  010       no 89000424  ¶
▶   2  040       MnHi ǂc MnHi ¶
▶   3  110 20    St. Peter's Church (Nottingham, England) ¶
▶   4  410 20    Saint Peter's Church (Nottingham, England) ¶
▶   5  410 10    Nottingham (England). ǂb St. Peter's Church ¶
▶   6  670       Nottingham parish registers. Marriages, 1900-1902: ǂb v. 3,
  t.p. (St. Peter's Church) ¶
```

```
▶ ARN:      2633427          Rec stat:      c
  Entered:   19891109        Replaced:   19891110
  Type:      z      Enc lvl:       n      Source:           Lang:
  Roman:     ▮      Upd status:  a      Mod rec:          Name use: a
  Govt agn: ▮      Ref status:  a      Subj:       a      Subj use: a
  Series:    n      Auth status: a      Geo subd: n      Ser use:  b
  Ser num:  n      Auth/ref:    a      Name:              Rules:    c ¶
▶   1  010       n 88212513  ¶
▶   2  040       DLC ǂc DLC ǂd DLC ¶
▶   3  110 20    St. Peter's Church (Hope, England) ¶
▶   4  410 20    Saint Peter's Church (Hope, England) ¶
▶   5  410 20    Hope Church (Hope, England) ¶
▶   6  410 10    Hope, England. ǂb St. Peter's Church ¶
▶   7  670       Porter, W.S. Notes from a Peakland parish, 1923: ǂb p. 2A (St.
  Peter's Church, Hope) p. 5 (Hope Church) ¶
▶   8  670       Crockford's clerical dir., 1980-1982 ǂb (Parish of Hope, St.
  Peter's Church) ¶
▶   9  675       Church of Eng. yrbk., 1987. ¶
```

```
▶ ARN:      847438           Rec stat:      n
  Entered:   19840823        Replaced:   19840823
  Type:      z      Enc lvl:       n      Source:           Lang:
  Roman:     ▮      Upd status:  a      Mod rec:          Name use: a
  Govt agn: ▮      Ref status:  a      Subj:       a      Subj use: a
  Series:    n      Auth status: a      Geo subd: n      Ser use:  b
  Ser num:  n      Auth/ref:    a      Name:       n      Rules:    c ¶
▶   1  010       n 82151415  ¶
▶   2  040       DLC ǂc DLC ¶
▶   3  110 10    United States. ǂb Army. ǂb Dept. of West Point. ¶
▶   4  510 20    United States Military Academy ¶
▶   5  670       U.S. Military Academy, West Point. General orders. Feb. 8,
  1881. ¶
▶   6  678       Military Academy and post of West Point were made a separate
  military department by 1877 ¶
```

```
▶ ARN:      307032           Rec stat:      n
  Entered:   19840819        Replaced:   19840819
  Type:      z      Enc lvl:       n      Source:           Lang:
  Roman:     ▮      Upd status:  a      Mod rec:          Name use: a
  Govt agn: ▮      Ref status:  a      Subj:       a      Subj use: a
  Series:    n      Auth status: a      Geo subd: n      Ser use:  b
  Ser num:  n      Auth/ref:    a      Name:              Rules:    c ¶
▶   1  010       n 79074300  ¶
▶   2  040       DLC ǂc DLC ¶
▶   3  110 20    United States Military Academy. ¶
▶   4  410 20    U.S.M.A. ¶
▶   5  410 20    West Point (Military academy) ¶
▶   6  410 20    USMA ¶
▶   7  410 10    United States. ǂb Military Academy, West Point. ǂw nna ¶
▶   8  510 10    United States. ǂb Army. ǂb Dept. of West Point ¶
▶   9  550 0     Military education ǂz United States ǂw nb ¶
▶  10  551 0     West Point, N.Y. ǂx Schools ǂw nb ¶
```

```
▶ ARN:        391084              Rec stat:      n
  Entered:    19840819            Replaced:      19840819
  Type:       z        Enc lvl:    n       Source:          Lang:
  Roman:      ▮        Upd status: a       Mod rec:         Name use: a
  Govt agn:   ▮        Ref status: a       Subj:       a    Subj use: a
  Series:     n        Auth status:a       Geo subd: n      Ser use:  b
  Ser num:    n        Auth/ref:   a       Name:     n      Rules:    c ¶
▶   1   010         n 80008526  ¶
▶   2   040         DLC ‡c DLC ¶
▶   3   111  20     Expo 67 ‡c (Montr´eal, Qu´ebec) ¶
▶   4   411  20     Universal and International Exhibition of 1967 ‡c (Montr´eal,
  Qu´ebec) ¶
▶   5   411  20     Exposition canadienne universelle et internationale ‡d (1967
  ‡c Montr´eal, Qu´ebec) ¶
▶   6   411  20     Expo 67 ‡w nnaa ¶
▶   7   550   0     Exhibitions ‡w nb ¶
▶   8   551   0     Montr´eal (Qu´ebec) ‡x Exhibitions ‡w nb ¶
▶   9   670         Expo 1967 (Motion ... ¶
```

Authority records for geographic names

```
▶ ARN:        564020              Rec stat:      c
  Entered:    19840820            Replaced:      19910507
  Type:       z        Enc lvl:    n       Source:          Lang:
  Roman:      ▮        Upd status: a       Mod rec:         Name use: a
  Govt agn:   ▮        Ref status: a       Subj:       n    Subj use: b
  Series:     n        Auth status:a       Geo subd: n      Ser use:  b
  Ser num:    n        Auth/ref:   a       Name:     n      Rules:    c ¶
▶   1   010         n 81018181  ¶
▶   2   040         DLC ‡c DLC ‡d DLC ¶
▶   3   151   0     Leopoldville (Congo) ¶
▶   4   451   0     Leopoldville, Congo (City) ‡w nnaa ¶
▶   5   451   0     Leopoldstad (Congo) ¶
▶   6   551   0     Kinshasa (Zaire) ‡w b ¶
▶   7   667         SUBJECT USAGE: This heading is not valid for use as a subject.
  Works about this place are entered under Kinshasa (Zaire). ¶
▶   8   678         Leopoldville, Congo renamed Kinshasa 7/3/66 ¶
```

```
▶ ARN:        208540              Rec stat:      c
  Entered:    19840818            Replaced:      19900622
  Type:       z        Enc lvl:    n       Source:          Lang:
  Roman:      ▮        Upd status: a       Mod rec:         Name use: a
  Govt agn:   ▮        Ref status: a       Subj:       a    Subj use: a
  Series:     n        Auth status:a       Geo subd: n      Ser use:  b
  Ser num:    n        Auth/ref:   n       Name:     n      Rules:    c ¶
▶   1   010         n 78073109  ¶
▶   2   040         DLC ‡c DLC ‡d DLC ¶
▶   3   151   0     Kinshasa (Zaire) ¶
▶   4   451   0     Kinshasa, Zaire ‡w nnaa ¶
▶   5   451   0     Kinshasha (Zaire) ¶
▶   6   451   0     Kinshasa (Congo) ¶
▶   7   551   0     Leopoldville (Congo) ‡w a ¶
▶   8   667         AACR 1 form: Kinshasa, Zaire ¶
▶   9   667         Leopoldville, Congo renamed Kinshasa 7/3/66 ¶
▶  10   670         Smit, H.M. Sharing material resources in African university and
  ... 1980: ‡b t.p. (Kinshasha, Zaire) ¶
```

```
▶ ARN:        275410              Rec stat:      c
  Entered:    19840819            Replaced:      19871005
  Type:       z        Enc lvl:    n       Source:          Lang:
  Roman:      ▮        Upd status: a       Mod rec:         Name use: a
  Govt agn:   ▮        Ref status: a       Subj:       a    Subj use: a
  Series:     n        Auth status:a       Geo subd: n      Ser use:  b
  Ser num:    n        Auth/ref:   n       Name:     n      Rules:    c ¶
▶   1   010         n 79041965  ¶
▶   2   040         DLC ‡c DLC ‡d DLC ¶
▶   3   151   0     Seattle (Wash.) ¶
▶   4   451   0     Seattle ‡w nnaa ¶
▶   5   551   0     Municipality of Metropolitan Seattle (Wash.) ¶
▶   6   670         U. S. Engineer Dept. Board of Engineers for Rivers and Harbors.
  Port and terminal facilities at the port of Seattle ... 1941. ¶
▶   7   670         NUCMC data from U. Washington Lib. for Brown and Caldwell.
  Records, 1956-1958 ‡b (METRO; Seattle, Wash.) ¶
▶   8   670         LeWarne, C.P. Washington State, 1986 ‡b (METRO; Municipality of
  Metropolitan Seattle; METRO governed by a board of reps. from King County and
  Seattle to build network of sewage lines and treatment facilities to clean up
  Lake Washington) ¶
```

Subject authorities records

```
▶ ARN:      2037239          Rec stat:    n
  Entered:    19871218       Replaced:    19871218
  Type:      z     Enc lvl:       n     Source:           Lang:
  Roman:     ▮     Upd status:    a     Mod rec:          Name use: b
  Govt agn:  ▮     Ref status:    b     Subj:             Subj use: a
  Series:    n     Auth status:   a     Geo subd: i       Ser use:  b
  Ser num:   n     Auth/ref:      a     Name:     n       Rules:    n ¶
▶  1   010        sh 85112201  ¶
▶  2   040        DLC ‡c DLC ¶
▶  3   150   0    Reference services (Libraries) ¶
▶  4   450   0    Libraries ‡x Reference department ¶
▶  5   450   0    Library reference services ¶
▶  6   450   0    Reference work (Libraries) ¶
▶  7   550   0    Information services ¶
▶  8   550   0    Libraries ‡w g ¶
```

```
▶ ARN:      2110560          Rec stat:    c
  Entered:    19871218       Replaced:    19891129
  Type:      z     Enc lvl:       n     Source:           Lang:
  Roman:     ▮     Upd status:    a     Mod rec:          Name use: b
  Govt agn:  ▮     Ref status:    b     Subj:      a      Subj use: a
  Series:    n     Auth status:   a     Geo subd: i       Ser use:  b
  Ser num:   n     Auth/ref:      a     Name:     n       Rules:    n ¶
▶  1   010        sh 85148150  ¶
▶  2   040        DLC ‡c DLC ‡d DLC ¶
▶  3   053        HD66 ¶
▶  4   150   0    Work groups ¶
▶  5   450   0    Groups, Work ¶
▶  6   450   0    Team work in industry ¶
▶  7   450   0    Teamwork in industry ¶
▶  8   550   0    Division of labor ‡w g ¶
▶  9   550   0    Industrial organization ‡w g ¶
▶ 10   550   0    Social groups ‡w g ¶
```

APPENDIX C
FIRST LEVEL OF DESCRIPTION

This appendix contains cataloging records for the items appearing on pages 55 to 62 prepared according to the rule for the first level of description (1.0D1). The examples below show the differences in the bibliographic description (i.e., title proper through physical description) between the first and second levels of description. AACR2R does not specify any differences between the two levels with regard to notes or the standard number(s). Furthermore, there is no indication in the rules of any differences between the levels with regard to choice of access points or forms of headings.

Figure 3-1: *First-level description:*

> Mass media/mass culture. — 2nd ed. — McGraw-Hill, c1992.
> xvii, 460 p.

Figure 3-2: *First-level description:*

> The Western experience / Mortimer Chambers ... [et al.].
> — 5th ed. — McGraw-Hill, c1991.
> 3 v.

Figure 3-3: *First-level description:*

> Minneapolis-St. Paul street map. — Scale [ca. 1:47,520].
> — Rand McNally, [1970]
> 1 map

Figure 3-4: *First-level description:*

> Music for four hands, 1 piano. — Chandos Records, c1990.
> 1 sound disc (64 min., 44 sec.)

Figure 3-5: *First-level description:*

> J.C.M. Hanson and his contribution to twentieth-century cataloging. — Dept. of Photoduplication, University of Chicago Library, 1970.
> 1 microfilm reel

Figure 3-6: *First-level description:*

Science in the college curriculum / [edited by] Robert
Hoopes. — [Oakland University], 1963.
x, 211 p.

Figure 3-7: *First-level description:*

Cataloging & classification quarterly. — Vol. 1, no. 1 (fall
1980)-   . — Haworth Press, c1981-
v.

APPENDIX D
GENERAL TABLES FROM THE
LIBRARY OF CONGRESS
CLASSIFICATION

Regions and Countries Table

Abyssinia *see* Ethiopia	
Afghanistan	.A3
Africa	.A35
Africa, Central	.A352
Africa, East	.A353
Africa, Eastern	.A354
Africa, French-speaking West	.A3545
Africa, North	.A355
Africa, Northeast	.A3553
Africa, Northwest	.A3554
Africa, Southern	.A356
Africa, Sub-Saharan	.A357
Africa, West	.A358
Albania	.A38
Algeria	.A4
America	.A45
Andorra	.A48
Angola	.A5
Antarctic Regions	.A6
Antigua	.A63
Arab countries	.A65
Arctic Regions	.A68
Argentina	.A7
Armenia	.A75
Armenia (Republic)	.A76
Aruba	.A77
Asia	.A78
Asia, Central	.A783
Asia, East *see* East Asia	
Asia, Southeastern	.A785
Asia, Southwestern *see* Near East	
Australasia	.A788
Australia	.A8
Austria	.A9

Regions and Countries Table (Continued)

Bahamas	.B24
Bahrain	.B26
Balkan Peninsula	.B28
Bangladesh	.B3
Barbados	.B35
Belgium	.B4
Belize	.B42
Bengal	.B43
Benin	.B45
Bhutan	.B47
Bolivia	.B5
Botswana	.B55
Brazil	.B6
British Guiana *see* Guyana	
British Honduras *see* Belize	
Brunei	.B7
Bulgaria	.B9
Burkina Faso	.B92
Burma	.B93
Burundi	.B94
Byzantine Empire	.B97
Cambodia	.C16
Cameroon	.C17
Canada	.C2
Canary Islands	.C23
Caribbean Area	.C27
Cayman Islands	.C29
Central African Republic	.C33
Central America	.C35
Central Europe	.C36
Ceylon *see* Sri Lanka	
Chad	.C45
Chile	.C5
China	.C6
Colombia	.C7
Communist countries	.C725
Comoros	.C73
Congo (Brazzaville)	.C74
Cook Islands	.C76
Costa Rica	.C8
Cuba	.C9
Cyprus	.C93
Czechoslovakia	.C95
Dahomey *see* Benin	
Denmark	.D4
Developing countries	.D44

Regions and Countries Table (Continued)

Djibouti	.D5
Dominican Republic	.D65
Dutch East Indies *see* Indonesia	
Dutch Guiana *see* Indonesia	
East	.E16
East Asia	.E18
Ecuador	.E2
Egypt	.E3
El Salvador *see* Salvador	
England *see* Great Britain	
Estonia	.E75
Ethiopia	.E8
Europe	.E85
Europe, Central *see* Central Europe	
Europe, Eastern	.E852
Europe, Northern	.E853
Europe, Southern	.E854
Europe, Western *see* Europe	
European Economic Community countries	.E86
Falkland Islands	.F3
Fiji Islands	.F4
Finland	.F5
Formosa *see* Taiwan	
France	.F8
French Guiana	.F9
Gabon	.G2
Gambia	.G25
Germany	.G3
Germany (Democratic Republic) *see* Germany (East)	
Germany (East)	.G35
Germany (Federal Republic) *see* Germany	
Germany (West) *see* Germany	
Ghana	.G4
Great Britain	.G7
Greece	.G8
Greenland	.G83
Grenada	.G84
Guadeloupe	.G845
Guam	.G85
Guatemala	.G9
Guinea	.G92
Guinea-Bissau	.G93
Guyana	.G95
Haiti	.H2
Holland *see* Netherlands	
Honduras	.H8

Regions and Countries Table (Continued)

Hong Kong	.H85
Hungary	.H9
Iceland	.I2
India	.I4
Indochina	.I48
Indonesia	.I5
Inner Mongolia *see* China	
Iran	.I7
Iraq	.I72
Ireland	.I73
Islamic countries	.I74
Islamic Empire	.I742
Israel	.I75
Italy	.I8
Ivory Coast	.I9
Jamaica	.J25
Japan	.J3
Java *see* Indonesia	
Jordan	.J6
Jugoslavia *see* Yugoslavia	
Jutland *see* Denmark	
Kampuchea *see* Cambodia	
Kenya	.K4
Kiribati	.K5
Korea	.K6
Korea (Democratic People's Republic) *see* Korea (North)	
Korea (North)	.K7
Korea (Republic) *see* Korea	
Korea (South) *see* Korea	
Kuwait	.K9
Laos	.L28
Latin America	.L29
Latvia	.L35
Lebanon	.L4
Lesotho	.L5
Liberia	.L7
Libya	.L75
Liechtenstein	.L76
Lithuania	.L78
Luxembourg	.L9
Macao	.M25
Macedonia	.M27
Macedonia (Republic) *see* Yugoslavia	
Madagascar	.M28
Malagasy *see* Madagascar	
Malawi	.M3

Regions and Countries Table (Continued)

Malay Archipelago	.M35
Malaya *see* Malaysia	
Malaysia	.M4
Maldives	.M415
Mali	.M42
Malta	.M43
Martinique	.M435
Mauritania	.M44
Mauritius	.M45
Melanesia	.M5
Mexico	.M6
Micronesia	.M625
Monaco	.M63
Mongolia	.M65
Mongolia (Mongolian People's Republic) *see* Mongolia	
Montenegro *see* Yugoslavia	
Montserrat	.M7
Morocco	.M8
Mozambique	.M85
Namibia	.N3
Near East	.N33
Nepal	.N35
Netherlands	.N4
New Guinea	.N43
New Zealand	.N45
Nicaragua	.N5
Niger	.N55
Nigeria	.N6
North America	.N7
Northern Ireland *see* Great Britain	
Northern Rhodesia *see* Zambia	
Norway	.N8
Nyasaland *see* Malawi	
Oceania	.O3
Oman	.O5
Outer Mongolia *see* Mongolia	
Pacific area	.P16
Pakistan	.P18
Palestine	.P19
Panama	.P2
Papua New Guinea	.P26
Paraguay	.P3
Persia *see* Iran	
Peru	.P4
Philippines	.P6
Poland	.P7

Regions and Countries Table (Continued)

Polynesia	.P75
Portugal	.P8
Puerto Rico	.P9
Qatar	.Q2
Reunion	.R4
Rhodesia, Northern *see* Zambia	
Rhodesia, Southern *see* Zimbabwe	
Romania	.R6
Rumania *see* Romania	
Russia	.R8
Rwanda	.R95
Sahel	.S15
Saint Kitts-Nevis *see* Saint Kitts-Nevis-Anguilla	
Saint Kitts-Nevis-Anguilla	.S17
Saint Vincent	.S18
Salvador*	.S2
San Marino	.S27
Saudi Arabia	.S33
Scandinavia	.S34
Scotland *see* Great Britain	
Senegal	.S38
Serbia *see* Yugoslavia	
Seychelles	.S45
Siam *see* Thailand	
Siberia *see* Russia	
Sierra Leone	.S5
Singapore	.S55
Slovenia *see* Yugoslavia	
Somalia	.S58
South Africa	.S6
South America	.S63
South Asia	.S64
Soviet Union	.S65
Spain	.S7
Sri Lanka	.S72
Sudan	.S73
Surinam	.S75
Swaziland	.S78
Sweden	.S8
Switzerland	.S9
Syria	.S95
Taiwan	.T28
Tamil Nadu *see* India	
Tanganyika *see* Tanzania	
Tanzania	.T34
Tasmania *see* Australia	

Regions and Countries Table (Continued)

Terres australes et antarctiques françaises	.T47
Thailand	.T5
Tibet	.T55
Togo	.T6
Tonga	.T63
Transvaal *see* South Africa	
Trinidad and Tobago	.T7
Tropics	.T73
Tunisia	.T8
Turkey	.T9
Uganda	.U33
Ukraine	.U38
United Arab Emirates	.U5
United States	.U6
Upper Volta *see* Burkina Faso	
Uruguay	.U8
Vatican City	.V3
Venezuela	.V4
Vietnam	.V5
Vietnam (Democratic Republic) *see* Vietnam	
Virgin Islands	.V6
Virgin Islands of the United States	.V63
Wales *see* Great Britain	
West Indies, British	.W47
Yemen	.Y4
Yemen (People's Democratic Republic)	.Y45
Yugoslavia	.Y8
Zaire	.Z28
Zambia	.Z33
Zimbabwe	.Z55

*Continue to cutter for earlier form of name.

United States

Alabama	.A2	Georgia	.G4
Alaska	.A4	Hawaii	.H3
Arizona	.A6	Idaho	.I2
Arkansas	.A8	Illinois	.I3
California	.C2	Indiana	.I6
Colorado	.C6	Iowa	.I8
Connecticut	.C8	Kansas	.K2
Delaware	.D3	Kentucky	.K4
District of Columbia		Louisiana	.L8
(see Washington, D.C.)		Maine	.M2
Florida	.F6	Maryland	.M3

United States (Continued)

Massachusetts	.M4	Oregon	.O7
Michigan	.M5	Pennsylvania	.P4
Minnesota	.M6	Rhode Island	.R4
Mississippi	.M7	South Carolina	.S6
Missouri	.M8	South Dakota	.S8
Montana	.M9	Tennessee	.T2
Nebraska	.N2	Texas	.T4
Nevada	.N3	Utah	.U8
New Hampshire	.N4	Vermont	.V5
New Jersey	.N5	Virginia	.V8
New Mexico	.N6	Washington (D.C.)	.W18
New York	.N7	Washington (State)	.W2
North Carolina	.N8	West Virginia	.W4
North Dakota	.N9	Wisconsin	.W6
Ohio	.O3	Wyoming	.W8
Oklahoma	.O5		

Canadian Provinces

Alberta	.A3	Nova Scotia	.N8
British Columbia	.B8	Ontario	.O6
Manitoba	.M3	Prince Edward Island	.P8
New Brunswick	.N5	Quebec (Province)	.Q3
Newfoundland	.N6	Saskatchewan	.S2
Northwest Territories	.N7	Yukon (Territory)	.Y8

APPENDIX E
KEY TO EXERCISES

CHAPTER 3

Exercise A

1. George Magoon and the down east game war : history, folklore, and the law / Edward D. Ives. — Urbana : University of Illinois Press, c1988. — xiv, 335 p. : ill. ; 24 cm. — (Publications of the American Folklore Society. New series)

2. Baroque oboe concertos [sound recording]. — New York, N.Y. : RCA Victor, p1990. — 1 sound disk : digital, stereo ; 4¾ in. — (Red seal)

3. Techniques of decision making [motion picture] / United States Office of Education. — Washington : The Office : Distributed by National Audiovisual Center, 1977. — 1 film reel (28 min.) : sd., col. ; 16 mm. + 1 workbook. — (You in public service)

Exercise B

1. The poet's poet, and essays / William A. Quayle. — 2d ed. — Cincinnati : Curts & Jennings, 1897.
352 p. ; 20 cm.

2. The contradictions of leadership : a selection of speeches / by James F. Oates, Jr. ; introduction by Blake T. Newton, Jr. ; with an interpretative essay by Robert K. Merton ; edited by Burton C. Billings — New York : Appleton-Century-Crofts, c1970.
viii, 161 p. ; 22 cm.

ISBN 0390-67490-7

3. The Short prose reader / [compiled by] Gilbert H. Muller, Harvey S. Wiener. — 6th ed. — New York : McGraw-Hill, c1991.
xxiii, 498 p. ; 21 cm.

Includes bibliographical references (p. 494-498)
ISBN 0-07-044135-9 : $15.95

4.   Symphonies 4 & 5 [sound recording] / Sibelius. — New York :
London Records, p1991.
1 sound disc (67 min., 50 sec.) : digital, stereo ; 4¾ in.

San Francisco Symphony ; Herbert Blomstedt, conductor.
Recorded at Davies Symphony Hall, San Francisco, May & June,
1989.
Compact disc.
425 858-2 (London Records)

5.   Schaum's outline of theory and problems of college mathematics
: algebra, discrete mathematics, trigonometry, geometry, introduction to calculus / Frank Ayres, Jr., Philip A. Schmidt. — 2nd ed. —
New York : McGraw-Hill, c1992.
viii, 459 p. : ill. ; 28 cm. — (Schaum's outline series)

Cover title: Theory and problems of college mathematics.
Spine title: College mathematics.
Rev. ed. of: First year college mathematics / Frank Ayres, Jr.,
c1958.
Includes index.
ISBN 0-07-002664-5

CHAPTER 4

Exercise A

1. Main entry under: William A. Quayle
Added entry under: Title

2. Main entry under: James F. Oates
Added entries under: Burton C. Billings
                     Title

3. Main entry under: Title
Added entries under: Gilbert H. Muller
                     Harvey S. Wiener

4. Main entry under: Sibelius
Added entries under: Herbert Blomstedt
                     San Francisco Symphony Orchestra
                     [Name. Title]: Sibelius. Symphonies, no. 5,
                     op. 83, E♭ major. 1991
                     [Name. Title]: Sibelius. Symphonies, no. 4,
                     op. 63, A minor. 1991
                     Title: Symphonies 4 and 5

5. Main entry under: Frank Ayres
   Added entries under: Philip A. Schmidt
   Title
   Title: Theory and problems of college mathematics
   Title: College mathematics
   Series

CHAPTER 6

Exercise A

1. Quayle, William A. (William Alfred), 1860-1925
   See reference from: Quayle, William Alfred, 1860-1925

2. Oates, James F.

3. Sibelius, Jean, 1865-1957
   See references from fuller form of name: Sibelius, Jean Julius Christian, 1865-1957
   See references from other language forms, e.g., Sibelius, Jan, 1865-1957

4. Onassis, Jacqueline Kennedy, 1929-
   See references from former names: Kennedy, Jacqueline Bouvier, 1929-   ; Bouvier, Jacqueline, 1929-
   See references from other language forms, e.g., Chia-kuei-lin, 1929-

5. Lawrence, D. H. (David Herbert), 1885-1930
   See references from other forms of name: Lawrence, David Herbert, 1885-1930
   See references from other name: Davison, Lawrence H. (Lawrence Herbert), 1885-1930
   See references from other language forms, e.g., Lorensu, 1885-1930

6. United States. Internal Revenue Service
   See reference from indirect heading: United States. Dept. of Treasury. Internal Revenue Service
   See references from initials: IRS
                                     I.R.S.

7. Association for Library Collections & Technical Services
   See references from initials: ALCTS
                                     A.L.C.T.S.
   See reference from variant spelling: Association for Library Collections and Technical Services

See reference from indirect heading: American Library Association. Association for Library Collections & Technical Services
See also reference from earlier heading: American Library Association. Resources and Technical Service Division

8. International Conference on Educational Measurement (1st : 1967 : Berlin, Germany)

CHAPTER 8

Exercise A

1. Papers on surface-enhanced raman scattering
   1. Raman effect, Surface enhanced.

2. Geometric function theory in several complex variables
   1. Geometric function theory.
   2. Functions of several complex variables.

3. The communicative ethics controversy
   1. Communication—Moral and ethical aspects.

4. Dictionary of concepts in recreation and leisure studies
   1. Recreation—Dictionaries.
   2. Leisure—Dictionaries.

5. Geography in the curriculum
   1. Geography—Study and teaching.

6. Proceedings of a conference on condensed matter, particle physics and cosmology.
   1. Condensed matter—Congresses.
   2. Particles (Nuclear physics)—Congresses.
   3. Cosmology—Congresses.

7. A handbook for counseling the troubled and defiant child
   1. Problem children—Counseling of—Handbooks, manuals, etc.
   2. Child psychotherapy—Handbooks, manuals, etc.

8. Construction materials: types, uses, and applications
   1. Building materials.

9. Control theory of distributed parameter and applications: proceeding of a conference
   1. Control theory—Congresses.
   2. Distributed parameter systems—Congresses.

10. An introduction to urban geographic information systems
    1. Geography—Data processing.
    2. Cities and towns—Data processing.

11. Paleontology of vertebrates
    1. Vertebrates, Fossil.

12. The adolescent in the family
    1. Parent and teenager.
    2. Teenagers—Family relationships.
    3. Adolescent psychology.

13. The rhythm and intonation of spoken English
    1. English language—Rhythm.
    2. English language—Intonation.
    3. English language—Spoken English.

14. The biblical doctrine of salvation
    1. Salvation—Biblical teaching.

15. An English-Swedish, Swedish-English dictionary
    1. English language—Dictionaries—Swedish.
    2. Swedish language—Dictionaries—English.

16. An historical study of the doctrine of the Trinity
    1. Trinity—History of doctrines.

17. ABC: A child's first book
    1. Alphabet rhymes.

18. Twenty-three days with the Viet Cong: a personal narrative
    1. Vietnamese Conflict, 1961-1975—Personal narratives.

19. The principal voyages and discoveries of the English nation to 1600
    1. Discoveries (in geography)—English.
    2. Voyages and travels.
    3. Great Britain—Exploring expeditions.

20. Public attitudes toward life insurance
    1. Insurance, Life—Public opinion.

Exercise B

1. a. Athens (Ga.)—Social conditions
        Athens (Greece)—Social conditions
        Brittany (France)—Social conditions
        Cambridge (England)—Social conditions
        Munich (Germany)—Social conditions
        New York (N.Y.)—Social conditions
        Ottawa (Ont.)—Social conditions
        Tennessee—Social conditions
        Rio de Janeiro (State : Brazil)—Social conditions
        Mississippi River Valley—Social conditions

   b. Art—Georgia—Athens
       Art—Greece—Athens
       Art—France—Brittany
       Art—England—Cambridge
       Art—Germany—Munich
       Art—New York (N.Y.)
       Art—Ontario—Ottawa
       Art—Tennessee
       Art—Brazil—Rio de Janeiro (State)
       Art—Mississippi River Valley

2. a. Events leading to the American Civil War, 1837-1861
     1. United States—History—1815-1861.
     2. United States—History—Civil War, 1861-1865—Causes.
 b. A history of slavery and slave trades in Sub-Saharan Africa
     1. Slavery—Africa, Sub-Saharan—History.
     2. Slave trade—Africa, Sub-Saharan—History.
 c. Profile of Ontario's provincial electoral districts based on statistics collected in the 1986 census
     1. Ontario—Census, 1986.
     2. Election districts—Ontario—Statistics.
 d. Popular culture in the United States during the cold war
     1. United States—Popular culture—History—20th century.
     2. Cold War—Social aspects—United States.
 e. Lobbying for social changes in the United States
     1. Lobbying—United States.
     2. United States—Social policy.
 f. Christian life and the church in the Holy Roman Empire during the tenth century
     1. Holy Roman Empire—Church history.
     2. Christian life—Middle Ages, 600-1500.
     3. Holy Roman Empire—Social conditions.
 g. Essays on the Hungarian Protestant Reformation in the 16th century
     1. Reformation—Hungary.
     2. Hungary—Church history—16th century.
 h. Violence in American families
     1. Family violence—United States.
 i. Managing social services in the United States: designing, measuring, and financing
     1. Social service—United States—Planning.
     2. Social service—United States—Evaluation.
     3. Social service—United States—Finance.

j. U.S.-Yugoslav economic relations since World War II
1. United States—Foreign economic relations—Yugoslavia.
2. Yugoslavia—Foreign economic relations—United States.

k. Social relations in Elizabethan London
1. London (England)—History—16th century.
2. London (England)—Social conditions.

l. Public school choice in American education
1. Public schools—United States.
2. School, Choice of—United States.
3. Education—United States—Parent participation.
4. Education and state—United States.

m. The Gypsies of Eastern Europe
1. Gypsies—Europe, Eastern.
2. Europe, Eastern—Ethnic relations.

n. The Taiwan uprising of February 28, 1947
1. Taiwan—History—February Twenty-Eighth Incident, 1947.

o. Working women look at their home lives
1. Home—United States.
2. Working mothers—United States—Attitudes.

p. Norman illumination of manuscripts at Mont St. Michel, 966–1100
1. Illumination of books and manuscripts, Norman—France—Mont St. Michel.

q. Life in a Japanese Zen Buddhist monastery
1. Monastic and religious life (Zen Buddhism)—Japan.

r. The German community in Cincinnati
1. German Americans—Ohio—Cincinnati.

s. A pictorial guide to San Francisco
1. San Francisco (Calif.)—Pictorial works.

t. A catalog of Great Britain railway letter stamps
1. Railway letter stamps—Catalogs.
2. Postage stamps—Great Britain—Catalogs.

Exercise C

1. A history of modern German literature
1. German literature—19th century—History and criticism.
2. German literature—20th century—History and criticism.

2. Essays on American and British fiction
1. American fiction—History and criticism.
2. English fiction—History and criticism.

3. A study of the themes of order and restraint in the poetry of Philip Larkin, a British author.
    1. Larkin, Philip—Criticism and interpretation.
    2. Self-control in literature.
    3. Order in literature.

4. Women and literature in France
    1. French literature—Women authors—History and criticism.
    2. Women and literature—France.

5. Irony in Rabelais
    1. Rabelais, François, ca.1490-1554?—Criticism and interpretation.
    2. Irony in literature.

6. Memoirs of Richard Nixon
    1. Nixon, Richard M. (Richard Milhous), 1913-
    2. Presidents—United States—Biography.
    3. United States—Politics and government—1969-1974.

7. Columbus and the age of discovery
    1. Columbus, Christopher.
    2. Explorers—America—Biography.
    3. Explorers—Spain—Biography.
    4. America—Discovery and exploration—Spanish.

8. Bibliographies of studies in Victorian literature for the years 1975–1984
    1. English literature—19th century—History and criticism—Bibliography.

9. A critical study of characterization in Jacobean tragedies
    1. English drama—17th century—History and criticism.
    2. English drama (Tragedy)—History and criticism.
    3. Characters and characteristics in literature.

10. A commentary on the epistles of Peter and Jude
    1. Bible. N.T. Peter—Commentaries.
    2. Bible. N.T. Jude—Commentaries.

11. A study of the theme of friendship in fifteenth-century Chinese literature
    1. Chinese literature—Ming dynasty, 1368-1644—History and criticism.
    2. Friendship in literature.

12. Mary Stuart in sixteenth- and seventeenth-century literature: a critical study
    1. Mary Stuart, Queen of the Scots, 1542-1587, in fiction, drama, poetry, etc.
    2. Literature, Modern—15th and 16th centuries—History and criticism.
    3. Literature, Modern—17th century—History and criticism.

13. A reader's guide to Walt Whitman
    1. Whitman, Walt, 1819-1892—Criticism and interpretation.

14. A journal of twentieth-century Spanish literature
    1. Spanish literature—20th century—Periodicals.

CHAPTER 9

Exercise A

1. Reading habits of adolescents
    1. Youth—Books and reading.

2. Advertising and selling by mail
    1. Advertising.
    2. Mail-order business.
    3. Direct selling.

3. Encyclopedia of science and technology
    1. Science—Dictionaries.
    2. Technology—Dictionaries.

4. *Library Journal*
    1. Library science—Periodicals.
    2. Libraries—Periodicals.

5. Handbook of chemistry and physics
    1. Chemistry—Handbooks, manuals, etc.
    2. Physics—Handbooks, manuals, etc.

6. History of the First World War
    1. World War, 1914-1918.

7. *Journal of Plant Pathology*
    1. Plant diseases—Periodicals.

8. A list of scientific journals
    1. Science—Periodicals—Bibliography.

9. *Time* (magazine)
    1. History—Periodicals.

10. A Russian-English dictionary of medical terms
    1. Medicine—Dictionaries.
    2. Russian language—Dictionaries—English.

11. A bibliography of library and information science
    1. Library science—Bibliography.
    2. Information science—Bibliography.

12. Opportunities in textile careers
    1. Textile industry—Vocational guidance

13. An amateur photographer's handbook
    1. Photography—Handbooks, manuals, etc.

14. *Sears List of Subject Headings*
    1. Subject headings.

Exercise B

1. Museums in New York City
    1. Museums—New York (N.Y.)

2. Popular songs in the United States
    1. Popular music.
    2. Songs, American.

3. History of Flemish painting
    1. Painting, Flemish—History.

4. Canadian foreign policy, 1945–1954
    1. Canada—Foreign relations.

5. *The Eisenhower Years: A Historical Assessment*
    1. United States—History—1953-1961.

6. Party politics in Australia
    1. Political parties—Australia.
    2. Australia—Politics and government.

7. Directory of hospitals in Athens, Georgia
    1. Hospitals—Athens (Ga.)—Directories.

8. The reign of Elizabeth, 1558–1603
    1. Great Britain—History—1485-1603.

9. A pictorial guide to San Francisco
    1. San Francisco (Calif.)—Description—Views.

10. *Famous American Military Leaders*
    1. United States—Armed forces—Biography.

11. *Norwegian Folk Tales: A Collection*
   1. Folklore—Norway.

12. *Getting to Know Iran and Iraq*
   1. Iran.
   2. Iraq.

13. *The Land and People of Switzerland*
   1. Switzerland—Civilization.
   2. Switzerland—Description.

Exercise C

1. Swedish word origins
   1. Swedish language—Etymology.

2. *Poems for Thanksgiving* (by various authors)
   1. Thanksgiving Day—Poetry—Collections.
   2. American poetry—Collections.

3. Russian grammar
   1. Russian language—Grammar.

4. *The Peace Corps in Action*
   1. Peace Corps (U.S.)
   2. Technical assistance, American.

5. *Chemicals of Life: Enzymes, Vitamins, Hormones*
   1. Enzymes.
   2. Vitamins.
   3. Hormones.

6. A history of the American Medical Association
   1. American Medical Association—History.

7. NATO and Europe
   1. North Atlantic Treaty Organization.
   2. Europe—History—1945-

8. The German community in Cincinnati
   1. German Americans.
   2. Cincinnati (Ohio)—Foreign population.

9. *Wonders of the Himalayas*
   1. Himalaya Mountains.

10. *Eastern Europe: Czechoslovakia, Hungary, Poland*
   1. Czechoslovakia.
   2. Hungary.
   3. Poland.

11. *The Department of Defense: A History*
   1. United States. Dept. of Defense—History.

12. Sparrows of Asia
   1. Sparrows.
   2. Birds—Asia.

Exercise D

1. *Lives of Famous French Dramatists*
   1. Dramatists, French—Biography.

2. *American Men and Women of Science*
   1. Scientists—Directories.

3. *French Short Stories: A Collection*
   1. Short stories, French.

4. *Stories of Maupassant*
   1. Short stories, French.

5. *Commentaries on the New Testament*
   1. Bible. N.T.—Commentaries.

6. *Life of Pablo Picasso*
   1. Picasso, Pablo, 1881-1963.

7. *Modern American Secret Agents*
   1. Spies.

8. *Famous New Yorkers*
   1. New York (State)—Biography.

9. *Life of Daniel Boone*
   1. Boone, Daniel, 1734-1820.

10. *The Agony and the Ecstasy* (an American novel based on the life of Michelangelo)
   1. Michelangelo Buonarroti, 1475-1564—Fiction.

11. *Best Sports Stories*
   1. Short stories.
   2. Sports—Fiction—Collections.

12. *A Day in the Life of President Johnson* (Lyndon B.)
   1. Johnson, Lyndon B. (Lyndon Baines), 1908-1973.

13. *The Combat Nurses of World War II*
   1. Military nurses.
   2. World War, 1939-1945—Medical Care—Biography.

14. *Book of Poetry for Children*
  1. Children's poetry.

15. *A Man for All Seasons* (an English drama based on the life of Sir Thomas More)
  1. More, Sir Thomas, Saint, 1478-1535—Drama.

16. *A Study of Mark Twain's Novels*
  1. Twain, Mark, 1835-1910—Criticism, interpretation, etc.

CHAPTER 12

Exercise A

1. India under the British rule
   954.03

2. Discipline of students through punishments in the public schools
   371.54

3. Television commercials
   659.143

4. A thesaurus of water resources terms
   025.4933391

5. Planning public library buildings
   022.314

6. A bibliography on diagnostic x-ray techniques
   016.61607572

7. Inbreeding in relation to human eugenics
   573.2133

8. Commentaries on the Gospel of John
   226.507

9. Colligative properties of electrolytic solutions
   541.3745

10. Unemployment in library services
    331.1378102

11. Embryology of vertebrates
    596.033

12. Curriculum design in schools
    375.001

13. *Dear Comrades: Menshevik Reports on the Bolshevik Revolution and the Civil War*
947.0841

Exercise B

1. Answers on p. 463.

2. a. Financial management of special education in Ohio
371.9042109771
   b. Brooklyn Public Library
027.474723
   c. History of classical languages
480.09
   d. A dictionary of modern music and musicians
780.922 (preferred) *or* 780.904
   e. Popular music in the United States
781.630973
   f. *American Libraries* (official journal of the American Library Association)
020.5
   g. The government of American cities
352.007240973
   h. *Journal of Physical Oceanography*
551.46005
   i. Foreign relations between Russia and Japan
327.47052
   j. The Nazi spy network in Switzerland during World War II
940.5487494
   k. Social conditions in Japan after World War II
952.04
   l. Masterpieces of painting in the Metropolitan Museum of Art: An exhibition catalog
750.747471
   m. Life and health insurance laws (United States)
346.7308632
   n. Illinois rules and regulations for fire prevention and safety, as amended 1968
344.7730537
   o. Arizona library laws (a compilation)
344.79109202632
   p. Tourist trade of Romagna, Italy, after World War II
338.47914540492   [04=hist per.; 92=1946–   ]
   q. Statistical methods used in social sciences
300.015195   [519.5=statistical math]

	United States	Tennessee	Scotland	Egypt
Area table notation	–73	–768	–411	–62
History of	973	976.8	941.1	962
Tourist guide to	917.304	917.6804	914.1104	916.204
Newspapers from	071.3	071.68	072.911	079.62
Folk songs from	782.4216200973	782.4216200768	782.4216200411	782.4216200962
Political condition in	320.973	320.9768	320.9411	320.962
Geology of	557.3	557.68	554.11	556.2

r. European immigrants in the United States during the 1930s
    325.24097309043 [−09043=1930–1939]
s. Computer aided proofs in numerical analysis
    519.40285 [519.4=Applied numerical analysis]
t. An exhibition of twentieth-century American art from a Long
    Island collection
    709.7307474725

Exercise C

1. Swahili grammar.
   496.3925

2. A bibliography of anonymous works in German
   014.31

3. A Chinese-English, English-Chinese dictionary
   495.1321

4. Islamic painting
   759.917671

5. Babylonian and Assyrian religion
   299.21

6. *La Raza: The Mexican-Americans*
   305.86872073

7. Mennonite colonization in Mexico
   305.6017671

8. The great Jewish families of New York
   305.89240747

9. A German version of the New Testament
   225.531

10. World War II letters of Barbara Wooddall Taylor and Charles E.
    Taylor
    940.5481730922

11. The Arabic linguistic tradition
    410.09175927

12. Teaching English reading in the secondary school
    428.40712   [−84=reading; 0712=2nd. educ]

13. The Spanish-speaking people from Mexico in the United States
    973.046872   [−004=Racial groups (vol. 3, p.710), −04 under
                  973; −68=Spanish American; −72=Mexico]

14. *Farewell, My Nation : the American Indian and the United States, 1820-1890*
973.0497   [–004=Racial groups; –97=Indians (T5)]

15. Italian-American women in Nassau County, New York, 1925–1981
974.7245004510082   [–747245=Nassau County, NY; –004= s.s; –51=Italians (T5); –0082=women (T1)]

16. The Jewish minority in the Netherlands
949.2004924   [–004924=Jews (T5)]

Exercise D

1. A collection of German literature for and by Jews
830.808924

2. Characterization in Jacobean tragedies: a critical study
822.05120927

3. A collection of devotional poetry from colonial America
811.1080382

4. A collection of seventeenth-century French drama
842.408

5. A history of science fiction in the United States
813.0876209

6. A study of the theme of friendship in fifteenth-century Chinese literature
895.109353

7. Abraham Lincoln in American literature: a critical study
810.9351

8. A study of the theme of alienation in twentieth-century American fiction
813.509353   [alienation as a social theme]
813.509382   [alienation as a religious theme]
813.509384   [alienation as a philosophic concept]

9. The diaries of Mark Twain
818.403

10. A history of Irish Gaelic poetry in the early period
891.621109

11. A study of the theme of death in twentieth-century American poetry
811.509354

12. A study of the characters in seventeenth-century French drama
    842.40927

13. A study of Shakespeare's tragedies by Clifford Leech
    822.33
    D-Lxx   [Lxx = Cutter number of author]

14. Collected poems of Byron
    821.7

15. The art of writing short stories
    808.31

16. An anthology of American short stories
    813.0108

17. Literary history of the United States: twentieth century
    810.9005

18. Women writers of contemporary Spain
    860.992870904

19. A study of feminine fiction in England, 1713–1799
    823.5099287   [−5=Queen Anne, 1702–45; −099287=woman (T3C)]

20. Study of literary criticism in Finnish universities
    801.9507114897

21. Essays on Russian and Polish literature
    891.709

22. A study of French Renaissance tragedy
    842.05120903   [−20512=Tragedy (T3B)]

23. Interpret the following decimal classification numbers:
    338.4769009421 = The building industry in London, England
    338.926091724 = Science and technology policy in developing
    countries
    551.2109989 = Volcanoes of the Antarctica
    782.4215520941 = Songs in British drama
    917.92003 = Utah place names

Exercise E

1. Magnetism of the earth
   538

2. Guidance and counseling in schools
   371.4

3. Cataloging and classification of books in libraries
   025.3

4. *Séance: A Book of Spiritual Communications*
   133.9

5. A bibliography of bacteriology
   016.5899 *or* 589.9016

6. Landscaping for homes
   712

7. Acquisition of audiovisual materials in libraries
   025.2

8. The causes of the Civil War
   973.7

9. A bibliography of local transportation
   016.3884 *or* 388.4016

10. The kinesiology of weight lifting
   613.7

11. Designing dormitories
   727

12. *Kentuckiana: A Bibliography of Books about Kentucky*
   016.9769 *or* 976.90016

13. A concordance to modern versions of the New Testament
   225.5

14. A critique of Marx's *Das Kapital*
   335.4

15. Smallpox vaccination
   614.5

16. Newspapers in Russia
   077

17. Position of women in Old Testament
   221.8

18. Paintings from the United States
   759.13

19. An atlas of the moon
   912

20. Public library administration
   025.1

21. Greek mythology
292.1

22. *How to Prepare for College Entrance Examinations*
378.1

Exercise F

1. How to teach cooking
641.507

2. *Is There Life on Mars? A Scientist's View*
574.999

3. Labor union discrimination against black American textile workers
331.6

4. Rocks from the moon
552.0999

5. Flora and fauna of Alaska
574.9798

6. Nursing education
610.7307

7. A history of Kentucky during the Civil War
976.9

8. Monetary policy of France
332.4

9. History of political parties in Australia
324.294009

10. An encyclopedia of engineering
620.003

11. A travel guide to Florida
917.5904

12. A bibliography of Ohio imprints
015.771

13. A history of Christian churches in Iowa
277.77

14. *Journal of Political Science*
320.05

15. Farming in Iowa
    630.9777

16. A history of New Orleans
    976.3

17. Interior decoration in Sweden
    747.285

18. Political conditions in the United States
    320.973

19. A history of Singapore
    959.57

20. A collection of fairy tales
    398.21

21. A gardener's handbook on diseases of flowers
    635.9

22. Political conditions in the United States
    320.973

23. Geology of Iran
    555.5

24. *American Restaurants Then and Now*
    647.9573   [647.95=Eating and drinking places]

25. United States policy toward Latin America
    327.7308

26. Kentucky folklore
    398.09769

27. Macroeconomic policy in Britain, 1974-1987
    339.50941

28. *Early Education in the Public Schools: Lessons from a Comprehensive Birth-to-Kindergarten Program in Brookline, Massachusetts*
    372.2109744

Exercise G

1. A history of American literature
    810.9

2. An encyclopedia of Austrian literature
    830

3. A biography of President Lyndon Baines Johnson
973.923092

4. A biography of Walter Cronkite
070.1092

5. A teacher's handbook of Latin literature
870.7

6. A critical study of twentieth-century drama
809.2

7. An English-Japanese, Japanese-English dictionary
495.6

8. A critical study of Russian novels
891.73009

9. A history of Chinese poetry
895.1

10. The collected works of Henry Fielding
823

11. A handbook for sign language teachers
419.07

12. A critical study of the Afro-American as a character in American fiction
813.009

13. Remedial reading for French
448.4

14. A collection of Portuguese essays (by various authors)
869.4008

15. A study of political themes in twentieth-century British literature
820.9

Exercise H

1. 973
Ad17h   Adams, Henry. *History of the United States of America.* 1962

2. 973
Ad17f   Adams, Henry. *The Formative Years: A History of the United States during the Administration of Jefferson and Madison.* 1948

3. 973
Ad18m   Adams, James Truslow. *The March of Democracy.* 1932–
33

4. 973
Ad19g   Adams, Randolph G. *The Gateway to American History.*
1927

5. 973
Ad19p   Adams, Randolph G. *Pilgrims, Indians and Patriots: The Pictorial History of America From the Colonial Age to the Revolution.* 1928

6. 973
B193s   Baldwin, Leland Dewitt, 1897–   . *The Stream of American History.* 1965

7. 973
B2215h   Bancroft, George. *History of the United States of America, from the Discovery of the Continent to 1789.* 1883–85

8. 973
B367a   Beals, Carleton. *American Earth: the Biography of a Nation.* 1939

9. 973
Sch38n   Schlesinger, Arthur Meier. *New Viewpoints in American History.* 1922

10. 973
Sch38p   Schlesinger, Arthur Meier. *Political and Social History of the United States, 1829–1925.* 1925

11. 973
Sch68h   Schouler, James. *History of the United States of America under the Constitution.* 1880–1913

12. 973
Se48s   Sellers, Charles G. *A Synopsis of American History.* 1963

13. 973
Sh16u   Shaler, Nathaniel S. *The United States of America.* 1894

14. 973
Sh35m   Sheehan, Donald H. *The Making of American History.* 1950

15. 973
Sh58c   Sherwood, James. *The Comic History of the United States.* 1870

16. 973
Si97   *Six Presidents from the Empire State.* 1974

17. 973
Sm54u   Smith, Dale O. *U.S. Military Doctrine: A Study and Appraisal.* 1955

18. 973
Sm57u   Smith, Goldwin. *The United States: An Outline of Political History, 1492–1871.* 1893

Exercise I

1. a. 92
C475ar   Arthur, Sir G. *Concerning Winston Spencer Churchill* [1874–1965]

b. 92
C475as   Ashley, M. P. *Churchill as Historian* [W.S. Churchill, 1874–1965]

c. 92
H638b   Bullock, A. L. C. *Hitler: A Study in Tyranny*

d. 92
C4745a   Churchill, Jennie Jerome, 1854–1921. *The Reminiscences of Lady Randolph Churchill*

e. 92
C475c   Churchill, Randolph S., 1911–1968. *Winston S. Churchill* [1874–1965]

f. 92
C475a   Churchill, Winston, Sir, 1874–1965. *A Roving Commission: My Early Life*

g. 92
C4747c   Churchill, Winston, Sir, 1874–1965. *Lord Randolph Churchill* [1849–1895]

h. 92
C4743f   Fishman, J. *My Darling Clementine* [wife of W.S. Churchill]

i. 92
C475g   Gardner, B. *Churchill in Power* [W. S. Churchill, 1874–1965]

j. 92
C475gr   Graebner, W. *My Dear Mr. Churchill* [W. S. Churchill, 1874–1965]

k. 92
H638aZh   Hackett, Francis. *What Mein Kampf Means to America*

l. 92
H638a   Hitler, Adolph. *Mein Kampf*

m. 92
H638aE   Hitler, Adolph. *My Battle*

n. 92
C4747j   James, R. R. *Lord Randolph Churchill* [1849–1895]

o. 92
C4745k   Kraus, R. *Young Lady Randolph* [Churchill, 1854–1921]

p. 92
C4745*l*   Leslie, Anita. *Jennie: The Life of Lady Randolph Churchill* [1854–1921]

q. 92
C4745*l*1   Leslie, Anita. *Lady Randolph Churchill: The Story of Jennie Jerome* [1854–1921]

r. 92
C4745m   Martin, R. G. *Jennie: The Life of Lady Randolph Churchill* [1854–1921]

s. 92
H638s   Smith, B. F. *Adolph Hitler: His Family, Childhood and Youth*

2. a. 823.8
D555zb   Brook, G. L. *The Language of Dickens*

b. 823.8
D555yc   Churchill, R. C. *A Bibliography of Dickensian Criticism*

c. 823.8
D555tG   Dickens, Charles. *Eine Geschichte von zwei Städten* [a German translation of *A Tale of Two Cities*]

d. 823.8
D555h   Dickens, Charles. *Hard Times*

e. 823.8
D555tS   Dickens, Charles. *Historia de dos Ciudades* [a Spanish translation of *A Tale of Two Cities*]

f. 823.8
D555tF   Dickens, Charles. *Paris et Londres en 1793* [a French translation of *A Tale of Two Cities*]

g. 823.8
D555hF   Dickens, Charles. *Les temps difficiles* [a French
            translation of *Hard Times*]
h. 823.8
D555hG   Dickens, Charles. *Schwere Zeiten* [a German trans-
            lation of *Hard Times*]
i. 823.8
D555t   Dickens, Charles. *A Tale of Two Cities.* 1934
1934

j. 823.8
D555t   Dickens, Charles. *A Tale of Two Cities.* 1970
1970

k. 823.8
D555tGd   Dickens, Charles. *Zwei Städte, Roman aus der fran-
            zösischen Revolution* [a German translation of *A Tale
            of Two Cities* by B. Dedek, 1924]
l. 823.8
D555zz   *Dickens Studies Newsletter*

m. 823.8
D555zzd   *The Dickensian: A Magazine for Dickens Lovers*

n. 823.8
D555yh   Hayward, A.L. *The Dickens Encyclopedia*

o. 823.8
D555tZ   *Twentieth Century Interpretations of A Tale of Two
            Cities: A Collection of Critical Essays*

CHAPTER 13

Exercise A

1. *Railway Imperialism* / edited by Clarence B. Davis and Kenneth E.
   Wilburn, Jr., with Ronald E. Robinson. 1991
   HE1041.R35 1991

2. *Beyond Ambition : How Driven Managers Can Lead Better and Live Better*
   / Robert E. Kaplan with Wilfred H. Drath and Joan R. Kofodimos.
   1991
   HD38.2.K37 1991

3. *Norbert Wiener, 1894–1964* / by Pesi R. Masani. 1989 [Wiener was a
   mathematician]
   QA29.W497M37 1989

4. *Creating Period Gardens* / Elizabeth Banks. 1991
   SB457.5.B36 1991

5. *Solomon's House Revisited : The Organization and Institutionalization of Science* / Tore Fransgsmyr, editor. 1990 [main entry under: Nobel Symposium (75th : 1989 : Stockholm, Sweden)]
   Q10.N63 1989

6. *Creativity in the Arts and Science* / William R. Shea and Antonio Spadafora, editors. 1990 (Proceedings of the Third Locarno International Conference on Science and Society, held in Oct. 1988; main entry under the title)
   Q174.C74 1990

7. *Accumulation of Organic Carbon in Marine Sediments : Results from the Deep Sea Drilling Project* / Ruediger Stein. 1991
   QE571.S74 1991

8. *Banach Lattices* / Peter Meyer-Nieberg. 1991
   QA326.M49 1991

9. *America and the New Economy : How New Competitive Standards Are Radically Changing American Workplaces* / Anthony Patrick Carnevale. 1991 [a book on labor productivity in the United States]
   HC110.L3C37 1991

10. *Yen for Development : Japanese Foreign Aid & the Politics of Burden-Sharing* / edited by Shafiqul Islam. 1991 [main entry under the title]
    HC60.Y46 1991

11. *Leadership : The Inner Side of Greatness : A Philosophy for Leaders* / by Peter Koestenbaum. 1991 (The Jossey-Bass management series)
    HD57.7.K46 1991

12. *Creating Effective Boards for Private Enterprises : Meeting the Challenges of Continuity and Competition* / John L. Ward. 1991
    HD2745.W37 1991

13. *Varieties of Social Explanation : An Introduction to the Philosophy of Social Science* / Daniel Little. 1991
    H61.L58 1991

14. *Taxation in the Global Economy* / edited by Assaf Razin and Joel Slemrod. c1990 [a book on tax on foreign income in the United States]
    HJ4653.F65T39 1990

15. *New Directions in Telecommunications Policy* / edited by Paul R. Newberg. 1989 [main entry under the title]
    HE7781.N49 1989

16. *Self Employment : A Labor Market Perspective* [for women in the United States] / Robert L. Aronson. 1991
    HD6072.6.U6A76 1991

17. *Translating Poetry : The Double Labyrinth* / edited by Daniel Weissbort. 1989 [main entry under the title]
    PN1059.T7T73 1989

18. *Paleontology of Vertebrates* / Jean Chaline. 1990 [an English translation]
    QE841.C4513 1990

Exercise B

1. *Financial Liberalization, Money Demand, and Monetary Policy in Asian Countries* / Wanda Tseng and Robert Corker. 1991
   HG1202.T74 1991   [Table VIII 551–555: Asia]

2. *Antonio Gramsci : Architect of a New Politics* / Dante Germino. 1990 [Gramsci (1891–1937) was an Italian communist]
   HX289.7.G73G47 1990

3. *Charlotte Brontë* / Penny Boumelha. 1990
   PR4169 .B68 1990

4. *Ben Jonson's 1616 Folio* [a textual criticism] / edited by Jennifer Brady and W.H. Herendeen. 1991
   PR2643.B46 1991

5. *The Masque of Stuart Culture* / Jerzy Limon. c1990
   PR678.M3L56 1990   [.M3=Masques]

6. *The Book of the Laurel* / John Skelton ; edited by F.W. Brownlow. c1990
   PR2347.B66 1990   [Table XXXV: 7=separate works: by title; .B66=Book]

7. *Last Lines : An Index to the Last Lines of Poetry* / Victoria Kline. c1992
   PN1022.K55 1991

8. *Medieval Literature : Texts and Interpretation* / edited and with an introduction by Tim William Machan. 1991
   PR275.T45M4 1991   [.T45=Textual criticism]

9. *The Makings of Happiness* / Ronald Wallace [20th century American author]. 1991
   PS3573.A4314M35 1991

10. *Close Connections : Caroline Gordon and the Southern Renaissance* / Ann Waldron. 1987
    PS3513.O5765Z97 1987

11. *The Second Part of King Henry VI* / William Shakespeare; edited by Michael Hattaway. 1990
   PR2815.A2H38 1990   [.A2=by editor]

12. *The Victorian Serial* / Linda K. Hughes and Michael Lund. 1991
   PR468.P37H84 1991   [PR468=History of Eng. lit.—19c.; .P37= Periodicals]

13. *Jane Austen and the Fiction of Culture : An Essay on the Narration of Social Realities* / Richard Handler and Daniel Segal. c1990
   PR4038.P6H36 1990   [Table XXXII: .P6=Political   and   social views]

14. *Mark Twain's Own Autobiography : The Chapters from the North American Review* / with an introduction and notes by Michael J. Kiskis. c1990
   PS1331.A2 1990   [Table XXXI: .A2=Autobiography]

GLOSSARY[1]

Access point. A name, term, code, etc. under which a bibliographic record may be searched and identified. *See also* Heading.

Added entry. An entry, additional to the main entry, by which an item is represented in a catalog; a secondary entry. *See also* Main entry.

Alphabetical catalog. *See* Dictionary catalog.

Alphabetical specific catalog. A catalog containing subject entries based on the principle of specific and direct entry and arranged alphabetically. *See also* Alphabetico-classed catalog; Classed catalog; Dictionary catalog.

Alphabetico-classed catalog. A subject catalog in which entries are listed under broad subjects and subdivided hierarchically by topics. The entries on each level of the hierarchy are arranged alphabetically. *See also* Alphabetical specific catalog; Classed catalog; Dictionary catalog.

Analytical entry. An entry for a part of an item for which a comprehensive entry is also made.

Analytico-synthetic scheme. *See* Faceted scheme.

Anonymous. Of unknown authorship.

Area. A major section of the bibliographic description, comprising data elements of a particular category or set of categories. *See also* Element.

Array. A group of coordinate subjects on the same level of a hierarchical structure, e.g., oranges, lemons, limes, but not citrus fruit.

[1]The following works were used in compiling this glossary:

The ALA Glossary of Library and Information Science. Heartsill Young, ed. Chicago: American Library Association, 1983.

Anglo-American Cataloguing Rules. 2nd ed., 1988 revision. Prepared under the direction of the Joint Steering Committee for Revision of AACR, a committee of: the American Library Association, the Australian Committee on Cataloguing, the British Library, the Canadian Committee on Cataloguing, the Library Association, the Library of Congress. Michael Gorman and Paul W. Winkler, eds. Chicago: American Library Association, 1988.

Lois Mai Chan. *Library of Congress Subject Headings: Principles and Application.* 2nd ed. Littleton, Colo.: Libraries Unlimited, 1986.

Melvil Dewey. *Dewey Decimal Classification and Relative Index.* Ed. 20. John P. Comaromi, ed., Julianne Beall, Winton E. Matthews, Jr., and Gregory R. New, assistant eds. Albany, N.Y.: Forest Press, a Division of OCLC Online Computer Library Center, Inc., 1989. 4 vols.

Consult these works for definitions of other terms.

Author. *See* Personal author.

Author number. A combination of letters or figures, or both, representing the name of an author in a call number. *See also* Item number.

Author-title added entry. *See* Name-title added entry.

Author-title reference. *See* Name-title reference.

Authority control. The process of maintaining consistency in access points in a catalog.

Authority file. A collection of authority records.

Authority record. *See* Name authority record; Subject authority record.

Bibliographic classification. *See* Close classification.

Bibliographic control. The operation or process by which recorded information is organized or arranged and thereby made readily retrievable. The term covers a range of bibliographic activities, including complete records of bibliographic items as published, standardization of bibliographic description, and provision of physical access through consortia, networks, or other cooperative endeavors.

Bibliographic description. The description of a bibliographic item, consisting of information, including title and statement of responsibility, edition, publication and manufacturing, physical description, notes of useful information, and standard numbers, that together uniquely identifies the item.

Bibliographic file. A collection of bibliographic records.

Bibliographic record. A record containing details with regard to identification, physical and other characteristics, and subject access information of a bibliographic item. In a catalog, it is also called a cataloging record.

Bibliographic utility. A processing center or network providing services based on machine-readable cataloging data.

Biographical heading. A subject heading used with biographies which consists of the name of a class of persons with appropriate subdivisions, e.g., **Physicians—California—Biography; Poets, American—19th century—Biography**.

Book number. *See* Item number.

Boolean operations. Logical or algebraic operations, formulated by George Boole, involving variables with two values, such as value 1 *and* value 2, value 1 *or* value 2, and value 1 but *not* value 2. Used in information retrieval to combine terms or sets, e.g., Children *and* Television, Children *or* Young adults, Children *not* Infants.

Broad classification. (1) A classification scheme that does not provide for minute subdivision of topics. (2) Arrangement of works in conformity with the provisions of such a scheme. *See also* Close classification.

Call number. A composite symbol consisting of the class number, book or item number, and sometimes other data, such as the date, volume number, and copy number, which provides identification of an individual item and its shelf location.

Cartographic material. Any material representing the whole or part of the earth or any celestial body at any scale; cartographic materials include two- and three-dimensional maps and plans (including maps of imaginary places); aeronautical, navigational, and celestial charts; atlases; globes; block diagrams; sections; aerial photographs with a cartographic purpose; bird's-eye views (map views); etc.

Catalog. (1) A list of library materials contained in a collection, a library, or group of libraries arranged according to some definite plan. (2) In a wider sense, a list of materials prepared for a particular purpose, e.g., an exhibition catalog or a sales catalog.

Cataloging copy. A cataloging record prepared by an agency to be used by other agencies or libraries.

Cataloging record. A basic unit in a catalog, containing cataloging data—bibliographic description, subject headings, and call number—of a particular item. The record may be displayed in different forms, such as a machine-readable record or a catalog card.

Centralized cataloging. The preparation of cataloging records by one agency to be used by other agencies or libraries. *See also* Shared cataloging.

Chain. A series of subject terms each from a different level of a hierarchy, arranged either from general to specific or vice versa.

Characteristic of division. *See* Facet.

Chief source of information. The source of bibliographic data to be given preference as the source from which a bibliographic description (or portion thereof) is prepared.

Chronological subdivision. A subdivision showing the period or span of time treated in a work or the period during which the work appeared. *Also called* Period subdivision.

Citation order. The order by which the facets or elements of a compound or complex subject are arranged in a subject heading or class number.

Class. (1) *(noun)* A group of objects exhibiting one or more common characteristics, usually identified by a specific notation in a classification scheme. (2) *(verb)* To assign a class number to an individual work. *See also* Classify (2); Classification.

Class entry. A subject entry consisting of a string of hierarchically related terms beginning with the broadest term and leading to the subject in question, in the form of a chain.

Class number. Notation that designates the class to which a given item belongs.

Classed catalog.   A subject catalog consisting of class entries arranged logically according to a systematic scheme of classification. *Also called* Class catalog; Classified subject catalog; Systematic catalog. *See also* Alphabetical specific catalog; Alphabetico-classed catalog; Dictionary catalog.

Classification.   A logical system for the arrangement of knowledge.

Classificationist.   A person who designs or develops a classification system or one who engages in the philosophy and theory of classification.

Classifier.   A person who applies a classification system to a body of knowledge or a collection of documents.

Classify.   (1) To arrange a collection of items according to a classification system. (2) To assign a class number to an individual item. *Also called* Class.

Close classification.   (1) A classification providing for minute subdivision of topics. *Also called* Bibliographic classification. (2) Arrangement of works in conformity with the provisions of such a scheme. *See also* Broad classification.

Coextensive heading.   A heading that represents precisely (not more generally or specifically than) the subject content of a work.

Collaborator.   One who works with one or more associates to produce a work; all may make the same kind of contribution, as in the case of shared responsibility, or they may make different kinds of contributions, as in the case of collaboration between an artist and a writer. *See also* Mixed responsibility; Shared responsibility.

Collection.   (1) Three or more independent works or parts of works by one author published together. (2) Two or more independent works or parts of works by more than one author published together and not written for the same occasion or for the publication in hand.

Collective biography.   A work consisting of two or more life histories. *See also* Individual biography.

Collective title.   A title proper that is an inclusive title for an item containing several works. *See also* Uniform title (3).

Compiler.   (1) One who produces a collection by selecting and putting together matter from the works of various persons or bodies. (2) One who selects and puts together in one publication matter from the works of one person or body. *See also* Editor.

Completely revised schedule.   Previously called *phoenix schedule,* a term used in the Dewey Decimal Classification meaning a completely new development of the schedule for a specific discipline. Except by chance, only the basic number for the discipline remains the same as in previous editions; all other numbers are freely reused.

Compound surname.   A surname consisting of two or more proper names, sometimes connected by a hyphen, conjunction, and/or preposition.

Conference. (1) A meeting of individuals or representatives of various bodies for the purpose of discussing and/or acting on topics of common interest. (2) A meeting of representatives of a corporate body that constitutes its legislative or governing body.

Content designation. A system of special codes (tags, indicators, and subfield codes) in a USMARC record used for the purpose of identifying a particular unit of information. *See also* Tag; Indicator; Subfield code.

Continuation. (1) A supplement. (2) A part issued in continuance of a monograph, a serial, or a series.

Controlled vocabulary. In subject analysis and retrieval, the use of an authorized subset of the language as indexing terms.

Conventional name. A name, other than the real or official name, by which a corporate body, place, or thing has come to be known.

Conventional title. *See* Uniform title.

Cooperative cataloging. *See* Shared cataloging.

Copy cataloging. The process of adapting an existing catalog record prepared by another library or agency. *See also* Original cataloging.

Corporate body. An organization or group of persons that is identified by a particular name and that acts, or may act, as an entity. Typical examples of corporate bodies are associations, institutions, business firms, nonprofit enterprises, governments, government agencies, religious bodies, local churches, and conferences.

Cross-classification. Placing works on the same subject in two different class numbers when a given work deals with two or more subdivisions of a subject, with each subdivision representing a different characteristic of division. Such a situation creates the possibility of inconsistent classification. Example: A work on weaving cotton cloth deals with two subdivisions of textile technology, cotton (material) and weaving (process), and may be classed with either. *See also* Citation order.

Cross-reference. *See* Reference.

Delimiter. A code (represented by the symbol ‡ or $) used to identify a subfield in a USMARC record.

Descriptive cataloging. That part of cataloging consisting of the presentation of bibliographic description and the determination of access points through personal names, corporate names, and titles.

Dictionary catalog. A catalog in which all the entries (author, title, subject, series, etc.) and the cross-references are interfiled in one alphabetical sequence. The subject entries in a dictionary catalog are based on the principle of specific and direct entry. *Also called* Alphabetical catalog. *See also* Alphabetical specific catalog; Alphabetico-classed catalog; Classed catalog.

Direct subdivision. Geographic subdivision of subject headings by the name of a local place without interposition of the name of a larger geographic entity. *See also* Geographic subdivision; Indirect subdivision.

Directory.   In the USMARC record, a series of entries that contain the MARC tag, length, and starting location of each variable field within the record.

Duplicate entry.   Entry of the same subject heading in two different forms, e.g., **United States—Foreign relations—France** and **France—Foreign relations—United States**.

Edition: Books, pamphlets, fascicles, single sheets, etc.   All copies produced from essentially the same type image (whether by direct contact or by photographic or other methods) and issued by the same entity. *See also* Reprint.

Editor.   One who prepares for publication an item not his or her own. The editorial work may be limited to the preparation of the item for the manufacturer, or it may include supervision of the manufacturing, revision (restitution), or elucidation of the content of the item and the addition of an introduction, notes, and other critical matter. In some cases, it may involve the technical direction of a staff of persons engaged in creating or compiling the content of the item. *See also* Compiler.

Element.   A word, phrase, or group of characters representing a distinct unit of bibliographic information and forming part of an area (q.v.) of the description.

Entry.   A record of an item in a catalog. *See also* Heading.

Entry word.   The word by which an entry is arranged in the catalog, usually the first word (other than an article) of the heading. *See also* Heading.

Enumerative scheme.   A classification scheme or subject headings system which lists subjects and their subdivisions and provides ready-made class marks or compound headings for them. *See also* Faceted scheme.

Explanatory reference.   An elaborated *see* or *see also* reference that explains the circumstances under which the headings involved should be consulted.

Facet.   A component (based on a particular characteristic) of a complex subject, e.g., geographic facet, language facet, literary form facet.

Facet analysis.   The division of a subject into its component parts (facets). Each array of a facet consists of parts based on the same characteristic, e.g., English language, French language, German language, etc.

Faceted scheme.   A classification scheme that identifies subjects by their component parts and requires fitting together the appropriate parts in order to provide a class mark for a work. For example, the Colon Classification is a faceted scheme, while the Dewey Decimal

Classification is partially so. *Also called* Analytico-synthetic scheme. *See also* Enumerative scheme.

Field.   A unit of data in a USMARC record, identified by a three-character numeric tag.

Field terminator.   A symbol used to signal the end of a field in a USMARC record.

Fixed field.   A field with a fixed (i.e., predetermined) length in a US-MARC record. *See also* Variable field.

Fixed location.   System of marking and arranging library materials by shelf and book marks so that their absolute position in room or tier and on the shelf is always the same.

Form heading.   A heading representing the physical, bibliographic, artistic, or literary form of a work, e.g., **Encyclopedias and dictionaries, Essays, Short stories, String quartets.**

Form subdivision.   A division of a class number or subject heading which brings out the form of the work, e.g., **–03** and **–05** in Dewey Decimal Classification, **—Dictionaries** and **—Periodicals** in Library of Congress Subject Headings.

Free-floating subdivision.   A subdivision that may be used by a cataloger at the Library of Congress under any existing appropriate subject heading for the first time without establishing the usage editorially.

Free text.   The use of natural language in information retrieval. *See also* Controlled vocabulary.

General material designation (GMD).   A term indicating the broad class of material to which an item belongs (e.g., sound recording).

General reference.   A blanket reference to a group of headings rather than a particular heading. *See also* Specific reference.

Geographic qualifier.   The name of a larger geographic entity added to a local place name, e.g., **Cambridge (Mass.), Toledo (Spain).**

Geographic subdivision.   A subdivision by the name of a place to which the subject represented by the main heading is limited. *See also* Direct subdivision; Indirect subdivision.

GMD.   *See* General material designation.

Half-title.   A title of a publication appearing on a leaf preceding the title page.

Heading.   A name, word, or phrase placed at the head of a catalog entry to provide an access point. *See also* Access point; Entry; Entry word.

Hierarchy.   The arrangement of disciplines and subjects in an order ranging from the most general to the most specific.

Imprint.   *See* Publication, distribution, etc. area.

Indicator.   One of two character positions at the beginning of each variable data field in a USMARC record containing values that interpret or supplement the data found in the field.

Indirect subdivision.   Geographic subdivision of a subject heading with the interposition of a larger geographic entity between the main heading and the local subdivision. *See also* Direct subdivision.

Individual biography.   A work devoted to the life of a single person. *See also* Collective biography.

Integrity of numbers.   The policy of maintaining the stability of numbers in a classification scheme. Such a policy is opposed to revision, especially when the relocation of a subject is involved.

International Standard Bibliographic Description.   An internationally agreed on standard format for representing bibliographic information.

International Standard Book Number (ISBN).   An internationally agreed on standard number that identifies a book uniquely.

International Standard Serial Number (ISSN).   An internationally agreed on standard number that identifies a serial publication uniquely.

Item.   A document or set of documents in any physical form, published, issued, or treated as an entity, and as such forming the basis for a single bibliographic description.

Item number.   That part of a call number which designates a specific individual work within its class. May consist of the author number and/or other elements such as a work mark and an edition mark. An item number for a book is also called a book number.

Key heading.   In Sears subject headings, a heading that serves as a model of subdivisions for headings in the same category.

Key title.   The unique name assigned to a serial by the International Serials Data System (ISDS).

Kit.   (1) An item containing two or more categories of material, no one of which is identifiable as the predominant constituent of the item. *Also called* multimedia item. (2) A single-medium package of textual material (e.g., a lab kit, a set of activity cards).

Leader.   Data elements (numbers or coded values identified by relative character position) that provide information for the processing of the MARC record.

Literary warrant.   (1) The principle which allows a category to exist in a classification or thesaurus only if a work exists for that category. (2) The use of an actual collection or holdings of a library or actual published works as the basis for developing a classification scheme or thesaurus.

Local subdivision.   *See* Geographic subdivision.

Machine-readable cataloging.   *See* MARC.

Main entry.   The complete catalog record of an item, presented in the form by which the entity is to be uniformly identified and cited. The main entry may include the tracing(s) (q.v.). *See also* Added entry.

Main heading.   In subject headings, the first part of a heading excluding subdivisions.

MARC (*machine-readable cataloging*).   A system in which cataloging records are prepared in a format that enables the computer to recognize the elements and manipulate them for various purposes.

MARC record.   A catalog record in machine-readable form.

Microfiche.   A sheet of film bearing a number of microimages in a two-dimensional array.

Microfilm.   A length of film bearing a number of microimages in linear array.

Microform.   A generic term for any medium, transparent or opaque, bearing microimages.

Mixed authorship.   *See* Mixed responsibility.

Mixed notation.   A notational system using a combination of two or more kinds of symbols, e.g., letters and numerals.

Mixed responsibility.   A work in which different persons or bodies contribute to its intellectual or artistic content by performing different kinds of activities (e.g., adapting or illustrating a work written by another person). *See also* Collaborator; Shared responsibility.

Mnemonics.   Recurring concepts denoted by the same notational symbols in a classification scheme.

Model heading.   *See* Pattern heading.

Monograph.   A nonserial item (i.e., an item either complete in one part or complete, or intended to be completed, in a finite number of separate parts).

Monographic series.   *See* Series (1).

Multimedia item.   *See* Kit (1).

Multipart item.   A monograph complete, or intended to be completed, in a finite number of separate parts.

Name authority file.   A collection of name authority records.

Name authority record.   A record that shows a personal, corporate, or geographic heading in its established form, cites the authorities consulted in determining the choice of form of name, and indicates the references made to the heading. *See also* Subject authority record.

Name-title added entry.   An added entry consisting of the name of a person or corporate body and the title of an item.

Name-title reference.   A reference made from the name of a person or a corporate body and the title of an item.

Network.   (1) Two or more organizations engaged in a common pattern of information exchange through communications links, for some common objectives. (2) An interconnected or interrelated group of nodes.

Notation.   Numerals, letters, and/or other symbols used to represent the main and subordinate divisions of a classification scheme. *See also* Mixed notation; Pure notation.

Notational synthesis.   *See* Number building.

Number building. The process of making a class number more specific through addition of segments taken from auxiliary tables and/or other parts of the classification. *See also* Synthesis.

Online catalog. A catalog based on MARC records accessible in an interactive mode.

Original cataloging. The preparation of a cataloging record without the assistance of outside cataloging agencies. *See also* Copy cataloging.

Other title information. A title borne by an item other than the title proper or parallel or series title(s); also any phrase appearing in conjunction with the title proper, etc., indicative of the character, contents, etc. of the item or the motives for, or occasion of, its production or publication. The term includes subtitles, avant titres, etc. but does not include variations (e.g., spine titles, sleeve titles) on the title proper (q.v.).

Parallel title. The title proper in another language and/or script recorded in the title and statement of responsibility area.

Part. (1) One of the subordinate units into which an item has been divided by the author, publisher, or manufacturer. In the case of printed monographs, generally synonymous with volume; it is distinguished from a fascicle by being a component unit rather than a temporary division of a work. (2) As used in the physical description area, part designates bibliographic units intended to be bound several to a volume.

Pattern heading. A subject heading that serves as a model of subdivisions for headings in the same category. Subdivisions listed under a pattern heading may be used whenever appropriate under other headings in the same category. For example, **Shakespeare, William, 1594-1616** serves as a pattern heading for literary authors, and **Piano** serves as a pattern heading for musical instruments. *Also called* Model heading.

Period subdivision. *See* Chronological subdivision.

Personal author. The person chiefly responsible for the creation of the intellectual or artistic content of a work.

Phoenix schedule. *See* Completely revised schedule.

Phonorecord. *See* Sound recording.

Plate. A leaf containing illustrative matter, with or without explanatory text, that does not form part of either the preliminary or the main sequences of pages or leaves.

Post-coordination. Combination of individual concepts into compound or complex subjects at the point of retrieval. *See also* Pre-coordination.

Pre-coordination. Combination of individual concepts into compound or complex subjects at the point of storage. *See also* Post-coordination.

Preliminaries.   The title page or pages of an item, together with the verso of each title page, any pages preceding the title page or title pages, and the cover.

Publication, distribution, etc. area.   An area in bibliographic description giving details regarding the manufacturing and distribution of a bibliographic item. Such details include place, name, and date. For a printed item, it is called imprint.

Pure notation.   A notational system using one kind of symbol only, e.g., arabic numerals or letters.

Qualifier.   A term (enclosed in parentheses) placed after a name heading or subject heading for the purpose of distinguishing between homographs or clarifying the meaning of the heading, e.g., **Paris (France), Indexing (Machineshop practice), PL/I (Computer program language), Mont Blanc (Freighter), Novgorod (Russia : Duchy).** *See also* Geographic qualifier.

Record.   A unit in a file or database. *See also* Bibliographic record; Cataloging record; Name authority record; Subject authority record.

Record terminator.   A symbol used to signal the end of a USMARC record.

Refer from reference.   An indication of the terms of headings *from* which references are to be made to a given heading. It is the reverse of the indication of a *see* or *see also* reference and is represented by the symbols *UF* (used for) or *x* (*see* reference from), and *BT* (broader term) and *RT* (related term), or *xx* (*see also* reference from). In the MARC authority record, these terms are stored in fields *4XX* and *5XX*.

Reference.   A direction from one heading or entry to another. *See also* Refer from reference; *See* reference; and *see also* reference.

Reference source.   Any publication from which authoritative information may be obtained. Not limited to reference works.

Relative location.   The arrangement of library materials according to their relations to each other and regardless of their locations on the shelves.

Relocation.   An adjustment in a classification system resulting in the shifting of a topic between successive editions from one number to another.

Reprint.   (1) A new printing of an item made from the original type image, commonly by photographic methods. The reprint may reproduce the original exactly (an impression), or it may contain minor but well-defined variations (an issue). (2) A new edition with substantially unchanged text.

Secondary entry.   *See* Added entry.

***See also* reference.**   A reference from a heading to a less comprehensive or otherwise related heading.

See **reference.**   A reference from a term or name not used as a heading to one that is used.

Segmentation.   The practice of breaking down a long Dewey Decimal class number into shorter segments. Libraries that decide to use shorter numbers can then cut off the long number at designated points, e.g., 574.1'92'05.

Serial.   A publication in any medium issued in successive parts bearing numeric or chronologic designations and intended to be continued indefinitely. Serials include periodicals; newspapers; annuals (reports, yearbooks, etc.); the journals, memoirs, proceedings, transactions, etc. of societies; and numbered monographic series. *See also* Series (1).

Series.   (1) A group of separate items related to one another by the fact that each item bears, in addition to its own title proper, a collective title applying to the group as a whole. The individual items may or may not be numbered. (2) Each of two or more volumes of essays, lectures, articles, or other writings, similar in character and issued in sequence, (e.g., Lowell's *Among My Books,* second series). (3) A separately numbered sequence of volumes within a series or serial, (e.g., *Notes and Queries,* 1st series, 2nd series, etc.). *See also* Serial.

Shared authorship.   *See* Shared responsibility.

Shared cataloging.   The preparation by one of several participating agencies or libraries of a cataloging record which is made available to the other participating agencies or libraries. *Also called* Cooperative cataloging. *See also* Centralized cataloging.

Shared responsibility.   Collaboration between two or more persons or bodies performing the same kind of activity in the creation of the content of an item. The contributions of each may form a separate and distinct part of the item, or the contribution of each may not be separable from that of the other(s). *See also* Collaborator; Mixed responsibility.

Shelflist.   A file of cataloging records arranged by call number.

Specific entry.   Entry of a work under a heading that expresses its special subject or topic as distinguished from an entry for the class or broad subject which encompasses that special subject or topic.

Specific reference.   A reference from one heading to another. *See also* General reference.

Standard subdivision.   In Dewey Decimal Classification, a subdivision that represents a frequently recurring physical form (dictionaries, periodicals, etc.) or approach (history, research, etc.) applicable to any subject or discipline.

Statement of responsibility.   A statement, transcribed from the item being described, relating to persons responsible for the intellectual or artistic content of the item, to corporate bodies from which the content emanates, or to persons or corporate bodies responsible for the performance of the content of the item.

Subdivision.   The device of extending a subject heading by indicating one of its aspects—form, place, period, topic. *See also* Form subdivision; Geographic subdivision; Chronological subdivision; Topical subdivision.

Subfield.   A subunit within a field in a USMARC record.

Subfield code.   A two-character code identifying a subfield in the MARC record, consisting of a delimiter (‡) followed by a data element identifier (a lowercase alphabetic or numeric character).

Subject.   The theme or topic treated by the author in a work, whether stated in the title or not.

Subject analysis.   The process of identifying the intellectual content of a work. The results may be displayed in a catalog or bibliography by means of notational symbols as in a classification system or by verbal terms such as subject headings or indexing terms.

Subject analytical entry.   A subject entry made for a part of a work.

Subject authority file.   A collection of subject authority records.

Subject authority record.   A record of a subject heading that shows its established form, cites the authorities consulted in determining the choice and form of the heading, and indicates the cross-references made to and from the heading. *See also* Name authority record.

Subject catalog.   A catalog consisting of subject entries only; the subject portion of a divided catalog.

Subject cataloging.   (1) The process of providing subject access points to bibliographic records. (2) The process of assigning subject headings.

Subject entry.   An entry in a catalog or a bibliography under a heading which indicates the subject of an item.

Subject heading.   The term (a word or a group of words) denoting a subject under which all material on that subject is entered in a catalog.

Subject-to-name reference.   A reference from a subject heading to a name heading for the purpose of directing the user's attention from a particular field of interest to names of individuals or corporate bodies that are active or associated in some way with the field.

Subordinate body.   A corporate body that forms an integral part of a larger body in relation to which it holds an inferior hierarchical rank.

Subseries.   A series within a series (i.e., a series that always appears in conjunction with another, usually more comprehensive, series of which it forms a section). Its title may or may not be dependent on the title of the main series.

Superimposition. The policy of adopting a new catalog code while leaving headings derived from an earlier code unrevised.

Syndetic device. The device used to connect related headings by means of cross-references.

Synthesis. The process of composing a class number, subject heading, or indexing term by combining various elements in order to represent a compound or complex subject. *See also* Number building.

Tag. A three-character numeric code that identifies a field in a US-MARC record.

Title. A word, phrase, character, or group of characters, normally appearing in an item, that names the item or the work contained in it. *See also* Title proper; Uniform title.

Title proper. The chief name of an item, including any alternative title but excluding parallel titles and other title information.

Topical subdivision. A subdivision that represents an aspect of the main subject other than form, place, or period. *See also* Form subdivision; Geographic subdivision; Chronological subdivision.

Tracing. (1) The record of the headings under which an item is represented in a catalog. (2) The record of the references that have been made to a name or to the title of an item that is represented in a catalog.

Uniform heading. The particular heading by which a subject or person that may be represented by different names or different forms of a name is to be listed in the catalog.

Uniform title. (1) The particular title by which a work is to be identified for cataloging purposes. (2) The particular title used to distinguish the heading for a work from the heading for a different work. (3) A conventional collective title used to collocate publications of an author, composer, or corporate body containing several works or extracts, etc. from several works (e.g., complete works, several works in a particular literary or musical form).

Union catalog. A catalog representing the holdings of a group of libraries.

Unique heading. A heading that represents only one person, corporate body, or subject.

Unit card. A basic unit in a card catalog containing the bibliographic record of an item, showing the main entry heading, bibliographic description in several short paragraphs, the tracings for subject and added entries, and various control numbers.

Variable field. A field with variable length in a USMARC record. *See also* Fixed field.

Verso of the title page. The back side of the title page.

Work mark. A part of call number based on the title of a work. *See also* Item number; Call number.

BIBLIOGRAPHY

ALA Filing Rules. Chicago: American Library Association, 1980.
ALA Glossary of Library and Information Science. Heartsill Young et al., ed. Chicago: American Library Association, 1983.
Aluri, Rao, D. Alasdair Kemp, and John J. Boll. *Subject Analysis in Online Catalogs.* Englewood, Colo.: Libraries Unlimited, 1991.
Anglo-American Cataloguing Rules. 2nd ed., 1988 revision. Prepared under the direction of the Joint Steering Committee for Revision of AACR, a committee of: the American Library Association, the Australian Committee on Cataloguing, the British Library, the Canadian Committee on Cataloguing, the Library Association, the Library of Congress. Michael Gorman and Paul W. Winkler, eds. Chicago: American Library Association, 1988.
Attig, John. "The USMARC Formats—Underlying Principles." *Information Technology and Libraries,* 1(2):169–174, June 1982.
Auld, Larry. "Authority Control: An Eighty-Year Review." *Library Resources & Technical Services,* **26**:319–330, October/December 1982.
Austin, Derek, and Jeremy A. Digger. "PRECIS: The Preserved Context Index System." *Library Resources & Technical Services,* **21**:13–30, Winter 1977.
Authority Control in the Online Environment: Considerations and Practices. Barbara B. Tillett, ed. New York: Haworth Press, 1989.
Avram, Henriette D. *MARC: Its History and Implications.* Washington: Library of Congress, 1975.
Bates, Marcia J. "Rethinking Subject Cataloging in the Online Environment." *Library Resources & Technical Services,* **33**:400–412, October 1989.
Bengtson, Betty, G. "Bibliographic Control." In Irene P. Godden, ed., *Library Technical Services.* 2nd ed. San Diego: Academic Press, 1991. Pp. 147–203.
Bliss, Henry Evelyn. *Bliss Bibliographic Classification.* 2nd ed. J. Mills and Vanda Broughton, eds., with the assistance of Valerie Lang. London; Boston: Butterworths, 1977–.
Bliss, Henry Evelyn. *A System of Bibliographic Classification.* 2nd rev. ed. New York: H. W. Wilson Company, 1936.

Bliss, Henry Evelyn. *The Organization of Knowledge in Libraries*. 2nd ed. New York: H. W. Wilson Company, 1939.

Boll, John. "The Future of AACR2 (In the OPAC Environment)." *Cataloging & Classification Quarterly*, **12**(1):3–34, 1990.

British Museum. Department of Printed Books. *Rules for Compiling the Catalogues of Printed Books, Maps and Music in the British Museum*. Rev. ed. London: British Museum; printed by order of the Trustees, 1936.

Brown, James Duff. *Subject Classification for the Arrangement of Libraries and the Organization of Information, with Tables, Indexes, etc., for the Subdivision of Subjects*. 3rd ed. Revised and enlarged by J. D. Stewart. London: Grafton & Co., 1939.

Buckland, Michael K. "Bibliography, Library Records, and the Redefinition of the Library Catalog." *Library Resources & Technical Services*, **32**:299–311, October 1988.

Byrne, Deborah J. *MARC Manual: Understanding and Using MARC Records*. Englewood, Colo.: Libraries Unlimited, 1991.

Cataloging & Classification Quarterly, **1**(1)–, Fall 1980–.

Cataloging Rules: Author and Title Entries. American ed. Chicago: American Library Association, 1980.

Cataloging Service. Bulletin 1-125, June 1945–Spring 1978.

Cataloging Service Bulletin, No. 1–, Summer 1978–. Published quarterly.

Chan, Lois Mai. "Functions of a Subject Authority File." In *Subject Authorities in the Online Environment: Papers from a Conference Program Held in San Francisco, June 29, 1987*. Karen Markey Drabenstott, ed. Chicago: American Library Association, 1991. Pp. 9–30.

Chan, Lois Mai. *Immroth's Guide to the Library of Congress Classification*. 4th ed. Englewood, Colo.: Libraries Unlimited, 1990.

Chan, Lois Mai. "Library of Congress Classification as an Online Retrieval Tool: Potentials and Limitations." *Information Technology and Libraries* 5:181-92, September 1986.

Chan, Lois Mai. *Library of Congress Subject Headings: Principles and Application*. 2nd ed. Littleton, Colo.: Libraries Unlimited, 1986.

Chan, Lois Mai, and Theodora Hodges. "Subject Cataloguing and Classification: The Late 1980s and Beyond." In Michael Gorman et al., eds., *Technical Services Today and Tomorrow*. Englewood, Colo.: Libraries Unlimited, 1990. Pp. 74–85.

Clack, Doris Hargrett. *Authority Control: Principles, Applications, and Instructions*. Chicago: American Library Association, 1990.

Classification of Library Materials: Current and Future Potential for Providing Access. Betty G. Bengtson and Janet Swan Hill, eds. New York: Neal-Schuman, 1990.

Coates, Eric. *Subject Catalogues: Headings and Structure*. London: Library Association, 1988.

Cochrane, Pauline A. "Universal Bibliographic Control: Its Role in the

Availability of Information and Knowledge." *Library Resources & Technical Services*, **34**(4):423–431, October 1990.

Comaromi, John P. *Book Numbers: A Historical Study and Practical Guide to Their Use.* Littleton, Colo.: Libraries Unlimited, 1981.

Comaromi, John P. "Conception and Development of the Dewey Decimal Classification." *International Classification*, 3:11–15, 1976.

Comaromi, John P. *The Eighteen Editions of the Dewey Decimal Classification.* Albany, N.Y.: Forest Press Division, Lake Placid Education Foundation, 1976.

Combined Indexes to the Library of Congress Classification Schedules. Compiled by Nancy B. Olson. Washington: U.S. Historical Documents Institute, Inc., 1974.

The Conceptual Foundations of Descriptive Cataloging. Elaine Svenonius, ed. San Diego, Calif.: Academic Press, 1989.

Crawford, Walt. *MARC for Library Use: Understanding Integrated US-MARC.* Boston: G. K. Hall & Co., 1989.

Cutter, Charles A. *Expansive Classification: Part 1: The First Six Classifications.* Boston: C. A. Cutter, 1891–1893.

Cutter, Charles A. *C. A. Cutter's Three-Figure Author Table.* Swanson-Swift revision. Chicopee, Mass.: H. R. Huntting Company, 1969.

Cutter, Charles A. *C. A. Cutter's Two-Figure Author Table.* Swanson-Swift revision. Chicopee, Mass.: H. R. Huntting Company, 1969.

Cutter, Charles A. *Cutter-Sanborn Three-Figure Author Table.* Swanson-Swift revision. Chicopee, Mass.: H. R. Huntting Company, 1969.

Cutter, Charles A. *Rules for a Dictionary Catalog.* 4th ed. Rewritten. Washington: Government Printing Office, 1904. Republished, London: The Library Association, 1953. First published under the title *Rules for a Printed Dictionary Catalogue* in 1876.

Dewey, Melvil. *Abridged Dewey Decimal Classification and Relative Index.* Ed. 12. John P. Comaromi, ed., Julianne Beall, Winton E. Matthews, Jr., and Gregory R. New, assistant eds. Albany, N.Y.: Forest Press, Division of OCLC Online Computer Library Center, Inc., 1990.

Dewey, Melvil. *Dewey Decimal Classification and Relative Index.* Ed. 20. John P. Comaromi, ed., Julianne Beall, Winton E. Matthews, Jr., and Gregory R. New, assistant eds. Albany, N.Y.: Forest Press, Division of OCLC Online Computer Library Center, Inc., 1989.

Dhyani, Pushpa. "Colon Classification Edition 7—An Appraisal." *International Classification*, **15**(1):13–16, 1988.

Dunkin, Paul S. *Cataloging U.S.A.* Chicago: American Library Association, 1969.

Dykstra, Mary. *PRECIS: A Primer.* Revised reprint. Metuchen, N.J., and London: Scarecrow Press, 1987.

Foskett, A. C. *The Subject Approach to Information.* 4th ed. Hamden, Conn.: Linnet Books; London: Clive Bingley, 1982.

Foundations of Cataloging: A Sourcebook. Michael Carpenter and Elaine Svenonius, eds. Littleton, Colo.: Libraries Unlimited, 1985.

Gorman, Michael. *"AACR2R:* Editor's Perspective." *Library Resources & Technical Services,* **33**(2):181–186, April 1989.

Gorman, Michael. "Descriptive Cataloguing: Its Past, Present, and Future." In Michael Gorman et al., eds., *Technical Services Today and Tomorrow.* Englewood, Colo.: Libraries Unlimited, 1990. Pp. 63–73.

Gorman, Michael. *The Concise AACR2, 1988 Revision.* Chicago: American Library Association, 1989.

Gorman, Michael. "Yesterday's Heresy—Today's Orthodoxy: An Essay on the Changing Face of Descriptive Cataloging (Views of Cutter and Panizzi)." *College & Research Libraries,* **50**:626–634, November 1989.

Hagler, Ronald. *The Bibliographic Record and Information Technology.* 2nd ed. Chicago: American Library Association, 1991.

Hamdy, M. Nabil. *The Concept of Main Entry as Represented in the Anglo-American Cataloging Rules: A Critical Appraisal with Some Suggestions: Author Main Entry vs. Title Main Entry.* Littleton, Colo.: Libraries Unlimited, 1973.

Hanson, J. C. M. "The Library of Congress and Its New Catalogue: Some Unwritten History." In *Essays Offered to Herbert Putnam by His Colleagues and Friends on His Thirtieth Anniversary as Librarian of Congress: 5 April 1929.* New Haven: Yale University Press, 1929.

Haykin, David Judson. *Subject Headings: A Practical Guide.* Washington: Government Printing Office, 1951.

Henderson, Kathryn Luther. "'Treated with a Degree of Uniformity and Common Sense': Descriptive Cataloging in the United States— 1876–1975." *Library Trends,* **25**:227–271, July 1976.

Hildreth, Charles. "Beyond Boolean: Designing the Next Generation of Online Catalogs." *Library Trends,* **35**:647–667, Spring 1987.

Holley, Robert P. "Subject Cataloguing in the USA." *International Cataloguing,* **14**:43–45, October 1985.

Hunter, Eric J. *Examples Illustrating AACR2, 1988 Revision.* London: Library Association, 1989.

An Index to the Library of Congress Classification. J. McRee Elrod, Judy Inouye, and Ann Craig Turner, eds. Ottawa: Canadian Library Association, 1974.

International Conference on Cataloguing Principles, Paris, 1961. *Report of International Conference on Cataloguing Principles.* A. H. Chaplin and Dorothy Anderson, eds. London: Organizing Committee of the International Conference on Cataloguing Principles, 1963; London: Bingley on behalf of IFLA, 1969.

International Conference on Cataloguing Principles, Paris, 1961. *Statement of Principles.* Annotated ed. Provisional ed. Commentary and examples by A. H. Chaplin and Dorothy Anderson. Sevenoaks (Kent): International Federation of Library Associations Secretariat, 1966.

International Federation of Library Associations. Working Group on the General International Bibliographic Description. *ISBD(G): International Standard Bibliographic Description (General): Annotated Text.* London: IFLA International Office for UBC, 1977.

Intner, Sheila S., and Jean Weihs. *Standard Cataloging for School and Public Libraries.* Englewood, Colo.: Libraries Unlimited, 1990.

Jewett, Charles C. *Smithsonian Report on the Construction of Catalogs of Libraries, and Their Publication by Means of Separate, Stereotyped Titles, with Rules and Examples.* 2nd ed. Washington: Smithsonian Institution, 1853. Reprinted, Ann Arbor, Mich.: University Microfilms, 1961.

Kelm, Carol R. "The Historical Development of the Second Edition of *Anglo-American Cataloguing Rules.*" *Library Resources & Technical Services,* **22**:22–33, Winter 1978.

LaMontagne, Leo E. *American Library Classification with Special Reference to the Library of Congress.* Hamden, Conn.: Shoe String Press, 1961.

Lehnus, Donald J. *Book Numbers: History, Principles, and Application.* Chicago: American Library Association, 1980.

Library of Congress. MARC Development Office. *Information on the MARC System.* 4th ed. Washington: Library of Congress, 1974.

Library of Congress. *Name Authorities Cumulative Microform Edition.* Washington: Library of Congress, 1977–. Also available on microfiche, in machine-readable form as *Name Authorities* (MARC tapes) and on CD-ROM as *CDMARC Names.*

Library of Congress. Network Development and MARC Standards Office. *Format Integration and Its Effect on the USMARC Bibliographic Format.* Washington: Library of Congress, Cataloging Distribution Service, 1988.

Library of Congress. Processing Department. *Studies of Descriptive Cataloging: A Report to the Librarian of Congress by the Director of the Processing Department.* Washington: Government Printing Office, 1946.

Library of Congress. Processing Services. *Library of Congress Filing Rules.* Prepared by John C. Rather and Susan C. Biebel. Washington: Library of Congress, 1980.

Library of Congress Rule Interpretations. 2nd ed. Washington: Cataloging Distribution Service, Library of Congress, 1989.

Library of Congress. *Rules for Descriptive Cataloging in the Library of Congress.* Adopted by the American Library Association. Washington: Library of Congress, 1949.

Library of Congress. Subject Cataloging Division. *Classification.* Washington: Library of Congress. 1901–.

Library of Congress. Subject Cataloging Division. *LC Classification—Additions and Changes.* Washington: Library of Congress. List 1–. March/May 1928–.

Library of Congress. Subject Cataloging Division. *LC Classification Outline.* 6th ed. Washington: Library of Congress, 1991.

Library of Congress. Subject Cataloging Division. *Library of Congress Classification Schedules: A Cumulation of Additions and Changes Through [year]* Rita Runchock and Kathleen Droste, eds. Detroit: Gale Research Co., 1974–. Published annually.

Library of Congress. Subject Cataloging Division. *Library of Congress Classification Schedules Combined with Additions and Changes Through [year].* Rita Runchock and Kathleen Droste, eds. Detroit: Gale Research Co., 1988–. Published annually.

Library of Congress. Subject Cataloging Division. *Library of Congress Subject Headings.* 8th ed.–. Washington: Cataloging Distribution Service, Library of Congress, 1975–. Published annually, with weekly updates issued quarterly. Also available on microfiche, in machine-readable form as *Subject Authorities* (MARC tapes) and on CD-ROM as *CDMARC Subjects.*

Library of Congress. Subject Cataloging Division. *Subject Cataloging Manual: Shelflisting.* Washington: Library of Congress, 1987.

Library of Congress. Subject Cataloging Division. *Subject Cataloging Manual: Subject Headings.* 4th ed. Washington: Cataloging Distribution Service, Library of Congress, 1991.

Library of Congress. Subject Cataloging Division. *Subject Headings Used in the Dictionary Catalogs of the Library of Congress.* 1st–7th eds. Washington: Library of Congress, 1914–1966.

Library of Congress Subject Headings: Principles of Structure and Policies for Application. Prepared by Lois Mai Chan for the Library of Congress. Washington: Library of Congress, 1990.

Library Resources & Technical Services, 1(1)–, Winter 1957–. Published quarterly.

List of Subject Headings for Use in a Dictionary Catalog. Prepared by a Committee of the American Library Association. Boston: Published for the ALA Publishing Section by the Library Bureau, 1895.

Lubetzky, Seymour. *Cataloging Rules and Principles: A Critique of the ALA Rules for Entry and a Proposed Design for Their Revision.* Washington: Library of Congress, 1953.

Lubetzky, Seymour. *Code of Cataloging Rules, Author and Title Entry: An Unfinished Draft.* Chicago: American Library Association, 1960.

Lubetzky, Seymour. "Principles of Descriptive Cataloging." In *Studies of Descriptive Cataloging.* Washington: Library of Congress, 1946. Pp. 25–33. Also in Michael Carpenter and Elaine Svenonius, eds., *Foundations of Cataloging: A Sourcebook.* Littleton, Colo.: Libraries Unlimited, 1985. Pp. 104–112.

Maltby, Arthur. *Sayers' Manual of Classification for Librarians.* 5th ed. London: Andre Deutsch, 1975.

MARC Format Integration: Three Perspectives. Michael Gorman, ed. Chicago: American Library Association, Library Information and Technology Association, 1990.

Markey, Karen. *Subject Searching in Library Catalogs Before and After the Introduction of Online Catalogs.* OCLC Library, Information and Computer Science Series No. 4. Dublin, Ohio: OCLC, 1984.

Markuson, Barbara Evans. "Bibliographic Systems, 1945–1976." *Library Trends,* **25**:311–327, July 1976.

Maxwell, Margaret F. *Handbook for AACR2 1988 Revision: Explaining and Illustrating the Anglo-American Cataloguing Rules.* Chicago: American Library Association, 1989.

McCallum, Sally H. "Format Integration Implementation Plans." *Information Technology and Libraries,* **9**:155–161, June 1990.

Miksa, Francis. *The Subject in the Dictionary Catalog from Cutter to the Present.* Chicago: American Library Association, 1983.

Miller, Rosalind E., and Jane C. Terwillegar. *Commonsense Cataloging: A Cataloger's Manual.* 4th ed. revised. New York: H. W. Wilson Co., 1990.

Mills, J. *A Modern Outline of Library Classification.* London: Chapman and Hall, 1967.

National Library of Medicine (U.S.). *Medical Subject Headings.* Bethesda, Md.: National Library of Medicine, distributed by National Technical Information Service, U.S. Dept. of Commerce, 1975–. Published annually.

National Library of Medicine (U.S.). *National Library of Medicine Classification: A Scheme for the Shelf Arrangement of Books in the Field of Medicine and Its Related Sciences.* 4th ed. revised. NIH Publication No. 81-1535. Bethesda, Md.: U.S. Department of Health and Human Services, Public Health Service, National Institutes of Health, National Library of Medicine, 1981.

NUC: Books. Washington: Library of Congress, 1983–. Microform.

The Online Catalogue: Developments and Directions. Charles Hildreth, ed. London: Library Association, 1989.

Osborn, Andrew D. "The Crisis in Cataloging." *Library Quarterly,* **11**:393–411, October 1941.

Osborn, Jeanne. *Dewey Decimal Classification, 20th Edition: A Study Manual.* Revised and edited by John P. Comaromi. Englewood, Colo.: Libraries Unlimited, 1991.

Panizzi, Sir Anthony, et al. "Rules for the Compilation of the Catalogue." In *Catalogue of Printed Books in the British Museum.* London: British Museum; printed by order of the trustees, 1841. Vol. 1, pp. v–ix.

Perreault, Jean. "Authority Control, Old and New." *Libri,* **32**:124–148, 1982.

Petersen, Toni, and Pat Molholt. *Beyond the Book: Extending MARC for Subject Access.* Boston: G. K. Hall & Co., 1990.

Pettee, Julia. *Subject Headings: The History and Theory of the Alphabetical Subject Approach to Books.* New York: H. W. Wilson Company, 1947.

Prevost, Marie Louise. "An Approach to Theory and Method in General Subject Heading." *Library Quarterly* 16:140-151, April 1946.

The Prussian Instructions: Rules for the alphabetical Catalogs of the Prussian Libraries. Trans. from the 2nd ed., authorized August 10, 1908, with an introduction and notes by Andrew D. Osborn. Ann Arbor, Mich.: University of Michigan Press, 1938.

Ranganathan, S. R. *Colon Classification.* Ed. 7, basic and depth version, revised. M. A. Gopinath, ed. Sarada Ranganathan Endowment for Library Science Series 19. Bangalore: Sarada Ranganathan Endowment for Library Science, 1987–.

Ranganathan, S. R. *Elements of Classification; Based on Lectures Delivered at the University of Bombay in December 1944 and in the School of Librarianship in Great Britain in December 1956.* 2nd ed., revised and rewritten. B. I. Palmer, ed. London: Association of Assistant Librarians, Section of the Library Association, 1959.

Satija, M. P. "A Critical Introduction to the 7th Edition (1987) of the Colon Classification." *Cataloging & Classification Quarterly,* **12**(2):125–138, 1990.

Saye, Jerry D., and Desretta V. McAllister-Harper. *Manheimer's Cataloging and Classification: A Workbook.* 3rd ed., revised and expanded. New York: Marcel Dekker, 1991.

Saye, Jerry D., and Sherry Vellucci. *Notes in the Catalog Record Based on AACR2 and LC Rule Interpretations.* Chicago: American Library Association, 1989.

Scott, Edith. "The Evolution of Bibliographic Systems in the United States, 1876–1945." *Library Trends,* 25:293–310, July 1976.

Sears List of Subject Headings. 14th ed. Martha T. Mooney, ed. New York: H. W. Wilson Company, 1991.

Sears, Minnie Earl. *List of Subject Headings for Small Libraries, Compiled from Lists Used in Nine Representative Small Libraries.* New York: H. W. Wilson Company; London: Grafton & Co., 1923.

Smiraglia, Richard P. *Music Cataloging: The Bibliographic Control of Printed and Recorded Music in Libraries.* Englewood, Colo.: Libraries Unlimited, 1989.

Studwell, William E. *Library of Congress Subject Headings: Philosophy, Practice, and Prospects.* New York: Haworth Press, 1990.

Subject Authorities in the Online Environment: Papers from a Conference Program Held in San Francisco, June 29, 1987. Sponsored by Resources and Technical Services Division, American Library Association;

Library and Information Technology Association; Association of College and Research Libraries; Public Library Association. Karen Markey Drabenstott, ed. ALCTS Papers on Library Technical Services and Collections No. 1. Chicago: American Library Association, 1991.

Subject Cataloging: Critiques and Innovations. Sanford Berman, ed. New York: Haworth, 1985.

Svenonius, Elaine. "Design of Controlled Vocabularies." In Allen Kent, ed., *Encyclopedia of Library and Information Science.* New York: Marcel Dekker, 1990. Vol. 45, suppl. 10, pp. 82–109.

Swanson, Edward. "Choice and Form of Access Points According to AACR2." *Cataloging & Classification Quarterly,* 11(3/4):35–61, 1990.

Taylor, Arlene G. *Cataloging with Copy: A Decision-Maker's Handbook.* 2nd ed. With the assistance of Rosanna M. O'Neil. Englewood, Colo.: Libraries Unlimited, 1988.

Taylor, Arlene G. "Research and Theoretical Considerations in Authority Control." *Cataloging & Classification Quarterly,* 9(3):29–57, 1989.

Theory of Subject Analysis: A Sourcebook. Lois Mai Chan, Phyllis A. Richmond, and Elaine Svenonius, eds. Littleton, Colo.: Libraries Unlimited, 1985.

Tillett, Barbara B. "Considerations for Authority Control in the Online Environment." *Cataloging & Classification Quarterly,* 9(3):1–13, 1989.

Universal Decimal Classification. International medium ed., English text. B.S. 1.000M. London: British Standards Institution, 1985–1988.

USMARC Concise Formats. Prepared by Network Development and MARC Standards Office. Washington: Cataloging Distribution Service, Library of Congress, 1991.

USMARC Format for Authority Data, Including Guidelines for Content Designation. Prepared by Network Development and MARC Standards Office. Washington: Cataloging Distribution Service, Library of Congress, 1987.

USMARC Format for Bibliographic Data, Including Guidelines for Content Designation. Prepared by Network Development and MARC Standards Office. Washington: Cataloging Distribution Service, Library of Congress, 1988.

USMARC Format for Classification Data, Including Guidelines for Content Designation. Prepared by Network Development and MARC Standards Office. Washington: Cataloging Distribution Service, Library of Congress, 1990.

USMARC Format for Holdings Data, Including Guidelines for Content Designation. Prepared by Network Development and MARC Standards Office. Washington: Cataloging Distribution Service, Library of Congress, 1989.

The USMARC Formats: Background and Principles. Prepared by MARBI,

American Library Association's ALCTS/LITA/RASD Machine-Readable Bibliographic Information Committee in conjunction with Network Development and MARC Standards Office, Library of Congress. Washington: Cataloging Distribution Service, Library of Congress, 1989.

Vatican Library. *Rules for the Catalog of Printed Books.* Trans. from the 2nd Italian ed. by the Very Rev. Thomas J. Shanahan, Victor A. Shaefer, and Constantin T. Vesselowsky. Willis E. Wright, ed. Chicago: American Library Association, 1948. 3rd ed. in Italian appeared in 1949.

Wajenberg, Arnold S. "Authority Work, Authority Records, and Authority Files." In Michael Gorman et al., eds., *Technical Services Today and Tomorrow.* Englewood, Colo.: Libraries Unlimited, 1990. Pp. 86–94.

Weihs, Jean, with Shirley Lewis. *Non-Book Materials: The Organization of Integrated Collections.* 3rd ed. Ottawa: Canadian Library Association, 1989.

Williamson, Nancy J. "The Library of Congress Classification: Problems and Prospects in Online Retrieval." *International Cataloguing,* **15**:45–48, October 1986.

Williamson, Nancy J. "The Role of Classification in Online Systems." *Cataloging & Classification Quarterly,* **10**(1/2):95–104, 1989.

Wilson, Patrick. "The Catalog as Access Mechanism: Background and Concepts." *Library Resources & Technical Services,* **27**(1):4–17, January/March 1983. Also in Michael Carpenter and Elaine Svenonius, eds., *Foundations of Cataloging: A Sourcebook.* Littleton, Colo.: Libraries Unlimited, 1985. Pp. 253–268.

Wilson, Patrick. *Two Kinds of Power: An Essay on Bibliographical Control.* Berkeley: University of California Press, 1968.

Wynar, Bohdan S. *Introduction to Cataloging and Classification.* 8th ed. by Arlene G. Taylor. Englewood, Colo.: Libraries Unlimited, 1992.

ACKNOWLEDGMENTS

The examples of MARC records are used with the permission of OCLC Online Computer Library Center, Inc.

The summary of the Dewey Decimal Classification is reproduced from DDC 20 of the Dewey Decimal Classification, published in 1989, by permission of Forest Press, a division of OCLC Online Computer Library Center, owner of copyright.

Photographs of the package case and photograph of the CD Sibelius, Symphonies 4 & 5 (No. 425 858-2) reproduced courtesy of The Decca Record Co. Ltd.

Ravel: Music for Four Hands; Louis Lortie and Hélène Mercier CHAN 8905—reproduced with permission from Chandos Records Ltd.

Title page and verso from G. Muller and H. Wiener, *The Short Prose Reader*, sixth edition, 1991, McGraw-Hill, Inc. reproduced with permission from McGraw-Hill, Inc.

Cover, title page, and verso from F. Ayres and P. Schmidt, *Theory and Problems of College Mathematics*, second edition, 1992, McGraw-Hill, Inc. reproduced with permission from McGraw-Hill, Inc.

Title page and verso from S. Wilson, *Mass Media/Mass Culture: An Introduction*, second edition, 1992, McGraw-Hill, Inc. reproduced with permission from McGraw-Hill, Inc.

INDEX

A and Z Cutter numbers in LCC, 347
AA (1908) (Anglo-American code) 35–36, 109
AACR (1967), 38–41, 43, 110, 128
AACR2 (1978), 43–45, 110, 128
AACR2R (1988), 45–46, 49–152
  development of, 45–46
  rules for access points, 107–122
  rules for description, 49–106
  rules for headings, 123–144
  rules for references, 145–152
Abridged DDC (*see Dewey Decimal Classification*, abridged edition)
Access points, 3–4, 9, 16, 107–122, 479
Accompanying materials, 88–90
Adaptations of original works, 114
Add instructions:
  in abridged DDC, 303–312
  in full DDC, 282–302
  in LCC, 351–366
Added entries, 5, 98, 121–122, 479
Additions:
  and changes to LCC, 338–339
  to name headings, 131–138
Address of publisher, 79
Adjectival phrase headings:
  in LCSH, 176–177
  in Sears, 213–214
Adoptions of LCC by other libraries, 327
ALA 1949, 37–38, 109
ALA Draft (1941), 37, 109
Alexandrian library, 6
Alphabetical specific catalog, 10, 157–158, 162, 479
Alphabetico-classed catalog, 157–158, 162, 479
American Library Association (*see* ALA entries)
Analytical entries, 97–99, 122, 479
Analytico-synthetic scheme, 261–262, 484–485

Anglo-American Cataloguing Rules (*see* AACR, AACR2, *or* AACR2R)
Anglo-American code of 1908, 35–36, 109
Annotated Card (AC) Program, 208–210
Anonymous classics written before 1501, 142–144
Anonymous works, 118
Areas tables:
  in abridged DDC (Table 2), 307–308
  in full DDC (Table 2), 288–291
Areas of description, 51–52, 69–97, 479
Arrangement of catalog records, 9–10
Arrays in classification, 261, 479
Art form [nature] of item note, 92
Aspects of subjects, 166
Audience note, 95
Author numbers (*see* Item numbers)
Author tables in LCC class P, 360–361
Author-title added entries (*see* Name-title headings)
Authority control, 3, 12–14, 123–144, 480
  (*See also* Name authority control; Subject authority control)
Authority files, 11–12, 123, 480
  (*See also* Name authority file; Subject authority file)
Authority records:
  in card format, 25
  MARC coding, 23–25
  in MARC format, 24, 125, 433–437
  (*See also* Name authority records; Subject authority records)
Authority work (*see* Authority control)
Authorized or preferred terms, 155–156
Authorship, 108–118
  (*See also* Corporate authorship; Personal authorship)
Autobiography (*see* Biography)
Automated catalog (*see* Online catalog)
Automatic switching to controlled terms, 158

Auxiliary tables or provisions:
  in abridged DDC, 305–313
  in full DDC, 285–302
  in LCC, 330, 346, 351–366, 441–448
  (*See also* Tables)

Bacon, Francis, 269–270
BC *(Bibliographic Classification)*, 392–397
Bias phase, 166
Bible, special rules for, 143–144
Bibliographic Classification (BC), 392–397
Bibliographic description:
  areas in, 50–53, 69–106
  chief sources of information for, 53–54
  defined, 480
  examples, with title pages, 54–62
  exercise, 99–106
  levels of, 67–69, 439–440
  punctuation in, (Table 3–1) 51–52, 63–67
  treated in depth, 49–106
Bibliographic files, 3, 11, 480
Bibliographic records:
  bibliographic access points for, 16,
    107–122
  in card format, 16, 423–425
  defined, 480
  information in, 4, 15–16
  MARC coding, 9, 14–23, 406–412
  in MARC format, 18, 426–432
  in online display, 20–21, 22
  (*See also* Authority records)
Bibliographic utilities, 11, 417–418, 480
Bibliography, treatment in NLM, 375
Biographical/critical works:
  in abridged DDC, 311
  entry for, 116
  in full DDC, 301,
  in LCSH, 203–204
  in Sears, 227–228
  work marks for, 319–320
Biography:
  classification of: in abridged DDC,
    312–313
  in full DDC (of authors), 301
  in LCC, 346–347, 355–356
  work marks for, in DDC,
    319–320
  subject headings for:
    in LCSH, 203, 205–208
    in Sears, 225–227
Biography table in LCC, 355
Bishops, headings for, 133

Blanket references, 163–164
Blind references, 147
Bliss, Henry Evelyn, 392
  [*See also Bibliographic Classification* (BC)]
Book catalog, 6–7
Book numbers (*see* Item numbers)
Books, [etc.], physical description of, 82,
    85, 86, 88
Boolean operations, 9, 480
British Museum Cataloguing Rules, 33–34
Broader term (BT) references in LCSH,
    196–197
Brown, James Duff, 387
  (*See also Subject Classification*)
BT (broader term) references, 163, 196

Call numbers (*see* Class numbers; Item
    numbers)
Callimachus, 6
Canadian provinces, LCC table for,
    354–355, 448
Card catalog, 6, 16
Cartographic materials:
  corporate entry for, 118
  defined, 481
  in microform, 78
  map example and record, 57, 427
  material specific details for, 77
  mathematical data [scale] area for, 77
  notes for, 94
  other physical details for, 85
  prescribed sources of information for, 54
  specific material designation for, 83
Catalog copy, 10–11, 413–418, 481
Catalog records (*see* Bibliographic records)
Cataloging codes, development of, 33–47
  (*See also specific names for particular
    codes, for example:* British Museum
    Cataloging Rules)
Cataloging copy, 10–11, 413–418, 481
Cataloging files, types of, 11–12
Cataloging-in-Publication, 415, 416
Cataloging operations, 10–15, 413–422
Cataloging records (*see* Bibliographic
    records)
Cataloging Service Bulletin, 41, 47
Catalogs, library:
  arrangement of, 9–10
  card examples, 16, 423–425
  defined, 4, 481
  forms of, 4–10
  integrity in, 45

Catalogs, library (Cont.):
  maintenance of, 123, 421–422
  production of records for, 413–422
  (See also specific forms of catalogs, for
    example: card catalog)
Catchword entries, 156–157
CC (Colon Classification), 389–392
CD-ROM catalog, 8
CDMARC Names, 414
CDMARC Subjects, 171, 414
Centralized cataloging, 414, 481
Chain strings:
  chain defined, 481
  in classification, 261
  in subject cataloging, 157, 162
Changes in responsibility for a work,
  120–121
Changes of names:
  corporate names, 126, 136
  geographic names, 134, 192
  personal names, 126, 129
Chief sources of information, 53–54, 481
Children's literature, LCSH headings for,
  208–210
Choices, principles governing:
  among variant names, 127, 134–136
  of class number, 263–266
  of form of name, 123–144, 182
    corporate names, 138–139
    geographic names, 134–135,182
    personal names, 130–134
Chronological subdivisions:
  defined, 481
  in LCSH, 188–189
  in Sears, 220
CIP (Cataloging-in-Publication), 415,
  416
Citation order:
  in general, 261, 481
  of literature facets in DDC, 296–297
  of subdivisions in LCSH, 193–194
Class entry, 157, 162, 481
Class numbers:
  choice of, 263–266
  MARC coding, 266–267
Classed catalog, 10, 157
Classification:
  DDC, 269–326
  in general, 13, 259–267, 482
  LCC, 327–367
  NLM, 369–379
  other modern systems, 379–397
  topics for discussion, 397–399

Classification by discipline:
  in DDC, 275–277
  in LCC, 329–332
Classification exercises (see Exercises)
Classification Research Group, 245
Classification systems:
  DDC, 269–326
  LCC, 327–367
  NLM, 369–379
  other modern systems, 379–397
Classified (or classed) subject entry, 157
Classified catalog, 10, 157
Closing the card catalog, 45
Coextensive heading, 167–168, 482
Collaborators, 113–114, 121, 482
Collections:
  definition of, 482
  descriptive cataloging of, 119
  of works of individual authors: in
    abridged DDC, 311–312
    in full DDC, 300
    in LCSH, 202
    in Sears, 228
  of works of more than one author: in
    abridged DDC, 310–311
    in full DDC, 297–299
    in LCSH, 201
    in Sears, 228
Collective biography:
  classification in abridged DDC, 313
  defined, 482
  LCSH headings for, 205–206
  Sears headings for, 226
  (See also Individual biography)
Collocation function of classification,
  259–260
Colon Classification, 389–392
COM catalog, 7
COMARC, 416–417
Commentaries, entry for, 115
Commission and committee reports,
  117
Compare and see references in LCC,
  341–342
Comparison phase, 167
COMPASS, 251–253
Compilers, 113, 116, 121, 482
Completely revised DDC schedules,
  274–275, 482
Compound surnames, 130, 482
Compound subject headings:
  in LCSH, 177
  in Sears, 213

Computer files, 430
  material specific details for, 77
  physical description of, 84, 86, 87, 89
Computer-accessed catalog (see Online
  catalog)
Computer-Aided Subject System, 251–253
Computer-assisted cataloging, 418–422
Computer-Output-Microform catalog, 7
Concepts and conditions of authorship,
  108–116
Conferences:
  defined, 483
  headings for, 140
  proceedings of: bibliographic
    description, 61
    entry for, 117
Conjunctive phrase headings, 176
Connecting symbols for UDC, 385–386
Consortia (bibliographic networks), 11,
  414–418
Content designation in MARC, 14, 17–25,
  406–412, 483
Contents note, 95
Continuous revision:
  in DDC, 272–273
  in LCC, 338–340
Controlled vocabulary:
  defined, 483
  for subject access, 155–156
Conversion of catalog records, 421
Cooperative (shared) cataloging, 10–11,
  413–418
Copy numbers in DDC, 324
Copy cataloging, 10–11, 413–421, 483
Copy-specific information note, 96
Copyright date, 81
Corporate authorship, 36, 40, 110–112
Corporate body:
  change in treatment of, 40
  defined, 135–136, 483
  main entry of, 110–111, 116–118
  name headings for: as main or added
    entries, 135–141
  authority record examples, 435–436
  cross-references for, 148, 150–151
  in LCSH, 180
  in Sears, 223
  qualifiers, 137–138
Corporate responsibility, 110–112
Criticism of literature, works of:
  in abridged DDC, 311
  in full DDC, 301
  in LCSH, 199–204

Criticism in literature (Cont.):
  in Sears, 227–228
  (See also Biographical/critical works)
Cross-references:
  for name headings: "blind" references,
    147
  defined, 489
  discussed, 145–152
  examples of, 26–28, 146–147, 150–152
  MARC coding for, 23–25, 124, 145
  public display in online catalogs,
    27–28
  tracings, 123, 147
  types of, 145
  in subject headings lists: in general,
    163–164
  in LCSH, 195–199
  in MeSH, 238–239
  in Sears, 214–217
Cumulative editions of LCC schedules, 339
Cutter, Charles A.:
  book numbering system, 315–318
  cataloging rules, 34–35
  Expansive Classification, 328, 379–382
  introduction of the alphabetical catalog,
    157–158
  levels of description, 67
  principles for subject access, 157–162
Cutter numbers:
  in DDC, 315–323
  exercises (see Exercises: DDC)
  in LCC, 335, 343–348, 352–355, 360–361,
    364, 365
Cutter tables, 315–317, 344

Dates:
  added to name headings, 133
  in LCC call numbers, 348–350
  of manufacture [in description], 82
  of publication, 81–82, 348–350
DDC (Dewey Decimal Classification),
  269–326
  for subtopics (see Dewey Decimal
    Classification)
DDC abridged (see Dewey Decimal
  Classification, abridged edition)
Delimiter defined, 410, 483
Descriptive cataloging, 12–13, 29–152
  defined, 483
  exercises (see Exercises: descriptive
    cataloging)
  topics for discussion, 149, 151

Dewey Decimal Classification, (DDC)
269–326
    abridged edition, 272, 303–314
    auxiliary tables in, 285–302
    basic principles of, 275–280
    biography, 301
    classification by discipline, 275–277
    early editions of, 270–272
    evaluation of, 280–282
    exercises (*see* Exercises: DDC)
    languages, 295
    literature, 296–301
    mnemonics in, 279–280
    notation for, 278–279
    number building in, 282–291
    outline of main classes, 276
    relative index to, 270,
    revision of, 272–275
    standard subdivisions, 285–288
    tables, 285–302
    (*See also* Tables in DDC full edition)
Dewey Decimal Classification, abridged
edition, 272, 303–314
    areas and persons table (Table 2),
        307–308
    auxiliary tables in, 305–314
    biography, 312–313
    exercises [*see* Exercises: DDC
        (abridged)]
    languages (Table 4), 312
    literature, 310–312
    number building in, 303–314
    single-zero rule, 306
    standard subdivisions (Table 1),
        306–307
    tables, 305–314
    (*See also* Tables in DDC abridged
        edition)
Dewey, Melvil, 269
Dewey numbers in Sears, 212
Dictionary catalog, 9–10, 157–158,
    161–162, 483
Dimensions of item, 86–87
Direct and specific subject entry, 161–162,
    167–168, 490
Direct geographic subdivision, 190–191,
    483–484
Direct or indirect subheadings of
    corporate bodies, 139
Directory in MARC record, 409–410,
    484
Discussion topics:
    classification, 397–399

Discussion topics (*Cont.*):
    descriptive cataloging, 149, 151
    subject cataloging, 253–254
Dissertation note, 60, 95
Distributor's name, 79–80
Divided catalog, 10, 158
Divisions in LCC, 332–333
Double Cutter numbers in LCC, 346–347,
    355–356

Early editions of DDC, 270–272
Early outline of LCC (Table 13–1), 329
EC (*Expansive Classification*), 328, 379–382
Editing catalog copy, 420
Edition and history of item note, 93
Edition area and edition statement, 75–76
Edition marks in DDC book numbers,
    323–324
Editor:
    added entry, 121
    defined, 484
Entries:
    defined, 484
    main and added, 4–5, 112–122
Entry elements in names:
    corporate names, 138–139
    geographic names, 182
    personal names, 130–134
Enumeration in LCC, degree of, 330
Enumerative scheme, 261, 484
Equivalence (USE) references in LCSH,
    195–196
Ethnic groups in DDC table, 294–295
Evaluation:
    of DDC, 280–282
    of LCC, 337–338
Exercises:
    descriptive cataloging: description,
        99–106 (Key, 449–450)
    main and added entries, 122 (Key,
        450–451)
    name headings, 149 (Key, 451–452)
    prescribed punctuation, 69 (Key, 449)
    DDC (abridged): schedules, 304–305
        (Key, 466–468)
    Tables 1 and 2, 309–310 (Key,
        468–469)
    Tables 3 and 4, 313–314 (Key,
        469–470)
    DDC: Cutter numbers, 318–319,
        (Key, 470–472), 325–326, (Key,
        472–474)

Exercises *(Cont.)*:
  literature, 301–302 (Key, 465–466)
  schedules, 284 (Key, 461–462)
  Tables 1–2, 291–293 (Key, 462–464)
  Tables 4–7, 295–296 (Key, 464–465)
  LCC: advanced, 366–367 (Key, 476–477)
    introductory, 350–351 (Key, 474–476)
  LCSH: literature and biography, 208
    (Key, 455–457)
    subdivisions, 189–190 (Key, 452–453);
    194–195 (Key, 453–455)
  Sears: complex subjects, 224–225 (Key,
    459–460)
    literature and biography, 229 (Key,
    460–461)
    local subdivisions, 221 (Key, 458–459)
    topical headings, 219–220 (Key,
    457–458)
Expansive Classification (EC), 328, 379–382
Explanatory references for name
  headings, 145, 484
Expressive notation, 262
Extent of item, 82–85

Facet analysis and synthesis, 260–262, 280,
  484
Faceted schemes, 260–262, 484–485
Family names, 179, 222
Field tags in MARC (*see* Fields and
  subfields; Subfield codes)
Field terminator, 409, 485
Fields and subfields in MARC, 14, 17–19,
  23–25, 409–412
File characteristics [of computer files]
  area, 77
Filing rules, 9–10
Fixed length data elements in MARC, 407,
  409
Form headings and subdivisions:
  defined, 485
  in LCSH, 176, 183
  in Sears, 213, 218–219
Free text, 155, 485
Free-floating phrase headings, 177–178
Free-floating subdivisions, 184–188, 485
Freezing the card catalog, 45
Fullness of names, 129, 133, 136–137

General material designation, 71–72, 485
General references:
  definition and discussion, 163–164, 485

General references *(Cont.)*:
  in LCSH, 198–199
  in Sears, 216
Generic qualifiers in geographic name
  headings, 181–182
Geographic area treatment:
  in DCC: in abridged edition, 307–308
    in full edition, 288–291
  in LCC: using Cutter numbers,
    352–355
    using special tables, 356–360
Geographic name headings:
  authority record examples, 436
  choice of name, 134–135
  in LCSH, 180–182, 190–194
  qualifiers, 134–135, 140, 181–182
  references for, 151
  in Sears, 222–223
  subdivisions for, 190–194, 220
Geographic qualifiers, 134–135, 140,
  181–182, 485
Geographic subdivisions:
  defined, 485
  in LCSH, 190–194
  in Sears, 220
Geographic tables:
  in DDC, 288–291
  in DDC abridged, 307–308
  in LCC, 352–355, 356–360, 441–448
  in NLM, 373–374
Given names, entry for, 131
GMD (General material designation)
  71–72, 485
Government bodies and officials,
  140–141
  (*See also* Heads of state and
  governments)

Headings (*see specific types of headings;
  subentry* headings for *under specific
  entities*)
Headings omitted:
  from LCSH, 172
  from Sears, 221–224
Heads of state and governments:
  entry and headings for, 118, 141
  subject headings for, 207–208
Hierarchical references in LCSH,
  196–197
Hierarchy in classification and notation,
  260–262, 277–279, 485
History [editions] of item note, 93

Holdings note, 96
Hospitality of classification notation:
  in LCC, 336
  in DDC, 281

Identical personal names, 133–134
Illustrations, 85–86
Illustrator:
  as added entry, 121
  as main entry, 114
Implementation of new cataloging codes,
  40–46
Imprint, 78–82, 485
In analytics, with example, 98–99
Index Medicus MeSH, 231, 233
Indexes to classification schedules:
  DDC (relative index), 270
  LCC, 340
  NLM, 374–375
Indicators in MARC, 14, 412, 485
Indirect geographic subdivision, 191–193,
  486
Individual biography:
  defined, 486
  classification of: in abridged DDC,
    312–313
  in full DDC (of authors), 301
  in LCC, 355–356, (Table 13–8) 355
  LCSH headings for, 206–208
  Sears headings for, 222, 225
  (*See also* Collective biography)
Individual literary authors:
  works about: in abridged DDC, 312
  in full DDC, 301
  in LCC, 360–361
  works by: in abridged DDC, 311–312
  in full DDC, 299–301
  in LCC, 360–361
Individual works of literature:
  in DDC, 301
  in LCC, 361
Influence phase, 166
Initials, 131, 134, 136–137
Inputting catalog records, 421
Integrity of catalog, 45
Integrity of numbers, 271, 486
International Conference on Cataloguing
  Principles, 39–40, 128*n*
International Standard Bibliographic
  Description:
  defined, 486
  ISBD(G), 42, 50–53

International Standard Bibliographic
  Description (*Cont.*):
  ISBD(M), 41–42, 53
  ISBD(S), 41–42
International Standard Book Number,
  96–97, 486
International Standard Serial Number,
  96–97, 486
International Standard Serial Number of
  series, 90
Inverted phrase headings, 177
ISBD(G), 42, 50–53, 486
ISBD(M), 41–42, 53
ISBD(S), 41–42
ISBN, 96–97, 486
ISSN, 96–97, 486
ISSN of series, 90
Item numbers:
  in DDC, 314–325
  defined, 486
  in LCC, 343–350
  MARC coding, 266–267

Jewett, Charles C., 34
Jewett's Rules, 34
Joint Steering Committee for the Revision
  of AACR, 44–46

Katz, William, in examples:
  authority record for, 23–25
  bibliographic record for, 16, 18, 20–22,
    408, 423–425
  cross-references for, 26, 146
Key headings in Sears, 219
Key title for serials, 96, 486
Keyword, 9, 155
Kit, 89–90, 486
Known-item searching, 155

Language of headings, 129, 134, 137,
  143
Language-aspect-of-topic table in full
  DDC (Table 6), 295
Language-of-item note, 92
Language tables for individual
  languages:
  in abridged DDC (Table 4), 312
  in full DDC (Table 4), 293–294
Larger-place qualifiers in headings,
  134–135, 181–182

LC (Library of Congress):
  filing rules, 10
  printed cards, 6, 38
  (*See also* Library of Congress *entries*)
LC 1949, 37–38
LC policies on descriptive cataloging:
  implementation of new rules, 40–41, 43,
    45, 46
  level of description used, 68
  on British titles of honor, 132
  rule interpretations, 47
  rule options followed, 46
LCC *(Library of Congress Classification)* [*see
  Library of Congress Classification
  (LCC)*]
LCSH *(Library of Congress Subject
  Headings)* [*see Library of Congress
  Subject Headings (LCSH)*]
Lead-in terms in subject lists, 156
Leader in a MARC record, 409, 486
Legal and governmental works,
  116–117
Levels:
  of bibliographic description, 67–69,
    439
  of fullness of names, 133
  of subject cataloging, 167
Library catalogs (*see* Catalogs, library)
Library classification systems, 259–260,
  269–397
  Bibliographic Classification (BC),
    392–397
  Colon Classification (CC), 389–392
  Dewey Decimal Classification (DDC),
    269–326
  Expansive Classification (EC), 379–382
  Library of Congress Classification (LCC)
    327–367
  National Library of Medicine Classification
    (NLM), 369–379
  Subject Classification (SC), 387–388
  Universal Decimal Classification (UDC),
    382–387
Library materials, types of, 49
Library of Congress (*see* LC *for entries
  about the library*)
Library of Congress Classification (LCC),
  327–367
  application of (how to use), 340–367
  biography, 346–347, 355–356
  classification by discipline in, 329–332
  Cutter numbers in class numbers, 335,
    340

Cutter numbers as book numbers,
    345–348
  early outline of (Table 13–1), 329
  economic advantages for libraries,
    327–328
  evaluation of, 337–338
  exercises, 350–351, (Key, 474–476),
    366–367, (Key, 476–477)
  history and development, 327–329
  literature, 360–361
  main and subordinate classes in,
    330–334
  Martel's seven points, 332
  notation, 328, 333–336
  overall characteristics, 329–330
  publication patterns for schedules,
    338–340
  revision of, 338–340
  table of classes, 331
  table of subdivisions in, 334
  tables, 341, 346, 351–366, 441–448
Library of Congress Subject Headings
    (LCSH), 171–210
  biography, 205–208
  children's literature, 208–210
  chronological subdivisions in, 188–189
  classes of headings omitted from, 172
  corporate name headings in, 180
  cross-references in, 195–199
  exercises (*see* Exercises: LCSH)
  form subdivisions in, 183, 184
  format of, 172–174
  free-floating subdivisions in, 184–188
  geographic names in, 180–182
  geographic subdivisions in, 190–194
  headings, syntax and semantics of,
    176–182
  history of, 159, 171
  literature, 199–204
  machine-readable form of, 159, 171
  main headings in, 176–182
  MARC coding for, 175
  pattern headings in, 185–187
  personal name headings in, 179
  pre-coordination in, 176
  proper names in, 179–182
  qualifiers used with, 178
  scope notes in, 178–179
  scope of, 172
  subdivisions of, 182–194
  Subject Authority File, 159, 171
  Subject Cataloging Manual, 171
  topical subdivisions in, 183–188

Library of Congress Subject Headings
    (LCSH) *(Cont.)*:
    types [syntax and semantics] of
        headings in, 176–182
Literary collections (*see* Collections)
Literary warrant, 330, 486
Literature:
    classification of: in abridged DDC,
        310–312
    in full DDC, 296–301
    in LCC, 360–361
    work marks for, in DDC, 320–323
    subject headings for: in LCSH, 199–204
    in Sears, 227–229
    works about: in abridged DDC, 311
    in full DDC, 299
    works of: in DDC, 301
    in LCC, 361
Literatures tables:
    in abridged DDC (Table 3), 310–312
    in full DDC (Table 3), 293
Local subdivision (*see* Geographic
    subdivision)
Lubetzky, Seymour, 39–40

Machine-readable cataloging [*see* MARC
    (Machine-Readable Cataloging)]
Machine-readable form of LCSH, 159,
    171
Magnetic tape distribution of MARC
    records, 416–417
Main and added entries, 107–122
    added entries, 5, 98, 121–122, 479
    exercise, 122 (Key, 450)
    main entry, 4–5, 108, 112–119, 486
Main and subordinate classes:
    in DDC, 269–270, 275–277, (Table 12–2)
        276
    in LCC, 330–332, (Table 13–2) 331
    in NLM, 370–372, (Table 14–1) 371–372
Maintenance of catalogs, 123, 422
Manufacturers' names, 78, 82
Manuscript catalog, 5
Manuscripts, 81, 83, 85, 87
Map example, 57
Maps (*see* Cartographic materials)
MARC (Machine Readable-Cataloging),
    14–28, 403–412, 487
    *(Note: MARC tags for record elements
        discussed in this book are given at the
        head of each section to which they
        pertain.)*

MARC as data structure, 409–412
    data fields and indicators, 411–412
    directory, 409–410
    leader, 409
    lists of tags (*see* MARC tags)
    types of formats, 405–406
MARC coding:
    bibliographic records, 9, 14–23, 406–412
        examples, 18, 426–432
    class and item numbers, 17–18, 266–267
        examples [*see* Bibliographic records
            in MARC format (fields 050 and
            082)]
    name authority records, 9, 23–25,
        123–125
        examples: corporate names, 435–436
        examples: geographic names, 436
        examples: personal names, 24, 125,
            433–444
    references, 147–148
    subject authority records, 173–174
        examples, 175, 437
    subject headings, 173–175
        examples [*see* Bibliographic records
            in MARC format (fields 6XX)]
MARC formats:
    for authority data, 406
    for bibliographic data, 405–406
    for classification data, 406
    for holdings data, 406
MARC records:
    in communications format, 408
    defined, 487
    full MARC display, 18, 24, 125, 426–437
    public catalog display, 20–21, 22
    sources of, 10–11, 414–418
MARC tags, explained, 17, 19, 21, 25, 124,
    174, 266–267, 411–412
Material specific details area, 76–78
    (*See also* Specific material designation;
        subentry material specific details
        for *under specific items*)
Material specific details of item note,
    93–94
Mathematical data (for cartographic
    materials) area, 77
Medical Subject Headings (MeSH) 231–244
MEDLINE, 231
Merits of classification schemes:
    DDC, 280–281
    LCC, 337
    UDC, 386–387
MeSH (*Medical Subject Headings*), 231–244

Methods of subject analysis:
    classification approach to, 262–266
    subject heading approach to, 166
Microform catalog, 5, 7–8
Microforms:
    defined, 7, 487
    dimensions of, 88
    example of description, 60
    extent of item information for, 85
    general material designation for, 71
    material specific details for, 85
    other physical details of, 86
Mixed responsibility, 114–116, 487
Mnemonics:
    in AACR2 rule numbers, 50
    in DDC, 279–280
    defined, 487
    in LCC notation, 336
    in MARC tag numbers, 19, 24, 412
Modern cataloging codes, development
    of, 33–47
Modern library classification systems (see
    Library classification systems)
Monographic series and multipart
    monographs, 98, 120
Monographs, descriptive cataloging of:
    changes in title, 120
    changes in responsibility for, 120
    defined, 487
    examples, 54–57, 61, 426–428
    physical description of, 82, 85, 86, 88
    series note for, 95
    series statements for, 90–92
Motion pictures, 80, 83, 85, 87, 89
Multimedia items, 89–90, 486
Multipart monographs, 98, 120
Multiple subjects (see Multitopical works)
Multiples in LCSH, 187–188
Multitopical works:
    classification of: in DDC, 263–266
        in LCC, 330
    subject headings for, 168–169
Music [in description], 428
    dimensions of, 87
    extent of item information for, 83
    material specific details for, 77
    in microform, 78
    other physical details for, 85
Musical presentation statement area, 77

Name authority control, 13–14, 123–144
Name authority data, sources of, 414–415

Name authority files, 12, 123, 172, 179,
    418, 487
Name authority records:
    content of, 23–25, 123–125
    defined, 487
    examples: corporate names, 435–436
    examples: geographic names, 436
    examples: personal names, 24, 25, 125,
        433–434
    LC distribution of, 414
    MARC coding for, 23–25, 123–125
Name changes, 126, 129, 134, 136, 192
Name headings:
    in descriptive cataloging, 123–144
        corporate, 135–141
        cross-references for, 145–151
        exercise on, 149 (Key, 451–452)
        geographic, 134–135
        personal, 126–134
        uniform titles, 141–144
    qualifiers, 131–135, 137–138, 140,
        181–182
    in subject cataloging:
        in LCSH, 179–182, 204
        in Sears, 221–224
    (See also Name-title headings)
Name reference examples, 26, 146–147,
    150–151
Name-title headings:
    defined, 487
    in descriptive cataloging, 107
    in subject cataloging, 204
Names of publisher, distributor, or
    manufacturer, 79–80, 82
Narrower term references in LCSH,
    196–197
National Coordinated Cataloging
    Program, 416–417
National groups in DDC, (table) 294–295
National Library of Medicine
    Classification, 369–379
National Union Catalog, 415
Natural-language searching, 155
Nature of item note, 92
NCCP (National Coordinated Cataloging
    Program), 416–417
Networks, 11, 417–418
New schedules in LCC, 339
NLM (National Library of Medicine
    Classification), 369–379
Nobility, titles of honor for, 132
Non-book materials:
    dates for, 81, 82

Non-book materials *(Cont.)*:
  examples of, 57–60, 427–428, 430–432
  physical description of, 83–89
  publisher information, 80
  *(See also entries for specific non-book
    materials, for example:* Sound
    recordings)
  treatment in early cataloging codes, 40,
    44
Notation, 262, 487
  in DDC, 278–280
  in LCC, 328, 333–336
  in NLM, 372–373
Notational synthesis *(see* Number
  building)
Note area, 92–96
NT (narrower term) references, 163,
  196–197
NUC (National Union Catalog), 415
Number building:
  in abridged DDC, 303–313
  in full DDC, 282–303
  in LCC, 351–386
  (See also Tables *entries)*
Number of LCSH headings applied, 168
Numbering within series, 90
Numbers found in item note, 96
Numerals used as authors' names, 131
Numeric designation area, 77

OCLC Online Computer Library Center:
  description of system, 11, 417–418
  examples of records in, 18, 24, 426–437
Official communications of heads of state,
  etc., 118
  (See also Heads of state)
Omissions:
  from corporate headings, 138
  headings omitted from LCSH, 172
  headings omitted from Sears, 221–224
  from statement of responsibility, 74
  from title, 71
Online catalog, 8–9, 488
  examples of records in, 20–22
  (See also Online cataloging; MARC
    entries)*
  subject retrieval capabilities of, 158
Online cataloging, 413–422
Online Computer Library Center *(see*
  OCLC Online Computer Library
  Center)
Open entry, 81

Options in AACR2R, 46
Order of subdivisions in LCSH, 193–194
Original cataloging, 11, 413, 488
Other physical details of item [in
  description], 85–86
Other title information, 72–73, 488
Outlines of main classes:
  BC (Table 14–7), 395–396
  CC (Table 14–6), 390
  DDC, (Table 12–2), 276
  EC (Table 14–2), 381
  LCC, (Table 13–1), 331; (Table 13–2), 333
  NLM (Table 14–1), 371
  SC (Table 14–5), 388
  UDC (Table 14–3), 384

Panizzi, Sir Anthony, 33
Parallel content designation in MARC,
  412
Parallel titles, 72, 488
Parallel titles note, 93
Paris Principles, 40, 108, 110–112, 128
Patriarchs, 118, 132
Pattern headings:
  defined, 488
  in LCSH, 185–187, (Table 8–1) 186–187
  in Sears [key headings], 219
Period subdivisions *see* Chronological
  subdivisions
Periods table in DDC, 288–291
Personal author:
  defined, 488
  main entry for, 110, 113–116
  name headings for *(see* Personal name
    headings)
Personal authorship or responsibility,
  108–116
Personal name headings, 126–134
  authority record coding and examples,
    23–25, 124–125, 433–434
  choice of entry element, 130–131
  choice of form, 129–130
  choice of name, 127–129
  cross-references for, 146–148
  in LCSH, 179–180
  in Sears, 222
Persons:
  with the same name, 131–133
  writing under different names, 127–129
Persons table in DDC, 295
Phase relations, 166–167
Phoenix schedules in DDC, 274–275

Phrases:
  as personal headings, 131
  in subject headings:
    in LCSH, 176–178
    in Sears, 213–214
Physical description area, 82–90
Physical description note, 94
Pinakes, 6
Place subdivisions (*see* Geographic
  subdivisions)
Place names (*see* Geographic name
  headings)
Places [in description]:
  of manufacture, 82
  of publication, 79
Popes, 118, 132
Post-coordination defined, 488
PRECIS, 244–251
Pre-coordination, 176, 488
Preferred subject terms, 156–156
Prefixes to call numbers, 324
Prepositional phrase headings:
  in LCSH, 177
  in Sears, 214
Prescribed punctuation, 63–69
Prescribed sources of information, 53–54
Preserved Context Indexing System
  (PRECIS), 244–251
Printed cards from LC, 6, 38
Proper names as subject headings:
  in LCSH, 179–182
  in Sears, 221–225
Provinces, LCC table for, 354–355, 448
Prussian Instructions, 36
Pseudonyms, 127–129
Publication and distribution note, 94
Publication date in LCC call numbers,
  348–350
Publication, distribution area:
  defined, 489
  rules for, 78–82
Publication patterns for LCC schedules,
  338–340
Publisher's name, 79–80
Punctuation, prescribed, 63–69

Qualifiers:
  defined, 489
  in geographic headings, 134–135,
    181–182
  in LCSH, 178
  in name headings, 131–135, 137–138, 140

Racial groups in DDC, (Table 5) 294–295
Ranganathan, S. R., 389
  (*See also* Colon Classification)
RECON Project, 416–417
Record structure in MARC, 14, 406–412
Record terminator, 409, 489
Refer from references for names, 123–125,
  489
Reference to published description note,
  95
References (*see* Cross-references; *specific
  types of references, for example:* BT)
Regions and countries in one alphabet,
  LCC table for, 353–354, 441–447
Reissues of LCC schedules, 339
Related bodies, 138–140
Related term (RT) references, 163,
  197–198
Relationship to original note, 96
Relationships among multiple subjects,
  166–167
Relative index to DDC, 270
Relative location, 270, 489
Relocations, 271, 273–274, 489
Repeatability of MARC fields, 410
Reports of commissions, committees, etc.,
  117
Research Libraries Information Network
  (RLIN), 11, 417
Retrospective conversion project, 416–417
Revised editions:
  entry for, 114–115
  of LCC schedules, 340
Reviser as main or added entry, 115
Revision:
  of DDC, 272–275
  of LCC, 338–340
RLIN, 11, 417
Roman names, entry for, 132
Royalty, entry for, 132
  (*See also* Heads of state and
    governments)
RT references, 163, 197–198
Rule interpretations of AACR2R, 47

S.l. [Sine loco]; s.n. [sine nomine], 79, 80
Sacred scriptures:
  entry for, 119
  uniform titles for, 143–144
Saints, headings for, 132
SC (*Subject Classification*), 387–388
Scale of map, 77

Scope:
    of item note, 92
    of LCSH, 172
Scope notes in LCSH, 178–179
Searching, 155–156, 420
Sears List of Subject Headings, 211–229
    cross-references in, 214–217
    exercises (*see* Exercises: Sears)
    form subdivisions, 218–219
    format of, 212
    headings for biography, 225–227
    headings for literature, 227–229
    headings omitted in, 221–224
    history, 211
    key headings in, 219
    period subdivisions in, 220
    place subdivisions in, 220
    proper names in, 221–225
    topical headings in, 213–214
    topical subdivisions in, 217–218
    types of main headings in, 213–214
    x and xx symbols in, 214–216
Sears, Minnie Earl, 211
See also references:
    for names, 145–151
    for subjects, 156, 195–198, 215–217
See and *compare* references in LCC,
    341–342
See from references for names, 123–125, 489
See references:
    for names, 145–151
    for subjects, 156, 197–198, 214–217,
        238–239
Segmentation, 302–303, 490
Serials:
    changes in names of, 120
    changes in responsibility for, 121
    defined, 490
    examples, with description, 62, 429–430
    general material designation for, 77–78
    material specific details for, 77–78
    in microform, 78
    treatment in LCC, 350
    treatment in NLM, 375–376
Series, 90–92, 122, 490
    Monographic series, 98
Series area and statement, 90–92
Series note, 95
Shakespeare, William:
    class number for, in DDC, 323
    key heading for, in Sears, 225
Shared cataloging, 10–11, 413–418, 490
Shared responsibility, 113–114, 490

Shelflist, 11–12, 157, 423, 490
Single responsibility, entry for works of,
    113
Single-zero rule in DDC, 286, 306
    (*See also* Zero as filler in DDC notation)
Size of item [in description], 86–88
Sound recordings:
    entry for, 118
    examples of record for, 58–59, 431
    physical description of, 83, 85, 87, 89
    publication, distribution information
        for, 80
Source of title proper note, 92
Sources:
    for cataloging copy, 10–11, 414–418
    of information for description, 53–54
Specific entry, 161–162, 167–168, 490
Specific material designation, 82–85
Spelling of names, 130, 133
Spirits, headings for, 132
Standard number and terms of
    availability area, 96–97
Standard subdivisions:
    in abridged DDC, 306–307
    defined, 490
    in full DDC, 285–288
Standardization, advantages of:
    in descriptive cataloging, 4–5, 33, 42, 44
    in subject cataloging, 158–159
Statement of responsibility, 73–75, 93, 490
States, LCC table for, 354, 447–448
Strengths of classification schemes:
    DDC, 280–281
    LCC, 337
    UDC, 386–387
Subclasses in LCC, 332–335
Subdivisions:
    defined, 491
    in LCSH, 182–194
    in MeSH, 236–238
    in Sears, 217–220
Subfield codes in MARC, 410, 412
Subject access, 155–169
Subject analysis, methods of:
    in classification, 262–266
    defined, 491
    in subject cataloging, 166–167
Subject authority control:
    authority data, sources of, 414–418
    authority file, 159, 164–166, 171, 414, 491
Subject authority records, 172–175, 437,
    491
Subject catalog, 9–10, 157–158, 491

Subject cataloging:
  brief discussion of, 13
  defined, 491
  discussion topics for, 253–254
  exercises *see* Exercises: LCSH and Sears
  general aspects of, 155–169
  guidelines for assigning headings,
    167–169
  LCSH, Sears, and MeSH, 171–244
  sources for subject authority data,
    414–418
Subject Classification (SC), 387–388
Subject headings:
  for children's literature, 208–210
  defined, 491
  discussed in depth, 155–254
  (*See also subentries under main entries for
    topics or entities, for example:*
    Collective biography: Sears
    headings for)
  systems of, 171–254 (Chapters 7–10)
    COMPASS, 251–254
    LCSH, 171–210
    MeSH, 231–244
    PRECIS, 244–251
    Sears, 211–229
  for works about individual works, 204
Subject subdivisions *see* Topical
  subdivisions
Subordinate bodies, 138–140, 491
Subseries, 90, 491
Subtitle, 72–73
Successive Cutter numbers in LCC, 347,
  365–366
Successive entry:
  for corporate bodies, 136
  for serial publications, 120
Summary of contents note, 95
Superimposition, 41, 45, 492
Supplementary items, 97
Supplied title, 70
Surnames, 130–131
Syndetic devices, 163–164, 492
  (*See also* Cross-references)
Synthesis:
  in DDC, 282–291
  in DDC abridged, 303–313
  defined, 492

Table of Cutter numbers, 315–317, 344
Table of regions and countries in LCC,
  353–354, 441–447

Tables in DDC abridged edition, 305–314
  areas and persons, (Table 2) 307–308
  exercises [*see* Exercises: DDC
    (abridged)]
  individual languages (Table 4), 312
  literatures and literary forms (Table 3),
    310–312
  standard subdivisions (Table 1), 306–307
Tables in DDC full edition, 285–302
  areas, periods, persons (Table 2),
    288–291
  exercises (*see* Exercises: DDC)
  individual languages (Table 4), 293–294
  languages [as facet of subject] (Table 6),
    295
  literatures and literary forms (Table 3),
    293
  persons (Table 7), 295
  racial, ethnic, national groups (Table 5),
    294–295
  standard subdivisions (Table 1), 285–288
Tables in LCC:
  biography table, 355
  Cutter table, 344
    (*See also* Cutter numbers)
  for geographic division by Cutter
    number, 352–355
    provinces of Canada, 354–355, 448
    regions and countries, 353, 441–447
    states and regions of the United
      States, 354, 447–448
  for internal subarrangement, 361–366
    ordinal value of table numbers, 363
    successive Cutter numbers, 365–366
  limited to use with a given class,
    356–366
    author tables in class P, 360–361
    geography tables in class H, 358–359
    geography tables in class S, 357
  translation table, 346
Terminology in subject headings, 162–163
Terms of availability, 97
Title and statement of responsibility area,
  70–75
Title and statements of responsibility for
  series, 90–92
Title entry:
  added entry, 122
  main entry, 118–119
Title proper, 70–71, 492
Titles of nobility as author's names, 131,
  132
Tool or application phase, 167

Topical subdivisions:
   defined, 492
   in LCSH, 183–188
   in Sears, 217–218
Topics for discussion:
   classification, 397–399
   descriptive cataloging, 149, 151
   subject cataloging, 253–254
Tracings:
   of added entries, 6, 16, 122, 124
   on catalog cards, 6, 16
   defined, 492
   of references, 123, 147
   of subject entries in manual records, 174
Translations:
   Cutter numbers for, in DDC, 321
   Cutter numbers for, in LCC, 346
   entry for, 115, 121
Tree structures:
   in classification, 260–262, 277
   in MeSH, 234–235

UBC (Universal bibliographic control),
   44–45
UDC (Universal Decimal Classification)
   382–387
UF (used for) references in LCSH, 196
Uncontrolled [subject] headings, MARC
   field tag for, 175
Uniform headings, 126–127, 161, 492
Uniform titles, 141–144, 148–149, 492
Union catalog, 4, 415, 492
Unique call numbers, 266, 317–324
Unique headings, 126, 133, 161, 492
United States table in LCC, 354, 447–448
Universal bibliographic control, 44–45
Universal Decimal Classification,
   382–387

University of Toronto Library
   Automation System (UTLAS), 417
Unknown or diffuse responsibility,
   118–119
USE references, 163, 195–196
Used for references in LCSH, 196
User and usage, 160
USMARC *(see MARC entries)*
USMARC Concise Formats [LC
   publication], 404
UTLAS (University of Toronto Library
   Automation System), 417

Variable fields, 14, 17–19, 407–412, 492
Variant names in headings, 127–129, 136
Variations in title note, 93
Vatican Code, 36–37
Volume numbers in DDC, 324

Weaknesses in classification schemes:
   DDC, 281–282
   LCC, 338
   UDC, 383, 386–387
Western Library Network (WLN), 11, 417
With (bound with) note, 96
WLN (Western Library Network), 11, 417
Work marks in DDC book numbers,
   317–323
Works of an administrative nature, 116
Works with four or more authors, 74, 118

x and xx symbols in Sears list, 214–216
X and XR symbols in MeSH, 238–239

Zero as filler in DDC notation, 278